Borges
and the
Literary
Marketplace

Borges and the Literary Marketplace

How Editorial Practices Shaped Cosmopolitan Reading

NORA C. BENEDICT

Yale UNIVERSITY PRESS/NEW HAVEN & LONDON

Published with assistance from the
Frank M. Turner Publication Fund.

Copyright © 2021 by Nora C. Benedict.
All rights reserved. This book may not be reproduced, in whole or in part, including illustrations, in any form (beyond that copying permitted by Sections 107 and 108 of the U.S. Copyright Law and except by reviewers for the public press), without written permission from the publishers.

Yale University Press books may be purchased in quantity for educational, business, or promotional use. For information, please e-mail sales.press@yale.edu (U.S. office) or sales@yaleup.co.uk (U.K. office).

Set in Mion type by Tseng Information Systems, Inc.
Printed in the United States of America.

Library of Congress Control Number: 2021930001
ISBN 978-0-300-25141-8 (hardcover : alk. paper)

A catalogue record for this book is
available from the British Library.

This paper meets the requirements of ANSI/NISO Z39.48-1992 (Permanence of Paper).

10 9 8 7 6 5 4 3 2 1

For my mother, who gave me my first books and with them the world.

Contents

Acknowledgments, ix

INTRODUCTION Sorting through the Stacks, 1

ONE Borges and the Book, 13

TWO Borges as Author, 47

THREE Borges as Critic and Collaborator, 86

FOUR Borges as Editor and Anthologist, 121

FIVE Borges as Publicist and Promoter, 185

SIX Borges as Publisher, 238

CONCLUSION Books after Borges, 272

Appendix: Books Produced by Editorial Sur (1933–1951), 279
Notes, 283
Bibliography, 327
Index, 353

Acknowledgments

This book already existed before I started to write it, but I never would have found it in the many hexagonal rooms of the library without the guidance of others. It started as nothing more than an idea early in my graduate career, back when I still called myself a medievalist and never dreamed of studying anything beyond the fourteenth century. All of that changed when I was awarded a Battestin Fellowship from the Bibliographical Society of the University of Virginia to study Borges's manuscripts in Special Collections during my first summer in Charlottesville, and I never looked back.

    I am grateful to my mentors who guided me through all of the researching and writing over the years. My first thanks go to Andrew A. Anderson, who believed in this project from the very start and worked with me tirelessly to perfect it. His feedback, advice, and friendship are rare gifts that I will always treasure. Warmest thanks to Michael Gerli for encouraging my work, even when I was no longer a medievalist, and to David Vander Meulen, who taught me the art of bibliography and the joys of being a scholar-collector. Daniel Balderston helped see this book through from an initial idea to its final stages; I am grateful for his early support of the project and his willingness to edit, critique, and workshop drafts along the way. I owe so much to Jared Loewenstein not only for developing the Borges Collection at UVA, but also for his advice, helpful contacts, and frequent conversations about my ideas over coffee and pumpkin muffins. I love knowing that this book might one day form a part of his collection.

My research for this book was supported by numerous grants and fellowships from the University of Virginia. Along with the previously mentioned Battestin Fellowship, I received funding from the Buice Scholarship Fund, the RBS-UVA fellowship program, and the Center for Global Inquiry and Innovation to attend three courses at the Rare Book School under the guidance of Michael Winship, John Kristensen, and Katherine McCanless Ruffin. I am grateful to each of these scholars for sharing their wisdom about books with me. The Department of Spanish, Italian, and Portuguese, as well as the Graduate School of Arts and Sciences and the Buckner W. Clay Endowment for the Humanities made my two archival trips to Buenos Aires possible. Thanks to Guillermo Martínez for pointing me in the right direction and putting me in contact with so many people before I arrived in Argentina. I benefited from many warm welcomes and insightful conversations during these two trips, especially those with Martín Hadís, Sara Luisa del Carril, María Kodama, Martina López, Ernesto Montequin, Alejandro Vaccaro, Nicolás Helft, Alfredo Breitfeld, and Alberto Casares. A special thanks to Laura Rosato and Gérman Álvarez for taking me under their wing and opening so many doors for my research. The Scholars' Lab at UVA granted me a Digital Humanities fellowship, which allowed me to lay the groundwork for the digital appendix to this book (https://norabenedict.github.io/borges/). I am thankful for Jeremy Boggs, Eric Rochester, Purdom Lindblad, and Shane Lin, all of whom collaborated with me and helped me make my digital vision a reality. Thanks also to Brandon Butler, who answered my countless questions about copyright and fair use over the years.

The Albert and Shirley Small Special Collections Library holdings were integral for the successful completion of my project. Their exceptional Borges collection was my original source of inspiration and truly made much of my work possible. I cannot say enough about the unparalleled Special Collections staff, who were always a constant source of encouragement and guidance for me; they made their stacks feel like my second home. I am particularly grateful for David Whitesell, Molly

Schwartzburg, Heather Riser, Regina Rush, Penny White, Holly Robertson, and Joseph Azizi.

Friends and mentors at Princeton University helped shape the manuscript and give it new life. Thanks to the Center for Digital Humanities for giving me the space and time to write, especially to Meredith Martin, Natasha Ermolaev, Rachael DeLue, Rebecca Munson, and Sarah Meadows for helping me through the process with ample tacos and emojis. Thanks to the Program in Latin American Studies for the opportunity to present parts of my book and receive feedback from the community. I am especially indebted to Gabriela Nouzeilles and Jeremy Adelman, who both took a special interest in my project and worked with me to make it better. I also thank Sandra Bermann, Marina Brownlee, Alberto Manguel, Javier Guerrero, Rob Karl, Jessica Mack, Pablo Pryluka, Gabriel Swift, and Eric White.

I moved to Athens and started a new job at the University of Georgia while I was in the process of editing and revising this book. I am grateful to all the members of the Department of Romance Languages who welcomed me with open arms, especially Betsy Wright, Nicolás Lucero, Rachel Gabara, Luis Correa-Díaz, and Stacey Casado for showing me the ropes. Many thanks also to the Franklin College of Arts and Sciences, which awarded me a first-book subvention grant.

I am grateful to Sarah Miller, my original editor, who took an interest in my project, and Jennifer Banks, who helped see the book through to the finish line. I thank Jessie Dolch for her exquisite copy editing and her personal appreciation for the bibliographical elements of my book. I also thank the editorial board and staff members of Yale University Press, especially Mary Valencia for designing the book jacket and Ash Lago, Abbie Storch, and Jeffrey Schier for their willingness to field my many questions and provide guidance throughout the process. Special thanks to my two anonymous readers, who provided detailed comments on the manuscript. Parts of the first chapter first appeared in my article "Books about Books and Books as Material Artifacts: Metabibliography in Jorge Luis Borges's *El jardín de senderos que se bifurcan*," *Revista Canadiense de Estudios Hispánicos* 42, no. 3 (2018). I thank Odile Cisneros and my two blind reviewers for their detailed comments and helpful suggestions that helped refine and clarify my arguments.

I have relied on the generosity of so many friends and family members in writing this book. Thanks to Micah McKay, for being a sounding board for much of my academic career; to Nicholas Wolters, for always being there to share ideas and scones; to James Ascher, for making me a better bibliographer; to Caitlin Beduhn and Bradley Haiar, for keeping me sane through it all; a mis queridas Élika Ortega y Alex Saum-Pascual, por siempre darme vida y ánimo; to Barnaby Nygren, for teaching me how to unpack and frame arguments; to Erin Goss, for reminding me of the importance of laughter; to Brian Norman, for helping me navigate the scholarly seas; to my in-laws, Douglas and Joanie, for their unconditional love; and to my brother, Dewey, for helping me build my personal library. And last, I owe so very much to my companion on this journey, Harrison. Thank you for reading countless drafts, for talking about my project with more enthusiasm than I ever could, and for letting me fill our home with books. Above all, thank you for letting me lean on you through it all.

My greatest thanks go to my mother, Aileen, who has always kept my mind busy and my heart full. She has seen all of the ups and downs of this project and taught me how to keep my head held high in the face of adversity. This book is for her.

Borges
and the
Literary
Marketplace

Introduction

Sorting through the Stacks

> Books constitute capital. A library book lasts as long as a house, for hundreds of years. It is not then, an article of mere consumption but fairly of capital, and often in the case of professional men, setting out in life, it is their only capital.
> —Thomas Jefferson, *The Jefferson Cyclopedia*

> El libro no es un ente incomunicado: es una relación, es un eje de innumerables relaciones.
>
> [A book is not an isolated being: it is a relationship, an axis of innumerable relationships.]
> —Jorge Luis Borges, *Otras inquisiciones*

The Argentine writer Jorge Luis Borges stands out as one of the most widely regarded and inventive authors in world literature. His mystifying labyrinths and boundless libraries have been the subjects of countless works following his explosion onto the global literary scene. Yet this book is not about his influence as a writer; instead, it centers on his curious jobs in the publishing industry, and how each of these positions influenced the overarching shape of cosmopolitan reading. In this way, *Borges and the Literary Marketplace* brings to light one writer's profound efforts to revolutionize and revitalize literature in Latin America. In short, Borges's place at the center of Buenos Aires publishing, a Spanish-language hub of twentieth-century print capitalism, reveals the fascinating history of how a writer crafts books—his own and others'—and how in turn these books craft an international literary marketplace.

This story begins far away from Latin America and the vibrant publishing hub of Buenos Aires. It begins, instead, "undergrounds," as it is called, in the Jorge Luis Borges collection at the University of Virginia.[1] Deep within these holdings I found myself leafing through copies and copies of different editions of Borges's work and scrutinizing variants that cropped up between, for instance, a manuscript version of a short story and its printed counterpart. I first thought that the key to analyzing the physical manifestations of these works would be in the variations between manuscript and printed text.[2] However, what stood out most to me during my initial study of the physical forms of his books was the extreme amount of variety from edition to edition. I discovered that Borges's earlier publications were not wedded to one specific publishing house, printer, or style and instead fluctuated considerably. Certain editions of works showed hints of a mass-market audience, with poor-quality paper and flashy covers, while others were nothing short of art objects. As I charted and catalogued paper types, printers' names, and publishing houses, I started to wonder how all of these distinct physical forms emerged and in what ways they were crafted for a specific type of reader.

But why *Virginia*? I've been asked this question time and time again. Why would one of the largest public collections of Borges's manuscripts, books, and print materials reside at the University of Virginia? In addition to the Borges collection being a logical extension of the Americana collection there, Borges felt that his works were at home in the Albert and Shirley Small Special Collections library.[3] "I discovered what is called North American literature in 1917, and I realized immediately that it was merely a part of the literature of the world," Borges said. "I have been much influenced by it, by Emerson and Poe. I also have much of English literature within myself, the literature of Shakespeare, all the way back to my Anglo-Saxon roots."[4] Borges's cosmopolitan view of literature foregrounds his aversion to the many categories and geographical boundaries imposed on writers and their works. Literature does not emerge from a vacuum nor does it belong to just one region; rather, it is universal and to be enjoyed by all. We immediately recognize Borges's suitable place in world literature with his works shelved alongside his precursors and literary muses and in the process are forced to reconsider the all-too-common north-south divide in American literature.[5] This anecdote on the curious location of one of Borges's archives also relates to his curious roles within the publishing industry. As I explain throughout this book, Borges's varied editorial activities speak to his continued efforts to promote literacy and democratize global literature, which reflects his worldviews.

This study draws on years of archival research undertaken in North and South America coupled with careful bibliographical analysis. A commonly overlooked fact of every book is the material evidence of its production and manufacture. As cultural artifacts, books help us determine social, economic, and even political undercurrents in play within a specific geographic and temporal space. My work relies on a careful study of the *whole* book—both its contents and its composition—in an effort to explore its role in shaping reading in Latin America. In other words, instead of examining variants from manuscripts to printed text, I rely on an analysis of the physical features (paper, typography, bindings) of Borges's print production to help tell the story of a book's creation, manufacture, and ultimate circulation. Paying close attention to the material properties of newspapers, magazines, and books foregrounds the importance of the physical form of a work and its design features for readers' responses and literary criticism. In the past decade there has been a marked uptick of interest in the history of the book in Latin America, yet these studies do not detail Borges's interactions with the publishing industry nor do they consider his editorial activities, which revolutionized the Latin American book world and forever changed reading in world literature.[6] My materially oriented investigations into Borges's place in the book world naturally lie at the convergence of various fields in the humanities and social sciences, most notably literary studies, book history, and sociology.

The scope of this book is limited to Argentina between the years 1930 and 1951. This time frame is a crucial period for Borges's formation as a writer of the short story and is when he produced some of his most canonical texts, such as *Ficciones* and *El Aleph*, among others. This twenty-one-year span also coincides with Borges's participation in the book industry. The end-date of 1951 pertains to a number of changes occurring in Borges's life during that year: health problems, political troubles, and his decision to work almost exclusively with one publishing house. While most critics tend to home in on one specific work of his from these years, I look comprehensively at his publications and editorial work during this time period to track and trace developments in his engagement with the physical form of the book. In this way I provide the first thoroughgoing study of the materiality of Borges's publications during one of the most active periods of his career while also drawing attention to his editorial activity and its value for understanding the development of cosmopolitan reading in Latin America.

Behind the Scenes in Buenos Aires

The books from the 1930s and 1940s that bear Borges's name—as author, editor, compiler, or translator—form a sprawling corpus of works: translations of Franz Kafka and William Faulkner, esoteric essays about kennings, literary reviews in flashy women's magazines, and anthologies dedicated to detective fiction brimming with snippets from Edgar Allan Poe, Nathaniel Hawthorne, and Ellery Queen. There is no end to the variety. Yet what all of these diverse print materials highlight is the newness of the publishing industry in Borges's Argentina. During these decades there is a marked increase in *porteño* book production coupled with a push toward increased professionalization in all of the industries surrounding publishing, including printing, editing, and binding.[7] At the beginning of the twentieth century, nearly all books written in Spanish that were sold in Buenos Aires were printed in Europe, mainly Germany, France, and Spain.[8] Even though a few local publishing firms emerged during this time, the high cost of paper and the elevated shipping taxes did not bode well for their success. That said, several factors aided in the growth of Argentine publishing houses as well as that of the modern editor. First, there was a significant expansion and improvement of the educational system from elementary to university programs. The establishment of national agencies that regulated, standardized, and modernized curricula in Argentina caused literacy rates to soar throughout the country.[9] Second, a more detailed version of the intellectual property law (Law No. 11.723) was enacted in 1933 to replace the earlier laws (7.092 and 9.510) and ensure authors absolute ownership over their written works. More specifically, Law No. 11.723 extended the length of copyright from ten years after the life of an author to thirty and also included a section on the crimes of plagiarism and copying, which were absent in the previous versions. Third, most existing libraries received more funding and as a result became the primary buyers of most published books in Argentina. One final reason for this sudden explosion of activity was the impact of the Spanish Civil War (1936–1939), which caused many exiles to flee from the Iberian Peninsula to Latin American countries (mainly Argentina, Mexico, and Cuba).[10]

In order to understand how Borges's many behind-the-scenes activities in the book world affected material production and reading habits in world literature, we must first consider the makeup of the global literary marketplace. Publishers, magazine and newspaper editors, printers, distributors, and booksellers all have an important role in the creation and circulation of print materials, yet many of their respective activities are often misunderstood or hard to distinguish. No attempt has been made to detail systematically the relationships that Borges maintained with members of the Argentine book trade. Was his interaction with each publisher or printer the same? Who else was working with these literary firms in the 1930s, 1940s, and 1950s? Did any editors or booksellers have particular reputations? By paying attention to Borges's role in and relation to the world of the book trade, I draw out connections between the physical forms of books and their larger political and cultural influences in Latin American reading, as well as their significance in the trajectory of Borges's career. I engage, therefore, in debates surrounding markets, commerce, and literary audiences in multilingual *porteño* material production, while also highlighting the importance of bibliographical study and book history for modern Latin American literature.

More often than not, publishers, especially those established during the twentieth century when Borges was producing the majority of his works—or those of other writers—would not have been responsible for the printing or even binding of their contracted authors' works. Rather, "publishing," broadly conceived, "is that set of activities that connect the production or manufacturing activities of the book trade [...] with the commercial or distributive activities. In a sense, the publisher is the entrepreneur of the book trade, making the decisions that bring together all the other activities and arranging for the coordination and credit— always important in a business where income realized from the sale of a product often comes months or years after the expense of production— and taking the risks necessary to make the whole book trade function."[11] Most important here is the characterization of publishing as a business. With the expansion of the literary marketplace and the book trade, it became possible for firms to specialize in certain activities, such as the manufacture or distribution of books, which meant that more parties became involved in the creation and circulation of print materials.

An important aspect of this multifaceted model of the book trade is the fact that "it is not possible to study publishing in a meaningful way as an isolated activity."[12] In other words, to best understand the creation and circulation of Borges's books—both his own and those of others—it is essential to explore not only the publishers with whom he associated at this time, but also the printers, distributors, booksellers, and various magazine and newspaper editors with whom he came into contact while producing his works. Generally speaking, most authors are either fully a part of the business of the book trade or have little to no interaction with its various industries. The former group tend to be book artists— such as William Morris or even Virginia Woolf—with their own presses and methods of production; the latter are what I would deem "regular" authors, who interface solely with an editor. Borges is an exception. He occupies a middle ground as someone who is aware of the newest technologies and methods of print production, as well as the elements of book design and manufacturing, yet chooses to maintain a certain distance. In essence, he challenges both models—the overly engaged author and the overly distant author—and demonstrates an understanding of and appreciation for labor practices in the global literary marketplace. For that reason, it is imperative to document and describe not only the physical manifestations of Borges's works, but also his interactions with publishers, such as Manuel Gleizer, Editorial TOR, Emecé, and Viau y Zona, as well as the relationships that he developed with printers, including Imprenta López and Francisco A. Colombo.

Alongside these networks of production, we must also consider the role of distribution in the book trade. Although this aspect of publishing is one for which there is little information or raw data, one of the ways to learn more about distribution is through subscription publishing and bookstore inventories or purchase forms. Another possible way to gauge the rate of distribution and the parties involved or targeted is to read and analyze the style of writing from any advertisements for forthcoming books (or other print material by a specific author) in newspapers, journals, or other print media, including the backs of books by the same publisher. Keeping in mind not only the language used for these advertisements, but also the venue or medium in which they are published reveals a great deal about the desired audience for a work (at least whether or not they might be considered lower, middle, or upper class). Consulting publishers' catalogues and the prices for items is also a good way of tracking distribution and consumption since, if the cost of a work is quite high, people in some social spheres are ruled out from purchasing it (although there is always the possibility that they might obtain a copy from a library or a friend). In general terms, publishers' catalogues, although they can at times be very hard to find from this early part of the twentieth century, can give us a great amount of raw data and material to sort through.

Crafting a Cosmopolitan Readership

"If a man grows up within a single culture, if he gets used to seeing other languages as hostile or arbitrary dialects," Borges said, "his mental development will be constricted."[13] This worldview, which is best characterized as a form of cynical cosmopolitanism, undoubtedly informs Borges's editorial activities and print production during the 1930s and 1940s. Most contemporary definitions and theorizations of cosmopolitanism base their arguments on certain ideas that stem from the Stoics or Kant and stress the moral and political attributes of the cosmopolitan.[14] However, if we consider the etymological roots of the term and the philosopher who coined it—namely, the Cynic Diogenes of Sinope—cosmopolitanism takes on much more negative connotations.[15] In the words of Simon Critchley, "Diogenes' 'cosmopolitanism' is much more of an anti-political stance than the sort of banal internationalism that people associate with the word today."[16] In direct contrast to the Stoics' or enlightenment thinkers' focus on maintaining a well-defined set of laws or norms, cynical cosmopolitanism rejects any and all types of political engagement or governance, as Gideon Baker points out: "Cynic contempt for constituted political power will not seek to reconstitute that power differently or elsewhere (the Cynic remains in the polities that he rejects), but rather to expose it as illusory."[17] As a result, cynical cosmopolitanism best captures Borges's well-established dislike of politics and nationalism as well as his desire to promote the writers whose work he valued the most (without concern for others' perceptions of his interests).[18] That is to say, Borges challenges the conventional norms of literary culture and educational standards by elevating minor genres and promoting foreign authors that might not fit within predetermined literary categories, whether national or international, local or global. Thus, alongside the publication of his own writings, his impeccably edited anthologies and volumes of collected literature, in conjunction with his extensive reviews of foreign authors and books, change both what people read and how people read.

Alongside the idea of cynical cosmopolitanism, I also draw on Borges's own conception of and writings about cosmopolitanism. I derive this language from two of his nonfiction essays: "El escritor argentino y la tradición" [The Argentine Writer and Tradition] and "Kafka y sus precursores" [Kafka and His Precursors]. These essays are arguably two of the most cited works by Borges and have shaped the work of foundational writers and literary critics including Umberto Eco, Harold Bloom, and Michel Foucault, among others. Both of these works originally appeared in 1951, the former as a lecture given to a class at the Colegio Libre de Estudios Superiores (Buenos Aires) and the latter as a published piece in the Argentine newspaper *La Nación*.[19] In "El escritor argentino y la tradición," Borges considers the place of Argentine writers, and Latin America more broadly, within the Western literary tradition and how they contribute to and shape it. The piece is structured around three central claims usually made about Argentine literary traditions: the need for local color, crucial links to Spanish literary traditions, and an inability to be European. Borges systematically refutes each of these through a series of clear, concise examples. He concludes that Argentina's literary tradition, and by extension that of Latin America in general, "is the whole of Western culture, and I also believe that we have a right to this tradition, a greater right than that which the inhabitants of one Western nation or another may have... the universe is our birthright."[20] In "Kafka y sus precursores," as the title suggests, Borges considers a series of writers (Zeno, Han Yu, Søren Kierkegaard, Robert Browning, Léon Bloy, and Lord Dunsany) whom he views as Kafka's precursors in light of the presence of distinct similarities across their work. Given the strong probability that Kafka never read several of these authors, Borges's analysis coyly paves the way for his groundbreaking conclusion: "The fact is that each writer *creates* his precursors. His work modifies our conception of the past, as it will modify the future."[21]

Although Borges makes unique claims in each of these two works, they are perfect companion pieces because of their common interest in literary history, canons, and a sense of cosmopolitanism. Moreover, when viewed together, these two essays serve as the ideal framing, in the form of a manifesto, for the current book. Borges's claim that literature is bound neither by language nor by region reflects his decisions to edit, translate, and anthologize a large number of foreign authors during the period this book examines. Second, his assertion that writers create their own precursors applies not only to the abstract realm of allusions and literary borrowings, but also to the concrete space of physically creating edited editions, anthologies, and books. While Borges does not use the term "cosmopolitan" explicitly in these two works, his central ideas that all literary histories and canons belong to all countries and regions of the world, and cannot be geographically restricted, echo the main tenets of cosmopolitanism. Moreover, his knowledge of global trends in book production—from preferences for eighteenth-century typography to paper spine labels—reveals how both his ideas and the books that physically contain them are cosmopolitan in nature. In essence, Borges's relationship to the literary marketplace is a global history of how books make the world and how the world makes books.

An Outline of the Chapters

Each chapter of this book focuses on a specific role that Borges performed within the Argentine book world. Chapter 1, "Borges and the Book," provides the foundation for my analysis of Borges's integration into the global literary marketplace. I take a closer look at how Borges thinks about books, how he writes about and imagines books, and how he engages with and understands trends in international book production. Drawing on unpublished manuscript evidence, I highlight the fact that he incorporates different varieties of editorial information into his writings and in the process demonstrates a detailed understanding of how books physically come into being. Alongside a literary analysis of many of Borges's works from the 1930s and 1940s, I also consider the physical features of these works in order to show how Borges approached books with both their contents and their form highly in mind. Chapter 2, "Borges as Author," considers the less-visible forces that helped bring Borges's creative fictions and philosophical essays into (physical) existence. Rather than providing another close textual reading of his well-known works, I instead look to the relationships that he developed with specific printers and publishers during the first half of the 1930s. More broadly, I examine the interactions of editors, publishers, printers, and authors in Buenos Aires book production during this time in an effort to foreground how these connections shaped Borges's international popularity later in life and his understanding of reading habits.

Chapter 3, "Borges as Critic and Collaborator," focuses on how Borges fills the void of foreign literary criticism and in the process develops a new type of marketing for book production and publishing. From his book reviews and short biographies of writers in the magazine *El Hogar* [*The Home*] to his creative collaborations with Adolfo Bioy Casares, I trace Borges's marked interest in promoting international literatures that previously lacked readership in Latin America. For instance, Borges's biweekly page on authors and foreign works in *El Hogar* and his collaborative work with the literary journal *Destiempo* directly influenced a number of emerging series with distinct publishing houses, including the Pajarita de Papel series of Editorial Losada and Colección Horizonte of Editorial Sudamericana. In like fashion, in Chapter 4, "Borges as Editor and Anthologist," I study how Borges showcases specific authors and their works for specific readers and in the process promotes underrepresented, forgotten, or unknown literatures from around the globe. As a way of highlighting his influence on readership and the literary marketplace, my analysis in this chapter centers on three themes: Argentine literature, detective fiction, and world literature. Working from Borges's theoretical conceptions of the anthology, I consider how these books were compiled, produced, and marketed and the roles that they played in the construction of world literature. Then in Chapter 5, "Borges as Publicist and Promoter," I argue that Borges's editorial work for various Argentine publishers—specifically his translations of foreign authors and prologues for their works—not only helped fill the previously mentioned literary void in Latin America, but also aided a number of firms in selling their books. All of this work is what I deem his editorial and/or promotional framing. I also consider the ways in which these works were physically framed (covers, prices, wrappers and bands, store window displays, etc.) as a way of deepening our understanding of the literary marketplace and Borges's central role in it. In Chapter 6, "Borges as Publisher," I show how Borges's interest in the physical form of the book culminated in his creation of two distinct publishing houses with his close friend Adolfo Bioy Casares. Their two firms, Editorial Destiempo and Editorial Oportet & Haereses, can be seen as the pinnacle of their ongoing critique of culture and methods of education. Here we see them problematizing conceptions of how books are made and how books should be used, especially when we consider the fact that the works that Borges produces as a publisher foreground his understanding of and engagement with global trends in book production.

    In the Conclusion, I consider the ways in which Borges's editorial activities and knowledge of the book as object impacted contemporary theorizations of the materiality of the book. More specifically, I return to a series of detailed examples of books in Borges's fictions as a way to think through his influence on the work of writers such as Gérard Genette and Roger Chartier. In particular, I show how Borges's behind-the-scenes positions from critic and editor to publisher and publicist inform his writings, which in turn inform Genette's and Chartier's marked focus on print culture and book history throughout the latter half of the twentieth century.

O • N • E

Borges and the Book

De los diversos instrumentos del hombre, el más asombroso es, sin duda, el libro. Los demás son extensiones de su cuerpo. El microscopio, el telescopio, son extensiones de su vista; el teléfono es extensión de la voz; luego tenemos el arado y la espada, extensiones de su brazo. Pero el libro es otra cosa: el libro es una extensión de la memoria y de la imaginación.

[Of all of man's tools, the most astonishing is, without a doubt, the book. All the others are extensions of his body. The microscope, the telescope are extensions of his vision; the telephone is an extension of his voice; later we have the plow and the sword, extensions of his arm. But the book is something else: the book is an extension of his memory and his imagination.]

— Jorge Luis Borges, "El libro"

In the midst of a lecture at the University of Belgrano in Buenos Aires in early 1978, Borges subtly mentions his desire to write a history of the book. Such a statement does not seem out of character since books, as both physical objects and conveyors of information, play an important role in Borges's writings. Yet, he quickly qualifies this statement by adding that such a work would *not* take into account the physical features of the book: "No me interesan los libros físicamente (sobre todos los libros de los bibliófilos, que suelen ser desmesurados), sino las diversas valoraciones que el libro ha recibido" [I'm not interested in books physically (especially not bibliophile's books, which tend to be excessive), but rather the different assessments that the book has received].[1] Borges's own writings, both fiction and nonfiction, paint a different picture with their detailed references to books, whether real or apocryphal. From descriptions of the material composition of books to an in-depth consideration of the specific publishers and printers that would produce his works, this Argentine writer is very much rooted in the physical. In their excellent study of Borges's books at the National Library in Buenos Aires, Laura Rosato and Germán Álvarez note a similar disconnect: "Hemos mencionado, como una característica del Borges propietario de libros, la ausencia de fetichismo por el objeto en sí. Sin embargo, esto no se contrapone con el modo hedónico en la elección de ejemplares" [We have mentioned, as a characteristic of Borges the book owner, the absence of any fetishism for the object itself. However, this does not go against his hedonic method of selecting copies of books].[2] Borges's personal library, currently housed (in part) at the Fundación Internacional Jorge Luis Borges in Buenos Aires and run by his widow, María Kodama, tells a different tale as well.[3] When I was given the opportunity to view this collection of nearly three thousand volumes, I was surprised to discover the incredible attention given to bibliographical details. The majority of the works are hardbound leather books, the most striking of which are, without doubt, the full runs of encyclopedias, a well-known interest of Borges.[4] Thus, much like the extensive passages in his prose that devote a great deal of attention to the material aspects of books, Borges's own personal habits and tendencies toward books emphasize, contrary to his statements in his lecture, a true affinity for the physical form of the book.

All of these details raise a number of questions. Most notably, what *is* Borges's relationship to the book, and why might he have such a strong aversion to its physical form? How can he disdain the physical features of books and simultaneously rely on their very material composition for many of his own writings? The inherent tension at play in such questions reflects the common divide between the bibliophile—who Borges mentions in his lecture—and the bibliographer. The former is interested in nothing more than the often ornate physical elements of the book, such as the leather bindings or gold-leafed edges, and the latter studies the physical features of books to learn and understand more about them. Thus, a bibliographer is someone who is interested in the *whole* book— both its contents and its composition—and aspires to create the most comprehensive study of these objects, not simply to collect them. Given Borges's love of encyclopedias, in particular the eleventh edition of the *Encyclopedia Britannica* (1910–1911), it is only fitting to turn to this work for a more detailed consideration of the work of the bibliographer. In the entry on "Bibliography and Bibliology" A. W. Pollard explains how the term "bibliography" originally referred to the writing of books and then in the eighteenth century transitioned to refer to the writing *about* books. As a field of study, bibliography thus is divided into four distinct subcategories: the examination and collation of books, the description of books, the enumeration of books, and the bibliography of bibliographies. The ways in which Borges writes *about* books coincide with these meticulous methods that comprise traditional forms of bibliographical inquiry and analysis. Although Borges has never been characterized as a bibliographer, this term best captures his understanding of the physical form of the book. In an effort to support this claim and foreground Borges's deep knowledge of the book as object, I analyze the ways in which he seamlessly incorporates bibliographical data—whether real or apocryphal— into his writings. In addition, I show how his early involvement in the publishing industry in the 1920s provides him with this deep knowledge of the physical features of books and their construction.

The Book as a Physical Presence in Borges's Writings

The most logical place to start any discussion of the role of the book in Borges's life is his father's library.[5] In his "Autobiographical Notes" for the *New Yorker* Borges describes the impact of this collection and how he has, to some extent, "never strayed outside that library."[6] Although his eyesight had gone long before this interview, he still had lucid recollections of the library: "It was in a room of its own, with glass-fronted shelves, and must have contained several thousand volumes... I vividly remember so many of the steel engravings in Chambers' Encyclopaedia and in the Britannica."[7] Even more telling are his memories of reading *Don Quijote* for the first time: "I still remember those red volumes with the gold lettering of the Garnier edition ... when I read the 'Quijote' in another edition I had the impression that it wasn't the real 'Quijote' ... I had a friend get me the Garnier with the same steel engravings, the same footnotes, and also the same errata. All those things form part of the book for me; this I consider the real 'Quijote.'"[8] This anecdote illustrates Borges's understanding of the fact that all physical manifestations of a work are unique, especially with his reference to the errata that can be found within the pages of *his* Garnier edition of *Don Quijote*. For Borges, the "real 'Quijote'" is the text—errata and all!—contained in the specific copy through which he first encountered the work.

Alongside his father's impressive library are the various bookstores that Borges was known to have visited and from which he at times purchased books. As Domingo Buonocore notes, "Buenos Aires fué centro librero antes que editorial" [Buenos Aires was a hub of bookstores before it was a hub of publishing].[9] Nearly eighty years have passed since the first publication of *Libreros, editores e impresores de Buenos Aires* [*Booksellers, Editores, and Printers of Buenos Aires*], yet Buonocore's observation still rings true today since, according to a recent study, Buenos Aires is the city with the largest number of bookshops per inhabitant in the world.[10] With such an exorbitant number of bookstores, the question of competition and survival comes to mind; however, what we find in the scant descriptions of these shops is their high level of specialization. Unlike our current conception of bookstores as all-inclusive in terms of their inventory, if you were in search of a title of German or English literature in Borges's Buenos Aires, you would be able to go to a unique shop, or even shops, that specialized in and sold only these types of books. For instance, Borges's passion for English literature frequently led him to bookstores such as Mackern's or Mitchell's, both of which specialized in imported foreign—predominantly English—literature.[11] Mackern's, founded in 1849 by George and Hector Mackern, initially sold mostly fine stationery items but soon branched out to focus on English literature, specifically popular detective fiction. Mitchell's, founded in 1907 by

Edward Bellet Mitchell, had very similar origins to Mackern's and also sold a great deal of fine stationery items before expanding into North American literary works.

Several of Borges's personal books from the Biblioteca Nacional contain tags from a number of other local shops, including Pygmalion, Goethe, Beutelspacher, and Viau y Cía. Lily Lebach, who fled Nazi-occupied Germany toward the end of the 1930s, ran Pygmalion, and the majority of her inventory consisted of books produced by British and German publishing firms. In addition to Borges purchasing books from this shop, it also was one of his known hangouts, where certain people, most notably Alberto Manguel, who was employed there in 1964, would read to the blind writer during the later years of his life.[12] Much like Pygmalion, Goethe and Beutelspacher were known for their German literature, which had become an interest of Borges after he first studied the language while at secondary school in Geneva. Finally, Viau y Cía specialized in luxury books with fine-quality paper and exquisite bindings.[13] This shop also held art exhibits and as a result functioned as a sort of cultural center for artists residing in Buenos Aires.

As Rosato and Álvarez aptly assert, "para Borges, el lugar de adquisición del libro era otro de los rasgos identitarios de un ejemplar, un atributo casi equiparable a la edición misma" [for Borges, the place where a book was acquired was another defining feature of a copy, an attribute that was almost comparable with the edition itself].[14] When we examine the unique store stickers that adorn his books, we find a pattern of regularity, revealing more often than not the names of shops that specialized in English editions. Estela Canto recalls this same tendency of Borges toward certain places and books in her memoir of the writer and also emphasizes his physical engagement with the book:

> Se sentaba en el suelo y empezaba a retirar los libros de estantes más bajos. Los examinaba y los leía con la página casi tocándole la nariz. (Le vi hacer esto en casa de los Bioy, en la biblioteca pública donde era un modesto empleado y en Mackern's y Mitchell's, las librerías inglesas, donde era conocido y se le permitía revolver todo lo que quisiera).

> [He would sit on the floor and start to take books from the lowest shelves. He would examine them and read them with the pages just about touching his nose. (I saw him do this same thing in Bioy's house, in the public library where he was a modest employee, and in Mackern's and Mitchell's, the English bookstores, where he was well-known and they let him riffle through anything he wanted.]¹⁶

The fact that Borges was seen as a regular in these bookstores—to the point where he could rummage through and disorder all of the books that he pleased—reveals that he was very much ensconced in the material world.

Although references to the physical aspects of books in any given Borges story or essay are subtle and more often than not overlooked by many a reader, they easily can be found once you start looking. For instance, within the pages of *Evaristo Carriego* (1930), arguably one of his lesser-read works, Borges dedicates an entire passage to describing the physical qualities of any book:

> [T]odo escritor empieza por un concepto ingenuamente físico de lo que es arte. Un libro, para él, no es una expresión o una concatenación de expresiones, sino literalmente un *volumen,* un prisma de seis caras rectangulares hecho de finas láminas de papel que deben presentar una carátula, una falsa carátula, un epígrafe en bastardilla, un prefacio en una cursiva mayor, nueve o diez partes con una versal al principio, un índice de materias, un *ex libris* con un relojito de arena y con un resuelto latín, una concisa fe de erratas, unas hojas en blanco, un colofón interlineado y un pie de imprenta: objetos que es sabido constituyen el arte de escribir. Algunos estilistas (generalmente los del inimitable pasado) ofrecen además un prólogo del editor, un retrato dudoso, una firma autógrafa, un texto con variantes, un espeso aparato crítico, unas lecciones propuestas por el editor, una lista de autoridades y unas lagunas ... Esa confusión de papel de Holanda con estilo, de Shakespeare con Jacobo Peuser, es indolentemente común, y

perdura (apenas adecentada) entre los retóricos, para cuyas informales almas acústicas una poesía es un mostrador de acentos, rimas, elisiones, diptongaciones y otra fauna fonética.

[Every writer starts out with a naively physical idea of what art is. To him a book is not an expression or a series of expressions but literally a *volume,* a prism with six rectangular faces constructed from thin sheets of paper that must include a title page, a half-title, an epigraph in italics, a foreword in larger italics, nine or ten parts that start with capital letters, a table of contents, an ex libris with a small hourglass and a Latin motto, a concise errata sheet, some blank leaves, a leaded colophon, and an imprint: items generally known to make up the art of writing. Some stylists (usually those of the inimitable past) also offer an editor's prologue, a dubious portrait, a facsimile signature, a text with variants, a weighty critical apparatus, a list of works consulted, a list of authorities, and some lacunae … That confusion of Holland paper with style, of Shakespeare with Jacobo Peuser, is terribly common, and it prevails (barely groomed) among rhetoricians, to whose simple acoustical souls a poem is a display case of stresses, rhymes, elisions, diphthongs, and other linguistic fauna.][16]

The level of detail here and Borges's emphasis on the material nature of books stand out.[17] From the opening line in which he informs his readers that art virtually always starts as a physical concept, to the intricate dissection of each of the parts of any book, the reader inevitably finds a deep interest in—and knowledge of—the book as object for this Argentine author. While these physical elements pertain specifically to Carriego's book, Borges displays a comprehensive understanding of and appreciation for them in his detailed outline. His closing comment on the fact that many individuals often confuse a high-quality paper with style or an author (Shakespeare) with a publisher (Jacobo Peuser) further affirms his familiarity with all of the elements and parties involved in the book industry, and also speaks to the previously established divide between bibliophiles and bibliographers.

In addition to *Evaristo Carriego,* Borges turns to the materiality of books and their composition in his collection *Discusión* (1932). In "Las versiones homéricas" [The Homeric Versions], for instance, he notes that "el concepto de *texto definitivo* no corresponde sino a la religión o al cansancio" [the concept of the *definitive text* does not correspond to anything except religion or exhaustion], highlighting the bibliographical idea, as expressed by G. Thomas Tanselle, that any given text is nothing more than an "arrangement of elements; and all can be the objects of emendation, for those elements (or their arrangements) can always be altered, producing different textures."[18] Borges continues his analysis of books and their translations with the example of the *Quijote* and claims that this work is "un monumento uniforme, sin otras variaciones que las deparadas por el editor, el encuadernador y el cajista" [a uniform moment, with no other variations aside from those offered by the editor/publisher, the binder, and the compositor/typesetter].[19] Instead of simply mentioning the possibility of error in any given copy of a book, Borges singles out the work of the editor, the binder, and the typesetter in creating a book.[20] References to these specific individuals, most notably the binder and the typesetter, are not frequent in early twentieth-century Latin American literature. Why, one must ask, does Borges acknowledge the role of these individuals in his essay as opposed to stating that the creation and composition of any book is a complex process that involves many parties and many steps? Perhaps he is trying to home in on the central issues that may arise in book publishing when discussing possible errors from one copy of a book to the next. The message conveyed in the manuscript (editor, publisher), the order of the pages in the book (binder), and the printed letters on the page (typesetter) are all important parts of any author's work, yet misunderstandings can arise at any moment in the intricate process of publishing that will result in a potential disconnect between the writer's work and the final printed document. Regardless of the specific reason, this reference demonstrates a concern for the complex world of publishing.

Another striking aspect that emerges in some essays in this collection is Borges's marked interest in book collecting and his own identification as a collector. In his essay "Paul Groussac," which, as the title indicates, pertains to the Argentine writer and former librarian of the National Library in Buenos Aires, Borges writes:

> He verificado en mi biblioteca diez tomos de Groussac. Soy un lector hedónico: jamás consentí que mi sentimiento del deber interviniera en afición tan personal como la adquisición de libros, ni probé fortuna dos veces con autor intratable, eludiendo un libro anterior con un libro nuevo, ni compré—crasamente—en montón.
>
> [I have ten volumes of Groussac in my library. I'm a hedonic reader: I've never let my sense of duty intervene with my very personal hobby of acquiring books, I've never tested my luck with an unrivaled author two times, avoiding an earlier book for a newer one, nor have I purchased—crassly—in heaps.][21]

Aside from describing book collecting as a very personal hobby, Borges hints at the necessity of specificity when selecting any given copy of a work. As Tanselle notes, "collectors not only preserve historical evidence; they also create a view of the past through their collections—by the scope they set for themselves and by the arrangement they impose on the artifacts."[22] In other words, looking to Borges's personal library and works that he was known to have sought out or treasured during his lifetime, such as the *Encyclopedia Britannica* or Pliny's *Naturalis Historia,* tells readers and critics alike a great deal about this Argentine author's "view of the past." For instance, Borges claims that he did not purchase a large number of books, yet he identifies ten volumes by Groussac in his own library. Which books did he possess? What were their themes or topics? Did the same publisher produce all these works? Did he purchase them from the same bookseller? As we consider the role of books in Borges's life, we being to see Borges not only as a creator of literature and culture, but also as a consumer of its physical manifestations.

There are fewer references to the physical book in Borges's next collection of essays, *Historia de la eternidad* [*A History of Eternity*] (1936), but the first of these four pieces, with the same title as the entire work, presents an intriguing conundrum.[23] While discussing the concepts of time and eternity, Borges states: "El mejor documento de la primera eternidad es el quinto libro de las *Enéadas* ... Quinientas páginas en folio no agotarían el tema: espero que estas dos o tres en octavo no parecerán excesivas" [The best document of the first ages is the fifth book of the *Enneads* ... Five hundred pages in folio would not exhaust the topic: I hope that these two or three in octavo do not seem excessive].[24] First is Borges's attention to the question of format, which is a very specific bibliographical detail relating to the size of a book. In his entry in the *Encyclopedia Britannica,* Pollard reminds readers of the complications involved in determining this aspect of a book: "The 'size' of a book is a technical expression for the relation of the individual leaves to the sheet of paper of which they form a part. A book in-folio means one in which the paper has been folded once, so that each sheet has made two leaves. In a book in-quarto, each sheet has been folded twice so as to make four leaves ... The recognition of what is meant by the size of a book has been obscured by the erroneous idea that the quires or gatherings of which books are made up necessarily consist of single sheets."[25] By drawing attention to the fact that this first edition of *Historia de la eternidad* is an octavo raises a whole host of other questions regarding materiality and the physical object of the book for Borges: If we read this essay in any other form but the first edition, does it carry the same meaning or message (if the format of this alternative object is not an octavo, but perhaps a quarto or duodecimo)?[26] How do we deal with the fact that the essay in question is twenty-four pages in total and the section from which the above citation is taken is five (yet Borges states that "these two or three" pages will be dedicated to the topic at hand)? Such material descriptions not only reveal Borges's knowledge of the creation and production of the book, but also call into question the importance of the physical edition for Borges (or, alternatively, the level of control he had over editorial decisions that went into each of these books).

Virtually all of the short stories collected in *El jardín de senderos que se bifurcan* [*The Garden of Forking Paths*] (1941) contain references to the materiality of books. In fact, even Borges's short prologue to this collection of fiction touches on the practice of writing books about (imaginary) books:

> Desvarío laborioso y empobrecedor el de componer vastos libros; el de explayar en quinientas páginas una idea cuya perfecta exposición oral cabe en pocos minutos. Mejor procedimiento es simular que esos libros ya existen y ofrecer un resumen, un comentario... Más razonable, más inepto, más haragán, he preferido la escritura de notas sobre libros imaginarios.
>
> [The composition of vast books is a laborious and impoverishing extravagance—to go on for five hundred pages developing an idea whose perfect oral exposition is possible in a few minutes. A better course of action is to pretend that these books already exist, and then to offer a summary, a commentary... More reasonable, more inept, more indolent, I have preferred to write notes about imaginary books.][27]

Even though Borges insinuates that many of the referenced books in *El jardín de senderos que se bifurcan* are not real, his engagement with and analysis of these media appears to be directly informed by bibliographical methods.[28] Readers will find that the very work that opens the collection, "Tlön, Uqbar, Orbis Tertius," presents an interesting bibliographical case. A mysterious reference to an imaginary region, Uqbar, in an article entry of an encyclopedia leads the unnamed narrator to search feverishly for any mention or indication of the actual existence of this place. During his search, the narrator encounters the region of Tlön and the planet of Orbis Tertius, both of which he discovers to be mere inventions of a team of scholars organized and financed by the millionaire Ezra Buckley. Generally speaking, "Tlön, Uqbar, Orbis Tertius" plays with many common themes that appear throughout a number of Borges's short stories, including the search for absolute truth, doubling, and the juxtaposition of binary oppositions, most notably the difference between history and literature—or the real and the imaginary. Borges himself claims that this story "es quizá el cuento más ambicioso mío. Es la idea de la realidad transformada por un *libro*" [is perhaps my most ambitious story. It is the idea of reality transformed by a *book*].[29]

From a material perspective, this story is nothing short of a bibliographical conundrum: How is it that these few pages dedicated to Uqbar ended up in only one copy of the encyclopedia? What are the unique physical features of the narrator's copy of the *Anglo-American Cyclopaedia?* Is the typeface used for these pages distinct from that of the rest of the book? What about the paper? The reader suddenly realizes the importance of these questions and the materiality of the dilemma facing the narrator when he attempts to find a copy of this encyclopedia with the entry on Uqbar. The quest quickly morphs into a wild goose chase in which we see him frantically checking numerous copies of this work throughout Buenos Aires. What we will discover through an analysis of "Tlön, Uqbar, Orbis Tertius" is Borges's conscious engagement with methods of descriptive bibliography, or the study of the physical features and production history of books, through his use of bibliographical data to enhance his narrative. In particular, descriptive bibliography serves as the foundation for virtually all other types of bibliography and, as Pollard writes, is "the ideal toward which all bibliographical work should be directed," since this kind of analysis informs later literary, historical, or even economic work related to the book.[30] Describing in detail the physical features of any given book is the most important branch of bibliography and as a result acts as the starting point for all other bibliographical pursuits.

After consulting a copy of the *Anglo-American Cyclopaedia* with no entry on Uqbar, the narrator's friend, Bioy, brings his personal copy of the work, with the desired article intact, to the narrator so that he can examine it: "El volumen que trajo Bioy era efectivamente el cuarenta y seis de la *Anglo-American Cyclopaedia.* En la falsa carátula y en el lomo, la indicación alfabética (Tor-Ups) era la de nuestro ejemplar, pero en vez de 917 páginas constaba de 921" [The volume that Bioy brought was indeed the forty-sixth of the *Anglo-American Cyclopaedia.* On the half-title page and spine, the alphabetical key was the same as in our copy, but instead of 917 pages, it had 921].[31] The fact that this copy of the *Anglo-American Cyclopaedia* contains a half-title page and four more pages of material than any other copy—precisely the pages that correspond to the article on Uqbar—highlights the importance of analyzing not only the text found within a book, but also the physical characteristics of this object, which serve as evidence when trying to discern the ways in which it was produced. Curiously, after analyzing the features of this specific copy of the *Anglo-American Cyclopaedia,* the narrator identifies it as a reprint of the tenth edition of the *Encyclopedia Britannica.* While the reference to this latter work is of great interest in light of Borges's affinity for the later eleventh edition, more intriguing is the use of the term "reprint." Bibliographically speaking, "*impression* and *printing* are synonymous terms for all copies of the sheets of a book printed by any one run of the presses from one setting of type or its equivalent in the form of plates or monotype rolls," and an impression (or reprint) can be created from standing type of the original impression, but in many cases, corrections, added material, or a new setting of type can be employed for its production.[32] More specifically, "impressions may vary somewhat from each other in certain typographical and even textual details and markedly in the size, quality, weight, or color of paper and in the details of the binding."[33] What is more, impressions are extremely difficult to identify, and "in the absence of any typographical differentiation, the best clue is likely to be found in the paper used" or at times in the bindings.[34] In light of the fact that it is difficult to identify a unique impression of a work, the narrator's description of a specific copy of the *Anglo-American Cyclopaedia* as such also alludes to the potential circulation of a pirated edition of this work.

Their initial examination of this curious four-page article on Uqbar takes Bioy and the narrator on a textually oriented journey in an effort to unearth its publication history. Thus we find them carefully investigating the bibliography that accompanies the article in question and discovering a series of unknown books that lead them to one of the many catalogues of Bernard Quaritch, a real-life bookseller in London and one of the most well-known figures in the book trade in all of Europe. As one bibliographer notes, Quaritch's cataloguing efforts, particularly his last *General Catalogue* of seventeen volumes (1887–1889), are without doubt "the greatest bibliographical monument ever produced around the stock of a second-hand bookseller."[35] Fernando de Toro also homes in on Borges's reference to Quaritch, yet he uses this allusion to accentuate the blurry divide between reality and fiction and does not delve into Borges's rationale for selecting this specific bookseller.[36] From a bibliographical perspective, the choice of Quaritch's catalogue is telling since it is extremely exhaustive and famed for including not just the best editions of a work, but rather all editions of a work. Even apocryphal works, such as the one mentioned by our narrator, might have appeared in one of these catalogues. Unable to unearth new evidence about Uqbar or their mysterious encyclopedia, the protagonists finally receive word from a friend that a set of the encyclopedia is for sale at a bookstore in Buenos Aires: "Carlos Mastronardi (a quien yo había referido el asunto) advirtió en una librería de Corrientes y Talcahuano los negros y dorados lomos de la *Anglo-American Cyclopaedia* . . . Entró e interrogó el volumen XLVI. Naturalmente, no dio con el menor indicio de Uqbar" [Carlos Mastronardi (to whom I had related the matter) noticed the black and gold spines of the *Anglo-American Cyclopaedia* in a bookshop on Corrientes and Talcahuano . . . He entered and examined Volume XLVI. Of course, he did not find the slightest indication of Uqbar].[37] Even though the article is missing from the copy that they find in the bookstore, it is noteworthy that the volumes are described using their physical features (black and gold spines).

This same level of material detail crops up later in "Tlön, Uqbar, Orbis Tertius" with the description of a book that the narrator receives in the mail days after the death of Herbert Ashe, a railroad engineer, furthering complicating his search for the truth about Uqbar: "Era un libro en octavo mayor . . . En el amarillo lomo de cuero leí estas curiosas palabras que la falsa carátula repetía: *A first Encyclopaedia of Tlön. Vol. XI. Hlaer to Jangr*" [It was a book in large octavo . . . On the yellow leather spine, and again on the half-title page, I read these words: *A First Encyclopaedia of Tlön. Vol. XI. Hlaer to Jangr*].[38] The use of this specific bibliographical terminology—whether an octavo, or even a quarto or a folio—seems reserved mainly for sixteenth-, seventeenth-, or even eighteenth-century title pages; booksellers' catalogues like Quaritch's; or publishers' advertisements, not contemporary fiction.

The closing postscript of "Tlön, Uqbar, Orbis Tertius" solidifies the meaningful engagement that this short story maintains with descriptive bibliography, since this section of the text presents readers with the solution to the enigma of the four-page article on Uqbar that is discovered through a close examination of the encyclopedias in question and their printing history. More specifically, we learn of the production of the secret edition of the encyclopedia of Tlön and how these volumes circulated, at first only among the members of Ezra Buckley's secret society, and then were later located in places as far away as Nashville, Tennessee. This in turn resulted in an explosion of "manuales, antologías, resúmenes, versiones literales, reimpresiones autorizadas y reimpresiones piráticas" [manuals, anthologies, summaries, literal versions, authorized reprints, and pirated reprints] of the original.[39] Understanding the history of the ways in which these mysterious encyclopedias have circulated and consequently have mutated underscores the role of descriptive bibliography in piecing together the physical evidence present in each book to re-create the circumstances of production for the unique copy of the *Anglo-American Cyclopaedia* that makes its way into the hands of Bioy and his friend. In short, we can identify a clear engagement with descriptive—and analytical—bibliography in this short story. Borges relies on this type of analysis to foreground the complex system of bringing any given text into physical existence since it must pass through various hands, from editors and graphic designers to typesetters and printers, before it reaches the reader. Thus, much like DNA replication, which continually introduces the possibility of mutation, books are the product of many highly orchestrated human interactions that can result in the introduction of errors at any moment in the process, and it is these errors that tell the story of each object's unique creation.

A second story from the collection, "Pierre Menard, autor del Quijote" [Pierre Menard, Author of the Quijote], is often cited for its questioning of key literary-critical concepts such as authorship, interpretation, and readers' responses. Yet throughout the pages of this work, we also find an engagement with bibliography. For instance, at the start of this story the narrator draws the reader's attention to the fact that Menard's oeuvre "es fácilmente enumerable" [is easily enumerated] and then lists his publications chronologically in an effort to correct a previous "catálogo falaz" [false catalogue] that lacked a number of his works.[40] In the process, the narrator produces the perfect example of an enumerative bibliography.[41] In addition, the central crux of this short story, Pierre Menard's literal (re)writing of the *Quijote*, perfectly aligns with issues of the examination and collation of books as well as their description, which are all inherently a part of bibliography and, more broadly, the creation of critical editions of works. Furthermore, considering the bibliographical aspects of "Pierre Menard, autor del Quijote" helps us to better understand and further enrich its literary-critical engagements with the ideas of canon formation, literary traditions, and cultural markets.

Immediately following this enumerative bibliography of Menard's published works, the reader is introduced to his latest literary project: "escribir un Quijote contemporáneo" [writing a contemporary Quijote].[42] The narrator is quick to clear up any confusion regarding the nature of this project, which initially might appear to be a creative work *in the style of* the *Quijote*. In fact, as we come to find out, Menard aims to "producir unas páginas que coincidieran—palabra por palabra y línea por línea—con las de Miguel de Cervantes" [produce pages that coincide—word for word and line for line—with those of Miguel de Cervantes].[43] After reading this description of Menard's next literary project, readers might think of it as an exercise in creative writing or a simulation of medieval practices of copying or even plagiarism.[44] As we read more about the process behind Menard's *Quijote* in the ensuing pages another thought springs to mind: he is crafting nothing other than an edition of this work and thus engaging directly with textual bibliography. In general terms, textual bibliography, also referred to as scholarly editing, looks to insight gathered from texts themselves, such as design features and variants, to prepare new documents that are either *critical,* which involves making emendations or changes in order to show authorial intention or a complete textual history of the document, or *diplomatic,* which involves no emending of the text. In a strange turn of events, Menard himself identifies these same two distinct methods of textual bibliography a few pages later: "Mi solitario juego está gobernado por dos leyes polares. La primera me permite ensayar variantes de tipo formal o psicológico; la segunda me obliga a sacrificarlas al texto 'original' y a razonar de un modo irrefutable esa aniquilación" [My solitary game is governed by two polar rules: the first allows me to try out formal or psychological variants; the second forces me to sacrifice them to the "original" text and to irrefutably justify those eradications].[45] As we shall see, the ways in which Menard undertakes his *Quijote* project directly correspond with the creation of an edition of a work, more precisely a *diplomatic* edition.

First is his profound interest in understanding the social and historical moment of Cervantes. He strives to re-create this moment in time for perhaps a heightened awareness of the forces placed on this Spaniard's writing process: "Conocer bien el español, recuperar la fe católica, guerrear contra los moros o contra el turco, olvidar la historia de Europa entre los años 1602 y de 1918, *ser* Miguel de Cervantes" [Learn Spanish, return to Catholicism, fight against the Moors or the Turks, forget the entire history of Europe from 1602 to 1918, *be* Miguel de Cervantes].[46] Menard notes that such a procedure is extremely difficult (and virtually impossible), but he will attempt it nonetheless. What is more, to describe his actions he uses the specific verb *componer,* which has the double meaning of composing (or writing) a text and setting a text in type.[47] The fact that both works—Cervantes's *Quijote* and Menard's *Quijote*—"son verbalmente idénticos" [are verbally identical] also connects Menard's project with the creation of a diplomatic edition. Finally, when discussing the reception of Menard's work, the narrator mentions that some individuals saw it as a literal transcription of the *Quijote,* which further links the methods analyzed in this short story with those of textual bibliography, since many diplomatic editions will consist of a series of facsimiles with their accompanying transcriptions. Thus, "Pierre Menard, autor del Quijote" illuminates Borges's role as a bibliographer since many theories and methods of (textual) bibliography operate at the heart of this short story and provide him with a unique point of departure for his creative fictions. On a deeper level, many of the editorial issues at stake in this short story both complement and complicate its established literary-critical interpretations since, for instance, each work included in any sort of canon must be evaluated for not only its literary qualities, but also its textual and physical qualities of composition.

"El acercamiento a Almotásim" [The Approach to Al-Mu'tasim] and "Examen de la obra de Herbert Quain" [An Examination of the Work of Herbert Quain], two additional stories from *El jardín de senderos que se bifurcan,* also incorporate methods associated with bibliography, including enumerative bibliography and descriptive bibliography. For instance, at the start of "El acercamiento a Almotásim," the first edition (*editio princeps*) of the work of the same name is printed on paper that "era casi papel de diario" [was almost newsprint quality], and within the first few months of its publication, "el público agotó cuatro impresiones de mil ejemplares cada uno" [the public bought up four printings of a thousand copies each].⁴⁸ The narrator of this short story also mentions the publication of an "edición ilustrada... que acaba de reproducir en Londres Víctor Gollancz" [illustrated edition... which has just been reproduced and issued in London by Victor Gollancz], a major mid-twentieth-century British publisher.⁴⁹ Borges's decision to include the name of an authentic publishing firm, as opposed to fabricating one, highlights his interest in blurring not only the line between reality and fiction, but also the world of print culture and its production. Thus, we find that even the references to places in which books are produced in any given Borges short story are worth further examination for the historical significance that they might bring to light.⁵⁰ Furthermore, after detailing the first printing and subsequent reviews of *Acercamiento a Almotásim,* the novel at the heart of "El acercamiento a Almotásim," the short story's narrator showcases his engagement with textual bibliography in compiling "un apéndice, que resume la diferencia fundamental entre la versión primitiva de 1932 y la de 1934" [an appendix, which summarizes the fundamental differences between the early 1932 version and the 1934 version].⁵¹

A similar situation occurs in "Examen de la obra de Herbert Quain," in which the ultimate flop of the protagonist's novel, *The God of the Labyrinth,* is due to failed marketing strategies and the publication of a competing novel by Ellery Queen.⁵² Since this short story masquerades as a type of obituary after the death of Herbert Quain, there are passing references to several of his publications accompanied by a brief summary and/or review of them, a feature that directly echoes much of Borges's work for the literary magazine *El Hogar* from 1936 to 1939. In fact, the enigma at the heart of Herbert Quain's *The God of the Labyrinth* is its textual similarity to Borges's review of Richard Hull's *Excellent Intentions* in the April 15, 1938, issue of *El Hogar*.⁵³ Nashieli Marcano expertly links this particular short story to the field of bibliography for its reliance on methods of textual bibliography, which serve to authenticate Quain's work:

> El hallazgo [de lo auténtico] se hace posible por medio de la creación de una bibliografía textual que le facilita al narrador-reseñista de "Examen" justificar la publicación de la obra de Quain (mediante la mención de fechas) y, a la vez, determina

la inestabilidad textual tanto de Quain como de Borges (por sus revisiones de "Examen") en su empresa literaria.

[The discovery [of what is authentic] is made possible through the creation of a textual bibliography that allows the narrator-reviewer of "Examen" to justify the publication of the work of Quain (through the mention of dates) and at the same time determines the textual instability of both Quain and Borges (in his revisions of "Examen") in their literary endeavors.][54]

Reading these short stories through a bibliographical lens allows us to grasp important aspects of Borges's writings that might otherwise go unnoticed or be dismissed as mere physical details. In fact, these bibliographical elements of Borges's work accentuate many of the larger philosophical themes that he most frequently writes about, such as authenticity, reality, and truth.

"La biblioteca de Babel" [The Library of Babel], also collected in *El jardín de senderos que se bifurcan,* contains many clear bibliographical resonances. Within the hexagonal rooms of this library not only are all of the books described as uniform, but their entire physical composition is specified in great detail: "cada libro es de cuatrocientas diez páginas; cada página, de cuarenta renglones; cada renglón, de unas ochenta letras de color negro. También hay letras en el dorso de cada libro" [each book is made up of 410 pages; each page, of forty lines; each line, of some eighty black letters. There are also letters on the spine of each book].[55] In addition, all of the books "constan de elementos iguales: el espacio, el punto, la coma, las veintidós letras del alfabeto" [are made up of uniform elements: the period, the comma, the space, the twenty-two letters of the alphabet].[56] Even though all of these books are uniform and composed in exactly the same way, the narrator of this short story specifically emphasizes the fact that "*no hay, en la vasta Biblioteca, dos libros idénticos*" [*there do not exist, in the whole vast Library, two identical books*], which touches on the bibliographical idea that every book is a unique physical object.[57] This concept of both textual and physical differences between copies of books is later suggested toward the close of the story, where the narrator reminds readers that even facsimiles of the works in this library differ from one another: "cada ejemplar [es] único, irremplazable, pero (como la Biblioteca es total) hay siempre varios centenares de miles de facsímiles imperfectos: de obras que no difieren sino por una letra o por una coma" [each book [is] unique, irreplaceable, but (inasmuch as the Library is total) there are always several hundreds of thousands of imperfect facsimiles of works that differ only by one letter or comma].[58] While facsimiles should not differ in content from their original sources, they can differ—and often do—in a physical sense. Thus, from a bibliographical perspective, the changes in scale, paper, quality of image, and coloration among facsimiles will always vary and as a result point to how no two copies in this library are the same.

Many of the key aspects of this short story show a marked engagement with a number of bibliographical branches such as descriptive bibliography (in the detailed description of each volume in the library) and enumerative bibliography (in the precise and methodical arrangement of all of its books). However, the most important form of bibliography that permeates the entirety of "La biblioteca de Babel" is the bibliography of bibliographies, or the systematic indexing—and organization—of all books, which I argue lies at the heart of not only *El jardín de senderos que se bifurcan,* but also much of Borges's oeuvre as a whole. In addition to the great sense of organization and classification of the works in the library (and of the library in general), every person in the story is described as a librarian as well, which further emphasizes the central role of books and their study for this work. What is more, an overarching message of "La biblioteca de Babel" is that every book is rare, and therefore every book should be catalogued and treated with care. This concept arises when the narrator describes how the "Purificadores" [Purifiers] invaded the library on several occasions to cleanse it of books that they considered "inútiles" [useless], which resulted in "la insensata perdición de millones de libros" [the senseless loss of millions of books].[59] Pollard evinces a similar sentiment in his own writings: "if [books] are to be of any use, they must be as living friends or acquaintances, and the whole art of forming and keeping a library consists in treating them on this footing, alike mentally and materially."[60] Part of the beauty of this library is the seeming uniformity of its contents, which, upon closer inspection, turns out to be a mere illusion since, as noted earlier, no two books in the library are exactly the same. As historical, social, and economic artifacts, every book presents readers with unique evidence regarding its production and place in a larger literary context, and thus, the physical features must be examined.

Throughout "La biblioteca de Babel" are several references to a certain book that serves as the perfect summary or condensation of every other book in the library, which I argue is equivalent to a bibliography of bibliographies. This is the "libro total" [total book] that the narrator describes at length. In other words, this is precisely the book that outlines the system through which individuals can find every book in the library, much like the Dewey Decimal System: "Para localizar el libro A, consultar previamente un libro B que indique el sitio de A; para localizar el libro B, consultar previamente un libro C, y así hasta lo infinito" [To locate book A, you must first consult a book B that indicates the location of book A; to locate book B, you must first consult a book C, and so on infinitely].[61] The *vademecum,* or manual, that surfaces in the short story's closing footnote also aligns with a bibliography of bibliographies: "bastaría un solo volumen, de formato común, impreso en cuerpo nueve o en cuerpo diez, que constara de un número infinito de hojas infinitamente delgadas" [one single volume would suffice, of a common format, printed in nine- or ten-point type, that consisted of an infinite number of infinitely thin pages].[62] Interestingly, Pollard classifies the bibliography of bibliographies as an example of a universal bibliography, which undoubtedly corresponds to the sense of an all-encompassing library as depicted in "La biblioteca de Babel." In addition, Pollard notes in his entry in the *Encyclopedia Britannica* that "universal bibliography was recognized as an impossibility," an observation that seems to play into the inherent dichotomy of fiction and reality that crops up in light of the narrator's notion of an infinite library.[63]

When I introduced the idea of bibliography at the start of this chapter, I turned to Pollard's detailed entry in the eleventh edition of the *Encyclopedia Britannica,* choosing this apt source for the high probability that Borges would have read these exact words at some point in his life. While the high potential that Borges consulted this source makes its selection particularly relevant, I also chose Pollard's words, as opposed to those of any other important bibliographer, for two of his major contributions to the field: his systematic organization of books at the British Museum and his role in the completion of *A Short-Title Catalogue of Books Printed in England, Scotland, and Ireland, and of English Books Printed Abroad 1475–1640* (1926). These two projects, the products of a lifetime of dedicated scholarship, point to the possible inspiration that a figure like Pollard might have had for Borges and *El jardín de senderos que se bifurcan*. His organizational methods, his bibliography of bibliographies, and his clear explications of the varying branches of bibliography suggest that Pollard enters into direct dialogue with Borges. That is to say, the "Hombre del Libro" [Man of the Book] who resides at the heart of "La biblioteca de Babel" is someone who is responsible for the complete systematization of the books and spaces in this library and as a result much resembles a bibliographer like A. W. Pollard.

In line with *El jardín de senderos que se bifurcan*, a few of the short stories in Borges's *Ficciones* rely on bibliographical details.[64] In the prologue to "Artificios" [Artifices], Borges masterfully links this second collection of short stories with the first (*El jardín de senderos que se bifurcan*) through a reference to Herbert Ashe, the railroad engineer who first appeared in "Tlön, Uqbar, Orbis Tertius." More specifically, he states that the central hotel in "La muerte y la brújula" [Death and the Compass], Triste-le-Roy, is precisely where Herbert Ashe "recibió, y tal vez no leyó, el tomo undécimo de una enciclopedia ilusoria" [received, and perhaps never read, the eleventh volume of an imaginary encyclopedia].[65] What is more, this explicit reference and its connection to "Tlön, Uqbar, Orbis Tertius" further highlights the important role of books for Borges's literary creations. Turning to the stories in this collection, we find the protagonist of "Funes el memorioso" [Funes the Memorious], known for his impeccable memory, comparing the forms of certain clouds with "las vetas de un libro en pasta española que sólo había mirado una vez" [the marbled grain in the design of a leather-bound book that he had seen only once].[66] It goes without saying that a large number of objects, or natural phenomena, in the world have a wispy design that echoes the form of certain clouds. The selection of the grains (or marbling) of a book as a foil to the previous image reiterates not only Borges's attention to detail, but also his interest in the physical details of books. At various points throughout this short story, Borges also makes references to Pliny's *Naturalis Historia,* which, as previously mentioned, was a work that Borges owned and valued highly.

Several additional, minor references to books in *Ficciones* include an "enorme biblioteca" [enormous library] filled with "libros controversiales e incompatibles" [controversial and incompatible books] in "La forma de la espada" [The Form of the Sword] and Marcelo Yarmolinsky's collection of books in "La muerte y la brújula" [Death and the Compass] that the protagonist, Erik Lönnrot, searches feverishly through to find an answer to the series of murders he is investigating.[67] Although there are no references to the physical features of books or specific editions in "Tema del traidor y del héroe" [Theme of the Traitor and the Hero], the central plot of this story relies on bibliographical details. In particular, at the start of the story the protagonist, Ryan, is investigating the assassination of a distant relative, Fergus Kilpatrick, in order to write "una biografía del héroe" [a biography of the hero], which involves a great deal of archival research. The last story in *Ficciones,* "Tres versiones de Judas" [Three Versions of Judas], recalls certain aspects of "Examen de la obra de Herbert Quain" and "Pierre Menard, autor del Quijote" since the story in question takes the form of a scholarly article that critiques the writings of Nils Runeberg by analyzing the books that he wrote during his lifetime, with an emphasis placed on their conception, creation, and production.

The question of materiality and the physical components of books also arises in *Seis problemas para don Isidro Parodi* [*Six Problems for Mr. Isidro Parodi*] (1942), which Borges co-wrote with his close friend Adolfo Bioy Casares. Take, for instance, "Las previsiones de Sangiácomo" [Free Will and the Commendatore], where we find very precise material references to a work written by one of the main characters, Ricky San Giacomo. Toward the end of the story we learn that Ricky's father, in an effort to quell his son's depression, "apresuró a lo somorgujo la impresión de la obra [*La espada al medio*], y, en menos que trepa un cerdo, le sorprendió con seiscientos cincuenta ejemplares en papel Wathman [*sic*], formato *Teufelsbibel*" [hastily sped up the printing of his work [*The Sword at Noon*], and, in the snap of a finger, he surprised him with 650 copies on Whatman paper, Devil's Bible format].[68] Though the mention of a precise type of paper—in this case Whatman, which normally is credited as the first example of wove paper, or paper without chain lines, wire lines, or watermarks—is intriguing, the given format of the work, *Teufelsbibel,* is much more puzzling. This curious German term translates to "Devil's Bible," which is a common name for the Codex Gigas, the largest extant medieval manuscript in the world. As with many of the other bibliographical details included in Borges's essays and short stories, this description raises a number of questions regarding the hypothetical printing of Ricky San Giacomo's book: What do Borges and Bioy Casares intend the term "format" to mean in this specific context? Are all 650 copies of *The Sword at Noon* this large? How do we deal with the inherent tension between the Whatman wove paper mentioned and the fact that the pages of the Codex Gigas, in its original form, are made of vellum, or animal skins? These questions highlight the potential richness in studying the question of materiality in Borges's work.

Along with *El jardín de senderos que se bifurcan* and *Ficciones,* one of the better-known collections of short stories that would later help Borges attain his international fame is *El Aleph.* Again, a number of stories in *El Aleph* reveal a close attention to the physical features of books.[69] The story that opens the collection, "El inmortal" [The Immortal], introduces the familiar conceit of the found manuscript, whose contents will form the text that follows. In setting up this common trope, the narrator goes to great lengths to describe the place where this supposed manuscript was found:

> En Londres, a principios del mes de junio de 1929, el anticuario Joseph Cartaphilus, de Esmirna, ofreció a la princesa de Lucinge los seis volúmenes en cuarto menor (1715-1720) de la Ilíada de Pope ... En el último tomo de la Ilíada halló este manuscrito.
>
> [In London, at the beginning of June 1929, the antiquarian Joseph Cartaphilus, from Smyrna, offered the Princess of Lucinge the six volumes in small quarto (1715-1720) of Pope's Iliad ... In the last volume of the Iliad she found this manuscript.][70]

Similar to what we saw in "Tlön, Uqbar, Orbis Tertius," "La biblioteca de Babel," and "Historia de la eternidad," Borges turns to the bibliographical concept of format by mentioning that the six volumes of Alexander Pope's work are in small quarto. This detail becomes even more intriguing when we consider the publishing history behind Pope's book, which was printed with subscribers funding the process, thus freeing up a great deal of capital for authors, publishers, printers, and all other parties involved in the book industry.[71] The choice of Alexander Pope also ties into Borges's bookish interests since, much like a number of other eighteenth-century English writers, Pope frequently included bibliographical details in his works and showed an interest in the physical aspects of books.

The last short story in *El Aleph,* which shares the collection's title, also weaves a few bibliographical details into its narrative. More specifically, one of the objects that the narrator, curiously named Borges, sees through the Aleph—"el lugar donde están, sin confundirse, todos los lugares del orbe, vistos desde todos los ángulos" [the place where there are, without converging, all of the places of the planet, seen from all possible angles]—is a book: "un ejemplar de la primera versión inglesa de Plinio, la de Philemon Holland, vi a un tiempo cada letra de cada página (de chico, yo solía maravillarme de que las letras de un volumen cerrado no se mezclaran y perdieran en el decurso de la noche)" [a copy of the first English translation of Pliny, that of Philemon Holland; I saw all at once each letter of each page (when I was small, I was always amazed by how the letters in a book never got mixed up and lost when the volume was closed at night)].[72] As opposed to just stating that he saw a copy of one of Pliny's books, the narrator includes precise details (of the edition, the language, and the translator) that make the work easily identifiable as his *Naturalis Historia,* which was one of Borges's most beloved books. Another detail that might go unnoticed is the passing reference in the postscript to an invented publishing house that produced the work of the protagonist, Carlos Argentino Daneri: Editorial Procusto (on "la calle Garay" [Garay Street]).[73] Once again, much as in *Ficciones,* Borges continues to blur the line between what is real and what is fiction.

Bibliographical Dead Ends: References to (Un)Real Books in Borges

As we have seen, books, as both material objects and containers of information, play an important part in Borges's writings. From the list of references to material aspects of books gathered in the first part of this chapter, it is clear that this Argentine writer had a keen eye for detail. That said, some of these details can be deceiving. Take, for instance, the mention of the first edition of *Acercamiento a Almotásim* described in the short story of the same name in *El jardín de senderos que se bifurcan*. The narrator goes to great lengths to provide the reader with precise and extensive information regarding the physical book in question, even the fact that it sold out quickly, yet this work does not actually exist outside of the pages of Borges's literary collection. In addition to masking this reality in detailed descriptions of the paper, Borges also makes sure to mention the "edición ilustrada ... que acaba de reproducir en Londres Víctor Gollancz" [illustrated edition ... which has just been reproduced and issued in London by Victor Gollancz], who, as previously mentioned, is a real-life publisher (1893–1967), thus blurring the line even further between reality and fiction. This example shows the need to disentangle the real from the apocryphal in virtually all of Borges's writings. Sylvia Molloy analyzes these types of citations and references in *Signs of Borges*: "it is equally pointless to systematically doubt all references and quotes. The irreverence and irony underlying Borges's erudition are not necessarily proof of its spurious nature. Borges makes no claim to authenticity; he goes beyond it, and even seems to invite the discovery of fraud, precisely because such a discovery in no way signals failure ... It is therefore vain to impose ethical criteria on an erudition that aspires to be literary, in the richest sense of the term."[74] Molloy also comments on Borges's tendency to distort citations and mix the real with the invented: "to quote irreverently as Borges does, vigorously shaking the problematic edifice of erudition, combining in wise disorder well known references and quotations with unknown or invented ones, does more than question the limits of that culture: it suppresses them, not through outright condemnation but through exaggeration and parody."[75] While imitation might be the highest form of flattery, Borges's imagined books and fictional citations serve to question and in a sense critique the cultural status quo.

Borges's ability to invent convincing bibliographical details with ease, especially ones that align with real trends in nineteenth- and twentieth-century publishing, speaks volumes. The inverse of this example is also true as we saw with "Tlön, Uqbar, Orbis Tertius," in which Borges no longer relies on true facts of the publishing world (such as publishing houses and printers) to spin the fictitious, but instead uses an existing book, the *Anglo-American Cyclopaedia,* as a jumping off point and in the process raises suspicion about the contents and state of this real-life object. When books form a part of the central plot of a story, they allude to the creation of other worlds.[76] Although the details used to reference these (imaginary) works are comprehensible, given our standardized system of citations, they do not match up with anything in our own world and as a result hint at Borges's desire to signal something *beyond* our material reality.[77] Along with the need to keep an eye on Borges's bibliographical "evidence," one of the more intriguing aspects in much of this writer's work is his unique citation style. Here I am not speaking of punctuation, but rather of substantive referents made after a quoted passage of another work. I was first struck by the fact that there is *no* regularity akin to standard styles, such as those in the *MLA Handbook* or *The Chicago Manual of Style,* which caused me to think critically about *why* Borges might have written his essays and short stories in such a way. Is there a deeper meaning or significance to the presence or absence of standards? If he includes a precise date or publisher for one work referenced but not another, does that *reveal* anything to readers? As Borges is characterized most frequently as the master of labyrinths, mirrors, and constantly forking paths, these inconsistencies, and even *mis*quotations, are his way of playing with his readers. We might even say that his imprecision with regard to citation is a virtue of sorts.

Citations in any Borges short story or essay that refer us to other, real works demonstrate his interest in placing himself within an existing body of knowledge or becoming part of what T. S. Eliot deems the historical sense, thus acknowledging an understanding of the relationship between the literary past and present. In a similar vein, the continual use of citations to existing works or bodies of knowledge, most notably in his essays, indicates the limits of time and space and the fact that it is virtually impossible to engage all aspects of a given work in one's writings. As a result, Borges appears to be encouraging his readers not only to check the validity of his sources, and by extension his arguments, but also to familiarize themselves with the works that have influenced him most as a writer and that serve as the literary and philosophical foundation for his own works. In addition to actual quotations from other sources, Borges also tends to reference entire books.[78] At times these mentions of supporting or consulted materials are nothing more than a title, lacking both author name and place of publication; at other times, he adds a date of publication. Although this extra piece of information might not seem terribly helpful at first, it allows readers to narrow down specific editions to which he was either referring or personally consulting while crafting his prose. Keeping this in mind, one can form a list of particular editions that Borges most likely worked with to write his essays and short stories.[79] Nevertheless, any one of these cited sources—or pieces of information from them—might be nothing more than an apocryphal text, invented by Borges himself.[80] Take, for instance, the page of consulted sources found at the end of *Historia universal de la infamia* [*A Universal History of Infamy*]. Although virtually all of the titles can be confirmed as *real* (after thorough bibliographic cross-checking), Borges has, indeed, included one false entry: Alexander Schulz's *Die Vernichtung der Rose*. As Sergio Waisman notes, "Alexander Schulz is a masked rephrasing of the name of Borges's friend, the Argentine artist Xul Solar, who never wrote such a text, and especially not in German."[81] Alongside these references to (un)real physical books is Borges's consistent use of established *forms* of writing—such as the book review, the biography, or even the detective story—as a type of parody or subversion of these genres, as well as the types of people writing them (i.e., academics).[82] Emir Rodríguez Monegal highlights this trend in Borges's work: "In parading his scholarship, Borges undermines it by introducing not only false leads but false sources, apocryphal books, misquoted texts."[83] Thus, Borges's engagement with books is both concrete (physical features, printings, publishers, etc.) and abstract (compositional and editorial theories, genres and forms of writing, etc.).

One possible way to interpret the varying citation practices and references to (un)real books in Borges's writings is that he ultimately wanted his work to remain anonymous. Borges expresses this sentiment in his own work as early as *Evaristo Carriego* and continues to reiterate these thoughts throughout his life. For instance, in a recorded phone conversation between Borges and C. Jared Loewenstein, the librarian responsible for starting and developing the Borges collection at the University of Virginia, Borges comments that he hopes that his writings will "continue to survive" and be read by many, but at the same time he preferred that "they do so anonymously."[84] Why, we might ask, would Borges not want his name attached to such groundbreaking texts as "La biblioteca de Babel" or "El jardín de senderos que se bifurcan," which immediately spring to mind with the mere mention of Borges's name? Perhaps we should consider Borges's own fascination with works that have remained anonymous over the years, especially *The Battle of Maldon* and many of the Icelandic sagas that he dedicated such a large portion of his later life to studying. By removing any type of authorial voice from these writings, readers are forced to focus solely on their content, which might be the idea behind Borges's desire for anonymity. Instead of *Ficciones*, *El Aleph*, or even *Historia universal de la infamia* appearing on recommended reading lists or syllabi *because* their author is Jorge Luis Borges, Borges might have wished for his writings to crop up in literary circles because of their carefully crafted messages in poetically precise prose.

Borges behind the Scenes: Crafting the Physical Book

From a very early time in his literary career, Borges not only was involved with the initial stages of crafting a manuscript to be sent to a publisher, but also was entrenched in the more editorial tasks of correcting proofs and even setting type to be printed. During an interview with Antonio Carrizo, curiously recorded in the same year as his lecture on the book, Borges recalls his intimate interactions with typesetters and designers while working as codirector of the *Revista Multicolor de los Sábados* [*Multicolor Saturday Magazine*]:

> Yo estaba en la misma sala en que estaban los dibujantes, y me hice amigo de todos ellos. Y además me gustaba mucho traba-

jar con los obreros en el taller, con los linotipistas. Y aprendí a leer los linotipos, como un espejo. Y aprendí a armar una página también.

[I was in the same room as the illustrators, and I made friends with them. I also liked to collaborate with many of the workers in the shop, with the linotypists. I learned how to read the Linotype slugs, like a mirror. And I learned to compose a page too.][85]

Carrizo later asked Borges whether he enjoyed this environment, to which he responded, tellingly: "Sí; me gustaba mucho. El ambiente de una imprenta es muy, muy agradable. Armar páginas, corregir pruebas: todo eso lo hacía yo y me pagaban la suma, entonces—no sé si muy pródiga, pero en todo caso, suficiente—de trescientos pesos por mes" [Yes; I liked it a lot. The environment of a print shop is very, very pleasant. Assembling pages, correcting proofs: I did all of this and they paid me—I don't know if it was very generous, but in any case, it was sufficient—three hundred pesos a month].[86] Ulyses Petit de Murat, Borges's codirector at the *Revista Multicolor*, confirms this sentiment in his memoir about the writer: "Borges accede a un mundo nuevo. Se le exige en la imprenta, junto a mí, que disponga la colocación de un grabado; que complete una página; que redacte allí mismo, cosa que no hubiera nunca soñado en hacer" [Borges gained access to a new world. In the print shop, with me there, he was told to arrange the location of a print; to complete a page; to edit right there, something that he had never dreamed of doing].[87]

Even though these job positions and interviews with co-workers attest to Borges's interest in creating and manipulating the physical aspects of his books, extant archives from his time working for the *Revista Multicolor* are not known. However, one of the recent manuscript acquisitions for the University of Virginia Borges collection, which to date is the only known material of its kind, supports the claim that this meticulous Argentine author was very much involved in the physical presentation of his works. Although this document predates Borges's job as codirector of the *Revista Multicolor*, the contents still tell us a great deal about his knowledge of and involvement with the precise formatting of

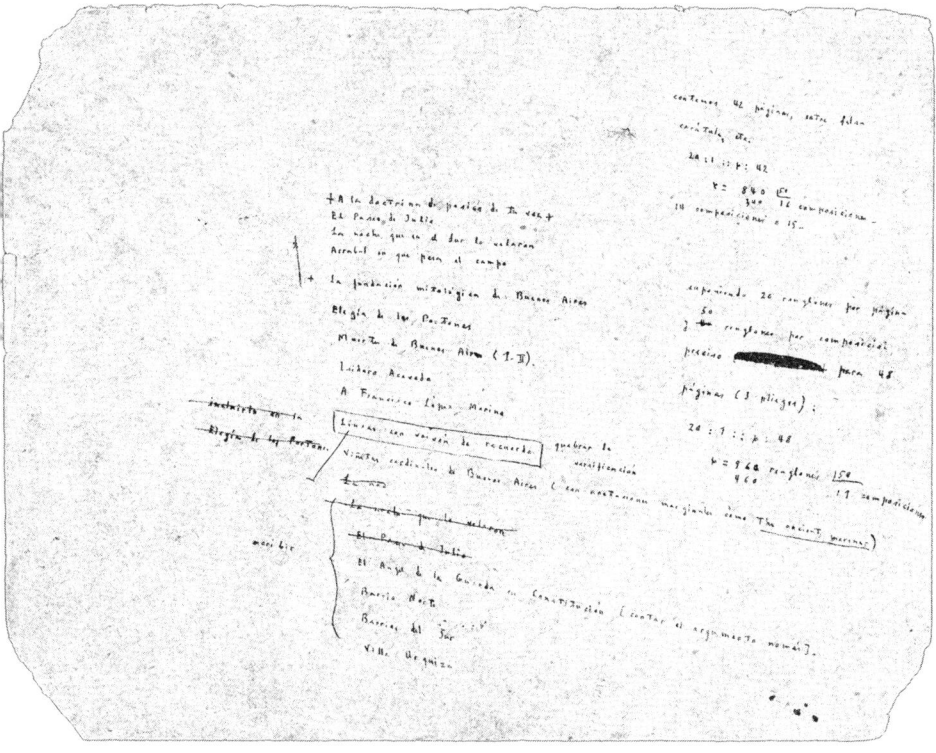

Collation formulations and a preliminary list of contents for *Cuaderno San Martín* (1929) in Borges's hand. *(Excerpt from "Two Covers of Cuaderno Chacabuco" by Jorge Luis Borges. Copyright © María Kodama, used by permission of The Wylie Agency LLC.)*

his books. Unlike other surviving Borges manuscripts that more often than not have the author's distinctive "insect-like handwriting" precisely printed on either ruled notebook paper or high-quality paper, the document in question appears to be a smattering of unconnected passing thoughts scribbled hastily on the covers of a notebook.[88] More specifically, as the first page of the manuscript clearly indicates, this is a Cuaderno Chacabuco, which was a typical Argentine schoolbook, but we have only its front and back covers; the interior pages are missing. The first, second, and fourth pages contain fragments of phrases or numerical equations, while the third page contains two drawn figures. Each of the pages of this manuscript deserves a more detailed description, but I devote my attention here to the second page (or verso of the front cover), which, given its contents, is crucial to the present study.

On the page in question we find a preliminary list of contents for Borges's 1929 book of poetry *Cuaderno San Martín* [*San Martín Notebook*] and a series of numerical calculations related to the physical layout of this volume. It might be commonplace for an author to decide on the individual works to be included in a collection of poetry, but unless an author also was an editor, it seems somewhat rare for this individual to decide on the number of lines per page and, as a result, how many pages will be necessary for the book. This is exactly the computation, clearly written in Borges's distinctive hand, that we find in this manuscript: "suponiendo 20 reglones por página y 50 renglones por composición, preciso para 48 páginas (3 plieges [sic]): 20 : 1 :: α : 48. α = 960 reglones 19 composiciones" [supposing 20 lines per page and 50 lines per composition, I require for 48 pages (3 gatherings): 20 : 1 :: α : 48. α = 960 lines 19 compositions]. Besides the peculiarity of an author designating a specific number of lines per page, Borges converting his total number of pages into groupings of gatherings ("3 plieges [sic]") is a very bibliographical detail.[89] When we read the colophon from the first printed edition of *Cuaderno San Martín*, we discover that it was printed by a high-quality printer (Francisco A. Colombo), was the product of a specific publishing firm (Editorial Proa), and was also part of a particular series directed by Alfonso Reyes (Cuadernos del Plata).[90] These facts make Borges's personal calculations all the more suspect and seem to indicate that he—or his father—may have been the party responsible for funding the production of this book. This newfound material evidence highlights the need to describe and analyze the physical features of Borges's various publications more closely, especially since he might have had more of a role in their physical production than initially thought.

Another interesting aspect of this hard-to-read manuscript is the following parenthetical note that appears alongside "Viñetas cardinales de Buenos Aires" [Cardinal vignettes of Buenos Aires], one of the possible titles to be included in the collection: "(con anotaciones marginales como

The ancient mariner)" [(with notes in the style of *The Ancient Mariner*)]. Before the arrival of book designers toward the end of the nineteenth century, the way in which individuals talked about how books looked was by comparing them to other books that already existed. In other words, authors might go to their publishers, or even to a printer, and explain that they wanted their work printed *in the style of* some other volume that they had seen. Since "Viñetas cardinales de Buenos Aires" was cut from the contents of the printed versions of *Cuaderno San Martín*, it is challenging to narrow down the particular edition of *The Rime of the Ancient Mariner* that Borges was referencing (from a design standpoint). That said, when we consider the publication history of Samuel Taylor Coleridge's poem, Borges was most likely alluding to the revised second edition (first published in 1817 as part of *Sibylline Leaves*), which incorporated a gloss that was not present in the first edition. Borges's desire to have his poem annotated in the style of Coleridge's well-known work highlights his strong preferences toward the physical presentation of the words on the page.[91]

As we have seen throughout this chapter, Borges has always had a keen interest in books and the printed text. From the formative years he spent within the walls of his father's library to his places of employment during this period (1930–1951), the physical media of books (as well as of newspapers and literary journals) are always a constant. What is more, dissecting and analyzing the ways in which he makes references in his own writings to the physical features of these media reveals a deep-seated engagement with books. By extension, it can be argued that he uses this detailed knowledge of the physical features and components of books to aid in his creation of the apocryphal texts and imaginary volumes that crop up throughout his works, most notably in *Ficciones,* since virtually every short story in this collection centers around a desire to have readers question their own conceptions of reality and contemplate the notion that history is not very different from fiction. Thus, it is the book (in terms of both its production process and its completed physical form) that lies at the heart of Borges's works. It is the book that speaks volumes about not only his formation as a writer and his intricate creation process, but also the historical and social moment in which he was writing. In a somewhat ironic turn of events, it is through the analysis of the physical features of Borges's books that we discover details about both the imaginary worlds that lie beyond our own reality (as so many critics have discussed) and the real constraints and pulls existing in this writer's contemporary Argentina.

T • W • O

Borges as Author

Jorge Luis Borges comes to mind first and foremost as an author. When we think of him within this specific role, we conjure up images and ideas of labyrinths, forking paths, and infinite libraries. We call to mind all of his fictions that fill the pages of *Historia universal de la infamia* [*A Universal History of Infamy*], *El jardín de senderos que se bifurcan* [*The Garden of Forking Paths*], and *El libro de arena* [*The Book of Sand*]. We muse over his *porteño* verses collected in *Fervor de Buenos Aires* [*Fervor of Buenos Aires*], *Luna de enfrente* [*Moon across the Way*], and *Cuaderno San Martín* [*San Martín Notebook*]. We contemplate all of his philosophical essays in *Inquisiciones* [*Inquisitions*], *Discusión* [*Discussion*], and *Otras inquisiciones* [*Other Inquisitions*]. In essence, we recall all of his works that make him one of the most important writers of twentieth-century world literature. In this chapter I consider the less-visible forces that helped bring these books into (physical) existence. Thus, rather than presenting another close textual reading of Borges's well-known works, I instead look to the printers and publishers whom he enlisted during the first half of the 1930s and ask several questions: What are the responsibilities of an editor, a publisher, or a printer in contrast with those of an author? How do all of these individuals interact? What were the general communities of book circulation like in Buenos Aires at this time? To answer these questions, I focus on the types of relationships that Borges developed with these diverse firms throughout the early part of his career and explore how these connections shaped his widespread popularity later in life.

Borges's literary production during the first half of the 1930s, which also is one of the most productive times in his career, reveals a great deal of diversity in terms of the publishers and printers with whom he worked and the possible readers whom he might have had at that time. What is most notable from this early period is the fact that he established close ties with fine printers known for their luxury editions (Francisco A. Colombo) and publishers whose work was also of a higher quality because they frequently sent their editions to these same luxury printers (Manuel Gleizer and Viau y Zona). At the same time, he worked for mass-media publications (*Crítica*) and produced his first volume of fiction with a publisher known for cheap, low-quality editions that were often rife with errors (Editorial TOR) (Table 1). In essence, this early stage in Borges's literary career is marked by a large amount of activity and variation in book production from one work to the next. Moreover, his decision to publish his writings in such disparate contexts and communities is notable and something that has yet to be analyzed in detail.[1] In her study dedicated to Borges's earlier works, and the author's constant manipulation of these texts, Annick Louis highlights the importance of contextualizing the venue in which Borges published his initial writings:

> El fenómeno se observa en lo que respecta a las editoriales; en este sentido, la elección de Colombo para *Las Kenningar* en 1933 y de TOR para *Historia universal de la infamia* en 1935 marca dos momentos radicalmente opuestos en cuanto a la calidad material de la edición, el precio del ejemplar y el circuito de difusión.
>
> [One observes the phenomenon (of manipulation and choice) in terms of the publishing firms; in this sense, the selection of Colombo for *Las Kenningar* in 1933 and of TOR for *Historia universal de la infamia* in 1935 marks two radically opposed moments in terms of the material quality of the edition, the price of the book, and the circuit of diffusion.][2]

Table 1. Works published by Borges from 1930 to 1936

Date	Title	Publisher	Printer
1930	*Evaristo Carriego*	Manuel Gleizer	Francisco A. Colombo
1932	*Discusión* [*Discussion*]	Manuel Gleizer	Francisco A. Colombo
1933	*Las Kenningar* [*The Kenning*]		Francisco A. Colombo
1935	*Historia universal de la infamia* [*A Universal History of Infamy*]	Editorial TOR	Editorial TOR
1936	*Historia de la eternidad* [*A History of Eternity*]	Viau y Zona	Francisco A. Colombo

Louis goes on to pose several significant research questions:

> ¿Dónde publicar qué? Parece haber sido una de las cuestiones que inquietaban al escritor de la época. Pero, llegado el momento de fabricar las antologías, el problema parece haber sido: ¿qué recuperar y qué orden otorgar a lo que se arranca al olvido, y por lo tanto, a su primer contexto de publicación?
>
> [*Where to publish what?* This seems to have been one of the questions that perplexed the author of that time. But, arriving at the moment of producing anthologies, the problem seems to have been: *What to save and what order to give the saved works, and, consequently, their first publication context?*]³

In general terms, Louis's study of Borges's career during the early 1930s, specifically his time at the *Revista Multicolor de los Sábados* as well as the production of his *Historia universal de la infamia*, is extremely thorough. That said, in addition to the research gap discussed above, Louis also highlights several other areas that deserve further attention, including

Borges's preference toward literary biography and how this genre leads to the development of his first fictions. These are some of the issues I address and the gaps I hope to fill throughout this chapter, especially in light of the fact that two of the works that Borges published during the early 1930s fall into the genre of biography (*Evaristo Carriego* and *Historia universal de la infamia*).

An important fact to keep in mind during this prolific period in Borges's early career is that virtually all of his writings, whether essays or fictions, were first published in small literary magazines or newspapers before their inclusion in the printed volumes dating between 1930 and 1936, which suggests the importance of examining all existing versions of a work for both differences in physical features and any alterations or variants in the written texts. One of the most notable tendencies in these earlier writings is a marked interest in the form of the biography, considered from a number of different angles. This trend becomes apparent with the early publication of *Evaristo Carriego* in 1930 and also Borges's preoccupation with the lives of various well-known criminals. Thus, in this early part of his career, Borges would send a literary biography of a minor Argentine poet (Evaristo Carriego) to a well-known publisher (Manuel Gleizer) that would be printed with a boutique luxury printer, Francisco A. Colombo, in a small (almost private) run.[4] A few years later, he would send his first collection of fiction based on the biographies of well-known criminals, *Historia universal de la infamia,* to the mass-market publisher Editorial TOR, known for printing books so cheaply that they were sold by the pound. The former edition was printed in a small run on fine paper, suggesting how the content within the book cohered with its external form and intended readership. In contrast, the affordable copy of *Historia universal de la infamia,* a collection of stories retelling the feats of criminals such as Billy the Kid, speaks to a popular audience. Keeping all of these factors in mind, I investigate how Borges shaped the distinct physical features of his works for specific and specifically different audiences. In addition, I take an important first pass at the relationship between markets, commerce, and literary audience in multilingual Argentine book production.

Francisco A. Colombo and the Art of Fine Printing

Two general trends emerged with the explosion of the book industry in Argentina during the first half of the twentieth century: one of popular culture for the masses (in the form of cheap paperback editions) and one of elite culture for the upper classes (in the form of fine, luxury editions). The latter trend, which starts to materialize in the 1920s, can be identified by book editions with limited print runs on high-quality paper that were illustrated with original prints or decorated with elaborate typographical ornaments and unique bindings. In other words, each of these types of volumes would "[aspirar] a la categoría de 'libro de bibliófilo'" [aspire to the category of "bibliophilic books"].[5] This production style would prove to be a constant during the first half of the twentieth century and can be traced to a number of factors not only in Argentina, but also throughout parts of Europe.[6] First, since up to this point many of the books sold throughout Argentina were printed and produced in Europe (most notably Germany, France, and Spain), a number of these foreign stylistic tendencies proved to be a large source of inspiration for the South American book market. In addition, the 1920s mark a crucial period in Argentine book history since during this early decade several organizations dedicated to the country's artistic production, including books, were formed. The two most notable of these groups were the Amigos del Arte [Friends of Art] (1924) and the Sociedad de Bibliófilos Argentinos [Society of Argentine Bibliophiles] (1928).[7] In order to better understand the output and overall importance of these two organizations, as well as the interest in luxury editions throughout Argentina at this time, I turn to one of the linchpins of this specialized industry, Francisco A. Colombo, a printer whose work is central to any investigation of Argentine bibliophiles' books during the twentieth century.

A native of Buenos Aires, Francisco A. Colombo (1878–1953) was best known for his typographical artistry.[8] Even though he was self-taught in the field of book production and had no professional training, the books that he printed over the years were held to superior standards and can be considered nothing short of works of art. At the beginning of the twentieth century in Argentina, luxury editions were rare, and as a result the work of Colombo was all the more exceptional.[9] Moreover,

Colombo printed all but two of the books associated with the Sociedad de Bibliófilos Argentinos, whose objectives align perfectly with much of this printer's work: "The Society has the objective of cultivating and fomenting the typographical art and the complementary decorative arts of good books, not only between its associates, but also in [the] public interest. The action ... will consist primarily in editing exclusively for its associates, publications that contribute to the progress and art of the book in the country; in organizing reunions, conferences, expositions, etc., related to bibliophilia; and [in] facilitating the relations of bibliophiles in Buenos Aires with those in the rest of the country and abroad."[10]

Before his association with the Sociedad de Bibliófilos Argentinos, Colombo was sought out by the well-known Argentine writer and bibliophile Ricardo Güiraldes.[11] In his speech marking the fiftieth anniversary of Colombo's work, Ricardo E. Molinari recognized the importance of this chance meeting of Güiraldes and the Argentine printer that would forever change fine printing in Argentina: "Le debemos a Güiraldes el descubrimiento de este distinguido artesano gráfico, que se une a su esclarecido nombre de escritor, como una flor a muchas hojas" [We owe to Güiraldes the discovery of this distinguished graphic artist, who joins his renowned writer's name, as a flower to its many leaves].[12] Their friendship began in 1922 and from that moment forward Colombo was marked as a luxury printer in the elite circle of many literary groups:

> Desde la primera edición de "Rosaura," hasta nuestros días, innumerables trabajos son testimonio de una singular dedicación en la realización del libro, como obra de arte. Desde la generosa dimensión de la tipografía de "Interlunio" de Girondo, con las magníficas aguafuertes de Spilimbergo, hasta la bella edición del "Matadero" de Echeverría, ilustrada por Melgarejo Muñoz, pasando por las exquisitas ediciones de Ricardo E. Molinari y Raúl Veroni, una sucesión de obras imperecederas, son testimonio de esa vocación por el arte gráfico, sentido como creación.
>
> [From the first edition of *Rosaura,* to our days, innumerable works are testament to a singular dedication to the produc-

tion of the book, as a work of art. From the generous dimension of the typography of Girondo's *Interlunio,* with Spilimbergo's magnificent etchings, to the beautiful edition of Echeverría's "El matadero," illustrated by Melgarejo Muñoz, passing through the exquisite editions of Ricardo E. Molinari and Raúl Veroni, a series of enduring works are testament to that vocation for the graphic arts, directed as creation.][13]

Along with the successful printing of *Rosaura* in 1922, Colombo also had great success with Güiraldes's *Don Segundo Sombra* in 1926. The first run of the novel, of two thousand copies, sold out in thirty days, which triggered a second printing of five thousand copies that same year.[14] The popularity of this work continued throughout the decade with two other print runs in 1928 and 1930, each consisting of a staggering five thousand copies.

In terms of the specifics of his printing and typographical style, Colombo is known for instituting the following standards: a cover with centered, uppercase typography (normally Garamond or Bodoni) printed on white or neutral paper, a title page in the same typeface with information about the publishing house and/or printer centered at the bottom of the page, typography of the text throughout in Garamond (size 10 or 12), and a justified colophon on the last page with handwritten numbering.[15] In other words, any one of Colombo's books printed during this time was known "por la pulcritud de su tipografía, compuesta a mano, por la habilidad de la puesta en página y por la calidad del papel" [for the beauty of his typography, set by hand, for the skill placed on each page, and for the quality of paper].[16] This style is exactly what we find throughout the pages of Borges's works that Colombo printed during the 1930s.[17]

It is quite clear from the authors and literary genres that Colombo gravitated toward and tended to produce that he was an elite printer. In addition to Borges's works and a number of translations of foreign works, some of the authors that Colombo frequently printed during the 1930s and 1940s included Adolfo Bioy Casares (*La nueva tormenta* [*The New Storm*], 1935), Leopoldo Lugones (*Romances del Río Seco* [*Romances of the Dry River*], 1938), Evaristo Carriego (*La canción del barrio* [*The Neighborhood's Song*], 1933), Oliverio Girondo (*Espantapájaros*

[*Scarecrow*], 1932), Victoria Ocampo (*Homenaje argentino a Claude Debussy* [*Argentine Homage to Claude Debussy*], 1928), Ricardo E. Molinari (*El pez y la manzana* [*The Fish and the Apple*], 1929, illustrated by Borges's sister, Norah; *La tierra y el héroe* [*The Land and the Hero*], 1936; and *La muerte en la llanura* [*Death on the Plain*], 1937; among others), and Ricardo Güiraldes (*Mi caballo y el hombre que pasó* [*My Horse and the Man Who Passed*], 1929). Besides the fact that the majority of these authors are poets, which in itself creates a narrowing of readership, virtually all of them also come from wealthy families and privileged backgrounds. Furthermore, each of these writers appears to have had some type of close relationship with Borges—such as being his intimate and lasting friend (Bioy Casares), starting a literary magazine with him (Güiraldes), or even serving as a great source of inspiration for him (Lugones). Regardless of the specifics of these relationships, it is an interesting fact that connects most of Colombo's printed work during this period. Borges's own support and interest in the high-quality works that Colombo printed is clear from the facts that his first four books from the 1930s are a product of this artist's handiwork and that both he and his sister, Norah, are listed as "supporters" of Colombo on the advent of his fiftieth anniversary of graphic work.[18]

Colombo's printed books circulated in the upper echelons of Argentine society and rarely would have found their way into the hands of the middle or lower classes because of their price and aesthetics. This is certainly the case when we consider the fact that Colombo was responsible for printing the first issue of Victoria Ocampo's literary magazine *Sur,* on "special paper" with "clear, bold print and twenty-four full pages of photographic illustrations."[19] Buonocore describes the quality of Colombo's work in the greatest detail:

> En efecto, en los tipos de letras escogidos, en las iniciales de capítulos, en el espaciado justo, en la intensidad uniforme de las tintas, hasta en la misma calidad del papel y en mil detalles, adviértese, indudablemente, junto a la acendrada preocupación por la belleza de cada libro, un dominio seguro e impecable del tecnicismo gráfico.

[In essence, in the sorts of the chosen letters, in the initials at the start of each chapter, in the justified spacing, in the striking uniformity of inking, to the extreme quality of paper and in a thousand details, one will find, undoubtedly, together with a refined preoccupation for the beauty of each book, a pure and impeccable dominion of graphic techniques.][20]

In short, what we find in the works that Colombo printed is a keen attention to detail and a knack for artistic beauty.

As previously mentioned, Colombo printed four of Borges's books during the first half of the 1930s: *Evaristo Carriego* (1930), *Discusión* (1932), *Las Kenningar* (1933), and *Historia de la eternidad* (1936) (see Table 1). In contrast to the equal distribution of published volumes of poetry and prose by Borges during the 1920s (three volumes of poetry and three volumes of prose), these four works highlight a notable shift in his writings in favor of prose that would continue throughout the 1930s and into the 1940s.[21] In addition, the publication of *Evaristo Carriego* is often seen as somewhat of an anomaly in Borges's oeuvre and as a result is overlooked (and understudied) by many critics; yet, as we shall see, it is an important early work that thematically echoes several other of Borges's writings during the 1930s. In an effort to best describe the relationship between form and content in these works, specifically in terms of their printer and publisher, I first briefly detail the subjects of these four books and then describe their physical features and attributes, which will help to complement and flesh out questions concerning markets, audiences, and the general reception of Borges's early works.

Evaristo Carriego is a biography of the minor Argentine poet of the same name, who happened to be a close friend of Borges's father. Yet, as Norman Thomas di Giovanni rightly notes, "it is not and never set out to be a conventional biography."[22] As a result, readers who are more familiar with Borges's *Ficciones* or *El Aleph* will take comfort in the common tropes and themes that emerge in this early work (and that will later serve as the crux of these more canonical collections of fiction). In fact, instead of presenting readers with a traditional biography of Carriego, Borges ends up revealing more about his own life and tendencies as a writer in this early work. Thus, from the very first section we find a lengthy description of Borges's native Buenos Aires, instead of material specifically related to the life of Carriego. Moreover, as previously mentioned in the first chapter, the entire opening of the third section of this book, which deals with Carriego's *Misas herejes* [*Heretical Masses*], details the physicality of books and how any first book should be designed. When we consider the fact that this work was anticipated before its first printing (by being listed in the front matter of Borges's *El idioma de los argentinos* [*The Language of the Argentines*] [1928] as a forthcoming work), it is clear that there was a great level of planning for and dedication to this work. Much like his other collections that appear during the early 1930s, *Evaristo Carriego* has its precedents in earlier works that Borges published throughout the 1920s, which maps onto his propensity for recycling and reusing parts of his writings in later works. In the case of this specific book, an earlier short essay, "Carriego y el sentido del arrabal" [Carriego and the Meaning of the City's Outskirts], initially collected in *El tamaño de mi esperanza* [*The Size of My Hope*] (1926), and an anonymous column printed in the literary journal *Martín Fierro*, "Homenaje al Carriego" [Homage to Carriego] (1927), both serve as initial drafts for this longer literary biography.[23] Even though all of these ideas would suggest a greater level of critical attention to *Evaristo Carriego,* hardly any studies are dedicated solely to this early literary biography.[24]

It is important to highlight the source of inspiration (and funding) for this particular volume, which Borges discusses in his "Autobiographical Notes" for the *New Yorker*. With his winnings from the Second Municipal Prize in 1929, Borges not only purchased his own set of the eleventh edition of the *Encyclopedia Britannica,* but also "was ensured a year's leisure and decided [he] would write a longish book on a wholly Argentine subject."[25] Borges goes on to describe the specifics of this "longish book": "My mother wanted me to write about any of three really worthwhile poets—Ascasubi, Almafuerte, or Lugones. I now wish I had. Instead, I chose to write about a popular but minor poet, Evaristo Carriego."[26] Borges's choice of Carriego is a very personal selection that allows him to write about himself and his own experiences through the guise of this popular Argentine poet. Although both the earlier short essay and the unsigned newspaper column appear quite different from the full biography, there are definite resonances, and the general emphasis on Palermo and Borges's Argentine neighborhoods is easily recognizable. One of the main differences between the earlier versions of this biographical essay and the book-length version is the level of detail and description in depicting his native Buenos Aires. There are also a larger number of poems analyzed in the book form of this work as well as several additional, somewhat tangential, essays that do not appear as part of either initial essay ("Páginas complementarias" [Supplementary Pages]).

Many of the physical features of the first edition of *Evaristo Carriego* reflect Borges's aesthetic preferences for clean lines and simplicity.[27] The soft-bound cover of this book, which includes no illustrations, displays a modern typeface with almost hairline serifs and an extreme level of vertical stress and contrast, which has the effect of drawing the eye up and down, rather than side to side.[28] In addition, the amount of balance in each of these letterforms gives the words a level of elegance. This pronounced type stands out even more with the soft, pastel colors of the cover (which were available in both light pink and light blue). Overall, these external features echo what we find in Borges's earlier *Inquisiciones* (1925) and *El tamaño de mi esperanza* (1926), suggesting a certain level of uniformity of style for Borges, especially when we consider the fact that each of these works was produced by not only different publishing houses (*Evaristo Carriego* versus *Inquisiciones* and *El tamaño de mi esperanza*), but also different printers.[29]

Even though these three covers possess many of the same design qualities, which suggests a certain stylistic preference that Borges might have conveyed to either his publishers or his printers, the high quality of Colombo's typographical work clearly surpasses that of the printers of *Inquisiciones* and *El tamaño de mi esperanza*. Consider, for instance, not only the already mentioned letters (perfectly spaced, thus adding to the visual appeal), but also the more adequately used space on the cover in comparison with the other two books, whose titles are slightly too close to the author's name at the top of the page. In terms of the other physical features of *Evaristo Carriego*, inside the pages of this book the wove paper is very thick and lacks both chain and wire lines, enhancing the book's modern feel (from the clean cover to the sleek choice of typeface). Furthermore, four images (in black and white) are inserted throughout

Cover of *Evaristo Carriego* (Manuel Gleizer, 1930). *(Reproduced from the Albert and Shirley Small Special Collections Library, University of Virginia.)*

Cover of *Inquisiciones* (Editorial Proa, 1925). *(Reproduced from the Albert and Shirley Small Special Collections Library, University of Virginia.)*

Cover of *El tamaño de mi esperanza* (Editorial Proa, 1926). *(Reproduced from the Albert and Shirley Small Special Collections Library, University of Virginia.)*

the text: a portrait of Evaristo Carriego, an example of one of his manuscripts, and two street scenes of Buenos Aires photographed by Horacio Coppola.

Colombo also printed Borges's second book from the 1930s, *Discusión*.[30] Covering a large number of philosophical and rhetorical questions, this book is also the first published work in Manuel Gleizer's series Colección de nuevos escritores argentinos [Collection of New Argentine Writers], which resulted in a great deal of critical attention for Borges in Argentina. More specifically, shortly after the publication of *Discusión*, the literary journal *Megáfono* dedicated an entire issue to the Argentine writer.[31] This periodical publication centers on his then recent publication of *Discusión*, described as a "libro en que consigue una completa identificación entre su pluma y su cerebro, por lo que, siendo él más conceptual, es el de más fácil lectura entre todos sus libros de prosa" [book in which he achieves a complete union between his pen and his brain, which is why, as a more conceptual book, it is the easiest to read of all of his prose works].[32] The introductory blurb from this special issue explains the rationale of choosing Borges:

> He elegido a Borges por tres razones: primero, porque me parece importante su obra literaria; segundo, por lo que este escritor representa y ha representado dentro de la "nueva generación"; y tercero, porque es el autor argentino que más influencia ha ejercido sobre los escritores más jóvenes.
>
> [I chose Borges for three reasons: first, because his literary work seems important; second, for what this writer represents and has represented for the "new generation"; third, because he is the Argentine writer who has most influenced the younger writers.][33]

Given that this special issue of *Megáfono* highlights the important role of Borges in the lives of the younger generation(s) of Argentine writers, it is only fitting that a large portion of the pieces are written by these same individuals. What is more, several of these writers have a direct (literary) connection with Borges during this time. Most notable is Ulyses Petit de Murat (1907–1983), who would help Borges in gaining his editorial position at the *Revista Multicolor de los Sábados* and serve as his codirector. Two other young writers who stand out in this issue of *Megáfono* are Ignacio B. Anzoátegui (1905–1978) and Sigfrido A. Radaelli (1909–1982). In addition to Anzoátegui and Radaelli being perfect representatives of this new group of young writers, their works would later form part of Editorial TOR's Colección Megáfono, in which Borges's *Historia universal de la infamia* also appears. On the interior flap of the first edition of *Historia universal de la infamia,* we see the names of Anzoátegui and Radaelli alongside Borges, as well as those of Lisardo Zia, Enrique Mallea, and Raúl Rivero Olazábal, all of whom also contributed to the special issue of *Megáfono*.

The majority of the essays in *Discusión* were previously published in a variety of literary journals or newspapers during the 1920s and early 1930s, which Borges himself highlights in the prologue to the first edition by calling the collection a series of "páginas recopiladas" [compiled pages] (Table 2).[34]

Even though *Discusión* had the same publisher and printer as *Evaristo Carriego,* this collection of essays differs from the earlier literary biography in terms of its physical features. First, and most notably, this collection of essays is the first book in the larger series Colección de nuevos escritores argentinos [Collection of New Argentine Writers] that Gleizer instituted in the 1930s. Strangely, the collection does not appear to have gained much traction since the titles that "sucesivamente irán apareciendo en esta colección" [successively will appear in this collection] by Eduardo Mallea, Julio Fingerit, and Armando Cascella, according to the inside flap of the first edition of *Discusión,* never appeared, making Borges's work all the more curious and rare. In contrast with the typographical details on the cover of *Evaristo Carriego,* the title of *Discusión,* while printed in a similar, modern typeface, is printed in a deep red-orange color. This striking use of color, and the larger size of the type, immediately draws the reader's attention to the title. The muted beige color of the cover also heightens the visual impact of the title. In addition, all of the text on the front cover (the name of the collection, the name of the author, the title of the work, and the publisher's information) is in a box,

Table 2. Previously published essays that appear in *Discusión*

Essay Title in *Discusión*	Journal/Newspaper in Which It Appeared
"Prólogo" [Prologue]	
"Nuestras imposibilidades" [Our Impossibilities]	*Sur* 4 (1931): 131–34
"La penúltima versión de la realidad" [The Penultimate Version of Reality]	*Síntesis* 2.15 (1928): 293–97
"El coronel Ascasubi" [Colonel Ascasubi]	*Sur* 1 (1931): 128–40
"La supersticiosa ética del lector" [The Superstitious Ethics of the Reader]	*Azul* 2.8 (1931): 11–14
"El *Martín Fierro*"	*Sur* 2 (1931): 134–35
"El otro Whitman" [The Other Whitman]	*La Vida Literaria* 14 (1929): 3; *Repertorio Americano* (San José, Costa Rica) 19 (1929): 280–82
"Una vindicación de la cábala" [A Vindication of the Cabala]	
"Una vindicación del falso Basílides" [A Vindication of the False Basilides]	*La Prensa*, January 1, 1932, 4
"La postulación de la realidad" [The Postulation of Reality]	*Azul* 2.10 (1931): 13–18
"Films"	*Sur* 3 (1931): 171–73
"El arte narrativo y la magia" [Narrative Art and Magic]	*Sur* 5 (1932): 172–79
"Paul Groussac"	*Nosotros* 23.65 (1929): 79–80; *Repertorio Americano* (San José, Costa Rica) 20 (1929): 162
"La duración del infierno" [The Duration of Hell]	*Síntesis* 2.25 (1929): 9–13
"Las versiones homéricas" [The Homeric Versions]	*La Prensa*, May 8, 1932, 1
"La perpetua carrera de Aquiles y la tortuga" [The Perpetual Race of Achilles and the Tortoise]	*La Prensa*, January 1, 1929, 1; *El Sol* (Madrid), December 1932, 2

immediately creating a different feel from *Evaristo Carriego* (or any of the earlier titles mentioned above). The differences in type size throughout the printed areas of the cover of *Discusión,* which create an almost graded or scaled effect, are quite striking when compared with those of *Evaristo Carriego.* Because it echoes the design features found on many of the covers from Borges's previous works of the 1920s, *Evaristo Carriego* creates a bookend with this earlier period, which suggests both an end to this initial stage of writing and production and the beginning of something entirely new. This idea is directly echoed in the physical presentation of the above two volumes; even though they have the same publisher and printer, there is a marked difference in the organization of space (and use of color) on the title page as well as the stress placed on certain information (through size variations and the use of bold text).

In line with all of Borges's writings discussed in this chapter, *Las Kenningar* was first published in a literary magazine before Borges had it printed separately with Colombo, which some critics explain as a desire on the part of Borges to eliminate a previous error in the title.[35] Echoing the erudite level of philosophical topics and themes found throughout the pages of *Discusión, Las Kenningar* takes the Old Norse linguistic formation most closely associated with our modern-day metaphor (the kenning) and examines its place in Old Norse poetry as a point of departure for this long essay. If this esoteric subject matter doesn't signal an elite, well-educated audience, the fact that Borges includes extensive examples in a myriad of languages, including Latin, English, and Old Norse, without translations, makes the connection quite clear. In terms of the critical studies devoted to this work, there is a great deal of scholarship (especially that authored by Borges himself) on Anglo-Saxon and Old Norse literature and Borges's interest in it, but there is not a great deal of material that parses the details of this early essay. In other words, the existing studies make only passing references to it.[36]

Unlike *Evaristo Carriego* and *Discusión, Las Kenningar* was not published by Manuel Gleizer and bears no other publisher's imprint, which seems to imply that Borges edited and paid for the printing of this volume himself. At first glance, the cover of *Las Kenningar* echoes that of *Discusión* for its modern typography and striking use of a red-orange ink

Cover of *Discusión* (Manuel Gleizer, 1932). *(Reproduced from the Albert and Shirley Small Special Collections Library, University of Virginia.)*

Cover of *Las Kenningar* (1933). *(Reproduced from the Albert and Shirley Small Special Collections Library, University of Virginia.)*

for the title. Although the letterforms are not spaced and appear much more streamlined and slender, there is a definite level of elegance in the spacing and overall modern simplicity of the cover. This same attention to detail is carried over to the modern typeface used on every page of the work. The large margins and high-quality paper (with visible chain lines) further emphasize the artistry of Colombo.

Borges's last work printed by Colombo from this time frame is *Historia de la eternidad* (1936). His long essay "Las Kenningar" is included in this collection alongside three other essays and two notes.[37] Virtually all of these writings are philosophical in nature, evoking the ideas of Plotinus, Plato, Saint Augustine, Nietzsche, and Schopenhauer, among others. Unlike the tendency found in *Discusión* to include previously written essays (usually slightly changed), *Historia de la eternidad* consists of mostly all previously unpublished material (with the exception of "Las Kenningar"). In addition to the work and ideas of these great thinkers, Borges also presents readers with two other favorite topics, the translation and review of literary works, both of which speak to his work for the *Revista Multicolor de los Sábados* (1933–1934) and the column that he would start writing for *El Hogar* [*The Home*] in 1936 ("Libros y autores extranjeros" [Foreign Books and Authors]).

The publisher of *Historia de la eternidad,* Viau y Zona, was known for the quality of its hand-set type, justified text, margin and line spacing, ink color, and paper, all of which was very much in line with the luxury work of Francisco A. Colombo.[38] According to one critic, the official start of Viau y Zona was "el 23 de Julio de 1925 ... por un plazo de dos años y con un capital de $40.000 m/n de curso legal aportado por los socios por partes iguales. Inmediatamente la sociedad arrendó el local bajo de la finca Florida 639 y 641" [on July 23, 1925 ... for a period of two years and with a capital investment of $40,000 Argentine pesos in legal tender supported equally by the two partners. The firm will immediately rent the space in the building between Florida 639 and 641].[39] In addition to the publishing house of Viau y Zona, Domingo Viau and Alejandro Zona also started their own bookstore, El Bibliófilo [The Bibliophile], which would soon become a "centro de arte y de cultura, a la cual concurrieon los estudiosos y amigos de las ediciones preciosas y raras" [center of art and culture, where scholars and friends of rare and precious editions would meet].[40] Given that Viau and Zona did not have their own printing house, they relied on others for the physical production of their works. Aside from five works that were printed in France or Berlin, all of their works were printed in Argentina and limited to between fifty and one hundred copies. Over the years many different names were created for (or can be associated with) the firm, including Viau y Zona, El Bibliófilo, Domingo Viau y Cía, and Domingo Viau-Editor.[41] Between 1927 and 1947,

> publicaron poco más de 150 libros. Muchos de ellos se distinguen por la calidad y elegancia de su construcción cumpliendo estrictamente las reglas de oro para la perfecta composición a mano, el adecuado tipo y cuerpo, la justificación proporcionada al formato, los márgenes e interlineados que hacen placentera la lectura, las tintas, los colores, los papeles y las ilustraciones que acompañan y comentan plásticamente al texto irreprochable como forma y contenido.
>
> [they published a few more than 150 books. Many of them were distinguished for the quality and elegance of their construction, which strictly followed the golden rules for perfectly hand-set composition, adequate type and body size, proportionate justification for the format, margins and spacing that would please any reader, inks, colors, papers, and illustrations that accompanied and artistically reflected the text's form and content.][42]

Parisian models were the clear influence of a great deal of these techniques and tendencies since, starting in the 1920s, Viau frequented the City of Lights. By the middle of the 1940s, Viau and Zona faced a number of problems that ultimately resulted in the closing of their firm in 1947.

Much like *Discusión* and *Las Kenningar*, *Historia de la eternidad* shows the hallmarks of Colombo's perfected aesthetics. Moreover, the typeface and use of space on the cover are virtually identical to what we find with *Las Kenningar*, the only blatant distinctions being the use of blue ink (as opposed to red-orange) and the spacing of the letterforms. Inside Viau y Zona's edition we find a modern typeface that is similar to that of Colombo's earlier works, but the paper used is of a much lesser quality than other editions printed by Colombo. In terms of the distribution and sale, this work was seen as a failure at the time since it was produced in too small of a press run. That said, Borges himself did not see the lack of sales as a failure, and shortly after its publication he "proudly announced that he had sold exactly thirty-seven copies of *Historia de la eternidad*."[43] Although the only copy of this book that I have analyzed is the one in the University of Virginia Borges collection, there appears to be a variant edition of this same work that was in circulation at the time and shows an even more striking resemblance to *Las Kenningar,* with the same red-orange ink used for the title as this earlier printed essay. A copy of this rare imprint was sold at a Sotheby's auction in 2018. According to the catalogue notes, it is a "first edition, a variant with the same setting of the text, and the same colophon as the Viau y Zona edition, but printed on thinner paper with a different colour wrapper."[44] Of note is the fact that the title for this separate imprint is the same red-orange color as *Las Kenningar.* If *Historia de la eternidad* was already promised to Viau y Zona, how was Colombo able to print this same work with the same setting of type, yet not mention the publishing house? Moreover, what would be the benefits of printing a separate edition that was most likely financed by the printer himself (as opposed to the publisher)? While it is virtually impossible to answer these questions, especially since the only visible change here seems to be the ink color on the cover and the elimination of Viau y Zona's name, it is most likely that this edition was produced for private use only, especially in light of the fact that the extant copy sold at Sotheby's came from Norman Thomas di Giovanni's personal library.

Accidental Publishers: Manuel Gleizer and Juan Torrendell

At the start of this new, expansive wave of publishing in Argentina, many editors focused on producing affordable books that would sell well. The

Cover of *Historia de la eternidad* (Viau y Zona, 1936). *(Reproduced from the Albert and Shirley Small Special Collections Library, University of Virginia.)*

majority of these early editor-publishers, for the most part, were interested in only marketing strategies and attracting new clientele in so far as it would help their profits. Since a large portion of these individuals came from immigrant families and were self-educated, most of their training in the book world was through experience and trial and error; it was not driven by an interest in the artistic qualities of these objects or a deep-seated desire to produce luxury items for specific readers. The profession of publisher thus came to Manuel Gleizer by accident.[45] Born in the tsarist Russian Empire at the close of the nineteenth century, Gleizer arrived in Entre Ríos, Argentina, with his parents around 1906 and would remain there, working the land, until 1918 when he moved to Buenos Aires. In this larger metropolis he started a business selling lottery tickets but soon realized that the odds for success were stacked against him, so he turned to selling books to eliminate his debt:

> tuvo la mala suerte de que le quedaran sin vender unos enteros que no pudo devolver y debió afrontar el pago de unos trescientos pesos, cifra monumental en la época para un hombre de escasos recursos y comercio limitado. ¿Cómo obtener el dinero para pagar? Se le ocurrió traer de su casa 230 libros de la Biblioteca Blanca de Sempere y los puso a la venta a un precio bajo, indicado en un cartelito: "0,40 el ejemplar." Los vendió rápidamente. Al día siguiente repitió la operación, pero al revés: puso un nuevo cartelito que rezaba: "compro libros." La desesperación y la responsabilidad de honrar su deuda lo habían convertido en un librero de viejo.

> [he had the bad luck of being stuck with a few sheets of lottery tickets that he was unable to return and was facing a payment of some three hundred pesos, an enormous amount during that time for a man with few resources and a limited business. How to obtain the money to pay the debt? It occurred to him to take 230 books from his home (that were part of the Blanca de Sempere Library) and sell them at a very low price, writing on a small poster: "40 cents a copy." He sold them all very quickly. The next day he repeated this same operation, but in

the reverse order: he created a new poster that read: "I buy books." The desperation and responsibility to honor his debt made him into a second-hand bookseller.]46

After this accidental encounter with book markets, Gleizer opened his own bookstore, Librería La Cultura, which soon evolved into a common hangout for young intellectuals (Borges, of course, among them). Not long after, in 1922, Gleizer turned to the publishing profession. It should be stressed that before this period in Argentina, it was very rare to find publishers. Even though there were any given number of printers and bookstores, publishers were a scarcer breed: "Antes de Gleizer, de Jacobo Samet, de Glusberg, de Antonio Zamora, en la Argentina no existía la figura del editor" [Before Gleizer, before Jacobo Samet, before Glusberg, before Antonio Zamora, the figure of the editor/publisher did not exist in Argentina].47 As a result, the work of publishers such as Gleizer was paramount for many young new Argentine authors in the early part of the twentieth century.48

At the start of his career Gleizer was known as a precursor of the phenomenon of producing cheap books by Argentine authors, which was a successful strategy in the book market. In fact, the second book that he published, Arturo Cancela's *Tres relatos porteños* [*Three Porteño Short Stories*], became a best seller shortly after its initial publication, "ya que en menos de 4 años se publicaron 18 mil ejemplares" [considering that in fewer than four years eighteen thousand copies were published].49 His success also can be measured by the fact that in less than a decade he published around two hundred works. That said, many writers and associates of Gleizer have noted his serious lack of marketing or commercial strategies and, more broadly speaking, his terrible financial decisions. For instance, Bernardo Ezequiel Koremblit recalls his experience upon visiting and selecting several books to buy in Gleizer's bookstore; when he asked the bookkeeper how much he owed him, his response was simply, "Dénme lo que quieran" [Give me what you want].50 Helvio I. Botana, the son of Natalio Botana (founder of the daily periodical *Crítica*), recounts a similar situation when his father wanted to purchase several of his wife's early works from Gleizer:

A mi requerimiento de cuanto le debía, contestó, no es nada, ¿por qué?—seguí insistiendo—. No recuerdo sus palabras exactamente pero su gesto al regalarme los libros era natural, los libros ya habían sido pagados al editarse.—Así, bueno como el pan era el viejo Gleizer.

[Upon my request of how much I owed him, he responded, it's nothing; why?—I continued insisting. I don't remember his exact words but his gesture of gifting me the books was natural; the books were already paid for when they went through the editing process. Thus, good as gold was the old Gleizer.][51]

Even though Gleizer arrived at the profession of bookseller and editor somewhat accidentally, it appears that he was not in it for the money, but rather for the love that he soon developed for his art.

In general terms, Gleizer published books within three collections that he established early on in his career: those dealing with Jewish topics, those touching on current (political) events, and any remaining books (something of a miscellany). It was this third collection "la que pasó a la historia. En ella pronto aparecieron *El idioma de los argentinos,* de Borges; *Molino rojo,* de Fijman; *No todo es vigilia la de los ojos abiertos,* de Macedonio ... y tantos más" [that became part of history. In it appeared *El idioma de los argentinos,* by Borges; *Molino rojo* (*Red Windmill*), by Fijman; *No todo es vigilia la de los ojos abiertos* (*Not All Open Eyes Watch*), by Macedonio ... and many more].[52] This third collection mostly was composed of young, lesser-known Argentine authors (usually those involved in avant-garde movements), and as a result, "muchas de las primeras ediciones de escritores que luego adquirirían renombre nacional (y a veces también internacional) llevan su sello editorial" [many of the first editions of writers that would later become famous in Argentina (and sometimes also internationally) bear the mark of his publishing house], which is most certainly true in the case of Borges.[53] Thus, Manuel Gleizer became synonymous with young (Argentine) writers and helped them in some way with their literary careers.

The question still remains of how such an accidental publisher crossed paths with the likes of Francisco A. Colombo, an elite, luxury printer. Since Borges's first two works during the early 1930s include both Gleizer's recognizable insignia and the clear indication of Colombo's printing presses in their colophons, the question is a valid and important one. According to Osvaldo Colombo:

> Mi padre tuvo con él [Gleizer] relaciones comerciales entre 1930 y 1933, hasta que pudo. Los "pagarés" firmados a mi padre no los podía cancelar, ya que los libros no se vendían y menos aún los de poesía y los de poetas argentinos, las librerías los rechazaban. Al no poder pagar sus ediciones a la imprenta de Francisco Colombo éste se desvincula de Gleizer como imprentero.
>
> [My father had commercial relations with Gleizer between 1930 and 1933, as much as he could. The "promissory notes" signed to my father he was unable to cancel, considering that the books didn't sell and even less the collections of poetry and those by Argentine poets; the bookstores refused them. Being unable to pay for Colombo's printing of his editions, Francisco Colombo severed ties with Gleizer as his printer.]⁵⁴

Osvaldo also recalls that 1933 was the last year that he and his father visited Gleizer's shop on Triunvirato Street. Although many of Borges's readers today may not recognize the name of Manuel Gleizer, he published two of his works during the 1930s (*Evaristo Carriego* and *Discusión*) and undoubtedly played an important role in the Argentine writer's literary career.⁵⁵

Another such accidental publisher who saw the book industry more for its potential profit margins was Juan Carlos Torrendell. Born in Barcelona, this Spaniard first worked at a bookstore before opening his own publishing house, Editorial TOR, on June 16, 1916.⁵⁶ This shift in profession, as we have seen, was a general trend in the first half of the twentieth century, and many publishers often maintained their bookshops in conjunction with their publishing houses. During the first years of Editorial TOR's existence, the publishing house was somewhat indistinguishable from other firms throughout Buenos Aires since its focus was on Spanish literature and best sellers. With the purchase of its first rotary press in 1930, Editorial TOR soon became synonymous with cheap paperbacks, usually of extremely poor quality.[57] One critic describes the majority of Editorial TOR's books during this period as "mal diagramados en papel de baja calidad, a un precio ínfimo, en algunos casos 50 centavos" [poorly designed and printed on paper of the lowest quality, at a negligible cost, in some cases 50 cents], which, of course, made ample circulation much more possible.[58] In comparison with other publishers that emerged during this period, Editorial TOR was very interested in "el aspecto commercial" [the commercial aspect] and "no poseía una motivación intelectual" [did not possess an intellectual motivation], which is evident by looking at the extreme diversity of its catalogues, the great variety of its titles, and its constant production of books.[59] Torrendell was also known to invent very unique marketing strategies, such as advertising fake books and creating fictitious publishing firms, to help sell more books. His most memorable (and radical) attempt to increase profits of book sales was a campaign during which the firm sold its books by weight.

Given Editorial TOR's constant obsession with profit and monetary gain, as opposed to the quality or content of the product that the firm was selling, it is quite curious that Borges would turn to this publishing house for his first collection of fiction.[60] *Historia universal de la infamia,* whose stories first appeared over the course of several months throughout the *Revista Multicolor,* was one of the four works published between 1934 and 1935 in Editorial TOR's Colección Megáfono. In general terms, this collection "estaba dedicada a ensayos más o menos orientados a la biografía ... Eran libros de formato grande, con tapa blanca y sin ilustraciones, con un promedio de 140 a 200 páginas de extensión" [was dedicated to essays more or less oriented toward biography ... They were books in a large format, with a white cover without illustrations, with an average length of between 140 and 200 pages].[61] Although the presence of a figure such as Borges in the collection seems odd, the fact that his *Historia universal de la infamia* is a series of biographies of historical figures fits perfectly with the most important criterion for inclusion in the collection: the topic. Furthermore, the fact that these essays were originally published in the *Revista Multicolor,* which highlights their appeal to the masses, might also have influenced Editorial TOR's decision to publish the work.

Advertisement for Editorial TOR. *(Reproduced from a copy of* Papel, Libro, Revista *housed at the University of Minnesota library.)*

Finally, a connection can be made between the journal *Megáfono*'s previously described publication of a special issue dedicated to Borges's work for the contributors and the fact that Editorial TOR frequently advertised in this journal (and even possibly financed it). Moreover, Raúl Rivero Olazábal, one of the young contributors, recalls that "los bourgeois no leen MEGÁFONO" [bourgeois readers do not read *Megáfono*], which speaks both to the journal and also to Editorial TOR's collection, thus highlighting the popular audience for each of these venues.[62]

Historia universal de la infamia is Borges's first published work within the genre of fiction. According to the Argentine writer himself, "I ... read up on the lives of known persons and then deliberately varied and distorted them according to my own whims."[63] This distortion and variation are most evident when we study the included biography ("índice de fuentes" [index of sources]) at the end of the work, which contains the first mention of apocryphal works. In addition to the clearly fictitious source by Alexander Schulz (Xul Solar), Borges also takes a great deal of liberty in recounting the exploits of the criminals he has chosen to spotlight. One critic calls this the "acculturation" of Borges in "appropriating and recontextualizing the narratives" that he uses as the basis for his own creations.[64] Thus, aspects from *Life on the Mississippi* by Mark Twain and *Mark Twain's America*, both cited as sources for "El atroz redentor Lazarus Morell" [The Cruel Redeemer Lazarus Morell], are echoed in such a way as to refer to South American demographics: "El Mississippi es río de pecho ancho; es un infinito y oscuro hermano del Paraná, del Uruguay, del Amazonas y del Orinoco" [The Mississippi is a large breasted river; it is a dark and infinite brother of the Paraná, of the Uruguay, of the Amazon, and of the Orinoco].[65] Many critics have studied these slight alterations of supposed sources in *Historia universal de la infamia*, so I do not dwell on this point further.[66]

In terms of the physical features of *Historia universal de la infamia*, there are initial echoes with Borges's earlier publications from this period, especially with the use of modern typefaces and a muted color for the softbound cover. However, on closer inspection, we soon realize that the artistic elements of this book have been completed hastily and lack the attention to detail that we saw with Colombo's works. The modern letterforms of the cover are neither spaced nor inked properly; instead, the bottom edges bleed onto the cover and give the title a blurring effect. The thick blue border that frames the cover has several gaps where one piece of type ends and another begins, which adds to the unpolished look of the edition. When we enter the book itself, we find similar sloppy tendencies. The wove paper is of an extremely poor quality and almost feels like it will break or tear with the slightest touch. Although the pages have been cut, they are anything but uniform, suggesting a certain level of carelessness. The aesthetic feel of the wide margins is minimized by the constantly smudged letterforms as well as the extraneous ink smears outside the central area of the text. All of these features speak to the low quality of books that Editorial TOR produced throughout the twentieth century in Argentina.

Mass-Market Audiences and Larger Print Runs: *Crítica* and *Revista Multicolor de los Sábados*

In examining the physical features of *Historia universal de la infamia*, we must also take into consideration the original publication of these fictions in the *Revista Multicolor de los Sábados,* as well as Borges's editorial role in creating this Saturday literary supplement to the daily periodical *Crítica*. As described in the first chapter, Borges's short stint as codirector of the *Revista Multicolor* (1933–1934) allowed him to interact with various writers and artists as they contributed their works and also with typesetters and more technical professionals. According to one of Borges's co-workers, Natalio Botana, founder of *Crítica,* wanted a specific type of editor-director for the *Revista Multicolor*:

> el que iba al taller y conocía de memoria el catálogo de tipos, la posibilidad de titulación, los que suministraba la máquina Ludlow. Borges había estado en imprentas de libros; pero prontamente se asimiló a las que daban tarea a las gigantescas rotativas Hoe. Hizo rápida amistad con linotipistas, matriceros y diagramadores.
>
> [one who would go to the (print) shop and know by memory the catalogue of sorts, the possibilities for titles, all of which

would be supplied to the Ludlow machine. Borges had been in print shops before; but he soon assimilated to the work of the gigantic Hoe rotary presses. He quickly made friends with the linotypists, the matrix cutters, and the individuals who were responsible for page layout.][67]

In addition to working closely with the physical formatting of the *Revista Multicolor,* Borges also proofread every text for any final errors, which speaks to his critical eye and attention to detail.

Botana was most known for his continual search for the newest (and at times the most attention-grabbing) trends for *Crítica,* and what we find in this periodical and its weekly literary supplement is nothing short of a spectacle.[68] One of the more recognizable aspects that set *Crítica* apart from other Argentine daily newspapers of the time, such as *La Prensa* or *El Hogar,* was the use of advanced technology for the production of each issue, which made this newspaper an extremely modern print medium. In order to keep up with the needs of its mass-market audience, "it acquired a building of its own and began to compete with *La Nación* in the areas of printing and Linotype equipment. *Crítica* adopted photoengraving a year before *La Nación* did, and in 1927 the newspaper [even acquired] a Hoe rotary press that turned out 160,000 copies per hour ... High technology was carving out both a concrete place and a virtual myth in the organization presided over by Natalio Félix Botana."[69] Alongside this use of modern technology, many of the articles included in each issue centered on contemporary issues of science and technology, which highlights the fact that *Crítica* was very attuned to the interests of its modern-day readers. Another noticeable feature was its impressive use of images: "At *Crítica,* the use of graphics—photographs, diagrams, drawings, and cartoons—was just short of lavish."[70] This claim appears to speak directly to what we find in all of the issues of its literary supplement.

The presence of vibrant imagery is not reserved for just the front page of the *Revista Multicolor,* but rather spills onto virtually every interior page. As a result, one of the most striking aspects of Borges's writings published here is their visual accompaniment, which critics have only briefly glossed.[71] Several studies have given an overview of the literary supplement and included transcriptions (or entire digital editions, in the case of Helft), but very few critics enter into the physical details of this early periodical and Borges's role in it.[72] In *Jorge Luis Borges: Obra y maniobras* Annick Louis mentions certain physical aspects of the *Revista Multicolor,* yet she provides virtually no analysis of the physical medium of this periodical or of the obvious changes involved with publishing several of the writings under the title *Historia universal de la infamia* with Editorial TOR. She notes that "la diagramación del texto e imagen ocupa tres cuartos de la página" [the layout of a text and an image occupies three-fourths of the page] yet leaves this somewhat vague idea hanging without further explication. She does, however, include Borges's personal sentiments toward Editorial TOR's publication of *Historia universal de la infamia*: "Este volumen (de no muy gloriosa presentación, aunque muy superior a otros productos de la culpable editorial que sabemos) no admite un juicio general" [This volume (of very poor presentation, although very superior to that of other works produced by this blameworthy publishing house) does not permit a general judgment].[73] Louis goes on to flesh out this statement with a general overview of the reputation of Torrendell's publishing house for its poor-quality books and even mentions the other titles included in the Colección Megáfono; yet she does not consider the place of this book in relation to Borges's other published books during the early 1930s, which is crucial for best understanding the relationship between form and content in his work.

Returning to the original publication of these writings, it is clear from the introductory text included with the first issue of the *Revista Multicolor* that its contents were intended for the widest (and most popular) group of readers possible:

> Nuestra costumbre es innovar. La nueva publicación de CRITICA significará un esfuerzo no igualado en el periodismo nacional. CRITICA, *REVISTA MULTICOLOR,* le proporcionará lectura para una semana, sin que su ejemplar le cueste un solo centavo más ... Desde el 12 de agosto Todos los Sábados 8 Págs. De Gran Formato Impresas a Todo Color[.] Una publicación moderna, destinada a todos los hogares argentinos. Se repartirá con las ediciones del día. La mejor lectura para el

más numeroso público. Exija su ejemplar de SÁBADO: Revista Multicolor.

[Our custom is to innovate. The new publication of *Crítica* signifies an unmatched effort in national journalism. *Crítica, MULTICOLOR MAGAZINE*, will provide readings for a week, yet each copy will not cost a cent more ... From August 12 Every Saturday 8 Pages. In a Large Format Printed in Every Color. A modern publication, destined for every Argentine home. It will be delivered with the daily editions. The best reading material for the largest public. Demand your copy of SATURDAY: Multicolor Magazine.][74]

According to one source, Borges's stories, which started to appear in the first installment of the supplement, figured prominently in its initial publicity: "el de Jorge Luis Borges ... anunciado excesivamente en el aviso del 8 de agosto como 'Vida, esplendor y muerte del espantoso redentor Lazarus Morell'" [that of Jorge Luis Borges ... excessively announced in the advertisement from August 8th as "Life, Splendor and Death of the Dread Redeemer Lazarus Morell"] (Table 3).[75]

The most obvious change from the *Revista Multicolor* to book format is the elimination of any images that accompany the writings in the former. In order to better understand these physical changes, one must consider the illustrations that appeared alongside the texts in the *Revista Multicolor*.[76] In addition to the use of extremely vibrant colors, what we see represented in these illustrations are certain key moments in each of Borges's stories. Thus, in "El impostor inverosímil Tom Castro" [The Unbelievable Imposter Tom Castro], the artist Parpagnoli highlights the dangerous sea voyage in which Tichborne dies, the physical transformation of Orton into Tichborne, and the gruesome tramping and ultimate death of Bogle.[77] A similar desire to focus on the more grotesque aspects of these stories appears in the drawings that accompany "El rostro del profeta" [The Face of the Prophet], which show the moment "Hákim fue cercado en Sanam por el ejército del Jalifa" [Hákim was surrounded in Sanam by Jalifa's army] and the ultimate climactic reveal of his hideous face:

Table 3. Textual overlaps between the *Revista Multicolor de los Sábados* and *Historia universal de la infamia*

Short Story	Revista Multicolor	Historia universal de la infamia
"El espantoso redentor Lázarus Morell" [The Dread Redeemer Lazarus Morell]	No. 1; August 12, 1933	Edited and retitled "El atroz redentor Lázarus Morell" [The Cruel Redeemer Lazarus Morell]
"Eastman, el proveedor de inquidades" [Monk Eastman, Purveyor of Iniquities]	No. 2; August 19, 1933	
"Historia universal de la infamia: La viuda Ching" [A Universal History of Infamy: The Widow Ching]	No. 3; August 26, 1933	Retitled "La viuda Ching, pirata" [The Widow Ching, Pirate]
"El brujo postergado" [The Deferred Sorcerer]	No. 4; September 2, 1933	Included under "Etcétera"
"Hombres de las orillas" [Men of the Neighborhoods]	No. 6; September 16, 1933	Edited and retitled "Hombre de la esquina rosada" [Streetcorner Man]
"El impostor inverosímil Tom Castro" [The Unbelievable Impostor Tom Castro]	No. 8; September 30, 1933	
"El espejo de tinta" [The Mirror of Ink]	No. 8; September 30, 1933	Included under "Etcétera"
"La cámara de las estatuas" [The Chamber of Statues]	No. 17; December 2, 1933	Included under "Etcétera"

"El incivil maestro de ceremonias Kotsuké no Suké" [The Uncivil Teacher of Etiquette Kotsuké no Suké]	No. 18; December 9, 1933	
"El rostro del profeta" [The Face of the Prophet]	No. 24; January 20, 1934	Edited and retitled "El tintorero enmascarado Hákim de Merv" [The Masked Dyer, Hakim of Merv]
"El teólogo" [The Theologian]	No. 46; June 23, 1934	Included under "Etcétera"
"Dos que soñaron" [Two Dreamers]	No. 46; June 23, 1934	Included under "Etcétera"
"El asesino desinteresado Bill Harrigan" [The Disinterested Killer Bill Harrigan]		Published for the first time
"Un doble de Mahoma" [A Double for Mohammed]		Published for the first time[a]

a. Also published in *Los Anales de Buenos Aires* 5, May 1946.

era en efecto blanco, pero con blancura peculiar de la lepra manchada. Eran tan abultada o increíble que les pareció una careta. No tenía cejas; el párpado inferior del ojo derecho pendía sobre la mejilla senil; un pesado racimo de tubérculos le comía los labios; la nariz inhumana y achatada era como de león.

[it was indeed white, but with a peculiar whiteness of spotted leprosy. It was so swollen or incredible that it seemed to them to be a mask. He didn't have eyebrows; the lower lid of the right eye hung on the senile cheek; a heavy bunch of tubers took over his mouth; the inhuman and flattened nose was like that of a lion.][78]

Thus we can identify a tendency to emphasize the monstrous or macabre elements of these works in their visual counterparts. The direct correlation between text and image further suggests that either the illustrators read the texts before completing their drawings or Borges explained them in detail. Given the nature of the venue and the fact that any literary supplement of its kind would have a large number of deadlines, it would seem that the latter possibility is closer to reality, which points to Borges's participation in all aspects of his work's production.

Critics frequently latch on to Borges's affinity for fusing elements of high culture with those of a more popular culture, "mixing pulp material—detective stories, sci-fi scenarios—with architectural structures and philosophical preoccupations," yet there has been no real discussion of the implication of or rationale for such diversity in his work with regard to the physical forms that these publications might take.[79] A consideration of the material aspects of Borges's works published between 1930 and 1936 reveals a great deal about the writer's interests and journey to becoming the international literary icon that he is known to be today. These varying levels of cultural production suggest the newness of the world of book production in Argentina at the time and the fact that many of the country's young writers were still trying to navigate this foreign terrain. The disparate forms that Borges's works took during this period, ranging from elite, esoteric essays produced with attention to detail to mass-produced, popular tales of criminals' exploits, speak to his personal interest in the burgeoning world of publishing and his desire to see his works through from start to finish. In a sense, Borges's role as author in the early 1930s is multifaceted; it implies not only a controlled approach to precisely worded texts, but also a controlled approach to how these compositions were physically prepared and printed.

T • H • R • E • E

Borges as Critic and Collaborator

Toda colaboración con Borges equivalía a años de trabajo.

[Every collaboration with Borges was equivalent to years of work.]

— Adolfo Bioy Casares, *Memorias*

"No a todos les agrada leer, y cuando lo hacen, prefieren, por razones que estoy lejos de censurar, leer a escritores extranjeros" [Not everyone likes reading, and when they do it, they prefer, for reasons that I'm far from denouncing, reading foreign authors].[1] This is how Borges responded when asked about his reading public in Buenos Aires in a 1946 interview for the magazine *El Hogar* [*The Home*]. Above all he stresses the interest of his local readers in *foreign* authors—as opposed to the works of Argentines or other Latin American authors. Writers such as G. K. Chesterton, Rudyard Kipling, and Anthony Berkeley typically filled not only the shelves of these readers, but also, as we shall see, the catalogues of numerous Buenos Aires publishing firms. Borges's careful selection of specific foreign authors to review and publish throughout the late 1930s and early 1940s—from William Faulkner and Virginia Woolf to Ellery Queen and Edgar Allan Poe—foregrounds his dedication to enhancing the literary tastes of his emerging cosmopolitan readers and also showcases his role in enabling Buenos Aires to enter the global literary marketplace.

After his successful publishing ventures during the first half of the 1930s, Borges began to branch out and explore new publishing possibilities in the second half of this decade: reviews of literature alongside brief biographies of new and foreign authors, editorial work on anthologies and collections, and collaborations on creative pieces of fiction with his new friend Adolfo Bioy Casares. All of these trends showcase Borges's efforts to fill the void of global literary criticism in Argentina and in the process develop a new type of marketing for book production and publishing in Buenos Aires. From his editorial position with *El Hogar* to his (playful) collaborative writings, in this chapter I trace Borges's marked interest in promoting international literatures that previously lacked (Argentine) readership. More specifically, I analyze how Borges singlehandedly developed reader interest in various literary genres, including High Modernism and detective fiction, through his behind-the-scenes roles, which would subsequently provide the necessary publicity for the books that he helped publish in the 1940s—of both his own writings and those of others.

Although Borges had written and published pieces for a number of Argentine periodicals during this period, he was not a full-time staff member at these firms, and as a result his work appeared only sporadically in these publications and he did not receive a salary. In contrast, Borges held a paid position with *El Hogar*, and his contributions were much more regular, similar to what we saw with the *Revista Multicolor de los Sábados* in the previous chapter. More specifically, he was the director for the "Libros y autores extranjeros" [Books and Foreign Authors] section of *El Hogar* from October 16, 1936, until July 7, 1939.[2] Alongside his monthly columns for *El Hogar*, and occasional essays and pieces of fiction for *La Nación*, Borges contributed a series of book reviews to Victoria Ocampo's literary journal, *Sur*.[3] In addition to these extensive periodical publications, Borges also worked with several of his close friends during this period to produce a number of anthologies. We can think of these early collaborative collections as a transformative redistribution of the newest global literatures rather than as an acceptance of already canonical texts, since Borges and his friends had to select, copy, translate, and (at times) shorten the texts to be included. Take, for instance, Borges and Bioy Casares's work to elevate the genre of detective fiction with their edited collection *Los mejores cuentos policiales* [*The Best Detective Tales*] (1943). Here they focused on stories and novels that developed enigmatic plots, in contrast to the North American and French tendencies for hardboiled violence and brutality.[4] I do not discuss the specifics of these anthologies and edited collections until the next chapter, but it is important to keep their formation in mind as I detail Borges's literary critiques and collaborative endeavors that laid the foundation for these later volumes.

Along with their editorial work on anthologies, Borges and Bioy Casares also produced collaborative pieces of fiction during the early 1940s. The first, and arguably best-known, collection of short stories by these two Argentine authors, *Seis problemas para don Isidro Parodi* [*Six Problems for Don Isidro Parodi*] (1942), was published by Editorial Sur under an invented pseudonym: Honorio Bustos Domecq. Borrowing names from their respective ancestors, the two men imbued the work of Bustos Domecq with amusing satire. A few years later, they created a second pseudonym, Benito Suárez Lynch, as a successor to Bustos Domecq. This persona had more serious connotations than his predecessor and tended to draw on the political tensions in Argentina under Juan Perón in his writings.[5] Regardless of the chosen name for their coauthored works, the end result was a resounding critique of contemporary Buenos Aires. These early collaborative endeavors also harmonized perfectly with Borges's desire to transform and rebrand the genre of detective fiction. More generally, there is a marked shift toward critique, criticism, and marketing in Borges's career during the 1930s and early 1940s, all of which complement the common trend of bringing foreign authors, works, and genres to Argentina through his literary reviews and the creative fictions that he produced with his close friends. Above all, many of Borges's literary endeavors during this time show the importance and the impact of the publishing industry for crafting (and branding) a particular product for Latin American readers.

Continued Contributions to Periodicals: *El Hogar, Sur,* and *La Nación*

Periodical publications are a constant in Borges's early career. Before working for *El Hogar,* Borges frequently contributed to *La Prensa, Crí-*

tica, Nosotros, and *Síntesis,* among others, not to mention his publications in the more avant-garde periodicals of *Prisma, Proa,* and *Martín Fierro* throughout the 1920s. As we saw in the last chapter with the *Revista Multicolor de los Sábados,* codirecting a literary supplement meant not only contributing articles and editing others, but also overseeing typesetters and illustrators. Contributing to *El Hogar* was no different. Borges went "metódicamente a las oficinas de *El Hogar*" [methodically to the offices of *El Hogar*] and in the process revolutionized its literary review page.[6] Most likely drawing inspiration from similar publications, such as the *Times Literary Supplement,* Borges's regular column for *El Hogar* introduced Argentine elites to new literary trends. His reviews of foreign authors and their works were a way of conditioning a cosmopolitan public to read and be interested in certain international authors and types of global literature. After Borges cast his net wide in the early 1930s and published works with disparate firms, in terms of their targeted audiences, his shift to working and publishing in venues that zeroed in on a predominantly elite audience shows a narrowing of focus that reflects an understanding of profitable book markets. In other words, after identifying a reading public that would be most captivated by his ideas surrounding genre, criticism, and the most important national and international literary trends, Borges slowly began to introduce key works to them through his reviews in *El Hogar.* These same reviews would also serve to promote his later edited collections and anthologies since, as we shall see, many of the authors he included in his column appeared throughout these volumes.

The majority of authors featured in Borges's section "Libros y autores extranjeros" hail from either the United States or a select few European countries, most notably England, France, and Germany. Alongside these reviews of foreign works and concise biographies of foreign authors, a handful of short original pieces by Borges about Argentine authors and literary trends in Buenos Aires crop up sporadically in *El Hogar.* Consider, for instance, his article from February 12, 1937, "Los escritores argentinos y Buenos Aires" [Argentine Writers and Buenos Aires], in which he discusses the debate between writers from Buenos Aires and those from other provinces in Argentina. Two weeks later he publishes "Las 'nuevas generaciones' literarias" [The "New Literary Generations"] (February 26, 1937), which focuses primarily on Borges's own generation ("la nueva generación" [the new generation], "la generación heroica" [the heroic generation], and the generation of *Prisma, Proa, Inicial, Martín Fierro,* and *Valoraciones*) and as a result complements the former piece. In addition to these more broadly themed articles about Argentine writers and their works, Borges also wrote a few pieces on individual authors from other countries, including Aldous Huxley, Miguel de Unamuno, Rudyard Kipling, Jorge Isaacs, Ramón Llull, and Alfred Henschke ("Klabund").[7]

Unlike many of the other periodicals for which Borges wrote regular pieces during the first half of the twentieth century, *El Hogar* stands out as distinct in terms of its format, physical features, and contents. In contrast to typical periodicals of the era, it primarily targeted middle-to-upper-class women in Argentina; therefore, the cover of any given issue looks similar to a popular novel or fashion catalogue rather than a regular periodical.[8] These flashy, feminine covers call to mind the well-known *Harper's Bazaar* (1867–present) or *Ladies' Home Journal* (1883–2014). Looking to the physical features of *El Hogar,* it might come as a surprise that Borges contributed a regular column to this periodical from 1936 to 1939.[9] Even though it advertised for a specifically female audience, a fact that is especially clear from its regular inclusion of dinner party recipes and the newest beauty tips and products, it was within the pages of this periodical that one of Borges's biographers, Emir Rodríguez Monegal, first encountered the Argentine's writings; he describes how he was "barely fifteen then and was promptly seduced by Borges's wit and impeccable style and the vast range of his reading."[10] He goes on to comment on how Borges's page in *El Hogar* "was, and still is, the best possible introduction to his mind and work."[11] Each page that Borges contributed to the magazine presented readers with a "biografía sintética" [concise biography] of one specific author, new publications in various languages (mainly French, English, and German), and, at times, tidbits about the lives of sundry writers. Over the course of several months, Borges slowly started to change the original format of this page in *El Hogar,* eliminating particular aspects until they altogether disappeared. As Rodríguez Monegal notes, Borges "had practically created a new form: the book review page, which is sort of a literary microcosm, a magazine inside a magazine."[12]

Cover of *El Hogar* (No. 1434, April 9, 1937). *(Reproduced from the Albert and Shirley Small Special Collections Library, University of Virginia.)*

Even though each issue highlighted different authors and books, the large majority of works and writers, as previously noted, hailed from England, France, and the United States.[13] Thus, Borges shows a marked preference for English-speaking countries (England, the United States,

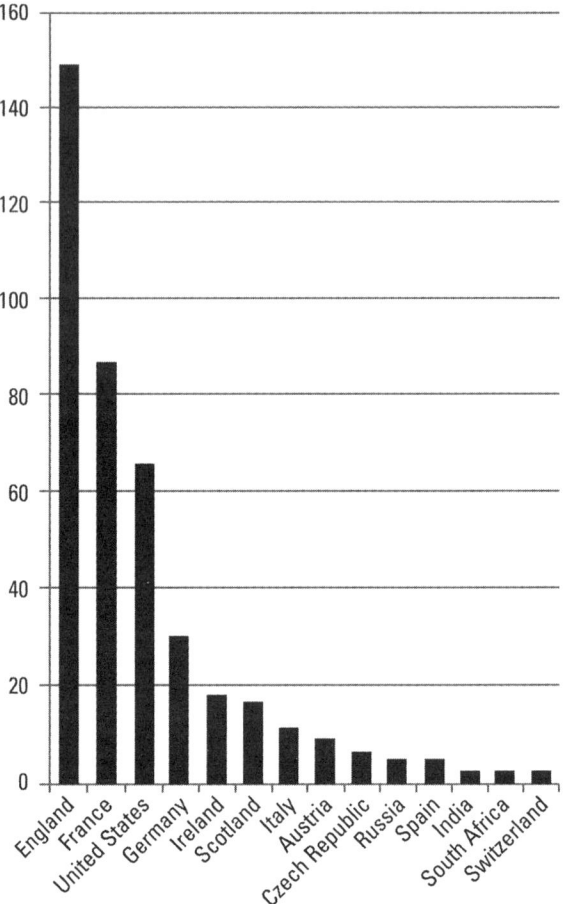

Countries of origin of writers mentioned by Borges in *El Hogar*. *(Line art courtesy of Christopher Westby.)*

Ireland, and Scotland), while Spain and any other Spanish-speaking country are sorely underrepresented.[14] In fact, Borges references Hispanic writers only four times throughout the course of his three-year appointment with *El Hogar,* and all of these references appear elsewhere than in his review column. Of these mentions, three are about Spanish-speaking authors (Miguel de Unamuno, Ramón Llull, and Jorge Isaacs), and one is a prologue to a novel (*La carreta* [*The Cart*] by the Uruguayan author Enrique Amorim) (Table 4).

Table 4. Hispanic writers Borges mentions in *El Hogar* outside of his review column

Author Mentioned	Borges's Article Title	Date
Miguel de Unamuno	"Presencia de Miguel de Unamuno" [The Presence of Miguel de Unamuno]	January 29, 1937
Jorge Isaacs	"Vindicación de la *María* de Jorge Isaacs" [The Vindication of Jorge Isaacs's *María*]	May 7, 1937
Enrique Amorim	"Prólogo de Jorge Luis Borges a la edición alemana de *La carreta* (por Enrique Amorim)" [Jorge Luis Borges's Prologue to the German Edition of *The Cart* (by Enrique Amorim)]	July 9, 1937
Ramón Llull	"La máquina de pensar de Raimundo Lulio" [Ramón Llull's Thinking Machine]	October 15, 1937

This limited selection of writers from Latin America and Spain raises the central question of who counts as a *foreign* author and what Borges categorizes as *foreign* literature.[15] In the most general sense, "foreign" is normally used to describe a country that is not one's own. Thus, all other Spanish-speaking countries outside of Borges's native Argentina would fit the bill to appear throughout the pages of "Libros y autores extranjeros." Yet this is certainly not the case. The small representation of authors and works from Spain might be explained by the outbreak of the Spanish Civil War in July 1936, only a few months before Borges's first published page and his appointed position at *El Hogar* (October 16, 1936). That said, many of these Spanish writers and artists fled Spain before the war so that they could continue writing and working from other countries. Furthermore, the Spanish Civil War does not explain the glaring absence of virtually any Latin American author or work throughout Borges's review column in *El Hogar*. Although Borges dedicates a short piece to Jorge Isaacs's novel *María* in May 1937, this work was first published in 1867 and is not representative of the literary scene in Latin America during the early part of the twentieth century. In a similar vein, the short prologue for Enrique Amorim's novel *La carreta*, which appears on July 9, 1937, is far from a representation of all of the current trends in Latin American literature and more accurately shows Borges's preference for including reviews of his friends' work. This idea is showcased by another Argentine writer, Ernesto Palacio, in a separate piece written for *El Hogar*: "¿Por qué no se leen libros argentinos?" [Why Aren't Argentine Books Read?] (March 19, 1937).[16] In addition to stressing the lack of profitability for publishers printing local authors, Palacio notes that Argentine literature lacks the tradition and history of criticism afforded to most foreign works and authors:

> La verdad es que de los libros extranjeros *se habla,* y de los argentinos, *no,* o se *habla mal.* Aquí, y no en otra parte, está la clave del problema. No es cierto que nuestros libros no se lean por su calidad inferior, ya que el público argentino consume en abundancia mala literatura extranjera, de todo precio. Lo cierto es que esta literatura es literatura protegida, y la nuestra, en cambio, es literatura desamparada ... El problema del libro argentino es, antes que nada, un problema de la crítica literaria ... No hay quien señale los valores. No puede saberse cuáles libros son buenos y cuáles no; qué debe leerse y qué evitarse; a quiénes cabe admirar y a quiénes repudiar; en qué consiste la originalidad o la utilidad o la belleza de lo que se publica y por cuáles razones.

> [The truth is that people *talk about* foreign books, and they *do not* talk about Argentine books, or they *speak poorly* about them. Here, and nowhere else, is the root of the problem. It's not true that our books aren't read for their inferior literary quality, considering that the Argentine populace consumes an abundant amount of bad foreign literature, of all prices. It's

true that this literature is protected, and ours, in turn, is abandoned... The problem of the Argentine book is, above all, a problem of literary criticism... There is no one who points out the values in it. You can't know which books are good and which are not; what one should read and what one should avoid; who should be admired and who should be repudiated; what originality or utility or beauty is in a publication and for what reasons.]¹⁷

Palacio goes on to discuss the fact that Argentine authors themselves are responsible for filling the void of literary criticism in their native country: "la solución de nuestro problema bibliográfico—que es el problema de nuestra cultura—está en manos de los mismos escritores" [the solution to our bibliographical problem—which is the problem of our culture—is in the hands of the writers themselves].¹⁸ Even though this short article deals solely with *Argentine* literature, Palacio's arguments concerning a lack of critical tradition, and as a result a lack of appropriate markets, can be extended to Latin American literature more generally. Moreover, Palacio's claims directly complement Borges's statement about his reading public in Buenos Aires that we saw at the start of this chapter.

Between the years 1936 and 1948, Borges wrote a total of forty-six book reviews for Victoria Ocampo's literary journal, *Sur*.¹⁹ In comparison with his review column in *El Hogar,* his contributions to *Sur* were much more academic and philosophical. In essence, they were intended for a more elite, educated audience. That said, the authors whom he reviewed for *Sur* did not differ drastically from those whom he included in his column for *El Hogar*. In fact, eleven of the forty-four authors (25 percent) whose works he reviewed in *Sur* also appeared in his pages in *El Hogar,* and most of these writers hailed from English-speaking countries. What is more, reviews of the following three works are published in *both* periodicals: Elvira Bauer's *Trau keinem Fuchs auf grüner Heid und keinem Jud auf seinem Eid* [*Trust No Fox on His Green Heath and No Jew on His Oath*] (Nuremberg: Stürmer Verlag, 1937), H. G. Wells's *Apropos of Dolores* (London: Jonathan Cape, 1938), and George S. Terry's *Duodecimal Arithmetic* (London: Longmans, Green, 1939). While the pieces vary in tone and length—with the *El Hogar* reviews being shorter and touch-

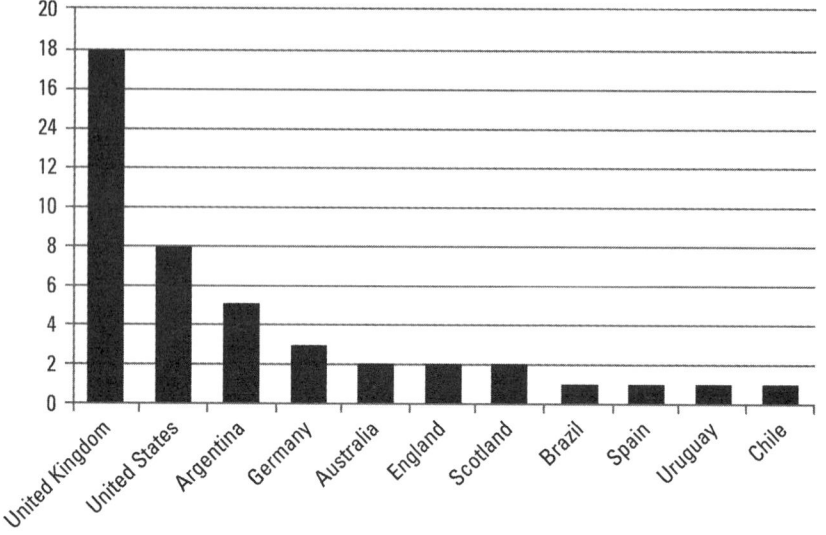

Writers reviewed by Borges in *Sur*. *(Line art courtesy of Christopher Westby.)*

ing on broader literary themes and traditions—it is telling that Borges includes reviews for these works in both publications. Moreover, the fact that they do differ in content and style reveals that Borges wrote versions of his reviews with distinct readers in mind. Consider, for instance, Borges's reviews of Bauer's work. While each medium certainly had length and formatting restrictions, the more neutral tone of the review in *El Hogar* appears stark and unconcerned when viewed alongside the review in *Sur,* even though both reviews ultimately reveal their distaste for Bauer's work. Thus, in the few phrases that bear structural similarity across periodicals, we see Borges framing the central argument of the book in particular ways and for particular audiences (Table 5).

Another shared aspect of Borges's contributions to *El Hogar* and *Sur* is the selection of several authors who would later become part of the *Antología de la literatura fantástica* [*Anthology of Fantastic Literature*] (1940), *Los mejores cuentos policiales* [*The Best Detective Tales*] (1943), and even the Séptimo Círculo (Seventh Circle) series produced by Emecé Editores and directed by Borges and Bioy Casares. Even though his publications in both periodicals predate all of these anthologies and collections by some years, Borges's initial reviews can be seen as the first phase

Table 5. Borges's collated reviews of Elvira Bauer's work in *El Hogar* and *Sur*

El Hogar (May 28, 1937)	*Sur* (May 1937)
"Ya se han vendido cincuenta y un mil ejemplares de este libro didáctico. **Su propósito es iniciar a los niños y niñas de las escuelas en los deberes y deleites inagotables del antisemitismo.** Oigo en Alemania que la crítica ha sido vedada a los críticos y no se les tolera sino la descripción de las obras."	"Las exhibiciones del odio pueden ser más obscenas y denigrantes que las del apetito carnal. Yo desafío a todos los *amateurs* de estampas eróticas a que me muestren una sola más vil que alguna de las veintidós que componen el libro para niños *Trau keinem Fuchs auf grüner Heid und keinem Jud auf seinem Eid*, cuya cuarta edición está pululando en Baviera. La primera es de 1936: poco más de un año ha bastado para agotar cincuenta y un mil ejemplares del alarmante opúsculo. **Su objeto es inculcar en los niños del tercer Reich la desconfianza y la abominación del judío.** Se trata, pues, de un curso de ejercicios de odio. En ese curso colaboran el verso (ya conocemos las virtudes mnemónicas de la rima) y el grabado en colores (ya conocemos la eficacia de las imágenes)."
[Fifty-one thousand copies of this didactic work have already been sold. **Its aim is to introduce school-age boys and girls to the duties and tireless pleasures of anti-Semitism.** I have heard that in Germany criticism has been banned by critics and the only thing that they will tolerate is a description of the works themselves.] (26)	[Displays of hatred can be more obscene and insulting than carnal desires. I challenge all of the *amateurs* of erotic imagery to show me even one example that is viler than any of the twenty-two images that make up the children's book *Trau keinem Fuchs auf früner Heid und keinem Jud auf seinem Eid*, whose fourth edition is multiplying in Bavaria. The first edition is from 1936: a little over a year was all it took to sell out of fifty-one thousand copies of the alarming minor work. **Its objective is to hammer into the children of the Third Reich distrust and abomination of the Jew.** It consists of, therefore, a series of exercises in hatred. In this course there are both verses (we already know the mnemonic virtues of rhyme) and colored prints (we already know the efficacy of images).] (80)

in a campaign to promote various works of High Modernism and detective fiction from around the globe. The later inclusion of similar authors in his edited collections and collaborative anthologies throughout the 1940s can be seen as the second phase of this same campaign to promote particular genres and literary tastes. When viewed together, the combination of his reviews in *El Hogar* and *Sur* and the series of anthologies that he later edited function as a conditioning or preparation of readers (in the Argentine middle-to-upper classes) for these assorted collections. Most notable are the reviews of Nicholas Blake's *La bestia debe morir* [*The Beast Must Die*] (*El Hogar,* June 24, 1938) and John Dickson Carr's *Los anteojos negros* [*The Black Spectacles*] (*Sur* 70 [1940]), which happen to be the first two books published in Emecé's Séptimo Círculo series in 1945. These works are the only ones Borges mentioned directly in his book reviews and also published in Emecé's series, but other authors from the Séptimo Círculo series appear throughout Borges's reviews, namely Michael Innes, Milward Kennedy, Hugh Walpole, Silvina Ocampo, Adolfo Bioy Casares, Manuel Peyrou, Richard Hull, Eden Phillpotts, Charles Dickens, Ellery Queen, and Graham Greene.[20] Similar overlaps of authors appear in the *Antología de la literatura fantástica* and *Los mejores cuentos policiales.* The correlation between the reviews of these authors in *El Hogar* and *Sur* and their later appearance in these three distinct venues also signals Borges's cultivation of cosmopolitan literary tastes for his readers. More specifically, all three of these publishing ventures deal with the genre of detective fiction, a genre that Borges and Bioy Casares were eager to elevate from its status as minor literature, which points to a general promotion of and investment in this type of literature.[21] What we find by analyzing the overlaps between Borges's reviews in *El Hogar* and *Sur* and the texts that he chooses to include in his edited series is that the majority of the writers are best known for their High Modernist fiction or their crime or detective fiction (Table 6). Thus, one of the key strategies in Borges's reviewing literature and collaborating with Bioy Casares (and also Silvina Ocampo) is the production of a new interest and market in Argentina for the previously overlooked genres of High Modernism and detective fiction.[22]

In addition to helping rejuvenate, rebrand, and popularize the detective fiction genre in Argentina, Borges's biweekly page on authors and

Table 6. Author overlaps among Borges's reviews and later publications

Author	El Hogar	Sur	Antología de la literatura fantástica	Los mejores cuentos policiales	Séptimo Círculo
Anthony Berkeley	X			X	X
Adolfo Bioy Casares		X		X	X
Nicholas Blake (Cecil Day-Lewis)	X				X
María Luisa Bombal		X	X		
Jorge Luis Borges			X	X	
John Dickson Carr	X	X		X	X
G. K. Chesterton	X	X	X	X	X
Jean Cocteau	X		X		
Wilkie Collins	X[a]			X	X
Lord Dunsany	X		X		
William Faulkner	X				X
James George Frazer	X		X		
Graham Greene	X			X	X
Richard Hull	X				X
Michael Innes	X			X	X
James Joyce	X		X		
Franz Kafka	X		X		
Milward Kennedy	X			X	X
Rudyard Kipling	X		X		
Silvina Ocampo		X			X
Manuel Peyrou		X	X		X
Eden Phillpotts	X	X		X	X
Edgar Allan Poe	X			X	
Ellery Queen	X	X		X	
Georges Simenon	X			X	
Olaf Stapledon	X	X	X		
Hugh Walpole	X				X

a. There is no biography dedicated to Wilkie Collins throughout Borges's pages of *El Hogar*, nor are any of his books reviewed. Borges references his novels only when he is discussing other authors as a point of comparison: "No en vano la primera novela policial que registra la historia—la primera en el tiempo y quizá en el mérito: 'The Moonstone' (1868) de Wilkie Collins—es, asimismo, una excelente novela psicológica" [Not in vain, the first detective novel recorded in history—the first in time and perhaps in merit: "The Moonstone" (1868) by Wilkie Collins—is, also, an excellent psychological novel] (September 3, 1937, p. 30; review of "Sic transit Gloria" by Milward Kennedy).

Table 7. Author overlaps between Borges's reviews and Editorial Losada's Pajarita de Papel series

Author	Work Included in Pajarita de Papel
Franz Kafka	La metamorfosis [The Metamorphosis] (1938) (translated by Borges)
Franz Werfel	La muerte del pequeño burgués [The Man Who Conquered Death] (1938)
Paul Claudel	El libro de Cristóbal Colón [The Book of Christopher Columbus] (1941)
George Santayana	Diálogos en el limbo [Dialogues in Limbo] (1941)
Walt Whitman	Canto a mí mismo [Song of Myself] (1941)
Jules Supervielle	La desconocida del Sena [The Unknown Woman of the Seine] (1941), with illustrations by Norah Borges
Aldous Huxley	El joven Arquímedes [Young Archimedes] (1943); El tiempo y la máquina [Time and the Machine] (1945)
Thomas Mann	Cervantes, Goethe, Freud (1943)
Paul Valéry	Política del espíritu [The Politics of the Spirit] (1945)

foreign works in *El Hogar* and his book reviews in *Sur* can be linked to a number of emerging series with distinct publishing houses. I first consider Editorial Losada's Pajarita de Papel (Paper Bird) series, directed by Borges's brother-in-law, Guillermo de Torre.[23] Not only do these collections contain works by authors highlighted throughout Borges's pages in *El Hogar* and *Sur*, but they also contain works that were translated by Borges himself (Table 7). In fact, the initial volume of the Pajarita de Papel series is none other than Borges's translation of Franz Kafka's *La metamorfosis* [*The Metamorphosis*] (1938), which serves to stress the impact of Borges's literary criticism and promotion on Argentina's entry into global book markets. The influence of his reviews on this collection is even more apparent when we consider the fact that the entire collection included only eighteen books. The director of the firm, Gonzalo Pedro Losada, described it as "la colección que más satisfacciones nos dio como editores" [the collection that has given us the most satisfaction as publishers].[24]

Many of the titles included in this early collection later appear (with new bindings and physical attributes) in Editorial Losada's Biblioteca contemporánea (Contemporary Library), another initial series started alongside Pajarita de Papel, which speaks to the publishing house's marketing strategies. There are a few studies dedicated to the Biblioteca contemporánea collection of works, especially in terms of its existence as an outlet for exiled Spaniards to edit works from their home country, but there is no extensive study, to date, on the Pajarita de Papel series.[25] The only mentions of this series are precisely that—mentions in passing to its existence rather than any detailed investigation into the design elements, prices, titles published, or parties involved in its production.[26] In addition to the importance that this series had for Editorial Losada, another intriguing aspect of the works included in it is the fact that every element of each book's production, from the selection of the texts to the translation and editing, appears to be somewhat of a family affair. In other words, not only did Borges's brother-in-law, Guillermo de Torre, serve as one of the directors of the publishing house and the specific person in charge of the series, but both Borges and his mother, Leonor Acevedo de Borges, contributed translations to the series, and Norah Borges de Torre provided illustrations.[27]

Each volume in the Pajarita de Papel series was carefully thought out, in terms of the specific work chosen and its physical features. The exiled Italian artist Attilio Rossi, a close friend and collaborator of Borges, was in charge of the design elements of each work, which accounts for the unique visual features found throughout their pages. Unlike any other of Editorial Losada's works published at this time, the volumes within the Pajarita de Papel series were hardcover books. We find the unique emblem for the collection—an origami paper bird—on each front cover and on rather flashy endpapers that artistically riff off of the series' name. Another aspect that helps these books stand out from other collections produced by competing publishing houses is the use of bright colors. More specifically, the covers of each volume range from deep,

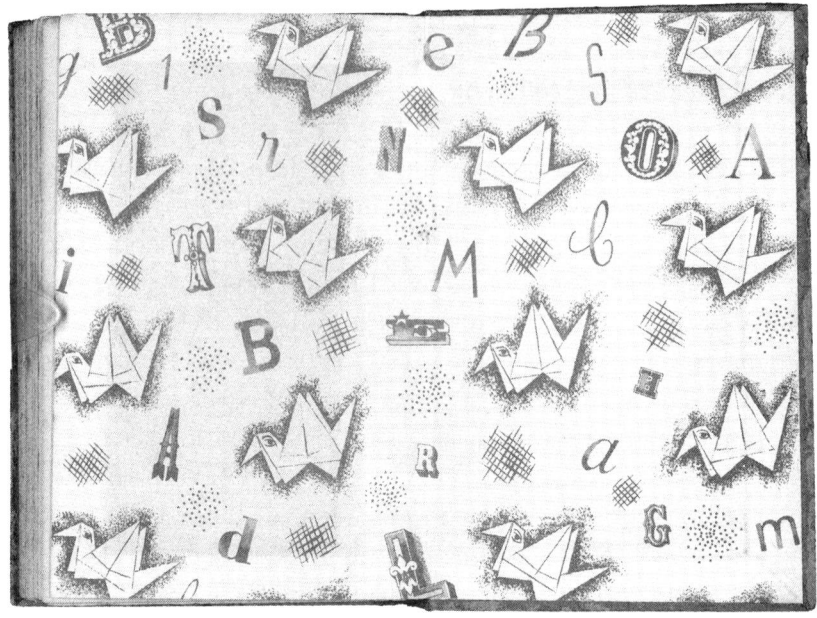

Endpapers found in Borges's translation of *La metamorfosis* (Editorial Losada, 1938), showing the origami paper bird emblem of the Pajarita de Papel series. *(Reproduced from the Albert and Shirley Small Special Collections Library, University of Virginia.)*

saturated reds to bright greens and pinks. In addition, virtually every volume, whether containing short stories or more lengthy writings by an author, has unique design headers at the start of every new section. Unlike competing series within Editorial Losada (or other collections produced by outside publishing houses, such as Editorial Sudamericana), these works were crafted artistically with the utmost care. Alongside their unique endpapers, we find ornately illustrated headers and at times full-page illustrations. Editorial Losada made sure to secure copyright for all of these design elements by printing "Marca y características gráficas registradas" [Registered brand and graphic characteristics] alongside the regular wording "Queda hecho el depósito que previene la ley núm. 11.723" [the deposit (of three copies of the book) has been made (to the National Intellectual Property Registry) in compliance with the law 11.723], which appears at the start of virtually every printed book during this period in Argentina. Thus, it is clear that aesthetics were very important to this publishing house and something that distinguished its works from those of its competitors.

Just as Borges's contributions to *El Hogar* and *Sur* affected publishing decisions at Editorial Losada, so too did they influence a series published by Editorial Sudamericana: the Colección Horizonte (Horizon Collection) (Table 8). Editorial Sudamericana's *Catálogo general* (1950) best summarizes the aim and content of this collection:

> La COLECCIÓN HORIZONTE agrupa una serie de obras que en conjunto componen el panorama más completo de la novela contemporánea, el cual va ampliándose aun a medida que con riguroso criterio estético se incorporan a ella los más notables valores de la literatura imaginativa. Cada uno de sus volúmenes representa un enfoque agudo y personalísimo del mundo; a través de sus páginas el lector penetra por laberintos de pasión, en los destinos atormentados o singulares de personajes que tienen todo el calor y la verdad de seres humanos. De todos los títulos puede decirse que destacan un valor representativo o un significativo matiz en la producción de este o aquel novelista, y asegurarse que, si bien separados naturalmente por las específicas cualidades de cada autor, todos se unen para constituirse en la muestra de mayor valor que en este género literario sea posible hallar entre las ofrecidas al lector exigente de nuestro tiempo.
>
> [The HORIZON COLLECTION groups together a series of works that provide the most complete panorama of the contemporary novel, which continues to expand on the most notable values of imaginative literature through rigorous aesthetic criticism. Each one of its volumes represents a pointed and very personal focus of the world; through its pages the reader enters into labyrinths of passion and into characters' tormented or unique destinies that have all of the reality and truth of real humans. All of the titles can be said to stress a representative value or a significant nuance in the produc-

Table 8. Author overlaps between Borges's reviews and Editorial Sudamericana's Colección Horizonte

Author	Work Included in Colección Horizonte
Liam O'Flaherty	*El alucinado* [*The Puritan*] (1939)
Julien Green	*Adriana Mesurat* (1939)
William Faulkner	*Las palmeras salvajes* [*The Wild Palms*] (1940) (translated by Borges)
William Somerset Maugham	*La otra comedia* [*Theatre*] (1941)
Thomas Mann	*Las cabezas trocadas* [*Die vertauschten Köpfe*] (1942)
Vicki Baum	*Marión* [*Marion Alive*] (1943)
Aldous Huxley	*Con los esclavos en la Noria* [*Eyeless in Gaza*] (1943);[a] *El tiempo debe detenerse* [*Time Must Have a Stop*] (1945)
Virginia Woolf	*Orlando* (1943)[a] (translated by Borges)
Evelyn Waugh	¡. . . *Más banderas!* [*Put Out More Flags*] (1947); *Primicia* [*Scoop*] (1947); *Retorno a Brideshead* [*Brideshead Revisited*] (1948)
Franz Werfel	*Estafa de cielo* [*Der veruntreute Himmel*] (1947)
John Dos Passos	*El número uno* [*Number One*] (1943); *Hombre joven a la ventura* [*Adventures of a Young Man*] (1951)

Note: Several other works were published in the Colección Horizonte series by authors whose names appeared in Borges's column in *El Hogar,* such as George Bernard Shaw (*El vínculo irracional* [*Irrational Knot*] [1953]), but since these books have a publication date after 1951, they are not included here.

a. Previously appeared with Editorial Sur in 1936 (Huxley) and 1937 (Woolf).

tion of this or that novelist, and assure yourself that, if they were separated out naturally by the specific qualities of each author, all of them would come together to form an example of the highest value in this literary genre that is possible to find among the works offered to the demanding reader of our time.][28]

The most salient characteristic of this collection that comes across through this description is that of literary and cultural value. More specifically, there is a marked interest in selecting and publishing works—from around the globe—that best represent contemporary authors' individual styles. In a certain sense, the Colección Horizonte provides readers with books that will add a level of value to their lives. Alongside this conceptually unifying idea of value, the books produced as part of the collection also possess similar physical characteristics. The cover of each volume is divided into four horizontal segments with varying color combinations, which aesthetically echoes the name of the collection itself. Even though the color schemes of this quadripartite division are hard to analyze for patterns (in light of the fact that with each new edition, each work appears to change and vary), they mimic trends in English publishing, specifically with regard to the Penguin Books series, which first emerged in 1935 and had a "basic horizontal tripartite division of the covers" similar to Editorial Sudamericana's collection.[29] In addition to their shared use of horizontal color blocking, both Penguin and Editorial Sudamericana choose a modern sans serif typeface for all of the printing on their books, which highlights their shared interest in a clean and modern design. Another shared trait is the inclusion of the price on the cover; however, unlike Penguin, Editorial Sudamericana prints these prices on the back cover.[30] All of these links unite Editorial Sudamericana's print production with that of Penguin and in the process emphasize the publisher's push to become a key player in the global literary marketplace.

Another oft-forgotten collection from a different publishing house appears to fit the same pattern as Editorial Losada's Pajarita de Papel and Editorial Sudamericana's Colección Horizonte: Emecé Editores's Cuadernos de la Quimera (Chimera's Notebooks).[31] This later series di-

Cover of Virginia Woolf's *Orlando* (Editorial Sudamericana, 1945). *(Reproduced from the Albert and Shirley Small Special Collections Library, University of Virginia.)*

rectly parallels what we saw with Editorial Losada's series, since the first volume is a translation of a literary classic produced by none other than Borges, and several of the authors published in the collection also appear within Borges's review pages in *El Hogar* and *Sur* (Table 9).[32] As a whole, the Cuadernos de la Quimera collection, directed by Eduardo Mallea, was dedicated to the "novella," a literary work that is typically fewer than one hundred pages long and thus falls somewhere between the short story and the novel.[33] Much like many of the collections that I argue stem from Borges's reviews for *El Hogar* and *Sur,* this particular series published works by only well-known, established—and more often than not international—writers, that is, works that had already been commercially successful in other countries (mostly Europe) or authors whose other writings had sold well. Once again, we see an overlap between the authors included in this series and several of Borges's publishing ventures.[34]

In terms of their physical features, each volume in the Cuadernos de la Quimera series more resembles a thin pamphlet (19 by 10.5 by 0.6 centimeters) compared with the other books that we have seen, which reflects the fact that the defining characteristic of all of these works is their shorter length. The cover of each work has a rectangle, in a different color than the rest of the cover, with the author's name, the title of the work, and the name of the series (printed in a cream color) along with the emblem of the series, a Chimera, printed in a smaller rectangle in the same color as the larger portions of the cover. In an effort to distinguish the titles of these works, Emecé uses a serif typeface, much resembling Caslon, for these parts of the cover, while the author's name and that of the series are printed in small caps in a sans serif typeface. The reason for the choice of the mythological figure of the Chimera is unknown, but its selection might allude to the sundry mix of works in the series that parallels the unique composition of the creature, which is traditionally described as having the head of a lion, the body of a goat, and the tail of a serpent.

Along with his influential reviews in *El Hogar* and *Sur,* Borges also wrote occasional pieces for *La Nación,* a well-established Argentine newspaper.[35] His contributions to it during this period were not as regular as those he made to *El Hogar,* nor did he hold a specific posi-

Table 9. Author overlaps between Borges's reviews and Emecé's Cuadernos de la Quimera series

Author	Work Included in Cuadernos de la Quimera
Herman Melville	*Bartleby* [*Bartleby, the Scrivener*] (1943) (translated and with a prologue by Borges)
Ezequiel Martínez Estrada	*La inundación* [*The Flood*] (1943)
José Bianco	*Sombras suele vestir* [*Shadows Tend to Dress*] (1944)
Adolfo Bioy Casares	*El perjurio de la nieve* [*The Perjury of the Snow*] (1944)
Charles Baudelaire	*La Fanfarlo* (1944)
Francisco Ayala	*El hechizado* [*The Cursed*] (1944)
Chaucer	*El cuento del perdonador* [*The Pardoner's Tale*] (1944)
Charles Dickens	*El velo negro* [*The Black Veil*] (1945)
Franz Kafka	*Informe para una academia* [*A Report to an Academy*] (1945)
Henry James	*La humillación de los Northmore* [*The Abasement of the Northmores*] (1945) (translated by Haydée Lange; prologue by Borges)
Julien Green	*El viajero sobre la tierra* [*Voyageur sur la terre*] (1945)

Note: Twenty-six works were published in this collection up through 1954, but given the scope of this book, I have limited the titles included to those that fall within the book's time frame. However, two other works that overlap with any other of Borges's publishing ventures appeared in 1954: Evelyn Waugh's *Amor entre ruinas* [*Love among the Ruins*] and Oscar Wilde's *El crimen de Lord Arturo Savile* [*Lord Arthur Savile's Crime*].

tion there, as he did with *El Hogar*. Moreover, the types of pieces that he wrote for *La Nación* differed drastically, in terms of their subject matter and style, from the literary reviews and short biographies of his "Libros y autores extranjeros." What we find in *La Nación* are short pieces of fiction, poems, and original essays, twelve of which would be revised and included in Borges's later collections or new versions of previously published works (Table 10). The differences between Borges's publications in *La Nación* and his reviews for *El Hogar* and *Sur* are quite clear. The large majority of his publications in the former periodical were original, creative pieces that would be republished in one of his own collections; the latter were focused solely on reviews of other authors and their works.[36] As a result, these outlets represent two distinct tendencies in Borges's publishing ventures during this moment in his career. On one hand, the reviews of foreign authors and their works for *El Hogar* and *Sur* would serve as a catalyst for his (successful) production of several anthologies, of both poetry and prose, with the help of his close friends. In addition to these edited anthologies, Borges's contributions to *El Hogar* and *Sur* would also help with the development of several collections for Editorial Losada, Editorial Sudamericana, and Emecé Editores. On the other hand, Borges's pieces published in *La Nación* reflect a simultaneous promotion of his own creative writings (in the form of short stories, essays, and poems), which would emerge more prominently on the scene with the release of his two most canonical collections during this decade: *Ficciones* (1944) and *El Aleph* (1949). Even though Borges's contributions to *El Hogar* and *La Nación,* or even his reviews in *Sur,* are not often considered as foundational as these later volumes, nor are they analyzed for their physical features or attributes, their importance for his formation as an author and his development of cosmopolitan reading habits cannot be emphasized enough.

Collaborative Foundations: Friendships and Shared Interests

Despite being extremely prolific during this early period of his career, Borges also managed to cultivate friendships with other writers, most notably Adolfo Bioy Casares. This relationship would result in the cre-

Table 10. Borges's subsequent publication of his pieces from *La Nación*

Title	*Historia de la eternidad* (1936)	*La Nación* (1940–1945)	*Ficciones* (1944)	*Otras inquisiciones* (1952)	*El otro, el mismo* (1969)	*Prólogos* (1975)
"Algunos pareceres de Nietzsche" [Some of Nietzsche's Views]		February 11, 1940				
"La noche cíclica" [The Cyclical Night]		October 6, 1940			X	
"Nota sobre 'The Purple Land'" [Note on "The Puple Land"]		August 3, 1941		X		
"Dos libros de este tiempo" [Two Books about This Time]		October 12, 1941		X		
"Tres formas del eterno regreso" [Three Forms of the Eternal Return]	X	December 12, 1941				
"El idioma analítico de John Wilkins" [The Analytical Language of John Wilkins]		December 14, 1941		X		
"Teoría de Almafuerte" [Theory of Almafuerte]		February 22, 1942				X
"Funes el memorioso" [Funes the Memorious]		June 7, 1942	X			
"La forma de la espada" [The Shape of the Sword]		July 26, 1942	X			

"Sobre una alegoría china" [On a Chinese Allegory]	October 25, 1942		
"La última invención de Hugh Walpole" [Hugh Walpole's Last Invention]	January 10, 1943		
"Sobre el *Vathek* de William Beckford" [On William Beckford's *Vathek*]	April 4, 1943	X	
"Poema conjetural" [Conjectural Poem]	July 4, 1943		X
"Poema del tercer elemento" [Poem of the Third Element]	March 5, 1944		X
"El propósito de Zarathustra" [The Purpose of Zarathustra]	October 15, 1944		
"La flor de Coleridge" [Coleridge's Flower]	September 23, 1945	X	

ation of literary alter egos whose names appear on several published works. Many sources pinpoint the first chance meeting of Borges and Bioy Casares to 1931 or 1932 at Victoria Ocampo's home in San Isidro:

> A poco del lanzamiento de *Sur*, Marta Casares de Bioy visitó a Victoria Ocampo. Iba a pedirle un consejo: su hijo Adolfito, un adolescente de diecisiete años y del que estaba orgullosa, tenía una profunda inclinación hacia la literatura; de hecho ya había escrito dos libros. Marta Casares quería saber a quién de entre los escritores conocidos recomendaba Victoria para que lo ayudara y lo guiara en el camino elegido por su hijo. Victoria, sin vacilar, le indicó a Borges ... Borges señala la fecha del encuentro en 1931, cuando él tenía treinta y dos años y Adolfito, diecisiete. Bioy, en cambio, afirma que ocurrió en 1932, y los dos dijeron que fue en la casa de San Isidro de Victoria Ocampo ... Borges quedó deslumbrado con este muchacho que en dieciocho años había leído los mismos autores y libros que él en treinta y tres.
>
> [Shortly after launching the literary magazine *Sur*, Marta Casares de Bioy visited Victoria Ocampo. She went to ask her advice: Her son Adolfito, a young seventeen-year-old of whom she was particularly proud, had a profound inclination toward literature; in fact he had already written two books. Marta Casares wanted to know who among Victoria's known writer friends she would recommend to help and guide her son on his chosen path. Victoria, without hesitating, pointed out Borges ... Borges chose the date of the meeting in 1931, when he was thirty-two and Adolfito, seventeen. Bioy, in turn, affirms that the meeting happened in 1932, and the two said that it was at Victoria Ocampo's home in San Isidro ... Borges was stunned with this boy who in eighteen years had read the same authors and books that he had in thirty-three.][37]

Following their initial encounter in San Isidro, Borges and Bioy Casares started to meet regularly to discuss literature and little by little began their collaborative endeavors. Around the time of their first meeting, Silvina Ocampo, one of Victoria's younger sisters, also started to attend their periodic *tertulias* and, as we shall see later, collaborate alongside these two Argentine writers.[38] One of the earliest instances of collaboration between Borges and Bioy Casares was "writing advertising copy on the health-giving properties—for 'intellectuals and sedentary types'—of La Martona's products," which were all produced by the latter's family-run dairy business.[39] Although copies of this pamphlet for La Martona are extremely rare, we know that the luxury printer Francisco A. Colombo printed it.[40] These early ads that Borges and Bioy Casares wrote for La Martona appeared in *Sur* (August 1935) and were also prominent throughout the literary journal *Destiempo* that the two writers created and directed from October 1936 to December 1937.[41]

Even though this periodical did not take off and consists of a mere three issues, it marks the inception of their collaborative endeavors, which would continue for almost the rest of their lives. The physical features of *Destiempo* immediately bring to mind several European and Latin American avant-garde periodicals from the early part of the twentieth century, which accentuate the duo's cosmopolitan sensibilities. Although *Destiempo* lacks a manifesto and the general sense of rupture that earlier avant-garde periodicals convey, the similar format, the typographical layout, and the kinds of materials included in its pages make it virtually impossible to ignore these earlier works as sources of aesthetic inspiration and influence. Two particular avant-garde periodicals, *ULTRA* (Spain: 1921–1922) and *Martín Fierro* (Argentina: 1924–1927), stand out for having an ample amount of physical features in common with *Destiempo*.[42] For instance, the use of one single sheet folded into thirds, much like a pamphlet, calls to mind the literary magazine *ULTRA*, and the combination of varying typefaces and multiple columns of text further echo the visual layout of this Spanish periodical. The publication of a series of *greguerías* by Ramón Gómez de la Serna in the last issue of *Destiempo* serves as a direct link between Borges and Bioy Casares's literary magazine and those of the historical avant-garde since this Spanish writer was very much involved in these types of periodical publications earlier in the twentieth century (both in his native Spain and abroad in various Latin American countries).

The shared traits between *Destiempo* and *Martín Fierro* are much more striking than those between *Destiempo* and *ULTRA*. First is the arrangement of details on the front page, especially the masthead, where the titles appear in serif and sans serif typefaces in bold and uppercase.[43] The layout of information pertaining to the city, year, and number of the issue is very similar between the two publications as well. Furthermore, and perhaps most intriguing, is the fact that there is a great deal of overlap between the writers and intellectuals associated with or published within *Martín Fierro* and those whose work also appears throughout the pages of *Destiempo*. Aside from Borges, Macedonio Fernández, Carlos Mastronardi, Nicolás Olivari, Xul Solar, and Silvina Ocampo are all involved (in some way) with both periodicals. Even though *Destiempo* does not have the same avant-garde driven edge of *Martín Fierro*, or any other periodical of its type, there is a possible link between the two in terms of their mutual desire to create or attract a new kind of cosmopolitan reader.

The writers and thinkers not associated with *Martín Fierro* who also contributed essays, poetry, and prose to the pages of *Destiempo* were close friends of either Borges or Bioy Casares. Many of these individuals would later work with Borges to produce a variety of literary anthologies or their writings would appear as part of these anthologies. For instance, Pedro Henríquez Ureña coedited the *Antología clásica de la literatura argentina* [*Classic Anthology of Argentine Literature*] (1937) with Borges in the same year as the last issue of *Destiempo*; and Franz Kafka, Manuel Peyrou, Macedonio Fernández, Ramón Gómez de la Serna, and Silvina Ocampo all appear within Borges, Bioy Casares, and Ocampo's *Antología de la literatura fantástica* (1940).[44] Furthermore, several of the writers who appear in *Destiempo* first made their appearance in Borges's literary reviews in *El Hogar* (e.g., Jules Supervielle and Franz Kafka), and others were codirectors of different magazines with Borges (e.g., Ulyses Petit de Murat). Finally, still more appeared in the collections created by Editorial Losada (Pajarita de Papel), Editorial Sudamericana (Colección Horizonte), and Emecé Editores (Cuadernos de la Quimera), a fact that supports my claim regarding Borges's marketing strategies in helping to create these collections that would revitalize Latin American reading habits.[45] In a similar vein, the curious "Museo" section included in each issue of *Destiempo* groups together fragments of works by European, American, and Latin American writers, which reflects Borges's interest in world literature. In the words of one critic, this particular section functions "as a device for mooting the temporal problem at the core of Argentina's cultural dilemma and as a figure through which to denationalize literary tradition and transform it into a global one."[46]

The Birth of Honorio Bustos Domecq

The collaborative work of Borges and Bioy Casares truly takes off with the creation of their first alter ego: Honorio Bustos Domecq.[47] The two men invented this pseudonym from a unique combination of their respective ancestors' surnames and in the process highlighted the importance of family lineage and the freedom that comes from writing with a name that is not recognizably their own.[48] To date, the majority of criticism surrounding the various works produced by Borges and Bioy Casares under this pseudonym (and that of Benito Suárez Lynch, the disciple of Bustos Domecq) tends to focus on aspects of humor and parody.[49] A large number of studies also address the importance of understanding the genre of detective fiction when approaching their collaborative pieces, especially their earliest joint book, *Seis problemas para don Isidro Parodi* [*Six Problems for Don Isidro Parodi*] (1942), which is considered "Latin America's first collection of short detective fiction."[50] Although these lines of thinking are valuable for studying the collaborative work of Borges and Bioy Casares, I focus on possible marketing strategies and editorial intentions involved with their collaborative fiction, specifically in terms of *Seis problemas*. In other words, the fact that Borges spends a great deal of time and energy reviewing works of detective fiction in his column for *El Hogar*, and then goes on to produce a number of anthologies and edited collections dedicated to this genre, signals a deliberate promotion of this type of literature that echoes trends in international publishing. Since Borges and Bioy Casares's creative collaboration falls within this same genre, a more complex aim seems to be at play that should not be boiled down simply to parody or humor, but rather, considered in light of publishing trends and global literary markets.

One of the most intriguing aspects of the creation of Honorio Bustos Domecq, particularly when we think about this pseudonym in conjunction with *Seis problemas,* is the desire on the part of Borges and Bioy Casares to flesh out this invented persona's biography and bibliography. Taking a pen name or writing under a pseudonym is common in the genre of detective fiction and thus a logical practice for the two men. For instance, J. I. M. Stewart wrote under the name Michael Innes; Frederic Dannay (Daniel Nathan) and Manfred Bennington Lee (Emanuel Lepofsky), under the name Ellery Queen; and Cecil Day-Lewis, under the name Nicholas Blake. That said, going to such lengths, as Borges and Bioy Casares did, to invent not only a pseudonym for one's work but also a life story and list of previously published synthetic works is much more than any of these well-known writers had done.[51] Thus, in addition to altering their names, these two Argentine writers open the first edition of *Seis problemas* with a short (fabricated) biography of Bustos Domecq, penned by Adelia Puglione (also fictional), that describes his life and works published to date.[52] Supposedly born in Pujato, a province of Santa Fe, Argentina, in 1893, Bustos Domecq published his first work, *¡Ciudadano!* [*Citizen!*], in 1915, which was followed by several others. Even though virtually all of these works are apocryphal, with the exception of *Entre libros y papeles* [*Between Books and Papers*], each title makes subtle references to important contemporary events in the lives of Borges and Bioy Casares.[53] For instance, the title of the first work, *¡Ciudadano!,* echoes the title of the cinematic blockbuster *Citizen Kane* (1941), which Borges harshly reviewed shortly after its release.[54] The undated *El Congreso Eucarístico: órgano de la propaganda argentina* [*The Eucharistic Congress: Body of Argentine Propaganda*] alludes to the conference of the same name that took place in Buenos Aires in October 1934 and brought hordes of people to the city. Another *porteño* reference that relates to both Borges and Bioy Casares is *Vida y muerte de don Chico Grande* [*Life and Death of Mr. Chico Grande*], which is the name of Juan Galiffi, the Argentine equivalent of Al Capone.

Alongside these more pointed references are two curious works that appear to be making a subtle commentary on the intellectual state of the Argentine populace: *¡Hablemos con más propiedad!* [*We Speak with More Authority!*] (1932) and *¡Ya sé leer!* [*I Know How to Read!*] (n.d.). Although these two works could be a commentary on the educational system in Argentina, it seems more probable that they are a reflection of the current reading habits of Borges and Bioy Casares's contemporaries.⁵⁵ This idea is supported further by the last work mentioned in this introductory note, *Los cuentos de Pujato* [*The Tales of Pujato*], which is described as the perfect example of Bustos Domecq's detective tales. Puglione stresses the fact that there is something in these tales for *every* kind of reader: "*Los cuentos de Pujato,* como cariñosamente los llama el autor, no son la filigrana de un bizantino encerrado en la torre de marfil; son la voz de un contemporáneo, atento a los latidos humanos y que derrama a vuela pluma los raudales de su verdad" [*The Tales of Pujato,* as the author affectionately calls them, are not the watermark of a Byzantine trapped in an ivory tower; they are the voice of a contemporary, attentive to human feelings and who sheds the torrents of truth quickly].⁵⁶ While these short detective stories focus on enigmas, as opposed to the violence and gore of so many other writings in this genre, they are accessible to all and show Borges and Bioy Casares's joint efforts to elevate this type of literature and at the same time cultivate more cosmopolitan literary preferences for Argentine readers.⁵⁷

Following this very bookish introduction to the invented author is a prologue by none other than one of the book's protagonists, Gervasio Montenegro. The first aspect of this *palabra liminar* (preliminary word) that stands out to readers is the emphasis placed on the fact that this book, *Seis problemas,* is the first work of detective fiction that does not fall within the traditional English or American traditions of the genre:

> ¡Insólito placer el de paladear, entre dos bocanadas aromáticas y a la vera de un irrefragable coñac del Primer Imperio, un libro policial que no obedece a las torvas consignas de un mercado anglosajón, extranjero, y que no hesito en parangonar con las mejores firmas que recomienda a los buenos amateurs londinenses el incorruptible Crime Club! También subrayaré por lo bajo mi satisfacción de porteño, al constatar que nuestro folletinista, aunque provinciano, se ha mostrado insensible a los reclamos de un localismo estrecho y ha sabido elegir para sus típicas aguafuertes el marco natural: Buenos Aires.

[What an unbelievable pleasure to relish, between two aromatic puffs and the edge of an irrefutable cognac of the First Empire, a detective novel that does not obey the fierce slogans of an Anglo-Saxon, foreign market and that does not pale in comparison to the best names that the incorruptible Crime Club recommends to good amateur Londoners! I will also stress discretely my *porteño* satisfaction, on confirming that our melodramatic novel, even though provincial, has demonstrated itself insensitive to the strategies of localism and has chosen for its typical etchings the natural frame: Buenos Aires.][58]

Thus, Borges and Bioy Casares not only carefully and conscientiously marketed this genre of detective fiction in their native Buenos Aires through anthologies and edited collections, but they now also emphasize the key *porteño* aspects that the tales of Don Isidro Parodi bring to potential readers. There are therefore several references in this prologue to how the figure of the gaucho, whose tradition is a central part of Argentine literature, serves as an important point of departure for a few of the short stories in the collection. Montenegro highlights this keen interest in pleasing the audience while also touching on the comical fact that Parodi is able to solve all of the enigmatic crimes presented to him from the confines of his own jail cell:

> H. Bustos Domecq es, a toda hora, un atento servidor de su público. En sus cuentos no hay planos que olvidar ni horarios que confundir. […] El lector menos avisado sonríe: adivina la omisión oportuna de algún tedioso interrogatorio y la omisión involuntaria de más de un atisbo genial, expedido por un caballero sobre cuyas señas particulares resultaría indelicado insistir…
>
> [H. Bustos Domecq is, at every hour, an attentive public servant. In his short stories there are neither false leads nor timetables to confuse. […] The least attentive reader smiles: he discerns the intentional omission of a tedious interrogation

and the unintentional omission of more than a brilliant insight, put forth by a gentleman on whose identifiable features it would be indelicate to dwell ...]⁵⁹

Nevertheless, these two Argentine authors have carefully sprinkled in references to other international writers of detective fiction, most notably Poe and Dickson Carr, for their more advanced audiences. Thus, there truly is something for every reader in these tales.

As we saw in the first chapter, direct references to the physical features of books and their production crop up in *Seis problemas,* which suggests that an interest in the material is not something reserved for Borges's solo publications but also is relevant to his coauthored pieces.⁶⁰ That said, the majority of such references, in conjunction with the unique preliminary materials, point to a marked interest in the idea of metafiction, which draws attention to the complex relationship between reality and fiction.⁶¹ For instance, in "Las previsiones de Sangiácomo" [Free Will and the Commendatore], one of the characters warns that it is necessary to "poner mucho ojo en lo que se publica. Acordate de Bustos Domecq, el santafecino ese que le publicaron un cuento y después resulta que ya lo había escrito Villiers de l'Isle Adam" [pay close attention to what one publishes. Remember Bustos Domecq, the person from Santa Fe who had a story published and then it turns out that it was already written by Villiers de l'Isle Adam].⁶² In this same story there is also a reference, made by Parodi, to the entire collection of tales that he relates:

> Mire, mozo; con tanta charla esta celda parece Belisario Roldán. En cuanto me descuido, ya se me ha colado un payaso con el cuento de las figuras del almanaque, o del tren que no para en ninguna parte, o de su señorita novia que no se suicidó, que no tomó el veneno por casualidad y que no la mataron. Yo le voy a dar orden al subcomisario Grondona, que en cuanto los vislumbre los meta de cabeza en el calabozo.
>
> [Look, kid; with so much talking in this cell it feels like Belisario Roldán (1873–1922; Argentine politican and orator). As soon as I get distracted, some clown gets in here with a story

about Zodiac signs, or about a train that doesn't stop anywhere, or about a young lover who doesn't commit suicide because she didn't drink the poison accidentally and who doesn't get killed. I'm going to give Deputy Superintendent Grondona the order to put all of these people in jail headfirst when he sees them.]⁶³

Even though these few references to the material are not nearly as precise as others we saw in the first chapter, they still exhibit a vested interest in the book as an object that must undergo some sort of physical production, packaging, and promotion before it reaches the hands of its readers.⁶⁴

In terms of the physical features of the first edition of *Seis problemas,* the light blue covers with white text (and a blue arrow as the logo for Editorial Sur) are quite distinctive when viewed alongside the other volumes published by Borges thus far in his career. That said, the positioning of the sans serif typeface on the cover is reminiscent of Francisco A. Colombo's works (see Chapter 2), which alludes to the development of a personal design style by Borges for elite audiences. This work is also one of the first that Borges published with Editorial Sur (not to be confused with the literary journal *Sur*).⁶⁵

As we have seen throughout this chapter, Borges's book reviews and short biographies of writers, his conscientious attempts to rebrand the detective fiction genre, and his creative collaborations with Adolfo Bioy Casares all show a marked interest in promoting global literature that previously lacked Argentine readership. In essence, Borges is filling the void of Argentine literary criticism and in the process developing a new type of marketing for book production and publishing in his native Buenos Aires. This trend also relates to the various edited collections and anthologies that he helped to produce during the late 1930s and early 1940s, a trend that highlights both his interest in literary criticism and his desire to influence and change reading habits and literary marketplaces in Argentina.

F • O • U • R

Borges as Editor and Anthologist

In his review of *The Albatross Book of Living Prose* for *El Hogar,* Borges comments on the curious form of the anthology. Above all, he marvels at the newly discovered meaning and virtue that arise from the unique, and often random, placement of textual fragments in an anthology: "La mera yuxtaposición de dos piezas (con sus diversos climas, procederes, connotaciones) puede lograr una virtud que no logran esas piezas aisladas. Por lo demás: copiar un párrafo de un libro, mostrarlo solo, ya es deformarlo sutilmente. Esa deformación puede ser preciosa" [The mere juxtaposition of two works (with their diverse atmospheres, origins, connotations) can achieve a quality that these two isolated works would never attain. Apart from that: copying a paragraph from a book, showing it alone, this is deforming it subtly. That deformation can be precious].[1] Borges calls this phenomenon "el encanto peculiar de las antologías" [the peculiar charm of anthologies].[2] But what is an anthology for Borges, and what role do these volumes play in introducing readers to new authors and their works? In order to demonstrate how Borges starts to fill the existing gaps in Argentine letters — gaps that he previously established in his literary reviews and critiques — I take a closer look at the anthologies and edited collections that he directed during the 1930s and 1940s. As a way of highlighting his influence on cosmopolitan reading, my analysis in this chapter centers on three themes:

Argentine literature, detective fiction, and world literature. Alongside an analysis of the overlaps in authors from one anthology to the next, I also examine the various physical features of these anthologies, since the ways in which authors are presented can provide a great deal of insight into the types of audiences that these works were trying to reach. More specifically, the information that is provided—or not provided—about each author, the format in which it is physically presented on the page in each volume, and the authors who are described in more detail than others tell us a great deal about Borges's larger project of enhancing reading habits in Latin America.

Generally speaking, an anthology

> es un conjunto de textos y/o fragmentos de textos que se agrupan a partir de ciertas características determinadas por un seleccionador, aunque no siempre argumentadas por el mismo, y cuya finalidad principal es divulgar las obras juzgadas representativas de un autor, un género, un tema, una tendencia, un movimiento, una región o una generación.
>
> [is an ensemble of texts and/or fragments of texts that are grouped together on the basis of certain characteristics determined by an editor, even though these attributes are not always put forth by the same person, and their principle purpose is to disseminate works that are judged as representative of an author, a genre, a theme, a tendency, a movement, a region, or a generation.][3]

We can expand this definition to include the freedom and level of choice that these types of books—in comparison with other literary forms—provide for readers. Moreover, the compact form of the anthology is much more manageable, both physically and thematically, and approachable for the average reader. This degree of accessibility also can be extended to that of affordability. In other words, someone would need extensive funds to purchase each individual work included as part of a literary canon, so buying an anthology is an affordable alternative for many readers.[4]

Another key aspect that must be stressed when discussing the form of the anthology is the challenging task of presenting the volume as a unified whole. Adán C. Diehl describes this complex process in his review of Pedro Henríquez Ureña and Borges's *Antología clásica de la literatura argentina* [*Classic Anthology of Argentine Literature*] (1937):

> La selección de las composiciones destinadas a formar una antología, es obra tan personal como la creación artística. Tantos criterios como autores. Infinidad de problemas que resolver: la extensión de tiempo, qué debe abarcar, la elección no sólo de los autores, sino también de las obras de éstos que deben figurar (lo que es muy distinto a "merecen" figurar), la responsabilidad que supone la presentación trunca o parcial de algunas piezas e innumerable cantidad de otros motivos de vacilación.
>
> [The selection of pieces that are destined to form part of an anthology is a very personal work, much like any artistic creation. Just as many rules as authors. An enormous number of problems to solve: the extension of time it should cover, the selection of not just authors, but also the works of these individuals that should be included (which is very distinct from those that "deserve" to be included), the responsibility of deciding whether or not to include shortened versions or full versions of works, and an innumerable quantity of other reasons for vacillation.][5]

In a sense, the care and precision required for crafting an anthology at times surpass those of editing and publishing a novel or collection of poems. Alfonso Reyes highlights this same level of labor as an essential characteristic of the well-made anthology by identifying two distinct types of anthologies: "las hay en que domina el gusto personal del coleccionista, y las hay en que domina el criterio histórico, objetivo" [those in which the personal tastes of the collector dominate, and those in which an objective historical judgment dominates].[6] While the first type of anthology has certain merits, its scope is determined purely by the likes (and dislikes) of its editors. As we shall see throughout this chapter, Borges, alongside a variety of collaborators, produces *both* types of anthologies during the 1930s and 1940s.

Ernesto Palacio's discussion of why readers have the tendency not to read works by Argentine authors that we saw in the last chapter prefigures much of the collaborative work that Borges undertakes during this time in the form of anthologies and edited collections. More specifically, the central concern Palacio expresses is the lack of critical tradition for Argentine literature, which serves as his rationale for the lack of readership in this area:

> Cuando surjan entre [los escritores] una o dos vocaciones críticas bien definidas, que se arroguen la tarea de poner orden en el caos actual de la producción bibliográfica argentina, destacando y definiendo los valores reales y descartando los ficticios, habría llegado a la hora de nuestra redención intelectual. La crítica señalará entonces al público, de manera segura, el camino que debe seguir para enterarse de la capacidad creadora de nuestro pueblo; servirá de intermediaria respetada y acatada entre la inteligencia y la masa.

> [When one or two well-defined critical vocations arise among (writers), they must take on the task of organizing the actual chaos of Argentine bibliographical production, emphasizing and defining real values and eliminating the fictitious ones, and then we will have arrived at the moment of our intellectual redemption. Their criticism will tell the reading populace, in a reliable way, the path that they should follow to understand the creative ability of our nation; it will serve as a respected intermediary between the intelligentsia and the masses.][7]

This is precisely the role that Borges fills during the late 1930s and early 1940s. Palacio continues his article by describing the specific ways in which the necessary void of literary criticism must be filled in Argentina:

No es labor de la gran prensa informativa. Por más restringido que sea el público que lee esas publicaciones sus juicios no caen en el vacío. Tienen, por el contrario, una gran influencia, si no directa, indirecta, sobre la colectividad. Obran, si así puede decir, por impregnación, de arriba bajo, desde las minorías cultas a las mayorías incultas. Los juicios de valor, emanados de tribunas respetadas, circulan y entran, poco a poco, en el lenguaje común. Una crítica seria y responsable desempeñaría un inestimable servicio a la causa de nuestra cultura.

[It is not the work of the large informative press. The more restricted the public is that reads these publications, the better the chance of these judgments not falling on deaf ears. They have, on the contrary, a large influence, if not direct, then indirect, over the collectivity. They work, if you can say it that way, through impregnation, from top to bottom, from educated minorities to uneducated majorities. Value judgments, which emanate from respected tribunals, circulate and enter, little by little, into the common language. A serious and responsible critique would perform an invaluable service to the cause of our culture.][8]

The idea of restricting the individuals who will read and develop an understanding of this literary criticism undeniably echoes the perspective of José Ortega y Gasset in *La deshumanización del arte* [*The Dehumanization of Art*] (1925). However, unlike the elite that Ortega y Gasset envisions, Palacio sees the Argentine elite as key in the dissemination of works of literary value. The presence of such an article in *El Hogar*, which had elite Argentine readership, also speaks to this instructive sentiment in Palacio's vision.

Borges shows a marked interest in the form of the anthology from a very early point in his career. While living in Spain with his family, he published two works that can be classified as antecedents to the collaborative anthologies of the 1930s and 1940s: the "Antología expresionista" [Expressionist Anthology] (*Cervantes,* Madrid, 1920) and "La lírica argentina contemporánea" [The Contemporary Argentine Lyric] (*Cosmópolis,* 1921). Although both of these works appear in literary journals, as opposed to being printed separately as their own entities, they mark an important moment in Borges's early career and play a crucial role in his later return to the form of the anthology. Even though the first anthology deals strictly with German expressionist poetry from the early twentieth century, the format is virtually identical to that of "La lírica argentina contemporánea" and as a result reveals much about the ways in which materials are presented and approached in these early works. Moreover, the last line printed in both anthologies, "Notas y traducción de Jorge-Luis BORGES" [Notes and Translation by Jorge-Luis BORGES], establishes Borges not only as the compiler, translator, and editor of these works, but also as an authority responsible for shaping a variety of national and international canons.

The importance of format and the general presentation of information cannot be emphasized enough, and the ways in which authors and their works are showcased for readers reveal a great deal about the intended audiences for these volumes. The facts that eight of the ten poets in Borges's "La lírica argentina contemporánea" (Macedonio Fernández, Marcelo del Mazo, Enrique Banchs, Rafael Alberto Arrieta, Alfonsina Storni, Álvaro Melián Lafinur, B. Fernández Moreno, and Héctor Pedro Blomberg) appear throughout various Argentine poetry anthologies from the first part of the twentieth century and five of the ten poets (Enrique Banchs, Rafael Alberto Arrieta, Alfonsina Storni, Álvaro Melián Lafinur, and B. Fernández Moreno) appear in Borges's *Antología poética argentina* [*Anthology of Argentine Poetry*] (1941) highlight the importance of this initial foray into the anthology for his future collaborative endeavors. This overlap, although seemingly small, is quite significant because it shows that Borges still valued several of his initial assessments of Argentine poets and their works, even twenty years after his ultraist tendencies.[9]

Argentine Canons and Local Color

A central thematic trend that emerges in Borges's collaborative work on anthologies and edited collections during this time period is his marked interested in *Argentine* literature. In essence, Borges takes on the task of "poner orden en el caos actual de la producción bibliográfica argentina, destacando y definiendo los valores reales y descartando los ficticios" [organizing the current chaos of Argentine bibliographical production, emphasizing and defining real values and eliminating the fictitious ones] that Palacio adamantly outlines in his article for *El Hogar*.[10] Within this grouping of his works, we see Borges not only creating definitive, authoritative editions of Argentine texts with extensive bibliographies, but also crafting unique versions of anthologies for his diverse audiences. Each of the anthologies that I analyze demonstrates Borges's interest in educating and exposing a wide array of readers—from elites to lower-to-middle-class individuals—to the essential poetic and prose instances of Argentine literature.

The *Antología clásica de la literatura argentina* (1937) is the first collaborative anthology that Borges crafts during the late 1930s. The philologist Pedro Henríquez Ureña worked with him to create this collection and determine the scope of its contents, which is clear from their joint prologue: "En la presente ANTOLOGIA CLASICA DE LA LITERATURA ARGENTINA se aspira a ofrecer a los lectores una noción sintética de lo que fue la obra de los escritores y poetas del pasado definitivamente concluso" [In the present CLASSIC ANTHOLOGY OF ARGENTINE LITERATURE we aspire to offer readers a concise idea of what the definitive works of writers and poets from the past were].[11] What stands out most here is the use of the word *sintética* (concise), which recalls Borges's "biografías sintéticas" for *El Hogar* that we saw in the last chapter. This subtle linguistic nod links Borges's reviews with his production of anthologies and literary collections. We also must recognize Henríquez Ureña and Borges's level of influence on readers for being the sole parties in charge of selecting the texts that will appear in their *Antología clásica*.[12] In other words, they alone make the decisions regarding what constitutes Argentine literary traditions and what does not. Finally, we see their keen awareness of textual variants through both their selection of texts and their appendix dedicated to sources.

Looking to Henríquez Ureña and Borges's initial commentary on their selection process, along with their cited bibliography, reveals their reliance on a unified editorial theory in crafting the *Antología clásica*. For starters, they stress the fact that many of the included authors have written extensive prose works, meaning that, as editors, they will have to pick and choose parts of their texts for the current anthology. While they convey their wish to "representarlos en todos sus aspectos" [represent them in all of their aspects], they also highlight their decision to "[evitar] las páginas demasiado conocidas, aunque sean magníficas" [avoid the overly known pages, even if they are wonderful], with specific reference to prose passages.[13] In direct contrast, the poetic selections for this work do not tend to be excerpted and more often than not are included as *obras íntegras* (whole works).[14] Following this brief explanation about the length of the selections, Henríquez Ureña and Borges discuss the more intricate aspects of their editorial roles and in the process impart a great deal about the provenance of their selected works: "Hemos buscado, para cada obra, la edición más autorizada, a fin de respetar las palabras auténticas del autor, muchas veces estragadas en las reimpresiones corrientes" [We have looked for the most authorized edition of each work, in order to respect the authentic words of the author, which are often corrupted in common reimpressions].[15] First, their biting criticism of certain circulating editions of works of authors included in this anthology shows a marked interest in the concept of authorial intention as well as a general understanding of editorial theories. By commenting on their desire to present readers with the most authentic version of texts, Henríquez Ureña and Borges further distinguish their work from other (lesser) editions and in the process highlight the superiority of their collection. We also note this level of precision in their description of the ways in which editorial intervention appears throughout the texts: "Todo corte en el texto se señala con puntos suspensivos. Cuando para compresión de algún pasaje es necesario intercalar una o más palabras, va indicado entre paréntesis angulares" [Every cut in a text is signaled by an ellipsis. When it is necessary to include one or two extra words in certain passages to make them understandable, these words are placed in square brackets].[16] In addition to this awareness of the level of variants among texts, the inclusion of a bibliography, or the *procedencia de los textos* (origin of texts), speaks to Henríquez Ureña and Borges's critical engagement with the publishing history of their included works. For instance, a number of their citations are not simple bibliographical entries that reference any version of an author's works, but rather give readers a sense of their level of authority for being revised and expanded editions.[17]

Henríquez Ureña and Borges's selection of texts for their anthology speaks to many issues at the heart of editorial theory, which can be divided into two central camps: documentary editing and critical editing. The first type of editing is also referred to as diplomatic or noncritical since it aims to reproduce (historical) documents without changing the text. The second type of editing, also called the eclectic method, is much more disputed since it invokes debates surrounding the ideas of copytext, accidentals versus substantives, and authorial intention.[18] Moreover, editors' roles, societal effects, and more performative issues are discussed at length with regards to critical editing.[19] To illustrate the textual aspects in play behind the scenes in the *Antología clásica,* I look to one selection in the collection: José Hernández's *Martín Fierro.* This poem is arguably one of the most canonical texts in Argentine letters, and Henríquez Ureña and Borges even describe it as "una de las obras más originales de la literatura de América. Alcanzó gran éxito popular y fué celebrada por escritores cultos; en épocas posteriores se la ha considerado al fin obra repesentativa [sic] y eminente" [one of the most original works in the literature of the Americas. It achieved great popular success and it was celebrated by educated writers; in Buenos Aires it was considered the most representative and eminent work].[20] The extreme popularity of *Martín Fierro* led various publishing houses and printers to produce copies of this work throughout the nineteenth and twentieth centuries, and as a result, changes gradually crept into the text, whether accidental or substantive.[21] Thus, in the *procedencia de los textos* we find a very precise entry for Hernández's poem: "*Martín Fierro,* comentado y anotado por Eleuterio F. Tiscornia. Buenos Aires, 1925. Contiene el texto de 1872 y en nota los retoques de 1878" [*Martín Fierro,* commentary and annotations by Eleuterio F. Tiscornia. Buenos Aires, 1925. It contains the 1872 text and the 1878 changes in the notes].[22] A similar footnote accompanies the actual text in the anthology: "Seguimos el texto de la primera edición del poema, en 1872, reproducido en el 'Martín Fierro' comentado y anotado por D. Eleuterio F. Tiscornia, Buenos Aires, 1925" [We followed the text of the first edition of the poem, the 1872 edition, reproduced in the "*Martín Fierro*" *commentary and annotations* by D. Eleuterio F. Tiscornia, Buenos

Aires, 1925].²³ We also find various footnotes throughout the text that highlight changes from edition to edition with, at times, personal commentary on these changes from Henríquez Ureña and Borges.²⁴ These textual details demonstrate the editors' desire to present readers with not just any text, but a well-thought-through version of a text.

Another curious aspect of the *Antología clásica,* which directly relates to questions surrounding the influence that Borges and Henríquez Ureña had on their readers, is its publisher: Editorial Kapelusz y Cía. Much like several other publishing houses that we have seen to this point—especially Manuel Gleizer and Editorial TOR—Editorial Kapelusz y Cía had its origins in a bookstore, started by Adolfo Kapelusz, that later expanded to a publishing house in 1905 with the aim to improve the quality of educational texts. In fact, many of the first authors published by the firm were known for being the best teachers in Argentina at that time. Over the years, this publishing house became associated with improvements in educational standards and the go-to firm for materials related to the classroom environment, including "láminas, mapas, carpetas de ejercicios, atlas, diccionarios y múltiples colecciones ... como las Grandes Obras de la Literatura Universal, que ha pasado definitivamente al imaginario escolar como la GOLU" [prints, maps, exercise books, atlases, dictionaries, and multiple collections ... like the Greatest Works of Universal Literature, which has been commonly referred to among imaginative scholars as GOLU].²⁵ The *Boletín bibliográfico argentino* [*Argentine Bibliographical Bulletin*] gives us a better sense of the kinds of works that Editorial Kapelusz y Cía published.²⁶ Another intriguing aspect of the *Antología clásica de la literatura argentina,* related to its publication with Editorial Kapelusz y Cía is the fact that this book is not listed under the section of "Antologías" in the *Boletín bibliográfico argentino* (1937), but rather appears in the category of "textos para la enseñanza primaria, secundaria y especial" [texts for primary, secondary and special education].²⁷ In contrast, the category of "Antologías" lists titles such as the *Antología de poetas y prosistas americanos* [*Anthology of American Poets and Prose Writers*] and the *Antología de poetas y prosistas españoles* [*Anthology of Spanish Poets and Prose Writers*], both edited by Oscar R. Beltrán.²⁸

As Henríquez Ureña and Borges outline in their prologue, the authors included in the *Antología clásica* are representative of Argentina's historical literary trends, meaning that no writers are included who were born after 1850. Their desire to focus on the past not only speaks to Palacio's claims regarding the lack of readership of Argentine works, but also showcases how the *Antología clásica* aims to fill this void: by creating an authoritative foundation of Argentine literary trends from which readers—with various interests and backgrounds—can benefit.[29] This historical focus and the desire to create a type of reference source for readers also emerges in the biographies of the authors that accompany each of the texts in the anthology. Unlike some other edited collections (see below), the *Antología clásica* presents readers with extremely detailed biographies of its writers. For instance, the biography for the first author in the collection, Ruy Díaz de Guzmán, gives not only his birth and death dates, but also the names and histories of his parents and a thorough analysis of his only written work, which is described as "escrita con claridad y sencillez" [written with clarity and simplicity].[30] Somewhat echoing the level of expertise and knowledge that we might find today in a Cátedra edition of a Spanish-language book, the biographical notes of each author in this anthology depict both the lives of the authors and the central traits of their written works. Thus, Luis de Tejeda is characterized as having a style "típico del siglo XVII: hay en él influencias del culteranismo y del conceptismo" [typical of the seventeenth century: there are influences of *culteranismo* and *conceptismo*].[31] This tendency to describe all facets of each writer's life recurs throughout the collection; at times, these descriptions are further enhanced by the inclusion of a portrait of the author in question.

    In addition to the content of these meticulous biographies, it is important to highlight their placement on the page. Unlike what we find in Borges's early anthologies that he published in *Cervantes* and *Cosmópolis*, the biographical information for each author is the first text that a reader encounters in each entry of the *Antología clásica*. Turning to the book's physical features, its pages are very brittle to the touch, and although the paper has a slight glossiness to it, it is very cheap. Alongside these fragile pages is the lackluster exterior of the volume, which is visually bland in comparison with the other anthologies I examine here. More specifically, the brown hardcover cloth covers are quite dull, yet the added gold color for the typography across the front cover and the spine provides the book with a bit more flair. All of these features—coupled with the textual presentation of the works included—point to the fact that Borges and Henríquez Ureña created this anthology with pedagogical ends in mind.

The next two anthologies that Borges collaborated on during this time, the *Antología de la literatura fantástica* [*Anthology of Fantastic Literature*] (1940) and the *Antología poética argentina* [*Anthology of Argentine Poetry*] (1941), were both produced by Editorial Sudamericana. Both of these anthologies form part of the Colección *Laberinto* (Labyrinth Collection), which, according to one of Editorial Sudamericana's catalogues, is "destinada a registrar lo perdurable y lo viviente de las diversas disciplinas de la literatura mundial" [designed to register what is everlasting and alive in all of the diverse facets of world literature].[32] The works included in the first anthology, dedicated to fantastic (prose) literature, "no se limita, como compilaciones análogas, a los clásicos del género (Poe, Villiers, de I'Isle Adam, Wells): incluye también los textos orientales . . . ; los místicos . . . ; los mejores artífices verbales . . . ; los maestros del terror escénico . . . y los metafísicos" [are not limited, like similar works, to classics of the genre (Poe, Villiers de I'Isle Adam, Wells): it also includes oriental texts . . . ; the mystics . . . ; the best verbal authors . . . ; the masters of dramatic terror . . . and the metaphysicians].[33] In a similar vein, the second anthology, dedicated to poetry, aims to showcase the most important poets of the early twentieth century (1900–1941) and follows an "objective criterion" that does not reflect the specific likes (or dislikes) of the editors: "Los compiladores han seguido un criterio objetivo, han procurado que esta selección no refleje una escuela ni un gusto personal" [The compilers have followed an objective criterion; they have ensured that this selection does not reflect a specific school or personal preference].[34] In addition to the broad range of literary trends that the Colección *Laberinto* purports to feature, the physical composition of each volume is also a defining feature of these anthologies: "Textos sabiamente elegidos, escrupulosas versiones de las obras extranjeras, clara y elegante tipografía, definen esta biblioteca de apasionante interés y de extraordinario valor cultural" [Texts wisely selected, scrupulous versions of foreign works, clear and elegant typography, will define this library of passionate interest and extraordinary cultural value].[35] The fact that the clear and elegant typography of this collection is discussed as a central feature of these works speaks volumes. What is more, the only two works included in the Colección *Laberinto* are the *Antología de la literatura fantástica* and the *Antología poética argentina*. It is essential to compare and contrast these two works and think more broadly about the so-called Colección *Laberinto,* but first I turn to the second, and final, volume in the collection, the *Antología poética argentina*.

One year after the publication of the *Antología de la literatura fantástica* in 1940, Editorial Sudamericana released Borges, Bioy Casares, and Silvina Ocampo's second coedited work: the *Antología poética argentina.* Unlike the first anthology in the collection, it has a clearly defined scope and organizational structure—not to mention the fact that all of the included poets are Argentine, as the title clearly indicates. Thus, the authors are arranged chronologically according to the date of their first publications and span from the mid- to late-nineteenth century to the middle of the twentieth century. Moreover, there has been a conscious effort to give all authors their own unique space in the anthology; that is, even if a short poem from one poet could fit typographically on a page with the work of another writer, the entries do not share any space. This spatial decision gives the book a much cleaner, sophisticated appearance, in contrast with the *Antología de la literatura fantástica,* which at times clumps two or three short fragments from different authors onto the same page.[36] In a similar vein, the paper used for the *Antología poética argentina* is much heavier in weight and of a higher quality than that of the previous book, which is also reflected in the price increase from $3.50 Argentine pesos for the *Antología de la literatura fantástica* to $4 Argentine pesos for the *Antología poética argentina*.

Unlike the prologue for the previous anthology, which bears Bioy Casares's name at its close, the introductory pages of the *Antología poética argentina* are signed by Borges. Even though both of these works are coedited, which makes it quite difficult to distinguish individual contributions from each writer, the fact that each of these prologues is signed by one of the three, rather than all three, is curious and more likely than not noteworthy. What is more, the voice of Borges is much more present in this prologue, which emphasizes his central role in crafting these words, and subsequently signing them. In particular, the punchy opening, filled with a slight amount of tongue-and-cheek humor, sounds like the start of many of his nonfiction essays on literature:

> Ningún libro es tan vulnerable como una antología de piezas contemporáneas, locales. En vano el agredido compilador se empeña en simular una erudición que linda con la omnisciencia, una imparcialidad que es inaccesible a las variadas tentaciones de la costumbre, de la pasión, del hastío, una perspicacia que prefigura el Juicio Final; el público (yo también soy el público) inevitablemente denunciará pecados de omisión y de comisión. ¡Qué injusta la omisión de B, la inclusión de C! ¿Cómo repitieron esa página de Lugones, que ya figura en otras antologías? ¿Cómo rehusaron esa página de Lugones, que todas las antologías publican? Esas interjecciones (y otras) requieren alguna respuesta.
>
> [No book is more vulnerable than an anthology of contemporary local works. The attacked compiler insists, in vain, on simulating an erudition that borders on all-knowing, an impartiality that is inaccessible to the various temptations of customs, passion, boredom, a cleverness that refigures the Final Judgment; the public (I am also included in the public) inevitably will denounce any sins of omission or commission. How unjust is the omission of B and the inclusion of C! Why have they repeated this page of Lugones, which is already present in so many other anthologies? Why did they not include this page of Lugones, which is in every other anthology? These interjections (and others) require some response.][37]

Here we find a marked echo of the prologue for the *Antología clásica* since, in this current work, the editors prefer to exclude oft-cited works simply because they are popular and well known: "Contrariando los métodos románticos de nuestro tiempo, no hemos optado por las más personales, características; hemos incluído [*sic*] las que nos parecen mejores. En muchos casos, las dos categorías coinciden. Hemos exluído [*sic*] los romances octosilábicos: forma rudimentaria y monótona" [In contrast with the romantic methods of our time, we have not opted for the most personal, characteristic works; we have included those that we think are best. In many cases, the two categories coincide. We have excluded eight-syllable ballads: a rudimentary and monotonous form].[38] Finally, Borges draws the reader's attention to one of the most taxing difficulties in crafting any anthology: space, that is, the need to limit the entries included in any anthology. More specifically, he describes the intellectual's interest in critiquing popular culture and, in light of its scope, the wide array of forms that this type of criticism may take:

> Es muy sabido que los literatos veneran lo popular: siempre que les permita un glosario y alguna pompa crítica, siempre que la indiferencia y los años lo hayan enriquecido de oscuridades o, a lo menos, de incertidumbre. Ahora celebran y comentan y a veces leen las payadas de los "gauchescos"; en un porvenir quizá no lejano deplorarán que las antologías argentinas de 1942 no incluyan el menor fragmento de la vasta epopeya colectiva que suman las letras de tango y que los discos de fonógrafo perpetúan... La dificultad de clasificar nuestra lírica demuestra su caudal heterogéneo, su variedad feliz.
>
> [It is well known that men of letters venerate the popular—whenever they are allowed to include a glossary and some pompous critique, whenever indifference and years have enriched their obscurity and sometimes their uncertainty. Now they celebrate and comment on and sometimes read gauchesque folk songs; in the not too distant future they will hate that the Argentine anthologies of 1942 did not include a small fragment from the extensive collective epic that is composed of the lyrics of the tango and that phonograph records perpetuate... The difficulty of classifying our lyrical poetry shows its varied worth, its happy variety.][39]

We can view these remarks as variations on a theme: no anthology or edited collection will ever be exhaustive.

In an effort to understand the evolution of the form of the *Antolo-*

Table 11. Argentine poetry anthologies (1921-1937)

Editor	Title	Date
Jorge Luis Borges	"La lírica argentina contemporánea" [The Contemporary Argentine Lyric]	1921
Julio Noé	*Antología de la poesía argentina moderna (1900-1925)* [*Anthology of Modern Argentine Poetry (1900-1925)*]	1926
Julio Noé	*Antología de poetas argentinos* [*Anthology of Argentine Poets*]	1926
Alberto Hidalgo, Vicente Huidobro, and Jorge Luis Borges	*Índice de la nueva poesía americana* [*Index of New American Poetry*]	1927
Julio Noé	*Antología de la poesía argentina moderna (1896-1930)* [*Anthology of Modern Argentine Poetry (1896-1930)*]	1931
Oscar R. Beltrán	*Antología de poetas y prosistas americanos* [*Anthology of Argentine Poets and Prose Writers*]	1937
José González Carbalho	*Índice de la poesía argentina contemporánea* [*Index of Contemporary Argentine Poetry*]	1937

gía poética argentina—and the place of this work within this evolution—I consulted a number of collections published in Buenos Aires between 1921 and 1937 (Table 11). These seven poetry anthologies published during this time, which focus mainly on Argentine poetry, emphasize Borges's claim in his prologue to the *Antología poética argentina* that "ninguno de los géneros literarios que practican los argentinos ha logrado el valor y la diversidad de la lírica" [none of the literary genres that Argentines practice has achieved as much value and diversity as lyrical poetry].[40] Borges's role as editor, or coeditor, for two of these earlier anthologies also serves to highlight their importance as antecedents to the current anthology. The first overlap between this series of anthologies and the *Antología poética argentina* are the poets themselves. Forty-seven poets (of sixty-nine) who appear in the volume published by Editorial Sudamericana also fill the pages of one of these earlier anthologies. In other words, nearly 70 percent of the poets included in the *Antología poética argentina* appear in earlier edited collections. Even though there is a great deal of overlap in the poets between all of these anthologies, virtually none of the earlier works outlines how the collections were composed, nor does any of them describe an overarching organizational principle with any depth. For instance, the prologue for Julio Noé's *Antología de la poesía argentina moderna (1900–1925)* [*Anthology of Modern Argentine Poetry (1900–1925)*] stresses the lack of interest in offering critiques for the included poems and instead refers to the editor as a collector.[41] In a similar vein, Oscar R. Beltrán's four-volume *Antología de poetas y prosistas americanos* [*Anthology of American Poets and Prose Writers*] continually accentuates his interest in following "los programas oficiales de los estudios literarios" [official programs of literary studies].[42] Moreover, three of these early works do not include any biographical (or bibliographical) information on the poets (*Índice de la poesía argentina contemporánea* [*Index of Contemporary Argentine Poetry*], *Índice de la nueva poesía americana* [*Index of New American Poetry*], and *Antología de poetas argentinos* [*Anthology of Argentine Poets*]) and are rife with typographical errors, both of which indicate a lack of precision and care in their production.[43]

One of the more distinctive aspects of the *Antología poética argentina* is the short biography that accompanies each of the included poets. Although there are slight variations from entry to entry, which suggests that each of the editors was responsible for specific biographies and textual excerpts, there also is a tendency toward two specific formulas for introducing an author's works: "Obras" [Works] (71 percent) and "Ha publicado" [Has published] (22 percent). That is to say, the list of an author's published works in each of these concise biographies would be introduced by one of these two phrases and immediately followed by a colon. For instance, Evaristo Carriego's biography reads "Nació en Paraná, en 1883; murió en Buenos Aies, en 1912. Obras: *Misas Herejes* (1908); *Los que Pasan* (1912); *Poesías Completas* (1913)" [He was born in

Paraná in 1883; he died in Buenos Aires in 1912. Works: *Heretical Masses* (1908); *Those Who Pass* (1912); *Complete Poems* (1913)], while Carlos Vega's entry states "Nació en Cañuelas, provincia de Buenos Aires, en 1898. Ha publicado: *Hombre* (1926); *Agua* (1931); *Danzas y Canciones Argentinas* (1936); *La Música Popular Argentina*, dos tomos (1941)" [He was born in Cañuelas, a province of Buenos Aires, in 1898. He has published: *Man* (1926); *Water* (1931); *Argentine Dances and Songs*, two volumes (1941)].[44] While it might be possible that these differences in biographical format line up with different entries by Borges, Bioy Casares, and Ocampo, it is also possible that these changes were the result of the general editor at Editorial Sudamericana, especially when we consider the fact that the title of this collection did not come from this trio but from the general editors, "que prefirieron la eufonía a la corrección" [who preferred euphony over correctness].[45] That said, the linguistic formulas used for each biography are not the most intriguing aspect of these entries, but rather the forward-looking tendency that surfaces with the use of phrases such as *en prensa* (in print) and *en preparación* (in preparation). More specifically, the biographical entries for twenty-eight of the sixty-nine poets included in the *Antología poética argentina*—more than 40 percent—contain one, and at times both, of these two phrases. It is more common to find and include works that are in the process of being printed, rather than tracking down and listing works that are still being written; thus it seems that the editors were in contact with all of their anthologized writers. For instance, Ricardo Rojas's biography lists two works "en preparación": *La Salamandra* [sic] and *El pensamiento vivo de Sarmiento* [*Sarmiento's Clever Thought*].[46] Both of these works were published with Editorial Losada shortly after their inclusion here. The case of Rojas's works "en preparación" actually being published is rare; the tendency is for works included in this category to never be published.[47]

The physical presentation of the *Antología poética argentina* is much more eye-catching than that of the *Antología clásica*, which speaks to the differences in their intended audiences and overall function. The use of multiple colors on the front cover immediately draws the reader in and reflects the value of the book since it would be costly to print and produce. The beige brick design that fills the background of the cover, coupled with the winged figure and the title of the collection (*Laberinto*),

Cover of *Antología poética argentina* (Editorial Sudamericana, 1941). *(Reproduced from the Albert and Shirley Small Special Collections Library, University of Virginia.)*

call to mind the mythological characters of Icarus and Daedalus. In other words, labyrinths and high (brick) walls echo the home that Daedalus built for the Minotaur on the island of Crete, while the central figure on the cover is reminiscent of Icarus flying with the wings that Daedalus crafted for him. This reading of the design elements on the cover of the *Antología poética argentina* is just one possibility, yet it aptly hints at the erudite contents contained in its pages.

The eighteen named authors on the cover of this poetry anthology can be linked to Borges's previous anthologies as well as the various literary organizations that he belonged to (such as the Argentine Society of Writers). Along with the authors' names and the titles of the two works, the only other (visible) difference between the two volumes in the Colección *Laberinto*, besides the prices and type of paper mentioned above, is the use of color. Even though the editors took great care in producing this volume—both physically and conceptually—Rodríguez Monegal goes so far as to say that "the anthology was the least successful venture attempted by Borges and the Bioys."[48] If this second volume was indeed a financial failure for Editorial Sudamericana, it might explain the publishing firm's rationale for discontinuing any subsequent editions or additional volumes by these three editors, as well as for terminating the Colección *Laberinto* series as a whole. That said, the exquisite design features and the types of works (and authors) included throughout the *Antología poética argentina* highlight the fact that it was intended for a distinct audience. More specifically, we can imagine both this publishing firm and this trio of Argentine editors targeting middle to-upper-class readers with the hopes that such learned individuals would disseminate the importance of these works to the rest of the Argentine populace, much like Palacio predicted in his article in *El Hogar*. Unlike the earlier *Antología clásica*, the fact that there is no explicit reason for the creation of this volume—other than the personal interests of the editors—further emphasizes the likelihood of an intended elite audience.

Emecé Editores, another publishing house that would be fundamental to much of Borges's career, was one of the many firms established in Buenos Aires during the late 1930s and early 1940s by Spanish exiles: Mariano Medina del Río, Álvaro de las Casas, and Carlos Braun Menéndez. The first two men served as the editorial board of this publishing house, and Braun Menéndez financed the operation. In light of the men's Galician roots, the first two books Emecé published were "obras relacionadas con la cultura galaica en gallego o castellano" [works related to Galician culture in Galician or Castilian]; as one might imagine, there was a general lack of interest in such topics in Argentina, and as a result no further works were added to their Biblioteca Gallega (Galician Library).[49] Following this initial failure, the directors of Emecé switched gears to focus on more canonical Spanish works and eventually incorporated more Latin American works as well. Alongside a number of artists and writers—from Argentina and other Spanish-speaking countries—Borges took employment with Emecé, contributing prefaces to works and translations of short stories by foreign authors, to help increase the meager wages he earned at the Municipal Miguel Cané Library (1937–1946). His presence at and interaction with Emecé over the years ultimately led to the firm becoming his central publisher in the Spanish-speaking world from 1951 until his death in 1986. Here I focus on just one of Borges's collaborative projects for Emecé: *El compadrito* [*The Thug*] (1945).

In addition to his better-known collaborative endeavors that promoted the genre of detective fiction in Argentina, Borges worked with Sylvina Bullrich Palenque to publish *El compadrito* as part of Emecé's Colección Buen Aire (Good Air Collection).[50] Subtitled "Imágenes y espíritu de América" [Images and Spirit of America], the Colección Buen Aire includes titles pertaining to the history and culture of Latin America in the broadest sense. Luis Seoane and Arturo Cuadrado also played an important part in initially editing and designing each volume for the collection.[51] Recalling his experience of starting this collection, Seoane said:

> Nosotros comenzamos en Emecé con una colección que se llamaba "Buen Aire," porque sólo el afán nuestro, de Cuadrado, Baudizzone y yo, que comenzamos los tres haciendo "Buen Aire," era el de hacer una pequeña colección de libros que fuesen muy bonitos, pero al mismo tiempo fuesen el reflejo de lo que era Latinoamérica.
>
> [We started in Emecé with a collection that was called "Good Air," because only our own pleasure, that of Cuadrado, Bau-

dizzone, and me, who all started the collection, was that of creating a small collection of books that were pretty, but at the same time reflected what was Latin America.]⁵²

Just as Seoane describes, each volume in the Colección Buen Aire presents readers with an important topic or figure in the culture and history of Latin America and has distinct physical features that set it apart from the books being produced by other Argentine publishing firms during the early 1940s. As Federico Gerhardt notes, there is a lot of diversity in the types of works that fall into the Colección Buen Aire; alongside travel narratives are also biographies, volumes of poetry, plays, and short stories.⁵³ Even though a great range of genres is present in this collection, the unifying characteristic of each work is "su relación con la cultura americana, fundamentalmente argentina y rioplatense, aunque también guardando un lugar a la brasileña" [its relation to American culture, fundamentally that of Argentina and the River Plate, though also saving a place for that of Brazil].⁵⁴

The publishing history of each volume in the Colección Buen Aire echoes the chaotic nature of the possible genres and themes covered by any given book's contents. Even though the design features of the books are somewhat uniform, the printers, editors, and illustrators fluctuate from volume to volume, making it difficult to attribute the layout and overall look of these works to one specific individual.⁵⁵ Each work is a colored hardcover book with a small square space on the front cover for the title and an illustration pertaining to the content of the work in question, but there are variations among books in type size, drawing quality, and the decision whether to include the volume number and price on the cover. Borges and Bullrich Palenque's *El compadrito* focuses on the *compadrito*, as the title suggests, who is broadly defined by Borges in the prologue as "el plebeyo de las ciudades y del indefinido arrabal" [the commoner of the cities and of the vague slum].⁵⁶ Thus, we can envision this figure as the urban counterpart to the Argentine gaucho, yet unlike this latter archetype, who has taken the form of Martín Fierro and Juan Moreira, among others, the *compadre* has yet to take form as a "símbolo inevitable" [inevitable symbol].⁵⁷ As a result, the purpose of this an-

Cover of *El compadrito* (Emecé, Colección Buen Aire, 1945). *(Reproduced from the Albert and Shirley Small Special Collections Library, University of Virginia.)*

thology is to spark readers' interest in this lesser-known figure "para que alguien escriba aquel verosímil poema que hará con el compadre lo que el *Martín Fierro* hizo con el gaucho" [so that someone can write that realistic poem that will do with the *compadre* what *Martín Fierro* did with the figure of the gaucho].[58] In other words, we see Borges coyly creating another opening for future readers to explore Argentine literary traditions.

The volume is organized into three parts that neatly fit into the categories introduced in the work's subtitle: "su destino, sus barrios, su música" [his destiny, his neighborhoods, his music]. The first section deals with the "ética de hombre que está solo y que nada espera de nadie" [ethics of the man who is alone and does not expect anything from anyone]; the second tackles "la cronología de su arrabal" [the chronology of his slum]; and the third provides examples of his music in the form of *milongas* and tangos.[59] Much like the other collaborative collections that we have seen in this chapter, Borges makes a point to tell his readers that he does not intend this anthology to be exhaustive and as a result has omitted some of the more well-known works, such as "[el] teatro nacional y las letras de tango" [the national theater and tango lyrics] and "los encantos itálicos del lunfardo" [the Italian charms of *lunfardo*].[60] These editorial decisions recall those he made for his *Antología clásica de la literatura argentina*, in which he also chose to exclude excerpts of popular prose.

Since each of the three sections of this anthology is organized around a theme, as opposed to a genre, we find short fragments of prose *and* poetry in each part. Borges and Bullrich Palenque achieve a further sense of unity in the work as a whole by carefully placing fragments of *milongas* or other popular verses in italics at the close of a number of excerpted texts in the collection. For instance, immediately following a series of poems by Evaristo Carriego is the following stanza:

> *Las rosas son rosas,*
> *Las hojas son verdes.*
> *El amor de mi china*
> *Nunca se pierde.*
>
> [Roses are roses,
> The leaves are green.

> The love of my china
> will never fade.]

After a poem by Borges (signed with his pseudonym Manuel Pinedo), we find a different stanza of popular verse:

> *Barraca' al Sur,*
> *Barraca' al Norte,*
> *A mí me gusta*
> *Bailar con corte.*
>
> [Ravine in the South,
> Ravine in the North,
> I like
> to dance with the court.]

Borges's own short story ends with the following lines:

> *Soy de los barrios del Norte,*
> *Soy del barrio del Retiro.*
> *Yo soy aquél que no miro*
> *Con quien tengo que pelear,*
> *Y en trance de milonguear,*
> *Naide* [sic] *se me puso a tiro.*
>
> [I am from the Northern neighborhoods,
> I am from the Retiro neighborhood.
> I am that one who doesn't look
> for anyone to fight with,
> And in the trance of a *milonga*,
> No one is within reach.]

Many more such examples can be found in the anthology, all pointing to a general interest in popular culture and the many forms that it takes throughout history.

The table of contents of *El compadrito* gives readers an immediate sense of déjà vu for the presence of many of Borges's preferred (Argentine) writers, including Evaristo Carriego, Ezequiel Martínez Estrada, Leopoldo Lugones, Ignacio B. Anzoátegui, Marcelo del Mazo, and Ricardo Güiraldes. Borges also includes himself among these writers. Unlike any of his other collaborative anthologies or edited collections, there are no biographies (or bibliographies) for the included individuals. Apart from their names printed below the titles of their works, no other clues are given regarding their careers or styles that might help readers discern why they have been included in these pages dedicated to the figure of the *compadrito*. This lack of detail is the case for all of the titles in the Colección Buen Aire, which might speak to a possible audience of more middle-to-lower-class readers with less of an interest in the writers. This format also points to the fact that the anthologized authors are merely a means to an end here, included in an effort to evoke the figure of the *compadre*. In contrast, most of the previous Argentine anthologies that we have seen provide readers with more details about an author's oeuvre and thus encourage further reading. That said, the Colección Buen Aire consisted of nearly one hundred unique titles, which points to a different type of further reading and literary consumption.

While the *Antología clásica de la literatura argentina,* the *Antología poética argentina,* and *El compadrito* might appear very different—in terms of both their content and their physical appearance—they all emphasize a similar desire to rebrand and promote the popular. This idea also emerges in the shared editorial decision to exclude canonical or well-known excerpts from each volume. Since Borges is the common denominator among the three anthologies, we can infer that this shared feature reflects his personal preferences. Returning to Palacio's claims regarding the role of the intellectual, we see Borges acting on his ideas by disseminating not only literary criticism, but also reliable, authoritative editions for readers. By not turning simply to canonical works, Borges unveils his desired scope for and vision of Argentine literature for his readers.

Detective Fiction and Enigmatic Texts

Much ink has been spilled over the intimate relationship between the genre of detective fiction—and its resurgence in Latin America during the middle part of the twentieth century—and the writings of Jorge Luis Borges. Regardless of their specific point of departure or theoretical framing, most critics situate Borges's burgeoning fascination with detection fiction in the early 1930s and mark its culmination in the early 1950s:

> los contactos explícitos de Borges con lo policial se restringen a una etapa de su vida—tentativamente el período que va desde mediados de los años '30 hasta comienzos de los '50—y a la postre a unos pocos textos ficcionales y ensayísticos específicos, tras los cuales el interés del autor se diluye y Borges no siempre parece convencido de la pertinencia de sus incursiones adventicias en el género.
>
> [Borges's explicit contact with the detective fiction genre is restricted to one specific moment in his life—tentatively between the 1930s and the start of the 1950s—and in the end refers to a few fictional texts and essays, through which the author's interest in the topic thins out and Borges doesn't always seem convinced that his writings pertain to the genre.][61]

Moreover, virtually all studies of Borges's writings from these few decades typically home in on the writer's interest in the "novela enigma," or the English-style mystery type of detective fiction.

Some critics mention the importance of Borges's literary reviews in *El Hogar* and his subsequent collaborative endeavors with Bioy Casares, but no one to date has considered in depth the physical forms that these writings take and the implications that they have for the development of global literary tastes and reading habits in Argentina.[62] My aim in exploring the physical forms that Borges's works take throughout this crucial part of his career is not to present readers with a new interpretation of his use of the genre of detective fiction, but rather to think critically about the ways in which his writings—and their physical manifestations as books, anthologies, and edited volumes—subtly promote certain types of literature. There is an extensive body of criticism pertaining to Borges and his central role in resuscitating detective fiction in Latin America from its status as a popular genre for the masses to one full of complexity fit for elite audiences, and other critics have already pinpointed the trajectory of his promotional efforts.[63] However, virtually all of these studies identify only this promotional strategy and do not attempt to dissect what such efforts mean for publishing markets and the book world at large.

Thus I now turn to the first volume in the two-volume Colección *Laberinto*. From its outset the *Antología de la literatura fantástica* claims to be nothing other than a selection of texts that are among the favorites of its three editors and what they deem the *best* representations of fantastic literature: "Analizado con un criterio histórico o geográfico, puede parecer irregular. Tampoco hemos buscado, ni rechazado, los nombres célebres. Este volumen es, simplemente, la reunión de los textos de la literatura fantástica que nos parecen mejores" [Looked at with an historic or geographic criterion, this volume can seem quite irregular. We also haven't looked for, or rejected, famous names. This volume is, simply, the gathering of texts of fantastic literature that we think are the best].[64] As a result, it is virtually impossible to place any sort of organizational principle on the texts included in this anthology. In his introduction to the collection, however, Bioy Casares offers a list of general observations about fantastic literature, dividing his thoughts into three unique categories: "el ambiente o la atmósfera" [the ambiance or the atmosphere], "la sorpresa" [the surprise], and "el Cuarto Amarillo y el Peligro Amarillo" [the Yellow Room and the Yellow Peril].[65] The first describes the creation of an ominous setting that may consist of "una persiana que se golpea, la lluvia, [o] una frase que vuelve" [a banging window blind, the rain, or a repeating phrase].[66] The second category can refer to something physical, something verbal, or something in the plot. The final group, which is most reminiscent of detective fiction, pertains to locked-room mysteries (based on Gaston Leroux's "The Mystery of the Yellow Room" [1907]) that occur "en un lugar limitado, con un número limitado de personajes" [in a limited place, with a limited number of characters] and fear of outside forces.[67]

In a way, Bioy Casares's tripartite grouping of fantastic traits gives readers a false sense of unity since he immediately goes on to enumerate any possible type of fantastic plot that might fill the pages of the *Antología de la literatura fantástica*:

Argumentos en que aparecen fantasmas ... Viajes por el tiempo ... Los Tres Deseos ... Argumentos con acción que sigue en el infierno ... Con personaje soñado ... Con Metamorfosis ... Acciones paralelas que obran por analogía ... Tema de la inmortalidad ... Fantasías metafísicas ... Cuentos y novelas de Kafka ... Vampiros y Castillos.

[Plots with ghosts ... time travel ... the Three Desires ... Plots with action that continues into hell ... With dreamed-up characters ... With metamorphosis ... Parallel actions that work as analogies ... Themes of immortality ... Metaphysical fantasies ... Short stories and novels by Kafka ... Vampires and Castles.][68]

Rodríguez Monegal echoes this sentiment by characterizing this work as "one of the most curious and unorthodox compilations on the subject."[69] In a similar vein, many of the debates surrounding this initial collaborative anthology deal with the fact that there appears to be no unifying element in the selections, and the chaotic feel of the volume is amplified by the lack of any overarching organizational principle. Thus, the collection opens with a lengthy thirty-one-page story by Max Beerbohm (1872–1956) ("Enoch Soames" [1916]), which is followed by a short fragment from George Loring Frost's (1887–?) *Memorabilia* (1923) and continues with a one-page excerpt from Alexandra David-Néel's (1868–1969) "La persecución del maestro" [The Persecution of the Master] (1931).[70] From this small sampling of the first three entries in the anthology we get a sense of its chaotic nature.[71] This lack of chronological, alphabetical, or even geographical organization further heightens the reader's feeling of disorientation. Moreover, short fragments of works are often squeezed onto the same page as other writings, which is reminiscent more of a miscellany than an anthology, especially when we consider the fact that many of these fragmented excerpts have no titles and are separated only by short dashes.

In contrast with anthologies, miscellanies are compiled with the popular tastes and interests of the moment in mind. These collections help readers stay informed of the newest trends and developments in the literary world, which speaks directly to Borges and Bioy Casares's rebranding of the genre of detective fiction since various authors in the *Antología de la literatura fantástica* later appear in *Los mejores cuentos policiales* as well as in their Séptimo Círculo series.[72] In other words, the miscellany is "designed to suit contemporary tastes" while "anthologies, in contrast, are generally selections of canonical texts which have a more established history and a greater claim to cultural importance. The miscellany, then, typically celebrates—and indeed constructs—taste, novelty and contemporaneity in assembling a synchronous body of material. It should be distinguished from the anthology which honours—and perpetuates—the value of historicity and the perdurance of established canons of artistic discrimination in gathering texts recognized for their aesthetic legitimacy."[73] The already established element of personal interest behind the formation of the *Antología de la literatura fantástica*, which stands in direct opposition to the types of materials included in Borges and Henríquez Ureña's *Antología clásica de la literatura argentina*, also serves to emphasize its likeness to a miscellany, as opposed to a traditional anthology that aims to emphasize writers and works that form part of an already recognized literary canon.

In line with the characterization of this work as a type of miscellany is the repetition of authors and works. More specifically, seven of the forty-seven authors in the *Antología de la literatura fantástica* appear twice in the book: Alexandra David-Néel, G. K. Chesterton, Tsao Hsue-Kin, Léon Bloy, Ramón Gómez de la Serna, James Joyce, and Franz Kafka. Of particular note is that the second excerpted works from four of these seven authors come from the *same* work as their first included text in the anthology. Thus, David-Néel's "La persecución del maestro" is from *Parmi les Mystiques et les Magiciens du Tibet* [*With Mystics and Magicians in Tibet*]; her second textual appearance nearly one hundred pages later is from this same work. In a similar vein, both of Chesterton's passages are drawn from *The Man Who Knew Too Much,* Hsue-Kin's "El espejo de viento y luna" [The Mirror of Wind and Moon] and "Sueño infinito de Pao Yu" [Infinite Dream of Pao Yu] are both parts of *El sueño del aposento rojo* [*The Dream of the Red Chamber*], and Joyce's two texts are both from *Ulysses.*[74] This odd repetition raises the question of why Borges, Bioy Casares, and Ocampo would choose to separate these excerpts rather than adjoin them with a possible section break to indicate that, while being from the same work, they are not continuous portions of the same text.[75] Moreover, the fact that many of the second texts from these repeated authors share space with other texts (by different, less-canonical authors) reflects a commonplace trend within any given miscellany where "works by major authors often [share] space with works by unknown" authors.[76]

The physical features of this anthology emulate those of the *Antología poética argentina*. We find the same brick-style background on the cover with serif and sans serif typefaces throughout and the same winged figure occupying the center of the cover. The names of eighteen authors also appear on the cover of this anthology, just as we saw with the *Antología poética argentina*. The particular authors included here are quite revealing and echo the promotional efforts of Borges in the late 1930s with his literary review column in *El Hogar*. The authors, in order of their appearance, are Jean Cocteau, Jorge Luis Borges, G. K. Chesterton, Macedonio Fernández, Franz Kafka, R. Gómez de la Serna, Leopoldo Lugones, James Joyce, Guy de Maupassant, François Rabelais, Thomas Carlyle, Giovanni Papini, Edgar Allan Poe, Herbert G. Wells, Rudyard Kipling, León Bloy, Engene [sic] O'Neill, and Max Beerbohm. In light of the fact that only forty-seven authors are included in the entire anthology, this list might appear at first glance to be a random sampling of authors, especially when we consider the fact that Kafka is the only author from the Austro-Hungarian Empire, Joyce is the only Irish author, Carlyle is the only Scottish author, and Papini is the only Italian author. That said, it is important to keep in mind that nearly half of the writers hail from either France or England, two of the primary countries spotlighted for their writers by Borges in *El Hogar*. The inclusion of three Argentine writers on the cover of this anthology suggests a desire to rethink and resituate the place of these authors in relation to their foreign counterparts. Of particular note is the fact that Borges himself not only surfaces within the pages of the *Antología de la literatura fantástica*, but also appears on the cover of this work—as both editor *and* contributor. Thus, we can identify a certain strategic positioning of Argentine literature alongside established global literary traditions. This idea is emphasized further when we consider the countries from which all of the included writers originate.[77]

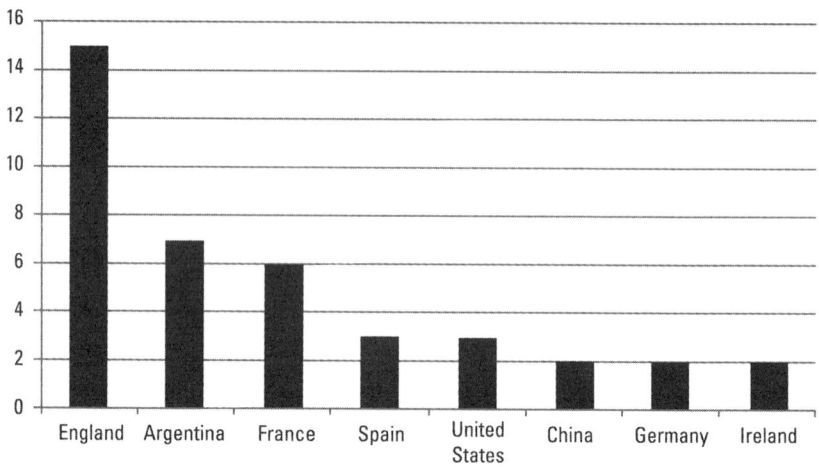

Countries of origin of the writers included in the *Antología de la literatura fantástica*. (Line art courtesy of Christopher Westby.)

Another unique aspect of the physical layout of this collaborative anthology is the biographical information that accompanies the excerpts. Even though these biographies are extremely truncated in comparison with what we have seen in earlier collections such as the *Antología clásica,* we find three key pieces of data in each one: nationality, the defining characteristics of each author's oeuvre, and a list of any fundamental works that they have published to date.[78] In a sense we see a desire to show the global impact of fantastic literature, the characteristics that define this genre, and possible suggestions for further reading that hint at establishing a canon. For instance Santiago Dabove is noteworthy for "el cuento fantástico" [the fantastic story]; Edgar Allan Poe "renovó el género fantástico" [renovated the fantastic genre]; "[a Villiers de L'Isle-Adam] la literatura fantástica le debe novelas, cuentos y obras de teatro" [fantastic literature has Villiers de L'Isle-Adam to thank for many novels, short stories, and theatrical works]; and "la literatura fantástica le debe muchos ejercicos coherentes [a H. G. Wells]" [fantastic literature owes many coherent practices to H. G. Wells]. Another intriguing feature of each biographical entry is the emergence of several linguistic patterns that differ slightly from what we saw with the *Antología poética argentina.*

For instance, information as basic as places and years of births and deaths is not always present for every writer, and the ways in which the authors' published works are introduced varies quite a bit from biography to biography.[79] That said, the majority of entries (twenty-four of forty-seven) are introduced with either "[es] autor de" [is author of] (38 percent) or "Ha publicado" [Has published] (13 percent). One of the first reviews of this work emphasizes the important contribution that the editors made in selecting titles and, more importantly, "el verdadero amor, la no fortuita inclinación con que el libro ha sido previsto, organizado y construido. No es una antología comercial: es el fruto de una inclinación muy segura en su facultad selectiva" [the true love, the not so fortuitous inclination with which the book was planned, organized, and constructed. It is not a commercial anthology: it is the fruit of a very sure inclination in terms of its selections].[80] Bioy Casares recalls how Editorial Sudamericana's director, Antonio López Llausás, asserted that this collection was a commercial failure, yet Bioy Casares negates this claim in his *Memorias*.[81]

After their collaboration on the *Antología de la literatura fantástica,* Borges and Bioy Casares approached Emecé with two unique projects intimately related to their personal interests in detective fiction: an edited collection of detective stories and the Séptimo Círculo series. The first, aptly named *Los mejores cuentos policiales,* is in line with their previous collaborative efforts. The texts included within the pages of this collection of detective fiction are by a myriad of national and international authors. Even though this book does not have a prologue, introduction, or any opening words to help readers understand the inclusion, or exclusion, of certain writers, the choice of some texts over others seems to resonate with Borges and Bioy Casares's tastes and preferences, thus aligning with what we found in their *Antología de la literatura fantástica.* That said, the book's organizational structure and its overarching purpose—as outlined in the book's interior flap—sets *Los mejores cuentos policiales* apart from Borges's earlier collaborative work with Editorial Sudamericana: "Este volumen quiere presentar un panorama completo de tan significativo sector de las letras contemporáneas" [This volume hopes to present readers with a complete panorama of such a significant part of contemporary letters]; and "el orden cronológico observado en la distribución de los cuentos permite al estudioso apreciar la evolución del género" [the observed chronological order allows scholars to appreciate the evolution of the genre].[82]

The large success of *Los mejores cuentos policiales* materializes most clearly when we consider its publishing history and the fact that this book went through multiple editions and even introduced a second series, which incorporated new authors and new texts.[83] In addition to these textual changes, the physical appearances of both series of *Los mejores cuentos policiales* are radically different. With the first edition of the first series, the flashy red, orange, and pink covers, filled with comic-strip-like drawings of scenes from select stories, distract from the title. The second series also presents readers with an eye-catching illustration—a geometric town in yellows, greens, and grays—but the title of the collection is printed in large serif capitals across the top third of the cover. Moreover, the first series prominently showcases the names of its two editors, which is a strategic move on the part of Emecé to boost sales since, according to the inside flap of the first, second, and third editions of the first series, these two Argentine writers are "reconocidos eruditos en la materia" [well-known experts in the subject], and "han puesto a contribución su largo y placentero conocimiento de los textos originales, sin olvidar, por cierto, los diversos aportes argentinos" [they have contributed their great and delightful understanding of these original texts, without forgetting, of course, the diverse Argentine contributions]. Bioy Casares also recalls that "[los editores de Emecé] sugirieron, eso sí, que la colección llevara nuestros nombres pero no el de la editorial" [the editors of Emecé suggested, this is true, that the collection bear our names but not that of the publishing firm].[84] In contrast, the names of Borges and Bioy Casares have disappeared from the covers of the second series.

In addition to the differences between the two covers of the first and second series, there is quite a bit of typographical difference among the various editions (1943, 1944, 1947) in the first series. Even though the same colorful design fills the background of all three dust jackets, there are curious typographical changes from edition to edition.[85] While the first and second editions share an identical serif typeface with high vertical stress for the title of the work, the presentation of the words "Selección de Adolfo Bioy Casares y Jorge Luis Borges" [Selections by Adolfo

Bioy Casares and Jorge Luis Borges] is noticeably changed from the first to the second edition. The typeface used for the words "Emecé Editores, S.A." is unique for both editions as well. The most apparent variations in the cover text emerge in the third edition of this first series. Here we see a completely new setting of type for the title along with the introduction of sans serif typefaces. In addition, the short dashes used to separate parts of the text on the cover are no longer black (as in the first two editions), but a vibrant red. Along with their aesthetic variants, the two series of *Los mejores cuentos policiales* also contain distinct contents, yet the various editions in each series do not change their contents. While there are several overlapping authors in the two series, there are no repeated stories (Table 12).

Since several of the authors found within the pages of these two series also surface in Borges's previous collaborative work—mainly in the *Antología de la literatura fantástica*—it is worthwhile to examine the ways in which these overlapping writers are presented to readers. The first notable feature of the biographies—and bibliographies—of these shared authors is the fact that many are transferred verbatim from Editorial Sudamericana's earlier anthology to Emecé's detective fiction collections.[86] More thought provoking, especially within the context of marketing and promotion, is the subtle inclusion of references to *other* collections produced by Emecé within the short biographies in both series of *Los mejores cuentos policiales*. For instance, within the first series, the editors make sure to indicate whether an author's work is included as part of Emecé's later Séptimo Círculo series; thus, we find parenthetical notes alongside Phillpotts's *Mr. Digweed and Mr. Lumb* (Séptimo Círculo no. 12) and Milward Kennedy's *The Murderer of Sleep* (Séptimo Círculo no. 6) and *Corpse in Cold Storage* (Séptimo Círculo no. 8). While these promotional asides might not be terribly surprising, especially in light of the fact that they are promoting similar types of literature that potential audiences might want to read, there are also references to works in other Emecé collections, which seems to suggest a different sort of agenda. More specifically, Hawthorne's short biography contains a footnote to *The House of Seven Gables* that brings readers' attention to the fact that this work was translated into Spanish and is a part of the Colección "La Quimera." In a similar vein, Poe's biography in this same series footnotes his work *Eureka* to alert

Table 12. Authors included in the first and second series of *Los mejores cuentos policiales*

First Series (1943–1947)		Second Series (1951–1956)	
Nathaniel Hawthorne	"La muerte repetida" [Mr. Higginbotham's Catastrophe]	Wilkie Collins	"Cazador cazado" [The Biter Bit]
Edgar Allan Poe	"La carta robada" [The Purloined Letter]	G. K. Chesterton[a]	"Los tres jinetes del Apocalipsis" [The Three Horsemen of the Apocalypse]
Robert Louis Stevenson	"La puerta y el pino" [Mr. Mackellar's Journey with the Master]	Hylton Cleaver	"Copia del original" [Copy of the Original]
Arthur Conan Doyle	"La Liga de los Cabezas Rojas" [The Red-Headed League]	Agatha Christie	"La señal en el cielo" [The Sign in the Sky]
Jack London	"Las muertes concéntricas" [A Thousand Deaths]	William Irish	"Si muriera antes de despertar" [If I Should Die Before I Wake]
Guillaume Apollinaire	"El marinero de Amsterdam" [The Sailor from Amsterdam]	Ellery Queen	"Aventura en la mansión de las tinieblas" [The Adventure of the House of Darkness]
G. K. Chesterton	"El honor de Israel Gow" [The Honor of Israel Gow]	Eden Phillpotts	"Tres hombres muertos" [Three Dead Men]
Eden Phillpotts	"El ananá de hierro" [The Iron Pineapple]	Graham Greene	"Una salita cerca de la calle Edgware" [A Little Place off the Edgware Road]

Ronald Knox	"El millonario que murió de hambre" [Solved by Inspection]	John Dickson Carr	"Personas o cosas desconocidas" [Persons or Things Unknown]
Anthony Berkeley	"El envenenador de Sir William" [The Avenging Chance]	Michael Innes	"La tragedia del pañuelo" [Tragedy of a Handkerchief]
Milward Kennedy	"El fin de un juez" [The End of a Judge]	**Jorge Luis Borges** and Adolfo Bioy Casares	"Las doce figuras del mundo" [The Twelve Figures of the World]
Ellery Queen	"Filatelia" [The Adventure of the One-Penny Black]	Harry Kemelman	"Nueve millas bajo la lluvia" [The Nine Mile Walk]
Carlos Pérez Ruiz	"A treinta pasos" [Thirty Steps]	William Faulkner	"Humo" [Smoke]
Georges Simenon	"La noche de los siete minutos" [The Night of the Seven Minutes]	**Manuel Peyrou**	"Julieta y el mago" [Julieta and the Magician]
Manuel Peyrou	"La espada dormida" [The Sleeping Sword]		
Jorge Luis Borges	"La muerte y la brújula" [Death and the Compass]		

a. Authors who appear in both series are shown in boldface.

readers to its translation and publication in Emecé's Colección "Grandes Ensayistas" ("Greatest Essayists" Collection), and Stevenson's introduction contains a reference to the presence of his *The Master of Ballantrae* within the Biblioteca Emecé (Emecé Library).[87] Even though a certain amount of biographical—and bibliographical—information might be borrowed from previous collaborative anthologies, there appears to be a much stronger desire on the part of Emecé to promote other collections that it was publishing during the 1940s.

Two other aspects to consider in relation to the publishing history of these works are their prices and their sales. While there are no extant records from the Emecé publishing house, we can analyze the physical features of each volume produced, particularly the back covers, which typically include a price, and the inside flaps, which discuss the demand for the books, and gain insight into the financial success that *Los mejores cuentos policiales* brought to the firm.[88] Specifically, the interior flap of the third edition of the first series highlights the high demand for this collection: "Al dar a la estampa la tercera edición de esta obra lo hacemos con la repetida satisfacción de ofrecer al público una nueva reimpresión urgentemente reclamada" [In producing the third edition of this work we do so with the repeated satisfaction of offering the public a new reprint that is urgently demanded]. The issuing of multiple editions—virtually without any changes in the contents—also points to a heightened level of interest from readers. Akin to the first series of *Los mejores cuentos policiales*, the second series also goes through multiple editions and, moreover, becomes part of several other collections created by Emecé, including the Selección Emecé de Obras Contemporáneas (Emecé Selection of Contemporary Works) and its Piragua series. The physical features of this second series do not change as much from edition to edition, but there is a noticeable shift in the design of each cover once they enter other Emecé collections. In addition, the quality of the paper in the third edition of the second series (1956) is much more brittle, indicating a move toward cheap paperback quality. These later editions are out of the scope of the current book because of their dates of publication, but it is worth noting these significant changes in price and quality for the information that they provide about the move toward popular, mass-produced paperbacks.

Following the successes of their collaborative detective fiction anthologies, Borges and Bioy Casares pitched an entire series of translated works to Emecé, the previously mentioned Séptimo Círculo series. The name of this series evokes Dante's *Inferno* and establishes a link between the works of detective fiction included in the series and this canonical Italian writer, which elevates the genre while also serving as a type of promotional strategy to draw a large audience. Borges and Bioy Casares directed this new series for Emecé from its start in 1945 until 1956 when Carlos V. Frías took over. During this period, the two writers were in charge of selecting the titles that the collection would publish (around 139) and determining the "estética distintiva y su ideología de género peculiar" [distinctive aesthetics and the ideology of the peculiar genre] that came to be a part of the series, which amounted to a complete aesthetic package, from content to covers.[89] Emecé did not accept Borges and Bioy Casares's idea immediately; Borges recalls that the editors "tardaron un año en aceptar la idea de la colección *Séptimo Círculo,* cuyo éxito ha sido enorme, porque decían que la literatura policíaca no era cosa digna de una editorial seria" [delayed a year in accepting the idea of the *Séptimo Círculo* series, whose success was enormous, because they said that detective literature was not dignified enough for a serious publishing house].[90] The initial doubts of Emecé with regard to an entire collection dedicated to detective fiction highlights the general attitude toward this type of literature in Latin America during the 1940s and, more importantly, Borges and Bioy Casares's great strides in rebranding and reestablishing its importance. Along with the collection's meaningful impact on reading habits, its previously mentioned financial successes were enormous:

> El éxito de *El Séptimo Círculo* se evidencia no sólo en la cantidad de títulos publicados (366), sino también en sus tiradas (14.000 ejemplares de cada título, según Frías, y a un promedio de uno por mes) y la venta de sus derechos a España, primero en *EDHASA* y luego en *Alianza Editorial.*
>
> [The success of the *Séptimo Círculo* series is evident not only in the number of titles published (366), but also in its print

runs (14,000 copies of each title, according to Frías, and an average of one per month) and the sale of its rights to Spain, first in *EDHASA* and later in *Aliazna Editorial*.]⁹¹

These statistics certainly speak for themselves and do not need further analysis with regard to highlighting the boom of the Séptimo Círculo series.⁹²

Much like many of the other anthologies and collections that Borges edited, the design elements of the Séptimo Círculo series, with virtually all of the cover illustrations and designs by José Bonomi (1903–1992), are particularly striking. In fact, it is quite easy to connect Borges and Bioy Casares's desired aesthetics for the series with Bonomi's elegant covers, which he designed and created until the 1970s. Bonomi discussed his role in creating the designs for the series:

> al realizar las tapas de esta colección nunca he intentado una explicación de la obra; no me he dejado atrapar por la mera anécdota, sino que he buscado una composición de los personajes, acaso una simbolización o he partido de algún elemento significativo para estilizarlo. Aunque no se vea, existe en todas esas tapas una trama previa; hay divisiones armónicas generalmente por mitades, con contrastes simultáneos y colores plenos. En resumen, todas ellas esconden una cruz que establece las simetrías; son bidimensionales y apelan a la planimetría.
>
> [in making the covers for this collection I never intended to explain the plots of the works; I did not let myself get caught up in mere anecdote; rather I looked for a composition of characters, perhaps a sort of symbolism or I started with a particularly significant element and stylized it. Even though you cannot see it, each cover has an initial connection (to the story); there are harmonious divisions, generally in halves, with simultaneous contrasts and full colors. In short, each one of them hid a cross that established symmetries; they are two-dimensional and appeal to planimetry.]⁹³

He also alludes to the fact that he read all of the works before designing their covers, which adds another level of complexity to the physical features of these works.

In general terms, each volume in the series has a similar geometric border around the edges of its cover and a small centered drawing that depicts an element of the text's plot. The cover of each book, which uses only three colors, was, in the words of Bioy Casares, a driving force behind the success of the series.[94] When we compare these books with similar collections of detective fiction produced by publishing houses such as Editorial TOR (Serie amarilla [Yellow Series]), we can identify almost immediately the impact of Emecé's artistically refined work.[95] While Editorial TOR's Serie amarilla uses more color on its covers, the images are flashy and melodramatic. The fact that the images do not quite line up with the other strips of color and text on the cover also illustrates a lack of care and precision in crafting these works. In contrast, each cover in the Séptimo Círculo series is much more visually appealing, with its geometric patterns, color limitations, and uniform typefaces throughout. This comparison also reinforces the claim that Editorial TOR was most concerned about profit and monetary gain, not design elements or prestige (see Chapter 2).

A clear genealogical line can be traced from Borges and Bioy Casares's *Los mejores cuentos policiales* to the works included in Emecé's Séptimo Círculo series when we consider the type of detective fiction that each of these collections favored. The only clear limitation placed on the titles to appear within the Séptimo Círculo series was that they must not be examples of detective fiction in the hard-boiled vein. This deep-seated interest in logic over violence is emphasized further by the logo created for the series—a chess piece—which one critic describes as a "fetishization of the intellectual game of problem-solving characteristic of the series."[96] Jorge Lafforgue and Jorge B. Rivera single out three thematic categories in this series' lengthy timespan: classic works employing an enigma or puzzle problem, works by authors who at first glance appear not to fit the bill of detective fiction writers, and a large inclusion of River Plate authors. These two critics also identify three unique historical moments of the Séptimo Círculo series: the direction of Borges

A cover from the Serie amarilla of Editorial TOR (1944).
*(Reproduced from the Albert and Shirley Small Special
Collections Library, University of Virginia.)*

A cover from the Séptimo Círculo series of Emecé
Editores (1945). *(Collection of the author.)*

and Bioy Casares, the direction of Carlos Frías, and the disappearance of Bonomi.[97]

Echoing what we find in not only *Los mejores cuentos policiales,* but also Borges's earlier review column for *El Hogar,* there is a marked preference for foreign authors and works in this detective fiction series.[98] The incorporation—and translation—of foreign works in the collection reflects Borges and Bioy Casares's desire to rebrand the genre of detective fiction in Latin America by introducing readers to writers they have never encountered before: "En El Séptimo Círculo publicamos excelentes novelas acaso condenadas al olvido por pertenecer al género policial. Un género de mucha venta, pero no siempre bien mirado por la gente seria" [In the Séptimo Círculo series we published excellent novels that were almost condemned to oblivion for pertaining to the detective genre—a genre with high sales, but not always well perceived by serious people].[99] By focusing solely on enigma-problem plots—as opposed to violent and immoral scenarios—Borges and Bioy Casares put their intellectual spin on this genre, which appealed to many of their elite audience members and intellectual friends. In turn, many of these same individuals, especially those associated with Victoria Ocampo's literary magazine *Sur,* helped to promote and popularize Emecé's Séptimo Círculo series.[100]

World Literature

Alongside a marked effort to endorse Argentine literature and detective fiction, Borges's anthologies and edited collections also celebrate international literary trends. Borges champions *all* literatures—from Russian authors and American poets to English writers and Austrian artists. More broadly speaking, each of the works I examine here reiterates his claim that Latin America's literary tradition "is the whole of Western culture," and not just those works and traditions that are native to Latin America.[101]

One of the most influential literary magazines for Borges's career was Victoria Ocampo's *Sur.* In fact, this literary magazine played a crucial role in putting Borges on the map.[102] This literary magazine, along with Editorial Sur, Ocampo's publishing firm of the same name, forms the heart of the next chapter, so here I keep my comments about Ocampo and the aims of *Sur* to a minimum. Before the creation of *Sur* in 1931, Buenos Aires and a large number of other major Latin American cities (such as Mexico City, São Paulo, Lima, and Havana) were known for their literary magazines, particularly those associated with avant-garde movements. Thus, Ocampo saw that the moment was right to establish a *new* type of literary magazine "for everyone with an interest in the Americas and [that] would serve as a bridge between America and Europe."[103] The general aim of *Sur*'s editors and its contributors was to be "arbiters of taste and commentators on certain aspects of society, while at the same time denying any ideological contamination."[104] To this end, the journal was most known for its "standards of literary decorum" that showed a notable interest in the ideas of intellectuals and those that involved women's rights.[105] In other words, what set the journal *Sur,* and the later works of its publishing house, apart from other kinds of literary production in Argentina was its highbrow elitism and affiliation with foreign authors, particularly those of France.[106]

Even though Borges contributed to many issues of *Sur,* and also formed part of the original editorial board, my analysis here centers on only two issues for their relevance to the theme of anthologies and edited collections: the March–April (double) issue from 1944 (nos. 113–114) and the January–March (triple) issue from 1947 (nos. 147–149). These issues of *Sur* are dedicated entirely to North American and French literature, respectively, and my analysis focuses on a series of poems that Borges (and Bioy Casares) translated in each issue.[107] The first group of poems (in nos. 113–114) is often described as the "Antología de la poesía norteamericana" [Anthology of North American Poetry].[108] The authors and poems translated by Borges and Bioy Casares that appear in its pages are as follows: John Peale Bishop, "Tema de las mutaciones del mar" [A Subject of Sea Change]; e. e. cummings, "Poema" [Poem] and "En algún lugar que nunca recorrí" [Somewhere I Have Never Traveled]; Hart Crane, "Poemio al puente de Brooklyn" [Poem to Brooklyn Bridge]; Wallace Stevens, "Domingo a la mañana" [Sunday Morning]; Karl J. Shapiro, "Carta de Nueva Guinea" [New Guinea Letter]; Robert Penn Warren, "Terror"; and Dustan Thompson, "Señor de Fantasmas" [Thane of Ghosts] and

"Memorare."[109] Even though there is no introductory note by Borges or Bioy Casares, Ocampo has written a general introduction that touches on the double issue's aim:

> Esta antología no tiene otro propósito que el de ofrecer al lector de lengua española la ocasión de echar una ojeada sobre la literatura y, a través de la literatura, sobre la vida contemporánea en los Estados Unidos, tal como la sienten y la piensan unos cuantos escritores aún poco leídos entre nosotros. Creemos que puede ser más instructiva y sutilmente reveladora que la mayoría de los artículos de la prensa.
>
> [This anthology does not have any other goal than to offer the Spanish-language reader the chance to take a look at literature and, through literature, (learn) about contemporary life in the United States, just as it's felt and thought by a few writers who are not commonly read by us. We believe that it will be more instructive and subtly revealing than the majority of articles that you can find in the newspaper.][110]

In addition to this short note that opens the issue, there is also a much longer piece by Morton Dauwen Zabel (translated by Frida Weber) dedicated to "La literatura en los Estados Unidos: Panorama de 1943" [Literature in the United States: Panorama of 1943] that appears immediately before Borges and Bioy Casares's translated poems and to a certain extent serves as the perfect introduction to their work that follows. Aside from providing readers with a truncated historical account of the late nineteenth and early twentieth centuries in the United States, this piece aims to emphasize the fact that "nuestro período puede recordarse como más fuerte en talento crítico que en talento creador" [our period can be remembered as stronger in critical talent than in creative talent].[111] Immediately following the creative explosion of a series of (avant-garde) movements at the turn of the twentieth century, the current moment in the United States is described by Zabel as one of a lull and tiredness with regard to newness and creativity. In the aftermath of World War I and the onset of World War II, Zabel sees a general interest in books either for information and critical reflection regarding these historic crises or as forms of pure diversion.[112] He therefore spends a great deal of time dissecting poets and their poetry from the 1930s and 1940s since he sees this specific artistic production as consistently dealing with "la crisis moral y el clima psíquico de su tiempo" [the moral crisis and psychological climate of his time].[113] Of particular note is the fact that Zabel singles out several of the poets that Borges and Bioy Casares translate in the next section of this double issue of *Sur*: "No es accidental que nuestra crítica social y moral más penetrante aparezca en la obra de escritores que antes fueron considerados primordialmente como técnicos o artífices del estilo—Marianne Moore, Katherine Anne Porter, Louise Bogan, Wallace Stevens, T. S. Eliot, E. E. Cummings, Allen Tate y Robert Warren" [It is no accident that our most penetrating social and moral critique appears in the work of writers before they were considered fundamentally as technicians and writers of the style—Marianne Moore, Katherine Anne Porter, Louise Bogan, Wallace Stevens, T. S. Eliot, e. e. cummings, Allen Tate, and Robert Warren].[114] He ends this lengthy panorama by describing the importance of such poets for their focus on moral responsibility that is indicative of this specific historical moment.

John Peale Bishop's "Tema de las mutaciones del mar" opens the section of poetry and echoes the concerns outlined by Zabel:

> Traicionado entre dos mundos, entre dos guerras,
> Nada más triste he soportado que el cambio,
> Nada más oscuro que la noche,
> Ningún espectáculo más terrible
> Que el de guerreros para quienes el honor es extraño.
>
> [Between two worlds betrayed, between two wars,
> I've had no sadder thing to bear than change,
> No darker thing than night,
> No more dread sight
> Than warriors to whom honor is strange.][115]

The central image of the sea that permeates his multipart poem also reflects the crisis of self that characterizes much postwar literature. This same watery imagery fills many of the other poems included in this section. Take, for instance, Karl Shapiro's "Carta de Nueva Guinea," which ends with the following lines:

> Requiero tranquilidad para agraciar mi página,
> Tolerancia absoluta como canon,
> Para mejorar los modales de nuestro tiempo,
> Y algún día, cuando sean hermosos los cielos,
> Y hayan perdido su escarlata los mares,
> Espero cenar contigo, con tu mujer y la mía.
>
> [Quiet I want to grace my page,
> Whole toleration for a gauge,
> To improve the manners of our age,
> And some day when the skies are fine,
> And seas have lost their incarnadine,
> Dinner with you, your wife and mine.][116]

Even though it does not reference the sea, Robert Penn Warren's aptly titled "Terror" also homes in on the atrocities of war that have left much of the world in a state of (moral) crisis. Much like the above-mentioned poems, the other verses (of other poets) translated and included in this section of *Sur* reflect similar concerns related to the critical stance of writers in this historical moment.[117]

Even though this special issue of *Sur* has yet to be analyzed strictly as an anthology, many of its features, apart from Ocampo's framing of the volume as an "antología," resonate with those of the other works discussed in this chapter. One of the key aspects is the biographies of the writers included in these works. While the "Antología de la poesía norteamericana" does not present readers with any such information on the same pages as the poems, there is a sort of appendix in the last few pages that fills that role. The section "escritores norteamericanos que han colaborado en este número" [North American writers who collaborated in this issue] contains short, concise biographies of the authors and poets that fill the pages of this issue of *Sur*. The linguistic forms used to present these writers is reminiscent of similar forms in the *Antología de la literatura fantástica,* the *Antología poética argentina, Los mejores cuentos policiales,* and the Séptimo Círculo series. In other words, each of the entries (organized alphabetically) contains information about the places and years of authors' births and deaths, any characteristic attributes of their writings, and, when available, a list of their published works. Even more curious is the inclusion of bibliographical references to the specific editions used for the cited passages, similar to the more scholarly *Antología clásica de la literatura argentina.*[118]

The "Antología de la literatura francesa" [Anthology of French Literature] differs from the previous special issue of *Sur* not only for its inclusion of various literary genres, but also for its lack of biographical information for the included authors. Ocampo does provide a brief introduction to the triple issue. Here she highlights the editorial decision to exclude well-known writers such as Paul Valéry and Antoine de Saint-Exupéry and focus instead on "deliberadamente [eligiendo] escritores todavía poco conocidos entre nosotros o no traducidos aún" [deliberately selecting writers who are still not known among us and who have yet to be translated], which is reminiscent of a number of Borges's previous anthologies, most notably the *Antología clásica de la literatura argentina.*[119] She also foregrounds the fact that this special issue will not provide readers with a complete panorama of *all* contemporary trends in French letters since "esta literatura es muy abundante" [this literature is so abundant].[120] However, we do find a sundry mix of essays, fiction, poetry, and even art reviews throughout its pages, several of which are penned by authors whose work has appeared or will later appear printed with Ocampo's Editorial Sur, including André Gide, Roger Caillois, André Malraux, and Albert Camus.

While the "Antología de la poesía norteamericana" included poems that were translated by both Borges and Bioy Casares, the "Antología de la literatura francesa" includes only a handful of poems—by Edith Boissonnas (1904–1989) and Francis Ponge (1899–1988)—translated by Borges alone. Unlike the works that he translated for the previous *Sur* anthology, Boissonnas's and Ponge's poems do not speak to a specific historic moment. Instead, they appear to be a representative sample of each poet's oeuvre. For instance, the four translated poems by Boissonnas— "Trama" [Plot], "Momentos" [Moments], "La animal" [The Animal], and

"El tiempo del insecto" [The Time of the Insect]—capture her introspective voice, which often takes the form of a male poetic voice, and showcase her attention to detail in everyday life. In fact, several of these poems recall the detailed, objective style of the contemporary American poet Elizabeth Bishop. While Ponge's two poems—"Del agua" [From Water] and "Orillas de mar" [Shores of the Sea]—echo a tendency toward describing everyday objects, his works are influenced by Surrealist poetry *in prose,* which gives them a different tone and overall feel. For instance, in "Del agua" he opens with a discussion of the properties of water and shifts to the image of a closet to explicate how all objects in the world do not need to obey any other law than that of gravity. Broadly speaking, the selection of Boissonnas's and Ponge's poems that Borges translates for the "Antología de la literatura francesa" reflects many of his own interests in philosophical topics, most notably that of time. In addition, both poets had never been translated into Spanish before this special issue, which highlights Borges's pivotal role in introducing new writers, genres, and trends to Latin American readers.

These two issues of *Sur* directly reflect Palacio's comments analyzed at the start of this chapter which note that this historical moment is one to establish a type of literary criticism that has been lacking. While his arguments pertain specifically to Argentine letters and the dwindling amount of readership with respect to these works, the idea of stepping back and evaluating the literary and artistic production of one's country certainly applies to works from other countries (such as the United States and France). We also must take into account the fact that the type of reader who would have encountered these anthologies in *Sur* would have been a middle-class or upper-class elite, which also resonates with Palacio's delineated strategy for future dissemination of key literary works. Thus, Borges's translations in the "Antología de la poesía norteamericana" and the "Antología de la literatura francesa" provide readers with access to previously unknown works from disparate regions and in the process aid in the democratization of global literatures.

In between his contributions to these two special issues of *Sur,* Borges accepted a new position as editor (and director) of the literary journal *Los Anales de Buenos Aires* [*The Annals of Buenos Aires*], which was "launched by an institution modeled on the Parisian Société des Annales."[121] Borges held this editorial appointment from March 1946 until the early part of 1948, and during his tenure he remodeled the entire look and feel of the periodical so that it was a true literary journal, as opposed to "a rather arbitrary" collection of "more or less distinguished writers, and assorted texts."[122] Seeming to capture a diversity of tastes and literary preferences, *Los Anales de Buenos Aires* featured articles that reflected the dry, academic tastes of the cultural institution that founded it as well as the more imaginative, creative tastes of Borges. While its most successful publications were Borges's own works, which would later fill the pages of *El Aleph* (1949) and *Otras inquisiciones* (1952), this journal also prominently featured foreign authors and their works. The first issue makes this cosmopolitan approach explicit in its opening statement:

> Cada día siéntese más la necesidad de periódicos que den a conocer la producción intelectual del país y del extranjero, ... sin prejuicios de escuela ni banderías de secta, en cuya lectura el pueblo encuentre una orientación de su gusto literario y una satisfacción a su afán de cultura. Críticas, artículos, poesías y cuentos de escritores nacionales alternarán con la producción literaria de los grandes escritores europeos ... Se propone también, esta dirección abrir sus páginas al talento de los escritores noveles, que hallan con frecuencia tantas dificultades para publicar sus primeros trabajos; pues desea, ante todo, estimular la creación espiritual de los nuevos talentos.

> [Every day we more and more feel the need for periodicals that allow us to learn of local and foreign intellectual production, ... without prejudice for schools or sects, through which the populace can learn about their own literary tastes and satisfy their desire for culture. Criticism, articles, poetry, and stories by national writers will mingle with those of the greatest European writers ... We also hope that these aims will attract new writers, who often find it very hard to publish their first works, with the desire, above all, of stimulating the spiritual creation of new talent.][123]

Even though Ocampo's *Sur* had similar objectives, there was such a need for these types of periodicals that the journals coexisted without much competition. Furthermore, many of the foreign contributions in *Los Anales de Buenos Aires* showcased the association's invited speakers during any given month, as opposed to reflecting a nuanced network of contacts like that of Ocampo.

In comparison with other literary periodicals that Borges wrote for or edited during this time, *Los Anales de Buenos Aires* is of a higher quality in terms of its physical features. The first eleven issues are printed on thick, glossy paper with wide margins on each page. A similar sans serif typeface runs throughout the publication, and each piece—with the inclusion of any illustration—is printed in black and white, which gives the periodical a clean, streamlined feel. The vibrantly colored cover of each issue presents readers with a unique illustration at the center and a list of contributors directly below. The fact that no one printer produced *Los Anales de Buenos Aires* throughout its nearly two-year run suggests that the physical presentation of the journal stems from the vision of its director.

While the periodical consistently features articles, poems, and prose excerpts from a variety of writers, there is an aesthetic refinement and inclusion of new types of material from the third issue on, which is precisely the moment when Borges becomes its director/editor. For instance, we immediately note a shift in the title's typographical presentation on the cover of the third issue. The shift to a modern serif typeface—in contrast to the more ornately flourished typeface of the first two issues—provides the journal with a level of sophistication and in a sense distances it from the more avant-garde periodicals of the 1920s, which reflects many of Borges's personal aesthetics. Alongside these visual changes, Borges also added a "Museo" [Museum] section to *Los Anales de Buenos Aires* that recalls his earlier *Destiempo* journal and several review sections—books, film and music, and art and theater—that echo similar sections in Ocampo's *Sur*; yet instead of promoting books published with Editorial Sur, many of the reviews in Borges's periodical highlight authors whom he included in his foreign authors' page for *El Hogar* or works that he edited for Emecé. Thus, we find the names of nineteen authors in both the "Museo" and review sections who also appear in Borges's *El Hogar* page (13 percent). Of these nineteen authors, eight surface in the *Antología de la literatura fantástica* (42 percent).[124] In short, Borges makes *Los Anales de Buenos Aires* relevant and approachable for a broader readership while also continuing to promote foreign authors and works that appear in his edited collections and anthologies (Table 13).

Although there is a marked presence of Argentine authors and artists throughout each issue of *Los Anales de Buenos Aires,* there also is a notable international presence. A survey of the contributors in every issue of the journal reveals that 72 percent are Latin American and 28 percent are from countries outside of Latin America. There are many French authors throughout the issues (eighteen), a surprisingly large group of Russian authors (twelve) and Austrian artists (fourteen), and a number of English authors (eleven). These more curious representations of foreign authors clearly speak to Borges's personal interests and literary preferences at the time. In addition, the largest group of foreign writers hail from Spain (thirty-six), which reflects the large population of Spanish exiles living in Buenos Aires and in various Latin American countries following the Spanish Civil War.

Rodríguez Monegal's perspective on *Los Anales de Buenos Aires* is particularly important since he, too, was a regular contributor to the journal and also met with the head of the association on several occasions. In his biography of Borges he points out, "Although [Borges] had been nominally the editor from the third issue onward, the head of the association had retained some power over the journal. She was a rather formidable woman whose literary tastes did not entirely coincide with Borges'. It seemed obvious to me then that she wanted to have Borges' name in the journal but that she was not terribly impressed with the way he edited it. By the end of 1947 she also seemed disappointed with the reception the magazine had. Borges and she parted company without regrets."[125] While the disparate visions of Borges and the head of the association are quite telling, what is more intriguing is the use of Borges's name for marketing and propaganda purposes. Perhaps partly because of the (financial) successes of Borges and Bioy Casares's detective fiction works with Emecé, we see individuals in the publishing industry taking note of Borges's ability to package, market, and sell literary works, especially foreign literary works. Even though the ultimate demise of *Los*

Table 13. Works reviewed in *Los Anales de Buenos Aires* that also appear in Borges's edited collections

Author	Work	Edited Collection
Nigel Balchin	*Las tinieblas descienden* [*Darkness Falls from the Air*]	Puerta de Marfil (Emecé, 1947)
James M. Cain	*El simulacro del amor* [*Love's Lovely Counterfeit*]	Puerta de Marfil (Emecé, 1947)
Wilkie Collins	*La piedra lunar* [*The Moonstone*]	Séptimo Círculo (Emecé, 1946)
Joseph Conrad	*Bajo las miradas del occidente* [*Under Western Eyes*]	Puerta de Marfil (Emecé, 1946)
Joseph Conrad	*Nostromo*	Puerta de Marfil (Emecé, 1946)
Louis Golding	*El perseguidor* [*The Pursuer*]	Puerta de Marfil (Emecé, 1947)
Arthur Machen	*Los tres impostores* [*Three Impostors*]	Puerta de Marfil (Emecé, 1947)
Margaret Millar	*Las rejas del hierro* [*The Iron Gates*]	Puerta de Marfil (Emecé, 1946)
H. G. Wells	*El gran Bulpington* [*The Bulpington of Bulp*]	Puerta de Marfil (Emecé, 1947)
Franz Werfel	*El ejército de las sombras* [*Army of Shadows*]	Puerta de Marfil (Emecé, 1946)
Franz Werfel	*Juárez y Maximiliano*	Teatro del Mundo (Emecé, 1946)

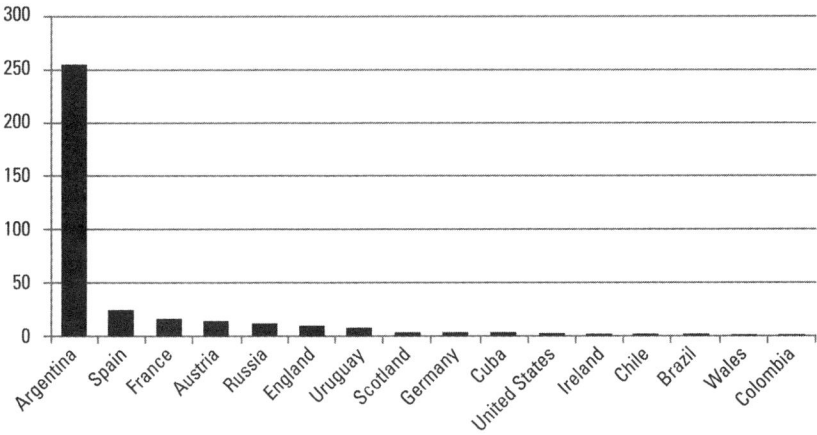

Countries of origin of authors in *Los Anales de Buenos Aires*.
(Line art courtesy of Christopher Westby.)

Anales de Buenos Aires seems to have been related to a lack of funds, its closure also points to the changing cultural climate in Argentina with the rapid rise of populism under Juan Perón.

Alongside his editorial duties for *Los Anales de Buenos Aires*, Borges also codirected another series for Emecé, the Puerta de Marfil [Ivory Door], with Bioy Casares, which presented readers with a similar focus on global literary trends (Table 14). Emecé most likely allowed these two writers to direct a second literary collection because of the monetary success of both their Séptimo Círculo series and *Los mejores cuentos policiales*. That said, Borges and Bioy Casares's Puerta de Marfil collection was quite different from their previous works. From Emecé's *Catálogo general perpetuo* [*Perpetual General Catalogue*] we learn that the name of the series is an erudite allusion to the *Odyssey* and the *Aeneid*, in which "la fantasía de los sueños atraviesa una puerta de marfil" [the fantasies of dreams pass through an ivory door].[126] Echoing many of the same global aspirations that we have already seen with regard to Borges's editorial endeavors, this series focused on established trends in world literature and published works by, among others, Joseph Conrad, Vera Caspary, Henry James, H. G. Wells, and James M. Cain. More specifically,

Table 14. Titles published in Emecé's Puerta de Marfil series (1946–1949)

Author	Title	Volume	Date	Translator(s)
Joseph Kessel	*El ejército de las sombras* [*Army of Shadows*]	1	1946	Roberto Mujica Láinez
Joseph Conrad	*Gaspar Ruiz*	2	1946	Ramón D. Perés, Gonzalo Guasp, and José Torroba
Joseph Conrad	*Cuentos de inquietud* [*Tales of Unrest*]	3	1946	Marco Aurelio Galindo and Cipriano de Rivas Cherif
Joseph Conrad	*Bajo las miradas de Occidente* [*Under Western Eyes*]	4	1946	Juan Mateos de Diego
Joseph Conrad	*Freya, la de las siete islas* [*Freya of the Seven Isles*]	5	1946	R. Vázquez Zamora
James M. Cain	*El suplicio de una madre* [*Mildred Pierce*]	6	1946	A. Caprile
Joseph Conrad	*La locura de Almáyer* [*Almayer's Folly*]	7	1946	Rafael Marquina
Joseph Conrad	*Nostromo*	8	1946	Juan Mateos de Diego
George Sessions Perry	*El amor a la tierra* [*Hold Autumn in Your Hand*]	9	1946	Jorge Ciancaglini
Joseph Conrad	*El negro del "Narcissus"* [*The Nigger of the "Narcissus"*]	10	1946	Ricardo Baeza
Joseph Conrad	*Victoria*	11	1946	Ramón D. Perés
Mikhail Artsybashev	*Sanin*	12	1946	G. Portnof
Joseph Conrad	*La línea de sombra* [*The Shadow Line*]	13	1946	Ricardo Baeza
Vera Caspary	*Bedelia*	14	1946	Vicente Diego Abad
Louis Golding	*El perseguidor* [*The Pursuer*]	15	1946	Estela Canto

Francis Jammes	*El señor cura de Ozeron* [*Reverend Father of Ozeron*]	16	1947	Andrés Guilmain
Margaret Millar	*Las rejas de hierro* [*The Iron Gates*]	17	1947	Teresa Reyles
George Douglas Brown	*La casa de los postigos verdes* [*The House with the Green Shutters*]	18	1947	Osvaldo Moyano
Joseph Conrad	*Lord Jim*	19	1947	Ramón D. Perés
James M. Cain	*El simulacro del amor* [*Love's Lovely Counterfeit*]	20	1947	Marta Acosta Van Praet
H. G. Wells	*El gran Bulpington* [*The Bulpington of Blup*]	21	1947	María Antonia Oyuela
Nigel Balchin	*Las tinieblas descienden* [*Darkness Falls from the Air*]	22	1947	Marta Velázquez
Arthur Machen	*Los tres impostores* [*Three Impostors*]	23	1947	Benjamín Hopenhaym
Joseph Conrad	*Un vagabundo de las islas* [*An Outcast of the Islands*]	24	1947	Antonio Guardiola
Henry James	*Los papeles de Aspern* [*The Aspern Papers*]	25	1947	María Antonia Oyuela
L. A. George Strong	*Los hermanos* [*The Brothers*]	26	1947	Susana W. De Ferkin
Nigel Balchin	*Mi propio verdugo* [*Mine Own Executioner*]	27	1948	Marta Velázquez
Joseph Conrad	*El agente secreto* [*The Secret Agent*]	28	1948	Marco Aurelio Galindo
L. A. George Strong	*Slocombe muere* [*Slocombe Dies*]	29	1948	Beatriz Florencia Nelson
Joseph Conrad	*El hermano de la costa* [*The Rover*]	30	1949	J. G. De Luaces
James M. Cain	*Carrera en Do Mayor* [*Career in C Major*]	31	1949	Aída Aisenson

the Puerta de Marfil aimed to "recoger lo más vivo, lo más intenso, lo más dramático de las muchas corrientes novelísticas de nuestro tiempo" [gather together the most vivid, the most intense, the most dramatic of the novelistic school of thought of our time] and did not limit its featured works to just the classics but also showcased "los valores novísimos de las letras europeas y americanas" [the most recent values in European and American letters].[127] In total, Borges and Bioy Casares edited thirty-one titles for the series, all of which were translations of foreign works. Even though each title is expertly edited, illustrated, and packaged, the Puerta de Marfil series was overshadowed by the ongoing Séptimo Círculo collection—and other prominent collections in Emecé's ever-expanding catalogue—and as a result does not receive much critical attention. That said, it is a fundamental series for understanding Borges's development of cosmopolitan reading in Latin America.

The Puerta de Marfil series showcased the works of authors who hailed from France (13.25 percent), England (27 percent), the United States (27 percent), Russia (6.5 percent), Canada (6.5 percent), Scotland (6.5 percent), and Wales (6.5 percent). The most overwhelming presence in the collection is that of Joseph Conrad, whose works account for more than 40 percent of all of the titles (thirteen of the thirty-one). Conrad was a well-known favorite of Borges for his ability to craft characters and weave tales of adventures, but his prevalence throughout the Puerta de Marfil series also reflects the complexities of the international literary marketplace. If we look to earlier Spanish-language translations of Conrad's works, we discover that every one of his titles that are published with Emecé's Puerta de Marfil series previously appeared with the Barcelona firm Editorial Montaner y Simón during the 1920s and early 1930s. Not only that, but they also were the exact same translations since both editions of each title bear the name of the same translator. Perhaps this textual recycling was an effort on behalf of Emecé to cut costs and pay less for securing authors' permissions, or perhaps it reflects Borges and Bioy Casares's desire to highlight the existing work of Spanish translators, some of whom, like Ricardo Baeza, were already linked to these two Argentines' print production.[128] It is also worth noting that several authors in the Puerta de Marfil series—Joseph Kessel, Louis Golding,

Francis Jammes, and Arthur Machen—first appeared in various sections of Borges's review column for *El Hogar*. Furthermore, readers will recall that a number of the works published in this Emecé series were reviewed in the book section of *Los Anales de Buenos Aires,* which further emphasizes Borges's efforts to influence publishing trends and reading habits.

In addition to their international literary focus, the works in the Puerta de Marfil series were also novel for their concurrent availability in both a paperback and a hardcover edition. This is the only collection that Emecé produced in two distinct formats. Aside from this anomaly, the physical presentation of each volume—in both paperback and hardcover formats—resembles the aesthetics of several other collections in Emecé's catalogue, namely the Séptimo Círculo series and the Colección Buen Aire. The modern covers with each title in a serif typeface and the name of the collection and publishing house in a sans serif typeface resemble Bonomi's designs for the Séptimo Círculo series, while the central cover illustrations, framed by a solid-color background, call to mind many volumes in the Colección Buen Aire. The clean lines and framing mechanisms in *Los Anales de Buenos Aires* also resonate with the style of each work in the Puerta de Marfil series, which further links Borges's editorial vision during this time. Many of these shared aesthetic styles more generally speak to the overlaps of artists and illustrators in both Emecé's collections and Borges's print production. For instance, Bonomi, known for his Séptimo Círculo cover designs, illustrated seven of the thirty-one titles in the Puerta de Marfil series and also contributed works to *Los Anales de Buenos Aires*. Guillermo Buitrago, Raúl Veroni, J. A. Ballester Peña, and Orlando Pierri all illustrated at least one title for both the Puerta de Marfil series and the Colección Buen Aire.[129] Edgar Koetz designed the cover art for five titles in the Puerta de Marfil series and also received an award for his illustrations in Franz Werfel's *Juárez y Maximiliano* (Emecé, 1946), which included a prologue by none other than Borges. Broadly speaking, the common ground among all of the works examined thus far is not a desire on the part of Borges and his close friends to share new types of literary production, but rather an interest in pausing to reexamine existing works (and their physical presentation) and in the process affect reading habits.

A cover from the Puerta de Marfil series of Emecé Editores
(1947). *(Reproduced from the Clifton Waller Barrett
Library of American Literature, Albert and Shirley Small
Special Collections Library, University of Virginia.)*

Foundations for Future Endeavors

All of the anthologies examined here—from Argentine local color to detective fiction and world literature—demonstrate Borges's desire to supplement his current Argentine literary traditions with underrepresented, and oftentimes unknown, works in an effort to influence global readership and broader literary consumption. These editorial endeavors also serve to distinguish Borges as a leading literary expert. As a way of concluding and accentuating Borges's impact on Latin American literature more broadly, I consider one final edited collection that he produced during this period: *Antiguas literaturas germánicas* [*Ancient Germanic Literatures*] (1951). Unlike the other works analyzed in this chapter, this collection was published *outside* of Argentina and as a result touches on the broader scope of Latin American publishing during the first part of the twentieth century. Aside from Buenos Aires, Havana and Mexico City were two other epicenters of publishing during this time. This anthology was produced in the latter of these three cities, with the well-known Fondo de Cultura Económica, reflecting not only the publishing climate of the period, but also Borges's ties to foreign presses and publishing houses.

Much like other Spanish-speaking publishing houses, Fondo de Cultura Económica organized its works into a large number of individualized collections. Thus, Borges's *Antiguas literaturas germánicas* is a part of the Breviarios series that this publishing house started in 1948 with the aim to "[poner] al alcance del hombre o la mujer no especializados los grandes temas del conocimiento moderno" [provide men and women who are not specialized with key topics of modern knowledge].[130] Although it might seem strange for Borges to work with a publishing firm in Mexico City when he was so well connected and established in the publishing world of Buenos Aires, the objective of the Breviarios collection might account for this anomaly.[131] The works in this series hoped to provide readers with solid introductory texts to a variety of subjects, so the director of this publishing firm called upon "especialistas de crédito universal" [universal specialists] to collaborate and edit the volumes in this collection, which certainly accounts for the presence of Borges and Delia Ingenieros as editors of *Antiguas literaturas germánicas*.[132] While

Ingenieros's name appears printed alongside Borges's, it is always with the phrase "con la colaboración de" [with the collaboration of], which seems to emphasize the central role that Borges held in crafting this volume and, perhaps, Ingenieros's editorial checking after the fact. This idea is supported further by the presence of only Borges's name on the front cover of the work and on the inside flap of the dust jacket. We might also view the presence of only Borges's name on the cover as a marketing strategy to sell more books, similar to what we saw with *Los Anales de Buenos Aires* and the intentional choice of Borges as director.

Similar to many of the organizational strategies of Penguin's collections that I touched on in the last chapter, the Breviarios books are grouped thematically by color. Within the established scheme, Borges's work appropriately falls into the category of literature and literary studies (orange).[133] The text printed on the interior flaps of the dust jacket for *Antiguas literaturas germánicas* echoes the generalist aim of the Breviarios collection and its creation for uninformed, general readers:

> Jorge Luis Borges ha escrito estas *Antiguas literaturas germánicas*—con la valiosa colaboración de Delia Ingenieros—y ha empleado un método en que no sólo presenta el desarrollo de los diversos hechos reflejados en los textos a que hace referencias, sino que vierte abundantes ejemplos que ayudan al lector a comprender la significación de lo ahí tratado.
>
> [With the hope of filling this gap, Jorge Luis Borges has written these *Antiguas literaturas germánicas*—with the valuable collaboration of Delia Ingenieros—and has employed a methodology that not only presents readers with the development of certain moments that are reflected in the texts, but also with various examples that will help the reader to understand the significance of the material itself.][134]

The joint desire of these two Argentine writers to expose their audiences to new types of literature is emphasized further through the presence of a detailed bibliography at the end of the work and, as the two editors note in their introduction, a large number of quotations and transcriptions, as opposed to criticism and opinions, so as not to overwhelm their readers.[135] Ultimately, Borges and Ingenieros hope to show Spanish-speaking audiences the important role that these ancient literatures, especially the form of the saga, have on the form of the novel and more contemporary writings.

The format of the volume and the presentation of the material also reflect an inclination on the part of the editors to make *Antiguas literaturas germánicas* as "user-friendly" as possible. The work proceeds in chronological order and is divided into three clear sections: Old English Literature, Old Norse Literature, and German Literature. Furthermore, each of these segments opens with a brief analysis of the central characteristics of the literature from these places and times. For instance, works of Germanic literature from England "insisten en el carácter militar y violento" [tend toward a militant and violent character], while Scandinavian works rely heavily on the poetic form of the kenning.[136] Unlike the previous anthologies and edited collections examined here, *Antiguas literaturas germánicas* does not consist of large fragments of these ancient texts, but rather presents readers with detailed historical accounts of these works along with summaries and a few passing textual examples. Thus, within the discussion of key works such as *Beowulf* or *La Edda Mayor* [*Elder Edda*], there are no large (translated) passages of these texts for readers to study—only the prose descriptions provided by the editors.

Another curious aspect of the textual framing of this volume is the connection that is ultimately made between the works described and analyzed in its pages and "las raíces de las literaturas modernas europeas" [their roots in modern European literatures].[137] As I detailed in the previous chapter, modern European literature—particularly that of Woolf, Joyce, and other High Modernists—is one of the types of literature that Borges promotes at length, along with the genre of detective fiction, through his reviews in *El Hogar*. In fact, several of his most notable translations from the late 1930s and early 1940s are of the works of modern European writers.[138] As a result, this seeming outlier in Borges's production of collaborative anthologies and edited collections from the 1930s and 1940s is more in tune with his promotional aspirations than one might initially think. In addition, the fact that many of the texts in *Antiguas literaturas germánicas* had not been previously translated—or available—in Spanish until its publication accentuates this idea of accessibility, especially when we consider that the first printing of this anthology in 1951 consisted of a massive eight thousand copies.[139] In essence, we might think of this work—and the larger Breviarios series—as a sort of precursor to the Very Short Introductions series that Oxford University Press launched in 1995 or the expanded successor to the essays that fill the pages of Borges's beloved *Encyclopedia Britannica*. It is an easily approachable, and digestible, work that leaves the reader feeling like an expert on a previously unknown topic.

Although disparate in scope, material, and organizational framing, all of the collaborative anthologies and edited collections analyzed in this chapter have one common characteristic: the promotion of underrepresented, forgotten, or unknown literature. Throughout the late 1930s and early 1940s we see Borges consciously promoting various kinds of literature through his (collaborative) edited volumes and in the process altering Argentine literary canons and changing his readers' view of foreign authors and their works. Rebranding the genre of detective fiction to ensure its reconsideration and (eventual) inclusion in the (Argentine) canon, compiling fragments of fantastic literature that will serve as the foundation for his own works of creative fiction, and thinking critically about popular and canonical literatures of the world are all key moments in the production of these works that speak to Borges's interests in shaping cosmopolitan reading throughout Latin America.

F • I • V • E

Borges as Publicist and Promoter

I n the "Palabras finales" [Final Words] for the *Antología de la moderna poesía uruguaya* [*Anthology of Modern Uruguayan Poetry*], Borges ruminates on the role of the prologue:

> El prólogo debe continuar las persuasiones de la vidriera, de la carátula, de la faja ... Se esperan de él un resumen práctico de la obra y una lista de sus frases rumbosas para citas y una o dos opiniones autorizadas para opinar y la nómina de sus páginas más llevaderas, si es que las tiene.
>
> [The prologue should continue the persuasions of the shop window, of the dust jacket, of the promotional band ... People expect it to provide a general summary of the work and a list of its most quotable phrases and one or two authorized opinions to believe and the numbers of its most easily understandable pages, if it has such things.][1]

Here we see his recognition that these preliminary texts serve as another form of promotional material for publishing houses. Thus, everything from the enticing shop window display, to the book cover and its unique promotional sash (or band), to the actual printed prologue—especially when penned by recognizable literary voices or public intellectuals—

functions as a type of literary marketing. In essence, introductory texts are yet another way for publishing houses to help sell their books and turn a profit. As I argue in the ensuing pages, Borges continues to fill a literary need, as he first did with *El Hogar,* through a series of carefully crafted translations of foreign works and expertly articulated prologues for the books of local and foreign authors. This work is what I deem his editorial and/or promotional framing; that is to say, each of the firms discussed here produces (and markets) works that are either translated by or contain a prologue by Borges. I show how these framing tendencies are not only a product of the publishing houses themselves, but also a deep-seated interest of Borges. My analysis to this point has progressed chronologically—highlighting the impact of Borges's specific jobs on the Argentine publishing industry—but the current chapter looks panoramically at the entire twenty-one-year period. The reason for this temporal shift is twofold. First, and most important, tackling the crucial role of the publishing house Editorial Sur requires an analysis of virtually all of the twenty-one-year span that I have established, in light of the fact that the firm was founded in 1933.[2] Second, and somewhat related to the central role of Editorial Sur, is the question of *elite* production, which pertains to all of the publishing houses discussed here.

Similar to the last chapter, I have grouped the works I consider into structural clusters—translations, prologues, and creative fictions. Moreover, the thematic parallels between this chapter and the previous one allow me to chart a gradual movement from the creation of a literary aperture with *El Hogar,* to filling it with small literary fragments vis-à-vis anthologies and edited collections, to penning (or endorsing) entire books. Many of the elements discussed and described in this chapter clearly align with what Gérard Genette deems a paratext, which, in his words, includes all of the elements that "[enable] a text to become a book and then [be] offered as such to its readers and, more generally, to the public. More than a boundary or a sealed border, the paratext is, rather, a *threshold,* or—a word Borges used apropos of a preface—a 'vestibule' that offers the world at large the possibility of either stepping inside or turning back."[3] His analysis of the "peritexts," or all of those elements that form part of the physical book (and text) that we hold in our hands, and "epitexts," or all of those elements that are *outside* and separate from the physical book (including an author's correspondence, book reviews, or interviews), complements much of my bibliographical analysis and heightens our understanding of the key role of all aspects of a book in informing readers and, more generally, in developing readership.[4] Of particular note for this current chapter is Genette's focus on the prologue, with "its chief function *to ensure that the text is read properly.*"[5]

Translations and Prologues: Framing the Reader's Encounter with a Text

In recent years, many critics have examined Borges's theories of translation and his own translations in great depth. For instance, Efraín Kristal's *Invisible Work: Borges and Translation* (2002) and Sergio Waisman's *Borges and Translation: The Irreverence of the Periphery* (2005) provide a vital springboard for understanding how Borges approached and wrote translations as well as his general ideas surrounding the art of translation and why this form of writing is at times superior to the original work. Throughout his work, Kristal focuses heavily on the merits that Borges sees in translation: "The idea that literary translations are inherently inferior to their originals is, for Borges, based on the false assumption that some works of literature must be assumed definitive. But for Borges, no such thing as a definitive work exists, and therefore, a translator's inevitable transformation of the original is not necessarily to the detriment of the work. Difference, for Borges, is not a sufficient criterion for the superiority of the original."[6] These ideas lie at the heart of much of Borges's writings and to a certain extent can be applied both to translations and to his essays, poems, nonfictions, and fictions.

The idea that works are always changing and evolving such that there is no such thing as a definitive version of a text is central for Borges, and we see it repeated time and time again throughout his writings.[7] In thinking about the act of translating, I cannot help but see a large number of similarities between this type of writing and the act of editing. That is to say, both the translator and the editor "cut, add, and transform for the sake of the work" and in the process highlight elements of any given text that might not shine through as well in the original.[8] This same idea is attributed to Borges in Kristal's work: "It is far easier to forget someone else's vanities than one's own."[9] Even though translation, in the broadest sense, provides readers with the opportunity to engage with works that they might not have been able to because of linguistic barriers, it also brings to mind questions of which works get translated (and which do not). In other words, in light of the fact that translation can be seen as a form of editing (for the common ties that these two acts share), it is important to think critically about not only *how* works are being translated, but also *which* works are being translated and what this selection might tell us about their promotion and, in turn, the interests of certain publishing houses.

Similar to translations, prologues also operate as a framing mechanism for texts.[10] Genette, who opts to call these types of texts "prefaces," outlines their possible function using as a point of departure a key question posed by Jacques Derrida: "But what do prefaces actually do?"[11] In order to answer this query, Genette provides his readers with several possibilities as to the type of prologue that they might encounter: "(1) the *original authorial preface* (*authorial* is to be understood, henceforth, as meaning authentic and assumptive); (2) the *original authorial postface*; (3) the *later authorial preface* ... ; (4) the *delayed authorial preface or postface* ... [and] type five: the *authentic allographic (and actorial) preface*."[12] Of all of these types of prologues, the fifth pertains most to my analysis in light of the fact that I am interested in prologues that Borges writes for *other* authors' works, not for his own.

Focusing solely on this category, we find that this type of prologue did not exist with great regularity before the nineteenth century, mostly because it required two writers (the author of the work and the writer of the preface).[13] Genette emphasizes the fact that "the functions of the allographic preface overlap with . . . the functions of the original authorial preface (to promote and guide a reading of the work)."[14] That said, the allographic preface tends to differ from the original authorial preface in its "high praise of the text" and the ways in which it presents information (about the text) to readers.[15] In terms of the latter idea, Genette stresses the fact that the allographic preface overlaps with the posthumous preface for their common tendencies to include biographical information about the author and to place the work in a larger context. One of the aspects that sets this type of preface apart from all others is its level of recommendation of or praise for the text, which comes in the form of a better-known writer vouching for the book and its author. This particular characteristic of an allographic preface emphasizes a clear level of promotion on the part of the preface writer and directly ties into other strategies publishing houses use to sell more books. The final two aspects of the allographic preface that we should keep in mind are its "critical and theoretical dimension," which aligns it with a type of critical essay, and the habit of preface writers to stray from the work and provide readers instead with a discourse that can be tangentially related to the subject matter.[16] In my discussions of the prologues that Borges wrote for other authors' works, it will be essential to touch on the following issues: Who are the authors and what is their relation to Borges? What would he tend to say about these individuals? What publishing houses would these works appear in? Where were they printed? Do any common trends crop up throughout Borges's large trajectory of prologue writing? Parsing the kinds of framing that these opening texts provide for the larger works they introduce will be essential in developing an understanding of how Borges promoted the writings of others. Throughout this chapter I evaluate not only the works of others that Borges translated and wrote prologues for, but also his own creative fictions—which he produced simultaneously with these other works—and how these overarching concepts of framing and promotion can help us better understand the production and existence of these canonical books.

In an effort to examine the function of all of these different framing devices, I analyze their use by three publishing houses that are constants in Borges's career: Editorial Sur, Emecé Editores, and Editorial Losada.[17] More specifically, I consider the ways in which Borges's translations and prologues function as textual frames in conjunction with how these publishing firms physically frame each book (covers, prices, wrappers and bands, store window displays, etc.) as a way of deepening our understanding of the Argentine book market and Borges's central role in this burgeoning industry. I also assess how Borges simultaneously publishes some of his most canonical collections alongside these translations and prologues (for the same publishing firms), which end up becoming wild successes perhaps partially because of the editorial groundwork that he lays throughout the 1930s and 1940s. In light of the fact that several publishing houses are involved in this discussion, I organize my analysis around the general framing categories of translations and prologues. It is my hope that this organizational decision will reveal not only the interconnectedness of these varied framing devices, but also the inherently tangled nature of the Argentine publishing industry during this time period (1933–1951).

Multilingual Translations and Global Perspectives: From Melville to Michaux

Borges has long been associated with the art of translation. In fact, his first published work is a translation: Oscar Wilde's "The Happy Prince," which appeared in *El País* on June 25, 1910. This initial venture into translation was encouraged by his mother, Leonor Acevedo de Borges, as were virtually all of his literary endeavors throughout his lifetime, and she became a key factor in his later works (both translations and original prose and poetry) as he gradually lost his sight.[18] Even though he translated a large number of works from English to Spanish throughout his lifetime, he also chose works in other languages, including French, German, Italian, and Anglo-Saxon. Alongside his translations, Borges wrote extensive essays and creative prose *about* translation, which solidifies the importance of this art for him. For instance, as early as 1926 he published "Las dos maneras de traducir" [The Two Ways of Translating] in the Argentine newspaper *La Prensa*, in which he spoke in favor of good translations and also outlined the differences between what he deemed romantic translations and classical translations: "Universalmente, supongo que hay dos clases de traducciones. Una practica la literalidad, la otra la perífrasis. La primera corresponde a las mentalidades románticas; la segunda a las clásicas" [Universally, I suppose that there are two types of translations. One practices the literal, the other periphrasis. The first corresponds to romantic mentalities; the other to the classics].[19] This central crux of Borges's first published piece on translation (i.e., literal versus circumlocution) seems to serve as the springboard from which many of his other writings on the subject, both fiction and nonfiction, emerge. For instance, as Suzanne Jill Levine demonstrates, "Las versiones homéricas" [The Homeric Versions], "Los traductores de las 1001 noches" [The Translators of the 1001 Nights], and even "Pierre Menard, autor del Quijote" [Pierre Menard, Author of the Quijote] all hark back to this first foray into what the act of translation means for Borges (and how it should be executed).[20] Even though my analysis in this chapter centers around Borges's translations of certain works, I note here that I do not delve into theories of translation or Borges's translations themselves; instead, I am interested primarily in the Argentine publishing houses and printers involved in the production process (and more broadly the specific authors whose works are chosen to be translated). In other words, as opposed to asking how Borges translates certain works during this period, I focus on tackling the question of why these works are translated and consequently promoted by a variety of publishing houses in Buenos Aires.

The majority of Borges's translations from this period appear with Editorial Sur, founded by Victoria Ocampo. Coming from a privileged upper-class background, Ocampo was highly educated and able to travel to Europe throughout her life, spending the majority of her time in its cultural capital of Paris and forming close relationships with a large number of writers and artists. For instance, during one trip (1928–1929), "she was introduced to Paul Valéry, Maurice Ravel, Gabriel Miró, Benjamin Fondane, Léon-Paul Fargue, Lev Chestov, Nikolai Berdiaeff, and Pierre Drieu la Rochelle."[21] Although Ocampo quickly made new friends and contacts throughout the Continent, who all expressed deep admiration of and appreciate for her creativity, intelligence, and aesthetic sensibilities, she still felt that she was an outsider, which was only confirmed when many of these same acquaintances displayed their ignorance about South America. Shortly after realizing her European friends' lack of interest in her native Buenos Aires (not to mention the entire South American continent), Ocampo met the US writer Waldo Frank, who shared many of her preoccupations: "He [Waldo Frank] has experienced in the North what we have been suffering in the South ... We miss Europe terribly, both of us, and yet when we reach Europe and live in it, we both feel she cannot give us the kind of nourishment we need."[22]

Fueled by her discontent with what she deemed the problem of Latin America, which was precisely its alienation and isolation from

Europe, Ocampo launched her literary journal, *Sur*—with a bit of encouragement from Waldo Frank and Eduardo Mallea—which she saw as "a cultural bridge between the Americas, a forum for the best thinkers of both continents."²³ More broadly, she conceptualized her journal as a way to connect not only North and South America, but also Europe and the Americas.²⁴ Even though Ocampo was not alone in formulating the idea behind *Sur*, she was responsible for virtually all of its design features. Thus, the high-quality paper, the exquisite typography, the inclusion of full-page illustrations, and even the downward-pointing arrow on the cover were all her ideas. These key details, in combination with the writings that fill the journal's pages, highlight the excellence of this publication in terms of both its content and its form.

It should come as no surprise to readers that Borges and *Sur* share an intimate history. Borges served on the initial editorial board for the literary magazine and also contributed regular essays, reviews, and pieces of fiction to many issues.²⁵ As John King notes, "*Sur* would be remembered not so much for its publication of scholars as for its promotion of the writer who made scholarship, and in particular philosophical enquiry, a teasing intellectual game: Jorge Luis Borges."²⁶ Thus, Ocampo's publishing endeavors tend to be remembered for their promotion of the works and writings of Borges.

Even though an extensive corpus of critical studies is dedicated to Ocampo's literary magazine, nothing more than a passing phrase is dedicated to the creation of her publishing house Editorial Sur.²⁷ Moreover, most scholars typically refer to its establishment as simply a way to help with the financial burden of running a literary magazine.²⁸ Although it is true that producing and publishing a literary magazine would be a costly expense—especially one that was started as a luxury magazine—establishing an entire publishing house to help offset these costs does not immediately spring to mind as the only solution to this financial conundrum. Considering Editorial Sur as nothing more than a type of cash cow for the efforts of its literary journal counterpart does not paint an adequate picture of the rationale for creating such a firm, especially in light of the fact that some of the works Editorial Sur published were distributed free of cost and others were luxury works not for sale and out of public circulation. Therefore, this analysis focuses on the works produced by

Editorial Sur instead of those writings that filled the pages of the literary journal of the same name. (See the Appendix for a list of works that Editorial Sur produced between 1933 and 1951.)

Editorial Sur emerged as a publishing firm in 1933 with the release of Federico García Lorca's *Romancero gitano* [*Gypsy Ballads*], D. H. Lawrence's *Canguro* [*Kangaroo*], and Aldous Huxley's *Contrapunto* [*Point Counter Point*]. In the opening pages of *Romancero gitano* we glean a sense of the general aim of Editorial Sur:

> SUR ha publicado, iniciando su serie de novelas argentinas y extranjeras, las obras *Canguro, de David H. Lawrence, y Contrapunto, de Aldous Huxley.* Publicará en breve ensayos, novela y poesía. Las primeras de estas obras serán de Victoria Ocampo, Eduardo Mallea, Francisco Luis Bernárdez, Leopoldo Marechal, Ricardo Molinari, Carlos Alberto Erro, etcétera.
>
> [SUR has published, starting its series of Argentine and foreign novels, the works *Kangaroo,* by David H. Lawrence, and *Point Counter Point,* by Aldous Huxley. It will publish essays, novels, and poetry. The first of these works will be by Victoria Ocampo, Eduardo Mallea, Francisco Luis Bernárdez, Leopoldo Marechal, Ricardo Molinari, Carlos Alberto Erro, etc.][29]

The September 1933 issue of the literary journal *Sur* provides more details about the firm:

> "SUR" acaba de iniciar con la novela "Canguro," de D. H. Lawrence, la publicación de sus ediciones especiales. "SUR" se propone crear en fecha próxima, diversas ramas que extenderán considerablemente su editorial. Iniciará, así, una colección de novelas argentinas, una colección de ensayos argentinos y una serie de volúmenes de poesía argentina. Paralelamente desarrollará la publicación de obras extranjeras que revistan para nuestro público un interés particular.

["SUR" started the publication of its special editions with the novel "Kangaroo," by D. H. Lawrence. "SUR" proposes to create in the next issue, diverse branches that will expand its publishing firm considerably. It will start, thus, a collection of Argentine novels, a collection of Argentine essays, and a series of volumes of Argentine poetry. At the same time it will develop the publication of foreign works that are of a particular interest for our reading public.][30]

Here we note a slight shift to distinct groupings of local Argentine works and foreign (European) works, versus the more general "novelas argentinas y extranjeras" [Argentine and foreign novels] put forth at the start of Lorca's *Romancero gitano*. A year later, in the opening pages of D. H. Lawrence's *La virgin y el gitano* [*The Virgin and the Gypsy*] (1934), we find that this publishing house's goal has evolved further to providing readers with a "colección de grandes novelas de este tiempo" [a collection of the best novels of our time] that will consist of key works that to date had not been available in Spanish. What is more, each of these editions, and many of the firm's future translations and publications, were "autorizadas por los autores" [authorized by the authors], which stresses not only Ocampo's large number of connections in the global literary world, but also the crucial role that Editorial Sur would play in disseminating new literary trends to Argentine readers (and making them readily available).[31]

The first aspect of these publications that stands out is the production of various types of editions, which further supports my claim that the creation of an entire publishing house for the sole purpose of financing a literary journal seems doubtful. For instance, looking to the unique printing details for Lorca's *Romancero gitano* reveals that three distinct editions of this work were produced—a popular edition, a luxury edition, and a private edition not for sale: "De este libro se han impreso aparte de la edición popular cien ejemplares de lujo ... de los cuales diez señalados de A a J fuera de comercio y noventa ejemplares numerados de 1 a 90 en papel Ingrés Italy ... todos firmados por el autor" [Apart from the popular edition of this book one hundred copies of a luxury edition have been printed ... of which ten are marked A to J and not for sale and ninety copies numbered 1 to 90 on Ingrés Italian Paper ... all signed by the author].³² When we compare this printing history with that of other publishing houses that were in the industry for the sole reason of making money—such as Editorial TOR (see Chapter 2)—the decision to generate not just one moderately priced edition but three seems like quite a novel publishing practice in Argentina. Although it is possible to interpret the publication of differing forms of Lorca's *Romancero gitano* as a way to cast the firm's net very wide and attract virtually all interested readers in Buenos Aires, regardless of their socioeconomic status, I firmly believe that other driving forces are involved.³³ In fact, Lorca's physical presence in Buenos Aires during this time and his tremendous success in the theater, not to mention his numerous literary and artistic contacts, might explain the existence of multiple formats of his book.³⁴ A related example is that of André Gide's *Regreso de la U.R.S.S.* [*Return from the USSR*] (1936), a brief piece outlining the shortcomings and failures of communism, which went through twenty-two editions in the course of one year. What is more, the twentieth edition of this work was printed in a run of one thousand copies, which speaks to its extreme popularity.

Another curious aspect related to the origins and overarching purpose of Editorial Sur is its general level of success, which led to its change of legal status. "Para la constitución de una sociedad editorial" [Forming an Editorial Partnership], a short pamphlet issued by Editorial Sur in 1937, provides a brief summary of the activities of the literary journal and publishing house of the same name up to that point.³⁵ Here we find that the publishing house had an immense amount of success with its sales and the overall popularity of its works: "No es menos importante consignar que las ediciones de SUR han alcanzado en el mercado librero un éxito totalmente fuera de lo común, como lo prueba la rapidez con que se han agotado los tirajes de diez títulos entre los 40 publicados" [It is important to note that the editions that SUR has put out into the book market have had a very unusual success, as the speed with which ten of its forty published titles have sold out shows].³⁶ The reader is then reminded of the importance of Ocampo in this publishing endeavor and the fact that much of it would not have been possible without her financial support and that of friends and acquaintances. The language throughout this pamphlet stresses the prestige and unique character of Editorial Sur, which, unlike many other contemporary publishing houses in Argentina, is "puramente argentina" [purely Argentine] and therefore "merecedor del apoyo más absoluto por parte de todos aquellos que desean elevar el nivel cultural de nuestro medio" [deserves absolute support from all of those who want to elevate the cultural level of our medium].[37] The main purpose of this pamphlet is to announce the expansion of the firm's editorial activities and its formation of a limited liability company with the help of interested parties buying stock at one thousand Argentine pesos a share: "Desde ahora podemos anticiparle que esta empresa, según está planteada, y con relación a los resultados positivos obtenidos ya en estos últimos años, ofrece las mayores garantías económicas, produciendo un beneficio neto equivalente al de cualquiera otra inversión de capitales" [From now on we can anticipate that this business, as it stands, and in terms of the positive results that it has achieved in the past few years, will offer the highest economic guarantees, producing a net benefit equal to any other type of capital investment].[38] Such boasting of the firm's ability to return on any investment with ease, not to mention the high demand for its unique editions, again suggests that Editorial Sur was much more than simply a way to help finance Ocampo's literary magazine.[39]

In addition to the publication of varied editions of works and its expanding business model, Editorial Sur at times named other publishing houses as authorized distributors of the books it published. It is hard to say exactly what these relationships entailed, but I imagine that Editorial Sur delivered packages of books to storefronts or booksellers associated with its authorized distributors. These other publishing houses then included Editorial Sur's works in their own promotional advertising. Among the firms that benefited from such relationships were Editorial Sudamericana, Editorial Losada, and Editorial Nova. I turn first to Editorial Sudamericana.

In addition to the fact that Editorial Sudamericana was directed by an exiled Spaniard, Antonio López Llausás, whose previous livelihood was also in the world of publishing, it is important to note that Ocampo, along with Oliverio Girondo and Alfredo González Garaño (both part of the initial editorial board for the literary journal *Sur*), was among the first writers for this publishing house. What is more, Editorial Sudamericana popularized the use of sales catalogues, which might account for Ocampo's close ties to this firm, given their effective promotional strategy: "La editorial intentaba, como vemos, llegar a un amplio abanico de lectores y ofrecía tanto entretenimiento como soluciones a problemas prácticos o reflexiones sobre el comportamiento social" [The publishing firm intended, as we saw, to reach a wide range of readers and offered both entertainment and solutions to practical problems or reflections on social behavior].[40] Regardless of the reason for Ocampo's choosing Editorial Sudamericana, the firm was distributing Editorial Sur's publications exclusively as early as 1944:

> Este prestigioso sello distingue a una empresa cultural fundada y dirigida por la escritora argentina Victoria Ocampo, a cuya influencia directa e indirecta tanto deben las letras argentinas. En efecto, su revista "Sur" fué uno de los primeros periódicos que, en su tiempo, se preocupó por dar a conocer a escritores argentinos y americanos cuya singularidad y sensibilidad los habían mantenido inéditos y que hoy son considerados entre los primeros del país y de América; sus páginas alternaban y alternan con las de los más finos escritores de Europa. Esta labor es complementada con conferencias dictadas por estos últimos que estimulan y fomentan constantemente nuestro movimiento intelectual. Finalmente, surgió la Editorial "Sur" —cuyas primeras publicaciones son distribuídas por la EDITORIAL SUDAMERICANA—, empresa que popularizó la obra de valores perdurables europeos desconocidos para los lectores de habla española, como el Conde de Keyserling, los hermanos Huxley y V. Woolf, entre otros.
>
> [This prestigious imprint pertains to a cultural business founded and directed by the Argentine writer Victoria Ocampo, whose direct and indirect influence has given so much to Argentine letters. In essence, her literary magazine "Sur" was one of the first periodicals that, in its time, concerned itself with exposing readers to Argentine and American writers whose singularity and sensibility left them unedited and that today are considered some of the best in the country and in America; its pages are always filled with the

most refined writers of Europe. This labor is complemented by conferences presented by these writers that constantly stimulate and foment our intellectual movement. Finally, Editorial "Sur" emerged—whose first publications are distributed by Editorial Sudamericana—a business that popularized the work of unknown key European values for Spanish-language readers, like Count Keyserling, the Huxley brothers, and V. Woolf, among others.][41]

Even though Editorial Sudamericana is at first responsible for only the distribution of certain titles produced by Editorial Sur, it appears that the firm slowly began to republish and distribute many of these same works as part of its own publications after seeing their successful sales.[42] Consider, for instance, the case of Virginia Woolf's *Orlando,* translated by Borges for Editorial Sur in 1937. In March 1943, nearly six years after its initial publication with Editorial Sur, Editorial Sudamericana produced an edition of *Orlando* for its Colección Horizonte, also translated by Borges; yet instead of being identified as the first edition (from its publishing house), it is described instead as the second edition.[43]

Turning to Borges's translation work for Editorial Sur, we find the following titles: André Gide's *Perséphone* (1936), Virginia Woolf's *Un cuarto propio* [*A Room of One's Own*] (1936) and *Orlando* (1937), and Henri Michaux's *Un bárbaro en Asia* [*A Barbarian in Asia*] (1941). Along with their unique physical characteristics, each of these books has quite complex publication and distribution histories, with a number of shared traits but also differences. Starting with the earliest, Gide's *Perséphone,* we discover that the size, placement, and style of the typography on the front cover more resembles the typography of the literary journal *Sur* than any other book published by Editorial Sur. More specifically, the downward arrow extending through both "SUR" and the title of the work brings to mind the cover of the literary journal. Much like a literary journal that might have a special issue dedicated to a specific theme or person, Editorial Sur's publication of Gide's *Perséphone* was produced in homage to Igor Stravinsky. This interest in honoring the work of Stravinsky runs throughout Editorial Sur since his *Crónicas de mi vida* [*Chronicles of My Life*] was published the previous year (1935), and the second installment,

Cover of André Gide's *Perséphone* (Editorial Sur, 1936). *(Reproduced from the Albert and Shirley Small Special Collections Library, University of Virginia.)*

Nuevas crónicas de mi vida [*New Chronicles of My Life*], appeared a few months later in 1936, following the publication of *Perséphone*. Of particular note with Borges's translation is the fact that Editorial Sur distributed this work free of cost, which certainly seems to be a promotional strategy.[44] While the free nature of this work might suggest that less care or precision was taken during its production (or that, perhaps, materials of a lower quality were used), we find that there is an inserted green page with "modificaciones" [modifications] at the start of the book, which stresses the fact that even though Editorial Sur would not have gained any revenue from this publication, the firm was still concerned about putting out a work of the highest quality. Furthermore, the fact that readers would have acquired this publication for free suggests that not every work published by Editorial Sur was for profit, which somewhat undermines many critics' arguments concerning the function of this firm.

Before diving into an analysis of Borges's next translation for Editorial Sur—Virginia Woolf's *Un cuarto propio*—I pause here to elaborate on the kinds of works produced by the printing firm Imprenta López in light of the fact that it is responsible both for a large portion of Editorial Sur's publications (and the majority of the early issues of the literary journal) and for many works published with other Argentine publishing houses discussed below. Founded in 1908 by Juan Bautista and José López García, Imprenta López started as a small business that reflected the interests of the entire family: the graphic arts. As the labors of their trade grew and expanded, the two men moved from their more modest offices at Tacuarí 634 to several other locations before finally settling at Perú 666, which is the firm's best known address and the one that appears printed on all of the works discussed below.[45] Over the years, Imprenta López perfected its craft and became known for the high quality of its works; consequently, the firm attracted numerous writers and editors from all corners of the Americas. Along with printing, this firm was also known in its initial years for binding and quality paper: "Imprenta, papelería y encuadernación de José López García, rezaban pomposamente el cartel de hierro que colgaba en la puerta, la vidriera y algunos impresos que acreditaron la existencia de aquel negocito" [Print shop, paper store, and bindery of José López García, stated the iron sign that hung above the door, the shop window, and some print shops that supported the founding of that small business].⁴⁶ We also know the various types of printing presses the firm used and the evolution of those machines over the years. When it first opened in 1908, Imprenta López had nothing more than two Minerva printing presses, a paper cutter, and a borer.⁴⁷ The machinery first changed to the more advanced flatbed press with the move to Perú 538. As work began to take off, it purchased two Linotype machines from another company that had gone bankrupt.⁴⁸ In terms of the typefaces López used, we see a great amount of diversity, which is emphasized in *Homenaje a Don José López García* [*Homage to Don José López García*] produced for the thirtieth anniversary of Imprenta López and composed "a mano, seleccionado del surtido de la Imprenta López, los tipos y adornos que rememoran las distintas épocas del establecimiento" [by hand, selected from Imprenta López's stock, the sorts and ornaments that call to mind each of the distinct eras of the business].⁴⁹

Imprenta López undoubtedly made waves in the Argentine book industry.⁵⁰ In fact, even though Francisco A. Colombo printed issues one through eight of Ocampo's literary journal *Sur*, Imprenta López took over, starting with the ninth issue, and printed virtually every subsequent issue throughout the 1930s and much of the 1940s. As a result, we find a fair amount of advertisement for this firm throughout the pages of each issue of *Sur*. Imprenta López also produced a full-color promotional book, *Cómo se imprime un libro* [*How to Print a Book*] (1942), in an effort to stress the quality of its craftsmanship and its dedication to producing the best work for each client's needs:

> Trabajamos con el lema de que la tipografía es un arte aplicado al servicio de la divulgación del pensamiento. Nunca caeremos en el vanidoso descarrío de proceder como si la tipografía fuese un arte independiente, de fueros ilimitados y con campo libre para buscar satisfacciones estéticas por sí misma sirviéndose del texto y no sirviéndolo. Nuestra posición en esto es bien clara: ante todo, reproducir fielmente el pensamiento en *forma del libro*; después dar dignidad y belleza a esa *forma* en coherencia estilística con las demás expresiones estéticas de nuestra época, pues la belleza tipográ-

fica de un libro será tanto más eficaz en su servicio de divulgación del pensamiento cuanto más concuerde con el estilo general de las tendencias artísticas actuales.

[We work with the slogan that typography is an applied art at the service of conveying thought. We never fall into the vain trap of thinking that typography is an independent art, of a limited status and with free rein to find aesthetic satisfactions for itself from the text and not serving the text. Our position in the matter is clear: above all, faithfully reproducing thoughts in the *form of a book*; after giving dignity and beauty to this *form* in stylistic coherence with the rest of the aesthetic expression of our era, thus the typographical beauty of a book is all the more effective when it serves to spread thoughts and is in sync with the general style of actual artistic tendencies.][51]

The ways in which Imprenta López describes its goals as well as the ways in which it promotes its work sets it apart from other competitors in the industry.

Borges's translation of Woolf's *Un cuarto propio* was printed by Imprenta López and was the "primera y única traducción española autorizada por la autora" [first and only Spanish translation authorized by the author].[52] It is clear that this edition of Woolf is of a high quality. For starters, the paper is thicker than usual and has visible (vertical) chain lines. The majority of works from Editorial Sur that were also printed by Imprenta López are on much more brittle paper that with aging has yellowed significantly and has neither chain nor wire lines. What is more, the text has very large margins on all sides throughout the work, which is a traditional trait of luxury works. In a similar vein, the serif typeface with its vertical stress is clean, neat, and easily readable. When we compare *Un cuarto propio* with *Orlando*—both of which were translated from the English by Borges, published with Editorial Sur, and printed by Imprenta López—we can see a number of stylistic differences. Although the title pages in each work use a very similar sans serif typeface, the letters are more drastically spaced in *Un cuarto propio,* which calls to mind the luxury printing work of Francisco A. Colombo that we saw in Chapter 2.

Moreover, *Orlando* maintains the same sans serif typeface for the copyright statement and indication of the original English title of the work (found on the verso facing the title page) while *Un cuarto propio* prints this information in a more elegant serif typeface. Entering the texts, one sees that *Un cuarto propio* presents each chapter title on a separate page from the text itself whereas *Orlando* has each chapter title as a heading directly above the text of these sections, which appears to indicate a desire to conserve space and use less paper and materials. In addition, *Un cuarto propio* is a much larger book than *Orlando,* with larger margins. All of these characteristics—the book's size, use of space, elegant typography, and high-quality paper—align *Un cuarto propio* with many traditional concepts of what constitutes a luxury book.

The last work that Borges translated for Editorial Sur is Henri Michaux's *Un bárbaro en Asia* (1941). In terms of its physical features we can start to identify a pattern that will become synonymous with Editorial Sur. As with *Orlando,* the crisp, clean green covers of *Un bárbaro en Asia* present the name of the author and the title in uppercase (white) sans serif type, while the name of the publishing house appears in a more elegant serif typeface with a downward red arrow behind the central "U" of the firm's name. Much like the paper used for *Orlando,* the pages of Michaux's work are brittle, yellowed, and worn from age and use, which points to a lower quality paper. A modern serif typeface is used throughout the work, even for the closing colophon, where the reader discovers that Imprenta López printed this work, which might account for the physical similarities between this book and the others analyzed thus far. The most curious aspect of Editorial Sur's edition of *Un bárbaro en Asia* is the following phrase, which appears printed on the back cover: "Concesionario exclusivo para la venta: EDITORIAL LOSADA, S.A.—BUENOS AIRES" [Exclusive authorized dealer for sale: EDITORIAL LOSADA, S.A.—BUENOS AIRES]. In light of the fact that Editorial Sur, much like the literary journal of the same name, did not have an established storefront from which Ocampo would be able to directly market and sell the works produced, it makes sense that each edition bearing this firm's name would be marketed and sold elsewhere. That said, it is peculiar that Editorial Sur would name *exclusive* authorized dealers for certain works that it produced, as it did with *Un bárbaro en Asia*.[53]

Even though Borges's translations are not the only translations produced for Editorial Sur, they give readers a good sense of the types of works translated: foreign works that more often than not appear originally in English, French, or German. In addition, much like many of the works that Borges reviewed in his column for *El Hogar*, a large number of the authors who are published, with or without translation, would be best characterized as High Modernist, elite, or hard-to-access writers. Thus, alongside Woolf, we find James Joyce, Albert Camus, Jean-Paul Sartre, Thomas Mann, Aldous Huxley, C. G. Jung, André Breton, H. G. Wells, and Roger Caillois, among others. Bearing in mind that Editorial Sur's publication of the works of these writers (and others) most likely would have been the first encounter that many Argentinians had with them in their full-length entirety, it is surprising that virtually all of these books lacked what might be deemed an essential component in aiding these readers: a prologue.[54] Perhaps this omission speaks to the type of audience that would read these works in the sense that these individuals would already know how to approach such works and as a result would not need a "road map" or guide of sorts from someone else.[55] This idea is further emphasized by the fact that prologues are scarce for the works produced by Editorial Sur, not just those translated by Borges.[56] Aside from his translations for Editorial Sur, Borges also translated works for Emecé and Editorial Losada: Herman Melville's *Bartleby* (Emecé, 1943) and Franz Kafka's *La metamorfosis* (Losada, 1938).[57]

Broadening the Reader's Conception of "American" Literature

Borges began writing prologues for other authors' works as early as 1925 and continued this practice for much of his life. Although he states in *Prólogos con un prólogo de prólogos* [*Prologues with a Prologue of Prologues*] that "nadie ha formulado hasta ahora una teoría del prólogo" [no one so far has developed a theory of the prologue], several of his introductory texts for *other* authors' works touch on what he deems the essential aspects of this kind of writing.[58] For instance, in his prologue for Elvira de Alvear's *Reposo* [*Repose*] (1934) Borges outlines two main functions of the prologue:

Considero que la función del prólogo es entablar la discusión que debe suscitar todo libro, y evitar al lector las dificultades que una escritura nueva supone ... En el libro común, el prefacio no tiene razón de ser, es un mero despacho de cortesías; en el excepcional, puede ser de alguna virtud. Entiendo que éste que propone Elvira de Alvear es de los segundos: por eso no me disculpo de prologarlo.

[I think that the function of the prologue is to initiate the discussion of the book, and eliminate any difficulties that a new type of writing can create ... In the ordinary book, the preface does not have a function, it is merely a place for courtesies; in the exceptional [book], it can be a virtue. I understand that Elvira de Alvear's book falls into the second category: for this reason I do not need to apologize for providing her work with a prologue.][59]

From this short excerpt we see a direct parallel with Genette's description of the allographic preface through Borges's discussion of what we might deem presentation ("evitar al lector las dificultades que una escritura nueva supone" [eliminate any difficulties that a new type of writing entails]) and recommendation ("puede ser de alguna virtud. Entiendo que éste que propone Elvira de Alvear es de los segundos" [it can be a virtue. I understand that Elvira de Alvear's book falls into the second category]). Writing his own prologue for a collection of his allographic prefaces, Borges also comments on the closeness of these types of texts to critical essays: "El prólogo, cuando son propicios los astros, no es una forma subalterna del brindis; es una especie lateral de la crítica" [The prologue, when the stars are favorable, is not an inferior form of a toast; it is a lateral type of critique].[60] A large number of Borges's prologues also present readers with biographical information about the author and tend to place their work in a larger context.[61] Still more show an interest in providing readers with a slightly alternative discourse that might not be entirely related to the work at hand.[62] In essence, what we find in surveying Borges's large oeuvre of prologues is the presence of virtually all of the characteristics outlined by Genette.

Another common thread that appears throughout a number of Borges's prologues for other writers' works is his recognition that these texts serve as another form of promotional material for publishing houses. In addition to the anecdote that opens this chapter, Borges's prologue to Roberto Godel's *Nacimiento del fuego* [*The Birth of Fire*] (1932) expresses a similar sentiment of promotion and marketing: "Un libro (creo) debe bastarse. Una convención editorial requiere, sin embargo, que lo preceda algún estímulo en letra bastardilla que corre el peligro de asemejarse a esa otra indispensable página en blanco que precede a la falsa carátula" [A book (I believe) should be enough. An editorial convention requires, however, that something stimulating precede it in italics that runs the risk of being too similar to that other indispensable blank page that comes before the half-title page].[63] This example shows not only a marked understanding of the function of the prologue as a type of promotional strategy employed by publishing firms, but also a clear understanding of the prologue as another physical aspect of the book that has a specific place within the book and a specific format ("en letra bastardilla" [in italics]).

Having outlined some of Borges's theoretical conceptions of the form of the prologue, I now turn to specific examples. Although Borges's greatest contribution to Emecé is most commonly cited as the Séptimo Círculo series, or even his complete edited works, he first started working with this publishing house in 1943 as what Sara del Carril calls an "asesor literario" [literary advisor]: "Leía libros y aconsejaba sobre su publicación, preparaba prólogos, corregía textos, etcétera" [He read books and advised about their publication, he prepared prologues, he corrected texts, etc.].[64] Unlike the large number of creative fictions and translations that Borges produced for Editorial Sur, his work for Emecé primarily consisted of writing prologues, selecting titles, and editing collections, not to mention republishing some of his own fictions. As a result, the common trend that we find in these works is not only a sense of framing, but also a deep-seated interest in producing successful works (i.e., works that will be popular and will sell well with the Argentine populace). This is precisely what we saw with Emecé's *Los mejores cuentos policiales* (see Chapter 4), which went through two separate series as well as numerous editions (primarily because of its large sales). Readers will recall that for the initial production of this edited collection of detective fiction, Emecé did not wish to have its name printed on the cover, just the names of the work's editors (Borges and Bioy Casares) as, perhaps, a sort of promotional strategy.[65] In line with this project, which resulted in the creation of an entire series of subsequent books (Séptimo Círculo), Borges was also invited to write prologues for a number of works that formed part of the following collections Emecé produced during the 1940s: Cuadernos de la Quimera (Chimera's Notebooks), El Navío (The Ship), Biblioteca Emecé (Emecé Library), Teatro del Mundo (Theater of the World), and Clásicos Emecé (Emecé Classics).[66] Before describing these framing texts and the physical formats of Emecé's works, it is necessary to detail the ways in which Emecé undertook the creation of its books, how the firm viewed its publications, and the efforts that it made to ensure that its works reached the greatest number of people possible.

The first volume of Emecé's *Catálogo general perpetuo,* a massive seven-volume reference source that allows readers to stay up-to-date on all of the works produced by the firm, opens by outlining the cultural importance of books and the great labor undertaken in their creation and circulation:

> No cabe dude ... que si la base intelectual de la cultura es el libro, la constitución de una biblioteca, por modesta que sea, en todos los hogares dignos de tal nombre es una necesidad fundamental, una exigencia imperativa de la vida espiritual ... Contribuir a esta empresa social, hacer asequible al mayor número posible la formación de esa biblioteca familiar, es el propósito cardinal de esta colección.
>
> [There is no doubt ... that the intellectual base of culture is the book; the formation of a library, as modest as it is, in all of the homes worthy to be called dignified is a fundamental necessity, an imperative requirement of spiritual life ... Contributing to this social business, making the formation of this familiar library accessible to the largest number of people, is the cardinal goal of this collection.][67]

In order to achieve this goal, Emecé focused on two aspects when producing each of its books: the textual presentation and the material presentation of the works. First, each work is painstakingly edited and corrected as well as annotated so that readers will have no trouble approaching any given book.[68] Second, the editors of Emecé stress their use of quality paper, legible printings, and beautiful and durable bindings. Thus, the works are valuable for both their content and their form. Emecé's twenty-fifth anniversary catalogue further stresses this high quality of the firm's work:

> Fue también idea del grupo iniciador presentar los libros irreprochablemente impresos, diagramados con el mayor cuidado posible, vigilados en la ejecución de todos los aspectos de la labor gráfica. Bajo la experta creación y dirección de Juan Antonio Spotorno los libros de EMECÉ fueron un verdadero ejemplo e influyeron grandemente en el perfeccionamiento de la industria del libro en la Argentina.
>
> [It was also the founding group's idea to present books that were perfectly printed, designed with the most care possible, watched through all aspects of their graphic production. Under the expert creation and direction of Juan Antonio Spotorno Emecé's books were a true example and they largely influenced a level of perfection in the book industry in Argentina].[69]

Most striking is the fact that Emecé's dedication to well-made works—in both content and form—served to influence other publishing firms throughout Buenos Aires and became one of its defining features. Thus, we find that Emecé was known for producing works that would contribute to the "obra cultural e intelectual" [cultural and intellectual work] of Argentina in all senses of the phrase.[70]

A new periodical publication that would be fundamental for the book world in Buenos Aires appeared around the same time that Emecé produced its *Catálogo general perpetuo*. The journal *Papel, Libro, Revista* [*Paper, Book, Journal*] tackled the various problems facing the publishing industry in Argentina including, but not limited to, paper shortages, transportation issues, and the production of cost-effective works of the highest quality. The first installment of *Papel, Libro, Revista* in March 1942 outlines the central aim in creating such a publication:

> Su lema será servir por igual al papelero, al editor y al librero, ponerlos en contacto por medio de sus páginas e informarles de cuanto se relaciona con sus propias actividades. En las páginas de esta revista colaborarán las figuras más destacadas de la industria, el comercio y la inteligencia; sus artículos abarcarán infinidad de temas que irán desde la venta en el mostrador de un artículo o libro hasta la decoración de vidrieras.
>
> [Its slogan will serve equally the paper seller, the publisher, and the book seller, putting them all in contact and informing them about their own activities. In the pages of this magazine the most prominent figures in the industry (and commerce) will collaborate; their articles will cover a variety of topics that range from the sales of an article or a book to the decoration of shop windows.][71]

True to its initial statements, *Papel, Libro, Revista* published articles such as "El arte de vender libros" [The Art of Selling Books] and "Base científica de la decoración de vidrieras" [The Scientific Basis of Decorating Shop Windows] in its June 1942 issue and dedicated an entire section to the "Feria del libro" [Book Fair] in its April–May 1943 issue, which also includes images of each publishing firm's booth, including that of Emecé.[72] In light of the fact that advertisements and other sections were dedicated to Emecé, such as a detailed description of the firm's funds and the type of company that it was, we can conclude that Emecé must have been aware of this periodical and also one of its readers.

In fact, one of the key factors that set Emecé apart from other Argentine publishing firms was its method of promotion — and awareness of the importance of promotion — which seems to suggest a possible engagement with the articles published in *Papel, Libro, Revista*. Leandro de Sagastizábal writes about Emecé:

> La empresa daba a conocer periódicamente, mediante folletos, otros aspectos: comerciales, promocionales, de capacitación del personal. Muy lejos de la improvisación que caracterizaba el trabajo del libro en esos días, proponía desde pautas de consumo, como, por ejemplo, la fabricación y promoción—verdadero anticipo del actual "merchandising"—de un mueble-biblioteca, hasta un estilo determinado de publicidad y difusión destinado a acrecentar la [sic] ventas: descripción de la [sic] virtudes de sus productos, elogio de su calidad y precio, y resumen de las acciones futuras de la editorial, a modo de adelanto.
>
> [The business publicized gradually, through pamphlets, and other aspects: advertisements, promotions, and training employees. Far from the improvisation that characterized the work of books in that moment, it proposed standards of consumption, like, for example, the fabrication and promotion—the true antecedents of "merchandizing"—of a movable library, even a particular style of advertising and dissemination intended to improve sales: a description of the virtues of its products, praising their quality and price, and a summary of the future actions of the firm, as a way of advancing.][73]

We see this strong sense of promotion that verges on our current understanding of marketing when we consider the fact that each of Emecé's catalogues was available to (and intended) for consumers. That is to say, in the initial pages of each volume of the *Catálogo general perpetuo* Emecé included a few lines that were aimed directly at potential buyers. In addition, at the close of each volume these same readers could find specific information about how to go about purchasing materials from the firm.

We now turn to the particular Emecé collections that contain Borges's framing contributions, in the form of prologues or *notas preliminaries* (preliminary notes). Unlike his work for Editorial Sur, which consisted exclusively of translations and original creative fictions, Borges provided Emecé mainly with prologues for a number of its books, which suggests that these works were intended for quite a different public. The earliest collection that Borges contributed to is the Cuadernos de la Quimera series. The series was directed by Eduardo Mallea and, unlike any other collection put out by Emecé, was dedicated to the lesser-studied form of the novella. Aside from Emecé's personal methods of promotion through its catalogues and connections with various booksellers, another key factor to consider when discussing this series is the central role of its director. In addition to being a well-known writer and a literary critic, Mallea was also the director of *La Nación*'s literary supplement from 1931 until 1955. This position allowed him to "[ejercer] una influencia decisiva en la literatura argentina y [contribuir] a moldear el gusto del público" [exert a decisive influence on Argentine literature and contribute to the molding of public tastes], which echoes much of what I argue are the effects of Borges's review column for *El Hogar* on the Argentine populace.[74] That said, the impact of *La Nación* was much greater since its distribution and circulation rates were quite high at this time.[75] When we see the names of the many invited foreign contributors, as well as the regular Argentine writers, whom Mallea chose to fill the pages of his literary supplements, we begin to understand the effect of networks, literary circles, and the interconnectedness of the book industry in Argentina. A short list of some of these usual suspects includes André Gide, Aldous Huxley, Pierre Drieu la Rochelle, Jean Cocteau, Jules Supervielle, Hermann von Keyserling, José Ortega y Gasset, Ramón Gómez de la Serna, Gregorio Marañón, Jorge Luis Borges, Adolfo Bioy Casares, Silvina Ocampo, and José Bianco.

As previously mentioned, Borges played a part in the production of two works in the Cuadernos de la Quimera series. Herman Melville's *Bartleby* (1943), which was translated by Borges and for which he wrote the prologue, appeared as the first title in the collection. From the opening words of his prologue, we clearly see that the book is intended for readers who might not be well versed in Melville's oeuvre. Borges spends a great deal of time chronicling the importance of *Moby Dick* and all of the criticism that that work received over the years, which would be common knowledge for a reader familiar with Melville's writings, especially when we consider the fact that this monumental work was first published in 1851 and most likely available at English-language bookstores in Buenos Aires such as Mackern's. Borges ends this introductory piece with a quick survey of the reception of Melville in which he tellingly cites his beloved eleventh edition of the *Encyclopedia Britannica*: "La grandeza de Melville es sustantiva, pero su gloria es nueva. Melville murió en 1891; a los veinte años de su muerte la undécima edición de la *Encyclopaedia Britannica* lo considera un mero cronista de la vida marítima" [Melville's grandeur is substantial, but his glory is new. Melville died in 1891; twenty years after his death the eleventh edition of the *Encyclopedia Britannica* considered him as a mere chronicler of maritime life].[76] The only other work in this collection that contains a prologue by Borges is Henry James's *La humillación de los Northmore* [*The Abasement of the Northmores*] (1945). Here the style has been altered slightly from that of Melville's *Bartleby* and much more resembles an extended version of the short biographies that Borges and Bioy Casares composed for *Los mejores cuentos policiales.* One might even argue that Borges is swiftly approaching the tone and technique of an *Encyclopedia Britannica* entry. Thus, readers can easily learn about the life, education, and various accomplishments of Henry James, while also perusing any of the cited critical works for further reading.

Another Emecé series directed by Mallea was El Navío, which is described in Emecé's *Catálogo general perpetuo* as a "Colección de Grandes Obras Continentales" [Collection of the Best Continental Works]. Curiously, instead of finding the name of a European author on each cover in this series, we find those of Americans, in the broadest sense: Domingo F. Sarmiento, Herman Melville, Henry David Thoreau, General José María Paz, Mark Twain, Walt Whitman, Thomas Wolfe, Lidia Besouchet, and José Lins do Rego. The emblem of the collection, an uppercase "N" in a boat on water, also speaks to the historical origins of the Americas. Echoing what we saw with the Cuadernos de la Quimera series, the first volume in Emecé's El Navío, Sarmiento's *Recuerdos de provincia* [*Provincial Recollections*] (1944), presents readers with a prologue by Borges. Even though this commonality might be a mere coincidence, I believe it points to an intricate web of connections among the elite circles of writers in Buenos Aires that would more often than not control the framing and presentation of texts for the Argentine reading public. The first striking elements of *Recuerdos de provincia* are the unique typographic details that characterize the entire collection. In contrast to the transitional serif

Cover of Domingo F. Sarmiento's *Recuerdos de provincia* (Emecé, 1944). *(Reproduced from the Albert and Shirley Small Special Collections Library, University of Virginia.)*

typefaces found on the covers of the Cuadernos de la Quimera series, Emecé's El Navío utilizes more lyrical and flowing typography—a subtle imitation of calligraphic form—that is reminiscent of many old-style serif typefaces that draw on the humble origins of typography. In light of the fact that this series contains some of the most important literary works in the history of the Americas, the use of such a typeface, which recalls the format and feel of many sixteenth- and seventeenth-century documents, not to mention the entire manuscript tradition, is fitting. That is to say, the covers in this collection highlight the artistry of Emecé and its constant striving to link form and content. What is more, from the colophon for *Recuerdos de provincia* we learn that this work was issued in two forms: a regular edition and a small luxury edition (of forty-seven copies) that was numbered, printed on Conqueror paper, and bound by the famous French binder Julien Leprêtre.

Borges's prologue for *Recuerdos de provincia* is much more theoretical and abstract in comparison with the detail-oriented examples from the Cuadernos de la Quimera series that immediately concentrate on the writer in question. He begins with a rumination on the art of literary analysis before placing the work of Sarmiento into one of his pre-established categories: "Otros, aún más misteriosos, no son analíticamente justificables … A esa categoría de escritores que no puede explicar la mera razón, pertenece nuestro Sarmiento" [Other writers, even more mysterious, are not analytically justifiable … To that category of writers that cannot be explained by mere reason, pertains our Sarmiento].[77] In essence, according to Borges, Sarmiento's prose is extremely complex even though it might appear quite simple alongside that of writers such as Lugones. That said, the importance of this work resides in the fact that Sarmiento's critiques of society and of its many tyrannies continue to resonate with Argentine history. Moreover, Borges stresses the changing viewpoints toward this work that naturally occur when new generations read it. Generally speaking, in this prologue we see a marked shift from chronicling the life and times of an author to focusing almost entirely on the work at hand, both in theoretical and in material terms.

Even though Mallea's Cuadernos de la Quimera and El Navío series are important for an analysis of the publishing trends and the depth and breadth of Emecé's production, its Biblioteca Emecé encapsulates the

Table 15. Biblioteca Emecé's twelve subject areas

I. Biografías y memorias; Epistolarios y oratoria [Biographies and Memoirs; Collections of Letters and Speeches]
II. Ciencias [Science]
III. Poesía y teatro [Poetry and Theater]
IV. Ensayo y crítica [Essay and Criticism]
V. Ficción (novela y cuento) [Fiction (Novel and Short Story)]
VI. Filosofía y religión [Philosophy and Religion]
VII. Clásicos castellanos [Castilian Classics]
VIII. Clásicos griegos y latinos [Greek and Latin Classics]
IX. Viajes y exploraciones [Travel and Explorations]
X. Historia y arqueología [History and Archaeology]
XI. Referencias y varios [Reference and Miscellaneous]
XII. Clásicos de la juventud [Classics for Youth]

firm's broader reach and goals. Divided into twelve subject areas, each with its own color scheme (again bringing to mind many of Penguin's editions), the Biblioteca Emecé is one of the firm's crowning achievements (Table 15).[78] According to the *Catálogo general perpetuo,* "esta biblioteca ... comprenderá las más grandes obras de la cultura universal en sus diversos órdenes" [this library ... will cover the most important works of universal culture in diverse orders].[79] The collection will not solely be for entertainment or leisure, but rather is an entire "orientación de cultura" [cultural orientation] and as a result will focus on "los clásicos de la literatura universal, antigua y moderna, y las obras maestras de historia o de crítica en los diversos órdenes del conocimiento" [the classics of universal literature, ancient and modern, and the master works of history or of critique in the various orders of knowledge].[80] Over the course of 1945 and 1946 Borges wrote four prologues for four works in this collection, each of which speaks to his personal literary interests: William James's *Pragmatismo* [*Pragmatism*] (1945; subject VI [see Table 15]), Thomas Carlyle's *Sartor Resartus* (1945; subject IV), Francis Bret Harte's *Bocetos californianos* [*California Sketches*] (1946; subject V), and Miguel de Cervantes's *Novelas ejemplares* [*Exemplary Novels*] (1946; subject VII).[81] In light of the fact that these works form part of an entire library that purports to educate interested parties on the most important literatures of the world, it should come as no surprise that each short description of the work in Emecé's *Catálogo general perpetuo* includes not only a short biographical note on the author, but also a brief analysis of the work.

Borges's prologues for several of the works in the Biblioteca Emecé are not this scripted. For instance, his prologue to Carlyle's *Sartor Resartus* focuses on the key role of idealism in the book and then gives a short synopsis of its central arguments, concluding, powerfully, that "No sé de un libro más ardido y volcánico, más trabajado por la desolación, que *Sartor Resartus*" [I don't know of a book that is more seething and volcanic, more crafted by devastation, than *Sartor Resartus*].[82] His *nota preliminar* for James's *Pragmatismo,* on the other hand, reads like many of his philosophical essays in *Historia de la eternidad,* with references to Plotinus, Bradley, and Parmenides. Here he places James's work within a larger philosophical tradition—starting with Aristotle and Plato—by providing a short, succinct summary of various philosophers' positions and simultaneously couching the theory of pragmatism alongside them. In contrast, his prologue for Harte's *Bocetos californianos* much resembles many of the concise biographies that he wrote for *El Hogar* during the 1930s. More specifically, we see an interest in describing the author's life, his upbringing, and how he and his work fit into more canonical trends in world literature, particularly that of the Americas. His prologue for Cervantes's *Novelas ejemplares* melds the abstract philosophical musings with the form of the concise biography. Here, Borges starts by positing two possible types of books—in an abstract sense—and then moves to the specifics of Cervantes and his writings to call these absolutes into question.

The general trend that we can observe, with regard to Borges's prologues for the Biblioteca Emecé, is that similar types of writings are grouped together. In other words, when Borges is writing about works that fall into this library's subject area of "Ensayo y crítica" [Essay and Criticism], such as Carlyle's *Sartor Resartus,* his prologues read like one of the essays out of his *Discusión* or the later *Otras inquisiciones* that tend to be more philosophical. The same case can be made for James's *Pragmatismo* and Cervantes's *Novelas ejemplares*. On the other hand, prologues for works from the subject area "Ficción (novela y cuento)" [Fiction (Novel and Short Story)], like Harte's *Bocetos californianos,* are akin to his many literary reviews published in *El Hogar, La Nación,* or even *Sur.* Therefore, with regard to this collection, there is not always a clear division between an essay or a short story by Borges and one of his prologues for another author's work, which makes the question of promotional framing all the more intriguing.

Emecé's Teatro del Mundo collection includes contemporary works of theater, as the collection's name suggests, by playwrights such as T. S. Eliot, Paul Claudel, Franz Werfel, Jean Cocteau, and Henry de Montherlant. As with the other Emecé collections discussed thus far, the Teatro del Mundo series has a unique emblem relating to the subject of its works: a bird's-eye view of a semicircular amphitheater. Even though the genre of this collection differs from those discussed above (with the exception of the Biblioteca Emecé, which has a theater subject area), Borges's prologue for Werfel's *Juaréz y Maximiliano* much resembles one of his critical essays fused with a sort of literary review. In particular, we see Borges immediately emphasizing one of his favorite themes at the start of this prologue: "En su clamoroso decurso, Werfel renueva un tema predilecto de las neurosis, de las literaturas y de los mitos: el doble, el *doppelgaenger*" [In his clamorous discourse, Werfel renews a favorite topic of neurosis, of literatures, and of myths: the double, the *doppelganger*].[83]

Borges also wrote a prologue for Emecé's Clásicos Emecé collection, which shares some similarities with the Biblioteca Emecé regarding the description and goals of the series: to present "las obras más ilustres y fundamentales de la cultura clásica" [the most illustrious and fundamental works of classical culture].[84] As a result, one of the distinguishing features of the Clásicos Emecé collection is the physical form of its titles, which imitates many sixteenth- and seventeenth-century bindings. More specifically, the hardcover bindings mimic a marbled calfskin, the unique emblem of the collection is printed in gold on a navy leather piece attached to the spine, the title of the work is printed in gold on a red leather piece attached to the spine, and the endpapers are marbled as well. Consider, for instance, Francisco de Quevedo's *Prosa y verso* [*Prose and Verse*], for which Borges wrote the original prologue in 1948.[85] Compared with his other prologues for Emecé's works, this text is much lengthier, which is due to the fact that Borges not only introduces the importance of the figure of Quevedo, but also describes his prose and poetry in great detail, going so far as to include a few poetic excerpts with their accompanying textual analysis. Thus, this prologue resembles what we might find in the opening pages of a Cátedra edition for its more erudite and scholarly nature.

The extremely wide net that Emecé casts over the Argentine book market is remarkable. A quick perusal of the *Catálogo general perpetuo* reveals twenty-five collections or series of works, each focusing on a specific aspect of the written word. Ranging from scientific manuals to contemporary crime novels, Emecé's output is exhaustive and points to both the firm's immediate saturation of the market from an early moment and to its uncanny ability to maintain this key position for many years. As I have shown, Borges's behind-the-scenes position at Emecé must also be considered in tandem with these successes since he created a number of profitable series and unique promotional framing for this firm.

The Spanish exile Gonzalo Losada founded Editorial Losada in Buenos Aires on August 18, 1938. Much like the founding members of other *porteño* publishing firms from this period, Losada had previously worked in the Spanish book industry—for a paper mill in Spain, which might account for his interests in the physical form and composition of the book. When he arrived in Argentina, he started working as a director for Espasa-Calpe's branch in Buenos Aires and soon after came up with the idea for its Colección Austral, which was "el primer intento de libros de bolsillo—los pockets—realizado en tierras sudamericanas" [the first attempt at small-format books—the pockets—made in South American lands], thus showing his understanding of book market needs and novelties.[86] Following the Spanish Civil War, Espasa-Calpe expressed its strong support of Francisco Franco by imposing certain kinds of censorship, and as a result Losada, along with some of his colleagues at Espasa-Calpe, including Guillermo de Torre, who was in charge of its Colección Austral, banded together to start a new publishing house. Attilio Rossi, Amado Alonso, and Pedro Henríquez Ureña also joined forces with Losada and de Torre as original members of Editorial Losada.[87] Over the years, a number of exiled Spaniards not only worked at this publishing house, but also had their writings published by it.[88] In fact, many of the Spanish works that Editorial Losada published during the 1930s and the 1940s had been banned or censored in Spain, especially those of Federico García Lorca. Thus, one of the defining characteristics of Gonzalo Losada, and of the publishing house that carries his name, is that of independence.

Losada always showed a certain affinity for the material aspects of his books, which explains his tendency to "[conservar] en su escritorio instrumentos para medir la calidad y el gramaje del papel" [conserve tools for measuring the quality and weight of paper in his desk].[89] The fact that Attilio Rossi was the design director for many of the firm's works during this time also speaks to their high aesthetic qualities.[90] Losada's particular interest in the physical features of the book emerges prominently in his writings for *Papel, Libro, Revista*. Most notably, his piece titled "Los problemas del libro" [The Problems of the Book] cites the shortage of paper and other sociocultural problems preventing the diffusion of the book:

> Creo que los grandes obstáculos que los editores tendremos que salvar habrán de influir mucho en la calidad de los libros pues no será posible invertir tiempo y materiales preciosos en la publicación de obras innecesarias o de mediana calidad, de suerte que lo que por una parte pierda el libro en su presentación material al tener que emplear para su confección papel y telas inferiores tanto por la carencia de clases finas como para poder mantener precios razonables, se ganará con la mejor calidad literaria, científica, etc., del conjunto de la producción editorial.

> [I think that the greatest obstacles that we publishers have to overcome will have a large impact on the quality of books since it is impossible to invest time and precious materials into the publication of unnecessary works or of works of poor quality, so that what a book loses in material presentation in order to account for the cost of paper and binding materials, and in order to maintain reasonable prices, will be made up for with the best literary quality, scientific quality, etc., in all of the publishing industry.][91]

Losada builds off of these ideas a few years later and advocates for the professionalization of editors in light of the fact that "ser editor en nuestro tiempo es sumamente difícil, pues exige amor al libro, una cultura general amplia y siempre ágil y despierta, conocimientos industriales y comerciales, gran probidad y un sentido de responsabilidad a toda prueba" [being a publisher in our day is extremely difficult, since it demands a love of the book, a very wide range of general culture, always agile and alert, industrial and commercial knowledge, immense integrity, and a sense of responsibility above all].[92] These deep-seated concerns for the entire book shine through in virtually all of Editorial Losada's published works.

Borges provided Editorial Losada with translations and prologues as well as two original works. While Guillermo de Torre's central role in the foundation and day-to-day operations of Editorial Losada might explain the noticeable presence of Borges, who was, after all, de Torre's brother-in-law, it seems highly unlikely that this correlation is the only reason that the firm published his prologues, translations, and original pieces. The only work that Borges translated for Editorial Losada, Kafka's *La metamorfosis,* is the first book in the Pajarita de Papel series, directed by de Torre (see Chapter 3).[93] Echoing the prologues for the Biblioteca Emecé, the opening text for *La metamorfosis* resembles the style that Borges adopted for his many literary reviews throughout the 1930s. In particular, we find a snapshot of Kafka's life and upbringing followed almost immediately by the two central themes in all of his works: "La subordinación es la primera de las dos; el infinito, la segunda" [Subordination is the first of the two; the infinite, the second].[94] From here Borges moves through some concrete examples from Kafka's writings and then briefly describes a few critical approaches to his works and the lasting effects of his prose. Sprinkled throughout this prologue are references to some of Borges's favorite philosophical topics, including Zeno's paradox, which is the subject of his early essay "La perpetua carrera de Aquiles y la tortuga" [The Paradox of Achilles and the Tortoise]. Such allusions elevate this prologue and equate it with any one of the writer's critical essays, which reinforces the claim that the prologue, for Borges, might take on various forms or shapes but all in all is just another form of writing.

With the exception of *La metamorfosis,* Borges's prologues for Editorial Losada are quite different from those that he wrote for Emecé.

More precisely, the two other prologues that he writes are for works authored by his close friends rather than for works by foreign authors whom he may have never met: Adolfo Bioy Casares's *La invención de Morel* [*The Invention of Morel*] (1940) and Attilio Rossi's *Buenos Aires en tinta china* [*Buenos Aires in Indian Ink*] (1951).⁹⁵ As we have seen, Borges and Bioy Casares were intimate friends.⁹⁶ Rossi, an Italian exile who lived in Argentina for nearly twenty years, is most known for his artistic affinities. Both a painter and a designer, he first worked for Espasa-Calpe in Buenos Aires as its graphic designer, creating the logo for the Colección Austral; and, with Losada and de Torre, he helped start Editorial Losada, for which he also designed the logo. The "Quién es quién" [Who's Who] section of *Papel, Libro, Revista* notes that

> su trabajo en la editorial Espasa-Calpe marca el comienzo de una nueva ruta para la industria editorial argentina. En efecto, crea, con la Colección Austral, la posibilidad de hacer libros al alcance de todos. Rossi declara que si bien esta modalidad tenía ya su precedente—los Penguin Books—en la Argentina era nueva, pues no se había llegado a la industrialización del libro.
>
> [his work for Espasa-Calpe marks the start of a new route for the Argentine publishing industry. In effect, he created, with the Colección Austral, the possibility of making books that were available to all people. Rossi declared that this modality already had its precedents—the Penguin Books—but it was new in Argentina, since the country had not yet arrived at the industrialization of the book.]⁹⁷

Rossi ultimately hopes that his artistic tendencies will help distinguish the Argentine book from the North American book and furthermore make it even greater than the European book. His unique artistic flourishes can easily be identified in Losada's Pajarita de Papel series (see Chapter 3). He also contributed his expertise to Ocampo's literary journal *Sur*, as Borges fondly remembers.⁹⁸ Similar to Borges's own involvement with numerous publishing houses and literary journals during this time, Rossi was immersed in all aspects of publishing, from editing to design.[99] Most notable is his aspiration to create the "libro de máquina perfecto para leer" [perfectly readable machine-produced book] that would surpass both the North American and European models.

Another common link between these two prologues that Borges wrote for Editorial Losada is the fact that neither includes any biographical information about Bioy Casares or Rossi. Borges's intimate relationships with each of these men might account for such an absence. Moreover, there is a greater level of praise for each work in these prologues, in comparison with what we saw in earlier prologues Borges wrote for Emecé. Thus, in his opening text for *La invención de Morel,* which Editorial Sur republished in 1948, Borges confidently describes this work as perfect: "He discutido con su autor los pormenores de su trama, la he releído; no me parece una imprecisión o una hipérbole calificarla de perfecta" [I discussed the details of the plot with the author, I have reread it; it doesn't seem imprecise or hyperbolic to describe it as perfect].[100] The main basis for such high regard stems from Bioy Casares's ability to negate Borges's claim, with great success, that the psychological novel is superior to a work of pure action. In addition, Borges lauds his friend for resuscitating the age-old concept akin to déjà vu that Saint Augustine first introduced: "Bástame declarar que Bioy renueva literariamente un concepto que San Agustín y Orígenes refutaron, que Louis Auguste Blanqui razonó y que dijo con música memorable Dante Gabriel Rossetti" [It's enough for me to say that Bioy literarily renews a concept that Saint Augustine and Origen refuted, that Louis Auguste Blanqui reasoned, and that Dante Gabriel Rossetti stated with memorable music].[101] In other words, as Borges concludes at the close of his prologue, Bioy Casares has, with this work, "[trasladó] a nuestra tierra y a nuestro idioma un género nuevo" [brought a new genre to our country and our language].[102]

This same idea of resuscitation and novelty resonates throughout Borges's prologue for Rossi's *Buenos Aires en tinta china*:

> En algún tiempo, el concepto de paisajes urbanos debe haber sido paradójico; no sé quién lo introdujo en las artes plásticas; fuera de algún ejercicio satírico . . . , su aparición en la litera-

tura, que yo recuerde, no es anterior a Dickens ... Este libro evidencia la felicidad con que Rossi cultiva tal género.

[At some moment in time, the concept of the urban countryside must have seemed paradoxical; I don't know who introduced it into the plastic arts; outside of some satirical exercise ..., its appearance in literature, that I remember, is not prior to Dickens ... This book demonstrates the happiness with which Rossi cultivates the genre.][103]

Much like his praises for Bioy Casares's prose, Borges celebrates the sheer artistry of Rossi's drawings: "déjese de bobadas en que cambiar el proscenio por sus dibujos, que son por lo demás mejores que aquél" [stop with the nonsense about changing the proscenium for your drawings, which are certainly better than that thing].[104] Moreover, we discover that Rossi himself had asked Borges to write the prologue to his book: "venga a mi vivienda sobre la calle Maipú 944. Allí me encontrará por la tarde y conversaremos sobre su prólogo ... Lo haré con gusto" [come to my house on Maipú Street 944. You will find me there in the afternoon and we can talk about your prologue ... I will write it with pleasure].[105] Although it is difficult to discern whether the practice of asking a friend, or a well-known writer, to compose the prologue for a work would have been normal or routine in Argentina during this time, the close connection between Rossi and Borges, in addition to their continued involvement with publishing, is more than likely the cause.

In terms of the physical features of these works, there is a shift from what we saw with Editorial Sur and Emecé to include more hand-drawn illustrations on the covers. In light of the fact that Bioy Casares was very close to Borges, it is only fitting that Borges's sister, Norah Borges de Torre, created the dust jacket and cover designs for *La invención de Morel*. Both original illustrations touch on elements from the plot of Bioy Casares's novel. The dust jacket depicts a map of the deserted island where the novel takes place, and the cover presents a portrait of a woman in profile, which alludes to the protagonist's love interest, Faustine. Both of these drawings serve as yet another type of promotional framing for the book. Rossi was responsible for the design and execution of his own cover illustrations. Much like the ink drawings that we find throughout *Buenos Aires en tinta china,* Rossi has included two illustrations of Buenos Aires street scenes on the dust jacket: a neighborhood scene on the front and a sketch of the iconic obelisk of Buenos Aires on the back. The white cover of the book depicts an ornate door knocker in gold. Even though both of these works are quite distinctive with regard to their illustrations, the presence of drawings that in these two cases relate to the content of the works marks a new tendency in this sphere of Argentine publishing. This artistic element will permeate all of the works discussed here, including the original works by Borges, which makes the production of Editorial Losada all the more striking.

In addition to its use of illustrations, Editorial Losada stands out among other publishing houses in the Argentine book market for being another exclusive distributor of the works of Editorial Sur. The perspectives and experiences of the founding members of Editorial Losada—especially those of Rossi, with his desire to reinvent the Argentine book so that it would stand out from the types of works produced in the United States and throughout Europe—might explain the choice of this publishing house to distribute Editorial Sur's works. The physical evidence linking the two firms can be found on the books themselves and throughout a number of the literary journal *Sur*'s advertisements for its publishing house's newest releases that list a specific distributor.[106] In light of the fact that *Sur* was available to readers on a subscription basis, it seems peculiar that Ocampo would not use a similar system for the books produced by her publishing house. Again, if the sole function of Editorial Sur was to support the running costs of the literary magazine of the same name, why limit the avenues of distribution? Regardless of Ocampo's reasoning, these material traces confirm the fact that she relied on specific modes of promotion for the circulation of her publications.[107] In terms of Editorial Losada and its central role in this network, we see the visual elements of its publications standing out from those of its competitors. What is more, the countless years of combined experience that its founding members share, both inside and outside of Argentina, suggest a deep-seated understanding of the ins and outs of the book industry. The combination of these two strengths, visual appeal and knowledge of the market, reinforce

Editorial Sur's logical choice of Editorial Losada as its authorized distributor for a number of years.

Another common trend that we see throughout the late 1930s and early 1940s in the Argentine publishing industry is the movement of employees from one firm to another. With the explosion of the book market during this time, editors and artists would often branch off from one publishing house to work at another or, even more frequently, start their own firm, as we saw with Editorial Losada. Another such case is that of Editorial Nova, founded in 1942 by two former employees of Emecé, Luis Seoane and Arturo Cuadrado. Upon discovering the broad diversification of Emecé's publications and the marked shift from its original interest in the production and distribution of solely Galician works, Seoane, a native of Buenos Aires, and Cuadrado, a native of Galicia, hoped that their Editorial Nova would "mantener viva la actividad cultural previa al estallido de la Guerra Civil existente en Galicia y en España" [keep the cultural activity alive that existed in Galicia and Spain before the outbreak of the (Spanish) Civil War].[108] Even though Seoane was born in Buenos Aires, his parents were exiles from Galicia and he spent much of his youth in La Coruña, which accounts for his avid interest in the preservation of Spanish culture. Both men had a significant amount of experience in the publishing industry—Cuadrado having worked for a variety of firms and several newspapers throughout Spain and Seoane boasting experience as an editor, artist, and typographer—which allowed them to enter the Argentine market quite easily. They also gained insight from their time at Emecé:

> Seoane y Cuadrado se desempeñarán en diferentes tareas, desde la lectura previa y selección de obras, el trabajo directo con la imprenta, la corrección de pruebas, e incluso la distribución. Además, el propio Seoane se encarga de cuidar el diseño y la diagramación de los libros hasta 1942, y las ilustraciones de algunos de ellos.
>
> [Seoane and Cuadrado performed different tasks, from reading and selecting texts, working directly with the printer, correcting galley proofs, and even distribution. Also, Seoane was

in charge of watching over the design and layout of books until 1942, as well as the illustrations of some of them].[109]

Along with these daily jobs, Seoane and Cuadrado were also responsible for the two main collections of Galician literature at Emecé: the Colección Dorna and the Colección Hórreo. They controlled virtually all aspects involved in the production and publication of works within these collections, from the typographic design to the endpaper selection.

The fact that Seoane and Cuadrado had worked previously for Emecé explains certain overlaps between the two firms, such as the common use of Imprenta López, which would be a founding partner of Editorial Nova and responsible for printing every work produced by this latter publishing house.[110] More striking is the level of similarity, in terms of both content and physical form, between Emecé's Colección Buen Aire and Editorial Nova's Colección Mar Dulce [Collection Sweet Sea], which is not surprising since Seoane and Cuadrado were responsible for both collections. In terms of content, both collections focus on a historic past: the Colección Buen Aire centers on that of Argentina, while the Colección Mar Dulce centers on that of America more broadly. In terms of form, the visual similarities between these two collections are striking. Along with the common use of a cover illustration related to the work in question, both collections present their works in a small hardcover format with comparable serif typography for the titles and the names of the series.[111] Inspection of the title pages of various works in these two collections reveals that each series made use of a drawing above the name of the collection as a type of branding. Even though each of these illustrations is unique and related to the collection that it represents, the style of the two drawings, in terms of their fluid lines and almost ethereal qualities, is very similar, not to mention the fact that both of these drawings depict mythic creatures: a figure inspired by the classical god of the wind for one and a mermaid for the other.

Another link between the Colección Buen Aire and the Colección Mar Dulce—albeit more tangential—is the presence of at least one prologue by Borges in each collection. He provided the prologue for *El compadrito* in Emecé's Colección Buen Aire, as we saw in Chapter 4, and one year later he composed a prologue for Estanislao del Campo's *Fausto*

(1946), which formed part of Editorial Nova's Colección Mar Dulce. Similar to his efforts in describing the important, often understudied, figure of the *compadre* in his previous collection for Emecé, Borges's prologue for *Fausto* immediately takes a defensive position, emphasizing the crucial role of local color and traditions. He positions himself against Rafael Hernández and Leopoldo Lugones, who had denounced del Campo for his ignorance and falseness, specifically with regard to his forced (unnatural) use of *criollo* language. While Borges cannot deny the linguistic oddities in del Campo's work, he focuses on the pleasure that these verses give him—and any other reader—as the most important aspect in play:

> lo que tal vez nos acompañará en la otra vida, es el placer que da la contemplación de la felicidad y de la amistad. Ese placer, quizá no menos raro en las letras que en la realidad corporal, es (lo sospecho) la virtud central del poema.
>
> [perhaps that which accompanies us into the next life is the contemplation of happiness and friendship. That pleasure, which is no less rare in words than in physical reality, is (I suspect) the central virtue of the poem.][112]

The physical features of this work serve to enhance the pleasure of reading it. More specifically, at the start of each section is an original illustration by Seoane, boldly printed in red, and the elegant serif typeface of the text is centered, leaving a large amount of marginal space. The contrasting red and black inks, the wide margins, and even the subject matter of the work (an epic of sorts) put this work in dialogue with medieval bookmaking traditions.

Following the initial establishment of Editorial Nova in 1942, Seoane and Cuadrado founded a second publishing firm in 1946: Ediciones Botella al Mar. Similar to their earlier publishing ventures with Editorial Nova, two works in the Ediciones Botella al Mar collections include a prologue by Borges—Ema Risso Platero's *Arquitecturas del insomnio* [*Architectures of Insomnia*] (1948) and William Shand's *Ferment* (1950). Subtitled "Cuentos fantásticos" [Fantastic Stories], Risso Platero's book contains nine short stories, all of which present themes, symbols, and concepts that can be linked to critical studies of dreams and the supernatural. Throughout the pages of these short stories are a series of Seoane's original—slightly spooky and jarring—illustrations. Borges's prologue opens by situating this work within the larger genre of fantastic literature and then provides readers with a succinct one-line analysis of each story—focusing predominately on Risso Platero's potential literary influences. For instance, Borges notes how "Presencias del silencio" [Presences of Silence] resonates with the work of Henry James and Poe for the prominence of "el mágico tema del *doppelgänger*" [the magical theme of the *doppelganger*], while her "El próximo testamento" [Next Testament] recalls many of Seneca's premonitions about the end of the world.[113] All of these allusions that Borges points out allow him to situation Risso Platero's work within the larger literary genre of the fantastic. Moreover, we see in his prologue his subtle nod to the importance of the form of the book as well: "Cada libro es un orbe ideal, pero suele agradarnos que el autor lo confunda con el universo común e incluya en su ámbito hechos que es tradicional ignorar: verbigracia, la existencia del propio libro" [Every book is an ideal world, but it tends to please us that the author confuses it with the common universe and includes in its sphere things that are normally ignored: for example, the existence of the book itself].[114]

In addition to the framing of Borges's prologue, Risso Platero's *Arquitecturas del insomnio* presents the following phrase printed on the back cover of the first edition, which further links Editorial Nova and Ediciones Botella al Mar: "Concesionario exclusivo para la venta EDITORIAL NOVA" [Exclusive authorized dealer for sale EDITORIAL NOVA]. This statement brings to mind Editorial Sur's exclusive sales with several *porteño* publishing firms such as Editorial Losada and Editorial Sudamericana. Curiously, around the same time that Seoane and Cuadrado founded Ediciones Botella al Mar, Editorial Sur begins to cite a new exclusive vendor for its works: Editorial Nova. A quick perusal of the June 1947 issue of *Sur* reveals several advertisements for available or forthcoming editions from Editorial Sur through its "distribuidor exclusivo [exclusive distributor]: EDITORIAL NOVA, Perú 613, Buenos Aires." The fact that Imprenta López was a founding partner of Editorial Nova and also one of the main printers for the large majority of the issues of Ocampo's literary journal, as well as the books produced by her publishing house, might account for this shift. The proximity of Editorial Nova (Perú 613) to the offices of Imprenta López (Perú 666), and the convenience that presumably would entail, might be another reason for the change.

William Shand's *Ferment* presents us with many of the same framing elements that we saw in Risso Platero's work. First, we find an original drawing—a portrait of the author—by Seoane in the opening pages of the book. Moreover, the cover of *Ferment* showcases Seoane's artistic talent and eye for design. Echoing part of the title of the publishing firm—Ediciones Botella al Mar—Seoane adorns this cover with a turquoise boat amidst a swirling sea of the same color. In terms of textual framing, Borges's prologue for Shand's work has a similar structure to the opening words that he penned for Risso Platero's work.[115] At the start of his "Foreword" for Shand's *Ferment*, Borges immediately places the Anglo-Argentine poet's work alongside that of other foundational poets, including William Butler Yeats and T. S. Eliot. Borges aptly puts Shand's work in dialogue with that of these poets for his focus on "el tedio, el horror y la gloria" [tedium, horror, and glory].[116] Thus, even though Shand's work is a collection of poems and Risso Platero's is a series of fantastic short stories, both of the prologues that Borges writes for these books situate them within historical literary trends. Throughout his prologue for *Ferment*, Borges also foregrounds the importance of poetry for this moment in the twentieth century and in the process highly praises Shand for his valuable contributions. At the same time, Borges alerts readers to the fact that this work—much like any published book—is a selection: "todo libro propone una selección. No sé qué piezas preferirá el porvenir de las congregadas en éste" [every book puts forth a selection. I don't know which parts of those that are gathered here the future [reader] will prefer].[117] Borges hints at the fact that if Shand's work had been published with a different firm, or in a different country, or at a different moment in time, it could have looked physically different, and it could have contained different texts. This idea runs throughout each of the prologues that I have analyzed here, as well as throughout any other framing device or element in a published book. It is the foundational idea that all of these objects are both *about* a variety of literary texts and produced by a variety of individuals at a specific moment and place. As a result, choices

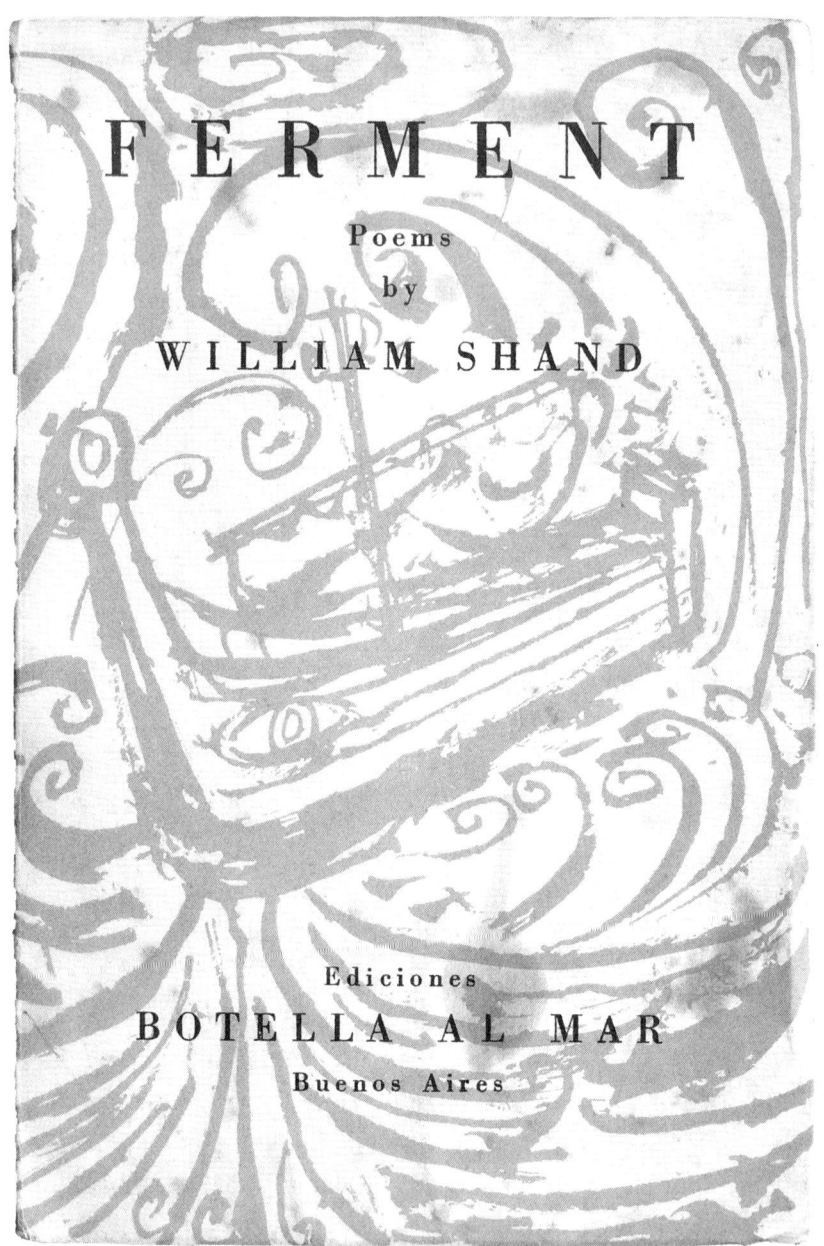

Cover of William Shand's *Ferment* (Ediciones Botella al Mar, 1950). *(Collection of the author.)*

will be made and errors may be introduced—by many different hands—which highlights the need for us to consider and analyze all elements of any given physical book—including all of the paratextual elements that we have seen here—for the clues that they provide about the object's production and circulation.

Reframing and Rebranding Borges's Creative Fictions

Any analysis of Borges's editorial or literary contributions to all of these Argentine publishing firms would be incomplete without a discussion of the illustrious collections of prose and poetry that he published with them during this period. First are his two most iconic works—*El jardín de senderos que se bifurcan* [*The Garden of Forking Paths*] (1941) and *Ficciones* (1944)—both published with Editorial Sur. Even though Borges was crafting and publishing short stories for a myriad of journals and newspapers with a certain level of regularity throughout the 1930s, *El jardín de senderos que se bifurcan* is one of the first book-length compilations of such writings.[118] From the advertising band that originally adorned this book, readers learn about its contents as a way of drawing them in: "Una muerte simbólica, una biblioteca infinita, una lotería implacable, un libro que abolirá la realidad" [A symbolic death, an infinite library, a relentless lottery, a book that abolishes reality]. Even though virtually all of Editorial Sur's works had similar bands, this one has a much more seductive and mysterious feel to it. For instance, compare it with the advertising band for Michaux's *Un bárbaro en Asia* (1941): "El libro más concreto, más vivido, a veces más cínico, sobre el Asia" [The most concrete, most vivid, and at times most cynical book about Asia]. These words are much more direct and provide readers with a clearer idea of what the book is about. We find similar cases with Victoria Ocampo's translation of Woolf's *Tres guineas* [*Three Guineas*] (1941), "Un libro constructivo y seductor. Todos los hombres conscientes deben leerlo; y no solo leerlo, sino estudiarlo, todas las mujeres responsables que tengan algún deseo de ayudar a la humanidad" [A constructive and seductive book. All conscious men should read it, and not just read it, but study it, [as well as] all responsible women who have any desire to help humanity], and even H. G. Wells's *El destino del homo sapiens* [*The Fate of Homo Sapiens*] (1941), "Los orígenes de la guerra actual. Juicio magistral sobre el nazismo, el comunismo y la democracia" [The origins of today's war. Flawless judgment about Nazism, communism, and democracy].[119] There is something much more poetic and enchanting about the advertising band for *El jardín de senderos que se bifurcan*, and much like the ways in which Borges described these promotional accouterments, it successfully helps draw the reader into the work.[120]

When we turn to *Ficciones*, published three years later by Editorial Sur, there is a marked shift from the lyrical and seductive quality of the language used on the advertising band to one of authorial promotion: "El público culto de America [sic] aguarda desde hace muchos años este libro: ¡Todos los cuentos de Borges reunidos en un solo volumen! Hondura, brillo, emoción, sabiduría, gracia. Una inteligencia proverbial. Un estilo perfecto" [The learned public of America will treasure this book for years to come: All of Borges's stories gathered in one volume! Depth, brilliance, emotion, knowledge, grace. A proverbial intelligence. A perfect style].[121] Of particular note is the identification of a specific type of reader, an educated or learned one, who has been anticipating the publication of this work for many years, which further stresses the link between Editorial Sur's (literary) production and an elite audience. We also see a subtle nod to the idea of rebranding and reframing on this band—"¡Todos los cuentos de Borges reunidos en un solo volumen!" [All of Borges's stories gathered in one volume!]—which is echoed by the contents of the collection itself since all of the short stories have been previously published elsewhere.[122] Another intriguing feature of the advertising band that adorns Borges's *Ficciones* is the fact that it changes within a few months after its first release in 1944. By June 1945, the text on this band reads, "Gran Premio de Honor de la Sociedad de Escritores" [Grand Prize of Honor from the Society of Writers]. The fact that Borges was the first recipient of this prize, a prize that was maybe unknown to readers at the time, might account for the need to highlight such a distinction.[123] Even with this change, which not only emphasizes Borges's importance, but also required the production of a new band for the book, the book's price did not change ($4 Argentine pesos). Thus, even though *Ficciones* is intended for a markedly elite audience, it is no more costly than most other editions produced by Editorial Sur during the 1940s. What is more,

Ficciones does not appear to have sold as well as other works, such as Albert Camus's *La Peste* [*The Plague*] (1948), which not only sold out and went through multiple editions, but also increased in price with each new edition.[124] This example highlights the fact that there is not yet an interest in Borges's works or a following of readers, whether of the middle, lower, or upper class.

Similar to his personal publications with Editorial Sur and Emecé, Borges also produced two original works with Editorial Losada: *Poemas (1922-1943)* (1943) and *El Aleph* (1949). Forming part of the firm's Poetas de España y América (Poets from Spain and America) series, directed by Amado Alonso and Guillermo de Torre, *Poemas* presented readers with a complete volume of virtually all of Borges's previously published poetry. This new volume provided a unique opportunity for interested readers since many of Borges's earlier poetry collections were very difficult to find, not to mention the fact that he was frequently critical of them. Along with a few new poems, *Poemas* consisted of the poems included in his *Fervor de Buenos Aires* (1923), *Luna de enfrente* (1925), and *Cuaderno San Martín* (1929).[125] That said, all of the earlier collections found in Editorial Losada's edition of *Poemas* reflect Borges's common tendency to edit, emend, and delete. For instance, several poems have been eliminated from *Fervor de Buenos Aires*: "Música patria" [Homeland Music], "Ciudad" [City], "Hallazgo" [Discovery], "Dictamen" [Judgment], "Alba desdibujada" [Indistinct Dawn], "Llamarada" [Outburst] "Cercanías" [Vicinities], and "Caña de ámbar" [White Ginger Lily]. What is more, certain titles have been changed, and much of the poetry has been edited.[126] This tendency toward republication—and what I consider a type of reframing and rebranding—carries over to Borges's creative fictions in *El Aleph*. Of the thirteen short stories included in the first edition, ten previously appeared in the literary journals *Sur* or *Los Anales de Buenos Aires*.[127]

Alongside the reframed and rebranded contents of both *Poemas* and *El Aleph* are the unique cover illustrations, both by Rossi.[128] As we saw with the two Editorial Losada works for which Borges wrote the prologues, the inclusion of eye-catching cover illustrations set their publications apart from those of most other Argentine firms. In fact, Losada praises the positive effects that these designs had on their overall sales

Cover of Jorge Luis Borges's *Poemas (1922–1943)* (Editorial Losada, 1943). *(Reproduced from the Albert and Shirley Small Special Collections Library, University of Virginia.)*

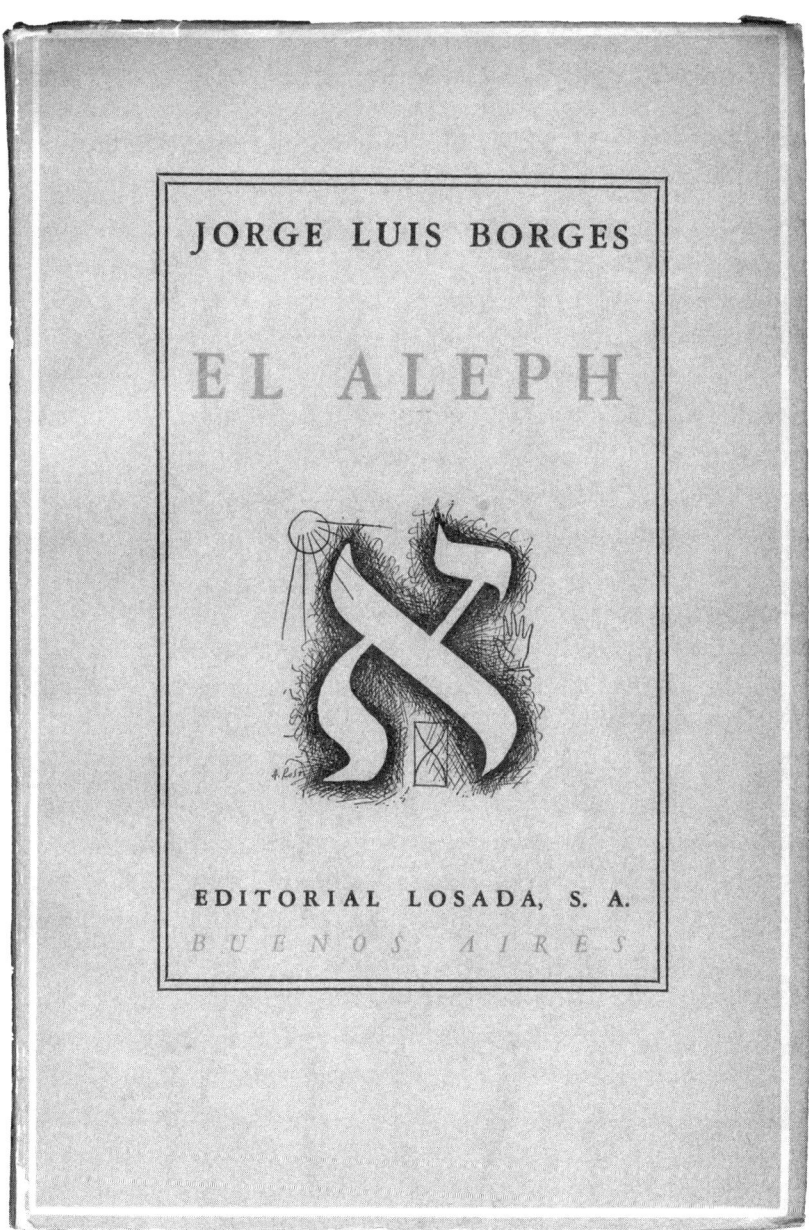

Cover of Jorge Luis Borges's *El Aleph* (Editorial Losada, 1949). *(Reproduced from the Albert and Shirley Small Special Collections Library, University of Virginia.)*

and reception, focusing on the series of which *El Aleph* is a part: "La gran revolución que nuestra casa provocó en el medio editorial ... fueron las tapas que Attilio Rossi dibujó para la colección Novelistas, de España y América" [The large revolution that our firm provoked in the realm of publishing ... were the covers that Attilio Rossi drew for the series Novelists, from Spain and America].[129] Although the typefaces and use of colors on each cover are similar, the images are distinct, which speaks to the different topics of each work. The somewhat cryptic cherub depicted on the cover of *Poemas,* who is chiseling away at a polygon in an open field and opaquely covered by a cobweb, might represent the almost unearthly experience of composing poetry. The illustration on the cover of *El Aleph* is much more straightforward since it shows an aleph, the first letter of the Hebrew alphabet. As a result, this image speaks to both the collection as a whole and its last story, "El Aleph," where this figure represents not just a letter, but also a single point in the world where the protagonist (or any other person) can see the entirety of the universe all at once. In essence, both of these illustrations encapsulate key aspects of the works that they adorn and therefore serve a purpose beyond simple visual appeal.

Borges also published a collection of short stories in 1951 with Emecé: *La muerte y la brújula* [*Death and the Compass*]. While this collection is certainly important for the history of Emecé and Borges's relationship with this publishing house, its contents are a variation on the theme of rebranding and reframing. That is to say, the short stories that make up *La muerte y la brújula* are from previously published collections: *Historia universal de la infamia, Ficciones,* and *El Aleph,* as well as the Argentine newspaper *La Nación.* Like *El jardín de senderos que se bifurcan* and *El Aleph, La muerte y la brújula* draws its name from the last piece included in the collection. One of the aspects that sets this edition apart from the previously published collections, aside from its price, is the elaborate color illustration by Friedrich (Fritz) Schonbach, which depicts a figure approaching an ornate mansion.[130] This unique artistic detail reminds us that Emecé was known for the quality and diversity of its products. It is also quite possible that the firm wished to distance its books from those of its competitors and as a result ensured that its edition of Borges's short stories was unique and eye-catching. In short, I argue that the analysis of Borges's framing devices for books by both foreign and local authors must also carry over to the creative fictions that he published with Editorial Sur, Editorial Losada, and Emecé. While three of these collections—*El jardín de senderos que se bifurcan*, *Poemas (1922–1943)*, and *El Aleph*—include a few new short stories or poems, these additions are overshadowed by Borges's trend toward recycling and rebranding his previously published work.[131]

Through an examination of Borges's translations, prologues, and creative fictions from this period, we have seen the enormous impact of elite publishers and their high levels of interconnectedness in the Argentine book market. In particular, the impressive efforts of Victoria Ocampo with her literary journal *Sur* and publishing house of the same name paved the way for the circulation and distribution of important works by foreign authors. As a part of the original editorial board for Editorial Sur, Borges was much involved in this process of cultural dissemination through his own translations, which were modes of promotion for certain types of literature. Even though he did not write any prologues for the works published with Editorial Sur (nor did many of that firm's works include prologues), he did write a large number of introductory pieces for Emecé and Editorial Losada, which highlights his affinity for promoting the work of other authors, for helping to establish an awareness among readers of literary trends, and for encouraging a local culture based on a literary sensitivity. Much like the type of prologue that he describes in his final notes for the *Antología de la moderna poesía uruguaya* that opens this chapter, Borges's prologues almost always promote and advocate for the work in question, which is a method of extending the enticing presentations of bookstore windows and the various pieces of advertising that might adorn these same books. Borges's almost fanatical interest in editing and helping to produce books from behind the scenes is complemented by his framing techniques of writing prologues or prefaces (and, in the case of Editorial Sur, producing translations), which can be equated with a kind of storefront adornment for interested readers. In essence, all aspects of the book matter for Borges.

S • I • X

Borges as Publisher

Borges's interest in the physical book culminates in the formation of two publishing houses with his close friend Adolfo Bioy Casares: Editorial Destiempo and Editorial Oportet & Haereses. As we have seen, Borges was involved with the publishing industry at various levels (editor, codirector of literary magazines, copy editor, translator, prologuist, author), but creating and running a publishing house is quite different from helping with one aspect of book production. As Michael Winship writes, and as pointed out in the Introduction to the present book, "the publisher is the entrepreneur of the book trade, making the decisions that bring together all the other activities and arranging for the coordination and credit."[1] In short, establishing and running a publishing house requires a new level of interaction with the book from start to finish and also the cultivation of relationships with other players in the industry such as printers and booksellers.

While these firms were not comparable to, or even as real as, others we have seen, they demonstrate Borges's ties to the entire process of book production in Argentina. Moreover, these almost secretive editorial endeavors stress the attention placed on all aspects of Argentine culture by a series of military coups in the early 1940s that ended with Juan Perón's rise to power in 1946. Perón's censorship mainly focused on popular modes of media transmission—newspaper, movies, and radio—but its looming presence throughout Argentina affected virtually all types of cultural production. In an effort to explore this idea in greater detail, I analyze the formation of each of Borges and Bioy Casares's publishing houses, the works that these firms produced—in terms of both their form and their content—and how their creations serve as the pinnacle of the two writers' critique of Argentine culture and methods of education.

Editorial Destiempo

As we saw in Chapter 3, Borges and Bioy Casares's first collaborative foray into the world of publishing came in the form of their short-lived literary magazine *Destiempo*, which lasted for a mere three issues between 1936 and early 1937. A small announcement in the third and final installment of *Destiempo* introduced their *porteño* readers to a series of books that would soon be available for their reading pleasure. Each of these works was to be published by a newly minted firm, Editorial Destiempo, and available through subscription.[2] Much resembling the somewhat spontaneous formation of Ocampo's Editorial Sur in 1933, Editorial Destiempo emerges unexpectedly with an advertisement in the last issue of *Destiempo* for six unique works, one of which had already appeared (Ulyses Petit de Murat's *Marea de lágrimas* [*Tide of Tears*]), which highlights the overlap between the creation of the publishing house and the last issue of the literary magazine.[3] Even though the literary journal *Destiempo* ceased production abruptly after its third issue, the works published by Editorial Destiempo cannot be seen as a simple side project with the goal of funding the literary journal of the same name. Moreover, neither of the two Argentine writers' names appears to be attached to this new publishing firm. Instead, interested parties are instructed to mail their subscriptions to "Ernesto Pissavini, secretario de la EDITORIAL DESTIEMPO Avenida QUINTANA 174 Buenos Aires." Curiously, Pissavini worked for Bioy Casares's family, and the Quintana address listed was that of Bioy Casares's parents. According to Sabsay-Herrera:

> Ernesto Pissavini no tenía antes de la creación de *Destiempo*, ni tendrá luego de la desaparición de la revista, ninguna relación con el medio literario argentino. Ya en este hecho se

puede vislumbrar sin duda una de las vetas que marcará la producción de Borges-Bioy: el único nombre que aparece como responsable de *Destiempo* tiene una existencia real ... pero su función en la publicación es una invención de los verdaderos directores de la revista, que logran de esta manera que ficción y realidad se confundan.

[Ernesto Pissavini did not have before the creation of *Destiempo,* nor will he have after the disappearance of the magazine, any relation with Argentine literature. In this fact we can see without a doubt one of the hallmarks of Borges and Bioy's productions: the only name that appears as responsible for the publication of *Destiempo* has a real existence ... but its function in the publication is an invention of the true directors of the magazine, who thus achieve a mixing of fiction and reality.]⁴

Thus, Borges and Bioy Casares's own publishing house is just as fun and playful as many of their collaborative fictions that appear in print under any number of inventive pseudonyms. As a result, a clear level of humor is present in their joint literary efforts, from the initial moment of creative inspiration to the final stages of production and distribution, which resonates with the first advertisement for Editorial Destiempo's publications.

Scanning the list of authors for the slated works in this advertisement reveals that these individuals are some of Borges and Bioy Casares's close friends and have appeared in a number of their previous publishing endeavors.⁵ Of the six works noted, only two come to fruition in the form of a physically published book: Ulyses Petit de Murat's *Marea de lágrimas* (1937) and Alfonso Reyes's *Mallarmé entre nosotros* [*Mallarmé among Us*] (1938); the remaining four works never appear in print. Even though Petit de Murat's collection of poems is the first advertised work, the first published book by Editorial Destiempo — and one that does not appear in the list at all — was authored by one of its two cofounders, Adolfo Bioy Casares, suggesting that the origins of this firm were very personal. In light of the fact that Bioy Casares and Borges published many of their own works in previous years without a unique publisher (in other words, they simply sent them to a printer), why would these two writers decide to invent a publishing house? This question, though certainly relevant for the other (apocryphal) publishing house discussed below, is particularly apt for Editorial Destiempo considering that multiple books by different authors appeared under the name of this firm, and not just works by Borges and Bioy Casares.

It is important to first consider the name of the firm and its unique insignia. "Destiempo," which translates literally as either "late" or "at the wrong or inopportune time," can be linked to Borges and Bioy Casares's mutual sentiments toward the perpetual onslaught of literary movements and trends during the early part of the twentieth century. In fact, Bioy Casares later recalls the choice of the name *Destiempo* for their literary magazine (and their later publishing firm of the same name) as arising from the two writers' frustration with contemporary traditions regarding the hierarchical importance of some literary works over others:

> El título indicaba nuestro anhelo de sustraernos a las supersticiones de la época. Objetábamos particularmente la tendencia de algunos críticos a pasar por alto el valor intrínseco de las obras y a demorarse en aspectos folklóricos y estadísticas sociológicas. Creíamos que los preciosos antecedentes de una escuela eran a veces tan dignos de olvido como las probables o inevitables trilogías sobre el gaucho, la modista de clase media, etc.

> [The title indicated our desire to distance ourselves from the superstitions of the time. We particularly objected to the tendency of critical scholars to overlook the intrinsic value of work and instead focus on aspects of folklore and sociological statistics. We believe that the precious antecedents of a school were often as forgettable as the probable or inevitable trilogies about the gaucho, the middle-class dressmaker, etc.][6]

Borges and Bioy Casares's marked level of discontent with certain standards of literary critique, and an irrational favoring of almost mythological lines of thought, lies at the heart of the foundation of both the literary magazine and the publishing house. In other words, aside from conveying a level of humor, the creation of this firm can be seen as satirizing and even mocking prevalent trends in their contemporary Argentine literary canons, which would make their firm literally "out of sync" with most trends.

A quick perusal of the physical features of each of the works published with Editorial Destiempo reveals an intriguing attempt to create a unique logo, or insignia, for the firm. Thus, the first work it produced, Bioy Casares's *Luis Greve, muerto* [*Luis Greve, Dead*] (1937), presents readers with an original drawing framed triangularly by the name of the firm. These triangulated words serve as a framing device for the original insignia of the publishing house, which resembles a flying fish, or a fish out of water, and as a result draw our attention to this odd figure.[7] This particular typographical formation disappears in subsequent publications, but the fishlike insignia remains a constant, along with the simplified word "DESTIEMPO" below it. Even though this illustrated logo is quite simple, its dreamlike, ethereal, and completely random quality echoes many historical avant-garde trends that can be found in the plastic arts associated with Modernism, Futurism, Surrealism, and even Dadaism and resonates with the firm's name.

Editorial Destiempo would publish six works over the course of seventeen years (Table 16). Bioy Casares's two works, which serve as bookends for the published works of the firm, are all fantastic stories, a fact which highlights the great influence that Borges had on this young Argentine writer. In fact, Borges himself reviews Bioy Casares's *Luis Greve, muerto* in the December 1937 issue of the literary journal *Sur* and praises him for bringing more fantastic literature to Argentine letters: "Nuestra literatura es muy pobre de relatos fantásticos. La facundia y la pereza criolla prefieren el informe 'tranche de vie' o la mera acumulación de ocurrencias. De ahí lo inusual de la obra de Bioy Casares" [Our literature is very lacking in fantastic tales. The glibness and laziness of our local narrators prefer the "slice of life" report or the mere accumulation of events. From there we can see the unusual quality of Bioy Casares's work].[8] In a sense, we can see this favorable review as a type of promotional strategy since, as one critic notes, these short stories are "flimsy

Original logo for Editorial Destiempo. *(Reproduced from a copy of Adolfo Bioy Casares's* Luis Greve, muerto *housed at Princeton University Library.)*

Table 16. Editorial Destiempo titles (1937–1954)

Adolfo Bioy Casares, *Luis Greve, muerto* (1937)
Ulyses Petit de Murat, *Marea de lágrimas* (1937)
Nicolás Olivari, *Diez poemas sin poesía* (con dibujos de Carybé) [*Ten Poems without Poetry* (with drawings by Carybé)] (1938) (not on the original subscription list)
Alfonso Reyes, *Mallarmé entre nosotros* (1938)
Antología de cuentos irreales [*Anthology of Unreal Stories*] (listed as forthcoming; ultimately unpublished)
Vicente Barbieri, *Cabeza yacente* [*Reclining Head*] (1945)
Adolfo Bioy Casares, *Homenaje a Francisco Almeyra* [*Homage to Francisco Almeyra*] (1954)

and clumsy."⁹ In general terms, *Luis Greve, muerto* is a collection of twenty-two short stories with "temas cada vez más irreales y peculiares" [increasingly unreal and peculiar subjects], while the other published bookend of Bioy Casares's, *Homenaje a Francisco Almeyra* [*Homage to Francisco Almeyra*] (1954), "es una alegoría de la suerte de los intelectuales bajo el régimen peronista" [is an allegory about the luck of intellectuals under the Peronist regime].¹⁰ The remaining works are either collections of poetry (Petit de Murat, Olivari, and Barbieri) or essays about poetry (Reyes). This unique combination of fantastic literature and poetry echoes the two anthologies that Borges and Bioy Casares would jointly edit in the early 1940s, the *Antología de la literatura fantástica* and the *Antología poética argentina*. In fact, I believe that the last book listed as forthcoming with Editorial Destiempo, *Antología de cuentos irreales* [*Anthology of Unreal Stories*], would actually develop into the *Antología de la literatura fantástica*. Moreover, the fact that this volume appears as a planned publication as early as 1937 suggests that its composition took Borges, Bioy Casares, and Ocampo more time to develop than initially supposed. As we saw in Chapter 4, Borges and Bioy Casares's editorial endeavors, whether for their own publishing firm or for another, continuously strive to promote underrepresented intellectual voices in literature that deserve to be part of the larger Argentine canon. In contrast, the subtle nuances of political and social critique that permeate both of Bioy Casares's Editorial Destiempo books emphasize the fact that these works were not intended for the average (Argentine) reader, but rather signal a more elite and well-educated individual.

In addition to the flying-fish logo that adorns four of the covers of Editorial Destiempo's publications, the books have a certain level of uniformity in terms of the paper, typography, and binding. In particular, the first four books published in 1937 and 1938 possess nearly identical stylistic aesthetics, from their burnt orange covers to their navy blue typography. What is more, many of the typefaces used for these works also appear throughout the pages of the short-lived literary journal *Destiempo*. These physical similarities can be accounted for when we consider the fact that each of these works (*Luis Greve, muerto*; *Marea de lágrimas*; *Diez poemas sin poesía*; and *Mallarmé entre nosotros*), and also the entire run of the literary journal *Destiempo,* was printed by Francisco A. Colombo.

While three of the four works make this connection to Colombo explicit by including his name in their colophons, Olivari's *Diez poemas sin poesía* excludes this information. The inclusion of no other information about this book's production other than the fact that it was printed for Editorial Destiempo stresses the importance of the publishing firm itself, yet the distinctive typeface and exquisite printing signal that it is the work of Colombo. Although *Diez poemas sin poesía* included drawings by the illustrator Carybé, the cover of this book includes no printing other than its typography.

Another curious feature of two of these four early books produced by Editorial Destiempo is their appearance in multiple forms. Much like the earliest works published by Editorial Sur that we saw in the last chapter, Editorial Destiempo produced certain books in both a luxury edition and a regular edition. For instance, in the opening pages of Petit de Murat's *Marea de lágrimas* we find a note alerting readers to the existence of two distinct formats of the book: "De esta obra se han impreso diez ejemplares en papel Croxley, numerados de I a X fuera de comercio, y trescientos ejemplares en papel pluma" [Of this work ten copies have been printed on Croxley paper, numbered from I to X not for sale, and three hundred copies on featherweight paper].[11] Bioy Casares's *Luis Greve, muerto* includes a similar note: "De esta obra se ha impreso, 500 ejemplares sobre papel Holanda y 10 ejemplares numerados de I a X, fuera de comercio, sobre papel hilo Croxley" [Of this work 500 copies have been printed on Holland paper and 10 numbered copies from I to X, not for sale, on linen Croxley paper].[12] There is no explicit information about the number of copies printed for each of the remaining works, but given the typical runs of works produced by Colombo, and the data gathered from *Luis Greve, muerto* and *Marea de lágrimas*, we can imagine that these books were published in smaller runs of no more than five hundred copies. In terms of their prices, Bioy Casares's *Luis Greve, muerto* is advertised as costing $1.50 Argentine pesos, while Petit de Murat's *Marea de lágrimas* and Reyes's *Mallarmé entre nosotros* sold for $2 Argentine pesos each (or $6 Argentine pesos for a subscription to a series of six works, four of which were never published, as we will see below).[13]

The remaining two works published by Editorial Destiempo, Vicente Barbieri's *Cabeza yacente* (1945) and Bioy Casares's *Homenaje a*

Francisco Almeyra (1954), show a marked shift in style and cohesion. In other words, neither of these two works is bound in burnt orange covers, nor do they bear the flying fish logo that appeared on each of the previous works. That said, the fact that both of these books are printed by Colombo links the group of works produced by Editorial Destiempo during the firm's seventeen-year existence. Similar to *Luis Greve, muerto* and *Marea de lágrimas,* Barbieri's *Cabeza yacente* provides readers with a "justificación del tiraje" [certification of the print run] at the opening of the work: "De esta obra se han impreso trescientos ejemplares en papel Polar, numerados y firmados por el autor" [Of this work three hundred copies have been printed on Polar paper, numbered and signed by the author].[14] The last aspect that sets Barbieri's work apart from the other Editorial Destiempo publications is its unique cover art by Gori Muñoz, an exiled Spanish painter, which depicts a platform in a wooded area with two candles in large urns. Along with this cover art, Muñoz also created a series of illustrations that appear throughout the book. In contrast, Bioy Casares's *Homenaje a Francisco Almeyra* resembles many of Borges's earliest publications that were printed by Colombo, such as *Las Kenningar* and *Historia de la eternidad,* for its clean, crisp covers and distinctive use of orange typography for the title.

Another five books, which were never published, were advertised either in the literary magazine *Destiempo* or on the inside-cover flaps of Editorial Destiempo's published works (Table 17). Readers will note the reappearance of certain names—Carlos Mastronardi, Ezequiel Martínez Estrada, and Macedonio Fernández, not to mention those of Borges and Bioy Casares.[15] As a result, Borges and Bioy Casares's initial foray into running a publishing house highlights the fact that many of their literary interests and concerns related to canon formation and literary education are perennial issues that surface in the majority of their collaborative endeavors. Moreover, virtually all of these collaborative endeavors point to an elite and well-educated audience.

Editorial Oportet & Haereses

The second publishing house that Borges and Bioy Casares create in the 1940s, Editorial Oportet & Haereses, is strikingly different from Edito-

Table 17. Works advertised in *Destiempo* that were never published

Carlos Mastronardi, *La rosa infinita* [*The Infinite Rose*]
Ezequiel Martínez Estrada, *Buenos Aires*
Novalis, *Fragmentos* (versión directa y notas de J. L. Borges) [*Fragments* (version and notes directly from J. L. Borges)]
Adolfo Bioy Casares, *Teseo fatal* [*Fatal Theseus*]
Macedonio Fernández, *Continuación de la nada* [*Continuation of Nothing*]

rial Destiempo and is what I would call an apocryphal firm for two reasons. First, "apocryphal" can refer to the *fictitious* nature of this publishing house, which seems to have appeared out of thin air and, unlike the earlier Editorial Destiempo, cannot trace its roots or emergence to a like-named literary journal or magazine. Moreover, the only works this firm published are three by its two founders, Borges and Bioy Casares: two collaborative works of fiction penned by the two men under pseudonyms — *Dos fantasías memorables* [*Two Memorable Fantasies*] (1946) and *Un modelo para la muerte* [*A Model for Death*] (1946) — and a philosophical essay about time by Borges — *Nueva refutación del tiempo* [*A New Refutation of Time*] (1947). For these reasons, the works produced by Editorial Oportet & Haereses are not very different from earlier works that Borges and Bioy Casares sent straight to a printer to be self-published without the name of a specific firm adorning the covers. Here, we see only the addition of an invented publisher's name, perhaps to give these works a greater sense of authority for having passed through the hands of an unbiased editor. The second reason I call this firm "apocryphal" is that, in addition to denoting something that is fake or false, the word, when applied to literature, takes on the meaning of *rare* or *secretive*: the 1911 *Encyclopedia Britannica* writes that the term "apocryphal" "was applied in a laudatory sense" to writings that "were kept secret because they were the vehicles of esoteric knowledge which was too profound or too sacred to be imparted to any save the initiated." The word apocryphal was also "applied to writings that were kept from public circulation" because of "their secondary or questionable value." Finally, "apocryphal" came to mean "what is false, spurious, bad, heretical."[16] All of the works published by Editorial Oportet & Haereses contain esoteric subject matters and writing styles and were printed in small runs of no more than three hundred copies, which most likely circulated only among close friends of Borges and Bioy Casares. The fact that the publication of these works (1946–1947) coincides with Juan Perón's initial reign in Argentina signals that these apocryphal characteristics can be seen as not only a possible strategy of avoiding censorship, but also a way of critiquing and subverting his rule.

There has been no in-depth study of this apocryphal publishing house to date, but Bioy Casares provides the following details about its significance in his extensive biography of Borges:

> el pie de "Oportet & Haereses" ... alude a I Corintios 9:19. La referencia podría ser indirecta, ya que: (a) en *Liturgies intimes* (1892), Verlaine incluye el poema "*Oportet haereses esse*"; (b) en su conferencia sobre "El romanticismo francés" (1920), Groussac recuerda que "según el Apóstol, hasta las herejías son útiles—*oportet et haereses esse.*"

> [the imprint "Oportet & Haereses" ... alludes to I Corinthians 9:19. The reference could be indirect, considering that: (a) in *Liturgies intimes* (1892), Verlaine includes the poem "Oportet haereses esse"; (b) in his conference about "French Romanticism" (1920), Groussac recalls that "according to the Apostle, even heretics are useful—*oportet et haereses esse.*"][17]

(Although Bioy Casares identifies the key words *nam oportet et haereses esse* as alluding to 1 Corinthians 9:19, they actually come from a passage that is two chapters later at 11:19.)[18]

Most references to these words *oportet et haereses esse,* whether drawn from the Bible or even from Verlaine's poem, translate them as "there must be heresies" (*que haya herejías*), which is not an adequate reflection of their meaning. That is to say, the word "heresy" mostly carries negative connotations today, so a more accurate translation would be "factions," since *haereses* does not always refer to a type of error but rather to a schism.[19] Even more puzzling is the fact that Borges understands the name of the firm as meaning something much different from

Bioy Casares's interpretation: "El sello editorial, Editorial Oportet & Haereses, aludía al Oporto y al Jerez" [The publishing firm, Editorial Oportet & Haereses, alludes to Port and Sherry].[20] To state that this publishing house was named after port and sherry might be a simple misdirection or inside joke, but it also might allude to the unique types of works that the firm produced, which, much like a nice after-dinner wine, are for a more refined palate. Even though Borges and Bioy Casares present readers with differing thoughts about the name Editorial Oportet & Haereses, the interpretations can be linked by their shared understanding of collaborative writings as a playful space for inside jokes that at times become so distorted that they lose all original sense of meaning: "Al comienzo hicimos bromas, y después bromas sobre bromas, como en álgebra; bromas al cuadrado, bromas al cubo ... y al final abandonamos el juego que volvía incomprensible" [At the start we made jokes, and later jokes about jokes, like in algebra; jokes squared, jokes cubed ... and in the end we abandoned the game since it because incomprehensible].[21]

A short anecdote from a work produced by Editorial Oportet & Haereses best serves as an introduction to the publishing house. "El signo" [The Sign], the second short story in *Dos fantasías memorables*, carefully weaves the thread of censorship into its central argument. Here, the protagonist, T. Mascarenhas, recounts his chance encounter with Wenceslao Zalduendo on a train bound for San Vicente. Although the narrator stresses the fact that he almost always maintains his distance from strangers, he becomes particularly interested in Zalduendo when he catches sight of "el lápiz Faber y un rollo de pruebas de imprenta, amén del diccionario de Roque Barcia" [the Faber pencil and a roll of galley proofs, as well as the Roque Barcia dictionary] that he is carrying with him.[22] A conversation sparked shortly thereafter reveals that this Don Wenceslao is none other than the proof corrector for Editorial Oportet & Haereses and that he is looking for help in completing his current editorial work. Before long Mascarenhas is entrenched in reading the proofs for Amancio Alcorta's *Instrucción secundaria* [*Secondary Instruction*]: "Exigua ¡qué canastos! fue la contribución que pude prestar esa primer mañana de consagración a las letras, pues, ... yo leía y leía, sin advertir las más garrafales erratas, las líneas traspuestas, las páginas omitidas o empasteladas" [Meager, oh my!, was the contribution I was able to give that first morning of devotion to letters, well, ... I read and read, without finding any tremendous errors, the lines were transposed, the pages were omitted or cleared of their wrong (typographical) sorts].[23]

Zalduendo's profession not only aligns perfectly with that of Borges and Bioy Casares at this very moment, but also involves their publishing house. In her case study of "El signo," Cristina Parodi cites a passage in Bioy Casares's biography of Borges that mentions the fact that a popular printer in Buenos Aires most likely served as the inspiration for the central character of Wenceslao Zalduendo:

> Borges me anuncia que esta noche va a una comida que le dan a José López Soto, el dueño de la imprenta López y de la editorial Nova. Yo le digo que iré también: López Soto, el probable original del héroe de una de las *Fantasías memorables* (la de los alimentos celestiales), es un hombre muy simpático ... Redondo, sereno y suave.

> [Borges told me that that night he was going to a dinner that they were giving in honor of José López Soto, the owner of Imprenta López and of Editorial Nova. I told him I would go, too: López Soto, the probable first hero of one of the *Fantasías memorables* (the one about the celestial foods), is a very nice man ... Round, serene, and suave.][24]

Aside from Bioy Casares's statement concerning the link between López and Don Wenceslao, there is another more obvious connection between this individual and *Dos fantasías memorables*: it was printed by Imprenta López.

These subtle allusions to real-world matters point to the need to examine the works that the narrator/protagonist and Zalduendo edit for this firm to discover further connections to other *porteño* material cultural production. Upon closer inspection, we find that all of the titles mentioned in "El signo" refer to real books. Moreover, all of these books, which can be grouped into two distinct categories, provide a type of commentary on Perón's level of censorship and reform in Argentina at the time. Thus, the first set of works that the narrator edits and corrects are all produced by the same publishing firm, José Ingenieros's La Cultura Argentina (Argentine Culture): Amancio Alcorta's *La instrucción secundaria* [*Secondary Education*] (1916), Raquel Camaña's *Pedagogía social* [*Social Pedagogy*] (1916) and *El dilettantismo sentimental* [*Sentimental Dilettantism*] (1916), Pedro Goyena's *Crítica literaria* [*Literary Criticism*] (1917), and José de Maturana's *Naranjo en flor* [*Flowering Orange Tree*] (1918). Four of these five titles immediately alert the reader to one of Ingenieros's main interests in producing books: education and curriculum. After traveling abroad to Europe, Ingenieros realized that his native Buenos Aires should strive to develop an educational system that was more separated from national institutions, especially the university. He also wanted to insert Argentina into the larger capitalist world by including "otras voces y otros recortes históricos y discursos" [other voices and other sides of history and discourses].[25] Instead of indoctrinating young students with a limited view of the world and its historical, social, economic, and literary formation, Ingenieros hoped to "formar ciudadanos libres" [form free citizens], which meant the inclusion in the curriculum of not just educators, but also writers, editors, and literary critics.[26]

As we have seen, in the story "El signo," Mascarenhas no sooner meets Don Wenceslao on the train than he begins reviewing galley proofs for Alcorta's *Instrucción secundaria*. In line with Ingenieros's interest in education, this book "examina el desarrollo de la [enseñanza misma] en todos los países civilizados, para hacer inferencias comparativas con [la enseñanza argentina]" [examines the development of education itself in all civilized countries, to make comparative inferences].[27] At the heart of Alcorta's work is his belief in the need for a secular school system without any kind of religious teaching. Alcorta also notes the heavy influence of Eduardo Wilde's earlier work, specifically his concept of the "escuela única" [unique school], or nonspecialized schooling:

> La "escuela única," decía el Dr. Wilde, como Ministro de la Instrucción Pública, la enseñanza sin bifurcaciones ni escuelas especiales, es la solución deseada y la que debemos mantener. En la escuela única se forma el hombre instruido, el que debe bastarse para determinar la dirección de sus fuerzas ejercitando sus deberes públicos y sus deberes privados, al par que

se forma también el que, con mayores ambiciones y una inteligencia bien equilibrada, busca un título profesional como la legítima realización de sus propósitos.

[The "unique school," Dr. Wilde said, as Minister of Public Education, teaching without bifurcation and without specialized schools, is the desired solution and what we should maintain. The unique school forms an educated man who must be capable of determining the direction of his strengths by exercising his public and private duties; at the same time, this individual, with better ambitions and a well-balanced intelligence, must be capable of searching for a professional title that legitimately fulfills his goals.]²⁸

Even though Alcorta's work was written almost half a century before Borges and Bioy Casares's collaborative fiction and also pertains to a much earlier educational debate in Argentine history, the central arguments of *Instrucción secundaria* almost eerily provide a retort to many of Perón's views on education at the start of his first political term (1946–1952).²⁹ Immediately after assuming his presidential position for the first time in 1946, Perón explicitly outlined several aspects of Argentine culture that he saw as problems to resolve, including the "immorality in public administration, the absence of God in public schools, ... the lack of moral authority of the judicial system, and the Communist threat."³⁰ Thus, Borges and Bioy Casares appear to be coyly commenting on Perón's level of control over educational methods and practices and by extension the degree of his general censorship of the Argentine populace.

Following this first editorial task, Don Wenceslao informs Mascarenhas that he has secured him a job at the Librería Europa. Similar to the list of edited works peppered throughout this short story, the Librería Europa, or the Librería *Europea,* was a real bookstore and publishing firm founded in Buenos Aires by Luis Jacobsen, a Danish immigrant, toward the end of the nineteenth century.³¹ In general terms, this shop "ofrecía libros técnicos en varios idiomas y revistas extranjeras, iniciando la importación con ritmo rápido de las novedades europeas, principalmente francesas" [offered technical books in various languages and foreign magazines, starting the importation, at a fast rate, of new European books, principally French ones].[32] Owing to the fact that Jacobsen was "culto, bibliófilo y políglota" [learned, a bibliophile and a polyglot], the Librería Europea quickly became synonymous with the highest quality imported foreign works.[33] Moreover, its key location on the "porteñísima calle" [very Argentine street] Florida in Buenos Aires, which was also the heart of the book industry, most definitely aided in the success of Jacobsen's business.[34] Along with its impressive catalogue of imported works, the Librería Europea was also an Argentine landmark for being a "punto de encuentro de importantes escritores" [place of contact for important writers] such as Miguel Cané, Paul Groussac, and Rubén Darío, which is quite a cast of intellectuals and easily could have included Borges a few decades later.[35] Each of these individuals, and their intellectual legacies, left a distinctive mark on Buenos Aires culture and is clearly another nod to Borges and Bioy Casares's subtle criticism of Perón's regime. In particular, the mention of Groussac, former librarian of the Biblioteca Nacional in Buenos Aires and one of Borges's idols, is telling. Much like Amancio Alcorta and Eduardo Wilde, Groussac, who was appointed to the position of the national inspector of education in Argentina in 1874, was in favor of secular education. He expressed these views clearly in his paper at the first pedagogical conference in Buenos Aires on "el estado actual de la educación primaria en la República Argentina, sus causas, sus remedios" [the actual state of primary education in the Argentine Republic, its causes, its remedies]. The fact that Don Wenceslao chooses this specific "sucursal muy seria" [very serious branch office] for Mascarenhas, therefore, appears to be no accident.

After announcing his newly gained position at the Librería Europ[e]a, the narrator of "El signo" goes on to list the remaining works that he corrects for Don Wenceslao, all of which, as noted earlier, were first published with Ingenieros's La Cultura Argentina. Similar to Alcorta's *Instrucción secundaria,* the two works by Raquel Camaña, *Pedagogía social* and *El dilettantismo sentimental,* pertain to desired changes in the Argentine educational system. From a sociological perspective, Camaña shows a marked interest in questions of social inequality as they relate to educational systems and the curriculum present in many schools. Throughout her *Pedagogía social* she advocates for a coeducational school that will be for all students, not only males and females but also children from any and every socioeconomic background. Alongside Camaña's work is Pedro Goyena's *Crítica literaria,* which might seem like an outlier in light of the fact that Goyena was a staunch Catholic and therefore against the secularization of schools in Argentina. However, this group of Goyena's texts is quite distinct from any of his dogmatic diatribes; instead, it is a series of critical essays on Argentina's literature during his lifetime, originally published in the *Revista Argentina* in the 1870s. Together with the other literary work listed in "El signo" (José de Maturana's *Naranjo en flor*), this collection of critical essays highlights the importance of not just books about educational standards for La Cultura Argentina, but also books that can be used in the classroom for educational purposes.

The second set of works that appears in "El signo," which only Don Wenceslao corrects for Editorial Oportet & Haereses, shows a marked deviation from the educational theme of the first group of texts. Instead of books that engage with pedagogical standards and curriculum, these other works are quite lewd and scandalous. Our protagonist's reaction to this lascivious subject matter, complete with obscene graphics, best summarizes the unexpected shift in published material: "rodó por el suelo uno de los pliegos que estaba corrigiendo don Wenceslao. Conozco mi obligación y, sobre el pucho me acomodé en cuatro patas para recogerlo. No haberlo hecho: vi una figura de lo más deslenguada, que me puse como un tomate" [one of the sheets that Mr. Wenceslao was correcting rolled to the floor. I know my obligation, and I got down on all fours near the cigarette butts to retrieve it for him. I should not have done it: I saw one of the most foul-mouthed figures, which made me turn bright red].[36] When the narrator celebrates his birthday a few days later, he decides to visit Don Wenceslao's home where he lays eyes on the finished books to which those prurient proofs belonged:

> había un alto de libros que me permití revisar. De nuevo le digo, eran de la Imprenta Oportet & Haereses y mejor no haberlo hecho. Bien dicen que cabeza en la que entra poco retiene el poco; hasta el día de hoy no puedo olvidarme de esos libros que hacía imprimir don Wenceslao. Las tapas eran con prójimas desnudas y de todos colores, y llevaban por

título *El jardín perfumado, El espión chino, El hermafrodita* de Antonio Panormitano, *Kama-sutra y/o Ananga-Ranga, Las capotas melancólicas,* las obras de Eléfantis y las de Arzobispo de Benevento.

[there was a shelf of books that I let myself look over. Again I will tell you, they were products of the printer Oportet & Haereses and it would have been better had I not. They say that once you get something in your head you can't get it out; to this day I still cannot forget those books that Don Wenceslao had printed. The covers were full of naked women and in all possible colors, and had titles such as *The Perfumed Garden, The Chinese Spy, The Hermaphrodite* by Antonio Panormitano, *Kama-Sutra and/or Ananga-Ranga, The Taciturn Condoms,* the works of Elephantis and those of the Archbishop of Benevento.][37]

All but one of the above cited titles are real books, with the common link of controversy. Three of the works are erotic literature or sex manuals (*El jardín perfumado, El hermafrodita,* and *Kama-sutra y/o Ananga-Ranga*), one is a critique of the social and political customs of the world (*El espión chino*), and the mention of the works of Elephantis conjures up her mysterious work on the art of love.[38] The only work from this second group that Borges and Bioy Casares invent, most likely for its humor, is *Las capotas melancólicas,* which Parodi links to a note from Richard Burton's *The Book of the Thousand Nights and a Night* that alludes to the invention and crafting of condoms:

> La nota de Burton aclara que, en árabe, *Al-Musrán* designa la bolsa rellena con sangre que Ali utiliza para disfrazarse de mujer y fingir un aborto; precisa que se trata un trozo de intestino delgado de oveja, un *cundum,* y agrega: "... *une capote anglaise,* a 'check upon child,' utilizado también para prevenir enfermedades venéreas" ... Es evidente que Borges y Bioy apreciaron la nota de Burton, evocando la imagen de los "condones taciturnos."

[The note of Burton clarifies that, in Arabic, *Al-Musrán* designates the bag full of blood that Ali uses to dress up as a woman and fake an abortion; more precisely it is a piece of sheep intestine, a *cundum,* and adds: ". . . an English hood, 'a check upon child,' used also to prevent venereal diseases" … It is evident that Borges and Bioy appreciated Burton's note, evoking the image of the "taciturn condoms."][39]

In essence, each of these volumes could easily appear on a list of banned books created for a conservative Catholic country, such as Argentina in the late 1940s. This claim is supported by the mention of the works of the Arzobispo de Benevento since his *Catalogo di diverse opere, compositioni et libri, li quali come eretici, sospetti, impii et scandalosi si dichiarano dannati et prohibiti in questa inclita città di Vinegia* [*Catalogue of various works, compositions, and books, which as heretical, suspect, impious, and scandalous are declared condemned and prohibited in this glorious city of Venice*] (1549) consisted of a list of 149 works that were prohibited by the Catholic Church in Venice because of their heretical nature. The scandal and shock that the narrator expresses upon seeing these titles aligns with the sad fate of his friend Don Wenceslao, who shortly after is "acusado de estafa y de traficar en libros infames" [accused of fraud and of trafficking in vile books] and therefore is sentenced to two years in jail, which undoubtedly echoes much of Perón's authoritarian control and censorship of Argentine print culture during his rule.[40]

In addition to the educational theme that emerges from the works that our protagonist corrects for Don Wenceslao, a very strong religious thread runs throughout the short story. We first see this motif in the epigraph from the book of Genesis: "Pondré mi arco en las nubes, y será señal de alianza entre mí y entre la tierra" [I have set my bow in the clouds, and it shall be a sign of the covenant between me and the earth].[41] Even though the content of this short story is quite removed from the biblical flood, after which the covenant is made between God and the earth, signaling a clean slate and a cleansing of the fallen peoples, there is an echo of this moment with the persecution and sentencing of Don Wenceslao for producing pornographic material. Moreover, while he is trying to pass the time in his jail cell, he decides to pray and subsequently starts to have strange visions: "Es verdad que el Señor me había deparado muchas visiones, todas francamente valiosas" [It is true that God provided me with many visions, all frankly valuable].⁴² We also see an extreme perversion and parodying of Noah's ark and the saving of certain creatures from the flood through one of these visions:

> Subían grandes cosas desde el monte del establecimiento rural Manantiales... Se dirigían en procesión al cenit ... El primero que distinguí ... era tamaña berenjena rellena ... La gran sorpresa bogaba a la derecha, a un nivel más alto, y era un solo puchero a la española, con su morcilla y su tocino.

> [Large things went up toward the mountain of the rural establishment Manantiales.... They all went in a procession toward the zenith ... The first that I saw ... was the size of a round eggplant. The biggest surprise rowed to the right, slightly higher, and it was a Spanish stew, with its blood sausage and bacon.]⁴³

Instead of having visions of animals and humans preparing to be saved and eventually ascend into heaven with God, Don Wenceslao has visions of food preparing for this same journey. After he is released from jail, our protagonist Mascarenhas still notes "un solo olor a fritangas" [a slight smell of fried food] outside of Don Wenceslao's home; then after Don Wenceslao's death a few days later, Mascarenhas is convinced that "su espíritu recto pudo ascender al firmamento, donde sin duda lo acompañan ahora todas esas minutas y postres" [his honorable spirit was able to ascend to the firmament, where without doubt all of these quick meals and pastries would accompany him].⁴⁴

The fantastic elements found at the end of "El signo" tie it to the other short story in Borges and Bioy Casares's *Dos fantasías memorables*. The structure of "El testigo" [The Witness] is very similar to that of "El signo" in that the reader is presented with a kind of monologue by the protagonist Mascarenhas to his friend Lumbeira.⁴⁵ That said, in contrast to the chance encounter with Don Wenceslao and the publishing industry in "El signo," in this short story Mascarenhas recounts some of his travels throughout the Argentine countryside (and some unpleasant meetings along the way) and then quickly moves to his employment with "la razón social Meinong y Cía" [the registered company Meinong and Cía], a tobacco factory run by Don Alejandro Meinong. When Don Alejandro must travel to La Plata for business, he entrusts Mascarenhas with watching his nine-year-old granddaughter and sole heir of his fortune. We soon learn that this young girl, Flora, is quite peculiar and begins to complain of frightening sightings in the basement after coming down with a severe fever:

> A la oración, hora que acostó a su muñeca, la divisé con fiebre en los pulsos, con alucinaciones y el miedo . . . Me dijo que la víspera había columbrado en el sótano una cosa tan rara que no podía describir cómo era, salvo que era con barbas. Yo di en pensar que esa fantasía con barbas no era causante de la fiebre, sino lo que el practicón llama síntoma.
>
> [At the hour of prayer, when she put her doll to sleep, I found her to be quite feverish, with hallucinations and fear . . . She told me that yesterday she caught a glimpse of something so strange in the basement that she could not even describe it, except that it had a beard. I told her that this fantasy with a beard was not the cause of the fever, but rather what a doctor would call a symptom.][46]

After Flora recovers, Mascarenhas asks her to return downstairs for some papers he needs, and although he stands at the top of the stairs to comfort her, it is not long before he hears her scream and runs down to find her dead. In shock, Mascarenhas tries to understand what transpired, and after surveying the space, he discovers the mysterious cause of her death, which appears to be her having seen the face of God:

> Vea, de a un tiempo, en un santiamén, los tres combinados que en una suerte de entrevero tranquilo animaban el sillón . . . Campeaba el Padre, que por las barbas raudales lo conocí, y a la vez era el Hijo, con los estigmas, y el Espíritu, en forma de paloma, del grandor de un cristiano.

[Behold, simultaneously, in a flash, the trinity give life to the rocking chair in a calm confusion of luck ... I caught sight of the Father, and recognized him for his flowing beard, and at the same time he was the Son, with the stigmata, and the Spirit, in the form of a dove, in the grandeur of a Christian.][47]

For fear of Don Alejandro's wrath, Mascarenhas moves Flora's body to her bed and flees town. He later learns that the home was demolished after some years with the expansion of Belgrano Street.[48] Much as in "El signo," many of these fantastic elements resonate with the story's opening biblical epigraph from Isaiah: "Y dije: ¡Ay de mí! que estoy perdido, pues soy un hombre de labios impuros, y entre un pueblo de labios impuros habito, que al rey Yahveh Sebaot han visto mis ojos" [Then said I, Woe is me! For I am undone; because I am a man of unclean lips, and I dwell in the middle of a people of unclean lips: for my eyes have seen the King, the LORD of hosts.][49] This biblical verse highlights the common idea throughout the Old Testament that the sight of God will bring about a person's death. Moreover, Isaiah exhibits a great sense of fear after seeing God and as a result sees himself to be in an unclean state.

When we consider the ideas of playful joking and parody used throughout Borges and Bioy Casares's fictions, particularly those produced by Editorial Oportet & Haereses, many of their strange elements make more sense. For instance, the visions that characters experience in both of the short stories in *Dos fantasías memorables* have strong religious overtones but also a fantastical character that corresponds to a sort of religious distortion. In tandem with these fantastical elements are the unique footnotes that crop up throughout both of the stories. For instance, in "El testigo" there is a grammatically oriented footnote provided by a Mario Bonfanti, S.J., who happens to be one of the central characters in *Un modelo para la muerte,* the second work published by Editorial Oportet & Haereses and is described as a "gramático y purista argentino" [grammarian and Argentine purist].[50] If this intertextuality were not already enough, this footnote by Bonfanti is footnoted further:

> Por un motivo que escapa a la perspicacia de esta Mesa de Correctores, el padre Mario Bonfanti, nerviosamente secun-

dada por el señor Bernardo Sampaio, pretendió a última hora retirar la nota anterior, abrumándonos con telegramas colacionados, cartas certificadas, mensajeros ciclistas, súplicas y amenazas.

[For reasons that escape the cleverness of this Table of Correctors, Father Mario Bonfanti, nervously seconded by Mr. Bernardo Sampaio, hoped to eliminate the previous note at an early hour, overwhelming us with collated telegrams, certified letters, bicycle messengers, pleas, and threats.][51]

A similar level of inside jokes continues in "El signo" where we find a footnote about Don Wenceslao's glasses by Gervasio Montenegro, a protagonist in *Seis problemas para don Isidro Parodi*.[52] Thus, Borges and Bioy Casares have coyly interwoven several of their collaborative fictions in these instances, which furthers the notion that their joint literary endeavors were a personal affair and, much resembling a type of palimpsest, built upon all previously coauthored writings.

The second book produced by Editorial Oportet & Haereses, *Un modelo para la muerte,* is a perplexing parody of the genre of detective fiction. Unlike *Dos fantasías memorables,* Borges and Bioy Casares have chosen a new pseudonym to adorn the cover of this work: B. Suárez Lynch. Much like the name of Honorio Bustos Domecq, the etymological origins of this name can be traced to ancestors in Borges's and Bioy Casares's families. To complicate matters even more, as we learn in the prologue to this book, Suárez Lynch is the disciple of Bustos Domecq, who also happens to be writing the prologue itself: "¡Tan luego a mí pedirme un 'A manera de prólogo'! En balde hago valer mi condición de hombre de letras jubilado, de trasto viejo. Con el primer mazazo amputo las ilusiones de mi joven amigo; el novato" [So to ask me for a "By way of a prologue"! In vain I will value my condition as a retired man of letters, an old container. With the first hammer blow I amputate the illusions of my young friend—the novice].[53] We soon find out that Bustos Domecq himself stumbled upon the central idea for *Un modelo para la muerte* and, as he had too much on his plate already, decided to pass the opportunity along to his student, B. Suárez Lynch: "La redacción de la novelita pertinente era un deber de mi exclusiva incumbencia; pero estando metido hasta el resuello en unos bocetos biográficos del presidente de un *povo irmão,* le cedí el tema del misterio al catecúmeno" [The composition of the short novel in question was a duty of my sole responsibility; but being up to my ears in biographical sketches of the president of a neighboring people, I gave the mysterious topic to the catechumen].[54] Curiously, Bustos Domecq mentions coming to his brilliant idea after reading "la columna de policiales" [the column of detective fiction], which brings to mind several of Borges's editorial positions during the previous decade, especially his role as codirector of the *Revista Multicolor de los Sábados* and his occasional columns for *El Hogar.*[55]

Generally speaking, *Un modelo de la muerte* is a story of revenge. That said, the central plot points of the narrative are muddled by the use of ornately antiquated language, nonlinear chronology, and the introduction of extraneous characters and story lines. Alfred MacAdam provides the best synopsis of this complex and perplexing short story:

> En el pasado pretextual, el criminal, Ladislao Barreiro, sufrió a causa de las acciones de Tonio Le Fanu (cuyo parentesco con el novelista gótico irlandés no existe). Le Fanu hace que Barreiro pierda su puesto como director de una biblioteca. Barreiro promete vengarse. Mucho más tarde, Barreiro conoce a Kuno Fingermann, que resulta ser el cuñado de Le Fanu. Este hecho hace de Le Fanu un bígamo *in potentia,* pues está a punto de casarse con Hortensia Montenegro, de la "alta sociedad" porteña. Barreiro convence a Fingermann para que extorsione a Le Fanu. Al mismo tiempo, Le Fanu descubre que Fingermann ha robado dinero de la Asociación Aborigenista Argentina. Le Fanu le informa a Barreiro (abogado oficial del grupo) que extorsiona a Fingermann. Le Fanu se entera de todo y—improbablemente—extorsiona a Barreiro. El dinero pasa de Le Fanu a Fingermann, a Barreiro y vuelve a Le Fanu. Barreiro decide romper el círculo matando a Le Fanu, y lo hace así: convence a Le Fanu que sería mejor matar a Fingermann, y cuando Le Fanu [lo] ha preparado todo para sorprender a Fingermann, Barreiro lo mata.

[In the pretextual past, the criminal, Ladislao Barreiro, suffered because of the actions of Tonio Le Fanu (whose relationship with the Irish Gothic novelist does not exist). Le Fanu made Barreiro lose his position as director of a library. Barreiro promised to seek vengeance. Much later, Barreiro met Kuno Fingermann, who turned out to be the brother-in-law of Le Fanu. This fact made Le Fanu a bigamist *in potentia*, because he was just about to marry Hortensia Montenegro, of the Argentine "high society." Barreiro persuades Fingermann to extort Le Fanu. At the same time, Le Fanu discovers that Fingermann has robbed money from the Aboriginal Argentine Society. Le Fanu informs Barreiro (official lawyer of this group) to extort Fingermann. Le Fanu finds out everything and—improbably—extorts Barreiro. The money passes from Le Fanu to Fingermann, to Barreiro, and returns to Le Fanu. Barriero decides to break the circle by killing Le Fanu and he does it in this way: he persuades Le Fanu that it would be better to kill Fingermann, and when Le Fanu has everything ready to surprise Fingermann, Barreiro kills him.][56]

Any reader familiar with the work of G. K. Chesterton will immediately identify this plot as that of "The Oracle of the Dog," which is one of the eight tales that make up *The Incredulity of Father Brown* (1926). MacAdam makes this crucial connection yet fails to tie it to Borges's previous work with the *Revista Multicolor,* which featured a Spanish translation of this short story ("La profecía del perro") in the May 12, 1934, issue. Knowing that this short story appeared within the pages of the *Revista Multicolor* while Borges held the position of codirector helps readers unpack the previously mentioned passage from the prologue to *Un modelo para la muerte* in which Bustos Domecq mentions that his inspiration for the story arose from reading "la columna de policiales."[57] Even more telling is the fact that Chesterton's story begins with his protagonist reading about the murder in question from a periodical clipping: "Pensé que había leído en los diarios todos los detalles ... Espere un segundo, creo que tengo un recorte que le servirá para informarse de todos los particulares" [I think that I read all of the details in the newspaper ... Wait a minute, I think I have a clipping that will give you all of the details].[58]

In contrast with their educational critiques in *Dos fantasías memorables,* Borges and Bioy Casares focus on linguistic complexity and esoteric literary allusions in *Un modelo para la muerte* as a way to critique Perón's populist discourse. One of the few studies dedicated to this complex short story focuses on how Borges and Bioy Casares parody the genre of detective fiction within their dizzying narrative in that very genre and exemplify "la parodia por medio de la repetición" [parody by means of repetition].[59] The first level of parody appears in the opening pages of *Un modelo para la muerte* with the humorous list of characters ("Dramatis Personae") that includes "Padre" Brown, a clear allusion to Chesterton's fictional priest, and Gervasio Montenegro, who was previously included among the characters in *Seis problemas para don Isidro Parodi* as well as in the footnotes in *Dos fantasías memorables*. Moreover, within the first few lines of the text itself, we enter an eerily familiar location: "Eligió el ángulo noroeste de la celda 273, se sentó en cuclillas y extrajo de los fondos del bombachón un trozo de caña de azúcar y lo chupó babosamente" [He chose the northeastern angle of cell 273; he sat in a squat and took out a piece of sugarcane from the depths of his pockets and sucked on it sluggishly].[60] This cell is none other than that of Isidro Parodi, Borges and Bioy Casares's crime sleuth extraordinaire from *Seis problemas para don Isidro Parodi,* which suggests that this narrative will imitate what we saw in this prior work. In other words, Parodi will serve as the sounding board for various characters as they try to work through the mysterious revenge plot that is unfolding before their eyes.

MacAdam does not connect this type of narrative structure with *Seis problemas para don Isidro Parodi,* but rather links it with the foundational work of one particular detective fiction writer, which serves to create yet another layer of parody and distortion: "La técnica de *Un modelo para la muerte* ... imita la de *The Moonstone* de Wilkie Collins: cada personaje presenta su versión de los hechos, y se enredan tanto que los hechos se pierden en la narrativa" [The technique of *A Model for Death* ... imitates Wilkie Collins's *The Moonstone*: each character presents his version of the facts, and they weave themselves together so much so that you lose yourself in the narrative].⁶¹ MacAdam's reference to Collins recalls Borges's column in *El Hogar* where he refers to *The Moonstone* on several occasions. For instance, in the June 24, 1938, issue of *El Hogar*, Borges establishes *The Moonstone* as "la primera novela policial que registra la historia" [the first detective novel in history]; almost a year later (May 5, 1939), while reviewing Faulkner's *The Wild Palms*, Borges returns to Collins's work and highlights his key technique of allowing characters to dictate the narrative:

> Que yo sepa, nadie ha ensayado todavía una historia de las formas de la novela, una morfología de la novela. Esa historia hipotética y justiciera destacaría el nombre de Wilkie Collins, que inauguró el curioso procedimiento de encomendar la narración de la obra a los personajes.
>
> [As far as I know, no one has written yet the history of the form of the novel, a morphology of the novel. That hypothetical and tough history will stress the name of Wilkie Collins, who inaugurated the curious procedure of making the narration the job of the other characters.]⁶²

In a sense, even though Borges and Bioy Casares are parodying the genre of detective fiction, they also seem to be paying homage to its foundational figures. This idea resonates with the various references and allusions to Chesterton and Borges and Bioy Casares's previous collaborative fictions.

Along with the complex language and literary allusions of *Un modelo para la muerte,* any discussion of this book requires a description of the peculiar series of seven drawings throughout it. Curiously, these drawings appear only in the first edition; none of them is reproduced in any subsequent editions, nor do critics or scholars mention their existence. The first image, which is reminiscent of Dante's half-man, half-bull minotaur in the *Inferno,* adorns the title page of the work. Throughout the remainder of the book, we find a unique, nonrepeating image at the close of each of its sections. No artist is credited for these images, nor do they seem to refer to any plot points or moments in the text. Rather,

B. SUÁREZ LYNCH

*UN MODELO
PARA LA MUERTE*

OPORTET & HAERESES
BUENOS AIRES
1946

Title page of *Un modelo para la muerte* (Editorial Oportet & Haereses, 1946). *(Reproduced from the Albert and Shirley Small Special Collections Library, University of Virginia.)*

The six drawings that appear in *Un modelo para la muerte* at the end of each section of its first edition (Editorial Oportet & Haereses, 1946). *(Reproduced from the Albert and Shirley Small Special Collections Library, University of Virginia.)*

these obscure drawings might be better suited to appear in the pages of Borges and Margarita Guerrero's *Manual de zoología fantástica* [*Manual of Fantastic Zoology*], and in fact, all of these illustrations—with the exception of the last one—appear reprinted beneath several sections in the first edition of that work.[63] Akin to the perplexing narrative style of *Un modelo para la muerte* itself, these drawings represent yet another layer of Borges and Bioy Casares's dizzying distortion of not only the genre of detective fiction, but also their conceptions of the relationship between text and image in books. In particular, the monstrous nature of these illustrations provides a striking visual contrast with their warlike imagery, which includes weapons, shields, and speared figures.

The third and final work produced by Editorial Oportet & Haereses, Borges's *Nueva refutación del tiempo,* is quite different from the other two, in terms of both its content and its physical form. For starters, this work is a critical essay published under Borges's real name. Moreover, the first part of this essay was published previously in the literary journal *Sur* in 1944, which makes this work not nearly as novel as the fictions that precede it. Aside from its different formal features, the content of *Nueva refutación del tiempo* is also quite distinct from that of the other two works published by Editorial Oportet & Haereses. A work of nonfiction, this essay stands out from the two creative short stories that comprise *Dos fantasías memorables* and the parody of detective fiction in *Un modelo para la muerte.* As with most of Borges's essays, the topic of *Nueva refutación del tiempo* is complex in nature and engages with the work of a number of metaphysical philosophers in an effort to demonstrate the unsoundness of the concept of time. Borges uses the writings of George Berkeley on idealism and those of David Hume on perceptions and sensations to rationalize his argument that the concept of time as we know it does not exist: "niego con argumentos del idealismo, la vasta serie temporal que el idealismo admite. Hume ha negado la existencia de un espacio absoluto, en el que tiene su lugar cada cosa; yo, la de un solo tiempo, en el que se eslabonan todos los hechos" [I deny, with arguments of idealism, the vast temporal series that idealism accepts. Hume negated the existence of an absolute space, in which everything has its place; I [negate] one of a single time, in which all things are linked together].[64] Thus, not only are the concepts difficult to understand for an average reader, but also much of the essay is repetitive and somewhat circular in nature, which complicates the central point further.[65]

I now turn to the physical forms of the books published by Editorial Oportet & Haereses. Two of the three—*Dos fantasías memorables* and *Un modelo para la muerte*—have identical bindings and typography and use similar paper throughout.[66] What is more, these two works are physically unlike most of the works that Borges published (or produced) during this time. First, and perhaps most curious, is the fact that these two hardcover books are quarter bound in a blue cloth with marbled paper on the frontboard and backboard. While this style of binding is commonly found throughout Europe and the United States, it is much less common in Argentina.[67] Coupled with this particular binding is the presentation of the title and author name on a small piece of paper adhered to the spine, which is quite atypical. In general terms, printed paper spine labels did not become commonplace in the book world until the eighteenth century when publishers and wholesalers began to use them as a kind of expedient packaging for the works that they produced. In other words, these add-ons were intended to be a temporary fix until the potential buyer was able to remove the somewhat shabby publishers' bindings for new, more elegant, materials. William Morris's Kelmscott Press, however, also favored quarter-linen binding with paper boards and printed spine labels at the end of the nineteenth century, thereby setting "a fashion among other publishers, so that for a generation or more after Morris's death English readers were afflicted with a plague of books issued in board covers with blue or grey paper."[68] With their peculiar use of similar printed spine labels on books that have more elegant marbled papers, Borges and Bioy Casares appear to be problematizing the conceptions of how books are made and how books should be used, especially when we consider the fact that these two works employ an antiquated high-brow language that is virtually incomprehensible (even for native Argentines) without the help of a dictionary.[69]

Unlike the previous two works, Borges's *Nueva refutación del tiempo* is not a hardcover book, but rather a softcover work composed of high-quality paper, much like a pamphlet. Thus, we are not presented with the beautifully marbled papers or quarter-bound blue spine, but rather a crisp cream-colored paper that harkens back to the physical features of

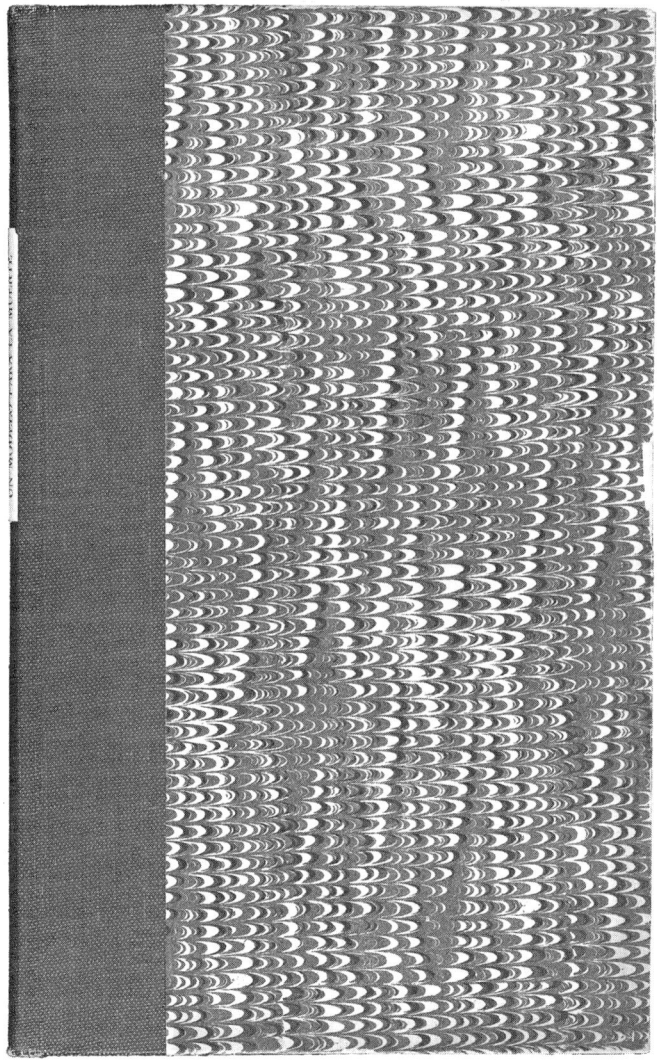

The marbled cover of Benito Suárez Lynch's *Un modelo para la muerte* (Editorial Oportet & Haereses, 1946). *(Reproduced from the Albert and Shirley Small Special Collections Library, University of Virginia.)*

Borges's earlier collections of essays such as *Las Kenningar* and *Historia de la eternidad,* particularly for their similar use of classical typography, color, and design.[70] An examination of the colophon printed at the close of this essay reveals that Francisco A. Colombo printed it, just as he had printed *Las Kenningar* and *Historia de la eternidad,* which accounts for the overlaps in design. However, unlike these earlier collections printed by Colombo, Borges's *Nueva refutación del tiempo* presents readers with an original hand-drawn image in the center of the cover, which distinguishes it from the rest of the works produced by this luxury printer.

Although the image of an hourglass echoes the theme of the essay, it is quite unfitting when compared with the rest of Borges's work. The fact that Borges did not favor cover art, and instead preferred clean covers with no more adornment than their typography, raises the question of the presence of this illustration.[71] Perhaps the best way to answer such an inquiry is by considering who created the image as opposed to why it might have been created. Directly below the drawing we find the clearly printed name of Amanda Molina Vedia. Aside from being an Argentine artist, Molina Vedia was also known to have caught the eye of a younger Borges, which might account for why he dedicated one of his most canonical short stories, "La muerte y la brújula" [Death and the Compass] to her. Rodríguez Monegal affirms this intimate connection between the two, with specific reference to details in "La muerte y la brújula," by citing the Argentine writer himself: "Triste-le-Roy, a beautiful name invented by Amanda Molina Vedia, stands for the now demolished Hotel Las Delicias in Adrogué. (Amanda had painted a map of an imaginary island on the wall of her bedroom; on her map I discovered the name Triste-le-Roy)."[72] Thus, much like Rossi's cover art for many of Borges's contemporaneous publications with Editorial Losada, or even his sister Norah's original designs for his early *Fervor de Buenos Aires,* Molina Vedia's illustration for *Nueva refutación del tiempo* exemplifies Borges's interest in publishing both his own thoughts and the works of his close friends.

Examining the works produced by Editorial Destiempo and Editorial Oportet & Haereses during the 1930s and 1940s serves as the ideal culmination to my analysis of the pivotal role of the book in Borges's early career. In his essay "Nota sobre (hacia) Bernard Shaw" [Note about (toward) Bernard Shaw] (1951), Borges describes how a book is not an isolated object, but rather "una relación, es un eje de innumerables relaciones" [a relation, an axis of innumerable relations].[73] If we read this phrase with the physical book in mind, it is the perfect encapsulation of the publishing industry and further complicates Borges's claim that he was not interested in the book's physical form since any given publisher inherently will be invested in the whole book, from idea to finished product. Moreover, in light of the fact that publishers connect all aspects of the book trade, from manufacture and production to distribution and sales, they will almost always see books as physical things, whether in the grouping of Linotype slugs, the galley proofs to review, or the finished products arriving from the bindery. By donning the role of publisher for Editorial Destiempo and Editorial Oportet & Haereses, Borges undoubtedly experiences the book as a physical entity. If we read the same idea about a book's innumerable relationships in an abstract sense, we can understand how books embrace their debt and intimate relationship to a vast array of historical, political, and literary works (or movements) by continually signaling to readers the various ways in which books recycle ideas and previously published material. What Borges creates in his works, whether authored by himself, collaboratively created with friends, or penned by other contemporary writers, is a type of palimpsest "en el que deben traslucirse los rastros—tenues pero no indescifrables—de la 'previa' escritura de [nuestros amigos]" [through which the traces—tenuous but not indecipherable—of [our friends'] "previous" writing should be translucently visible].[74] In a physical sense, Borges and Bioy Casares's works produced with Editorial Destiempo and Editorial Oportet & Haereses involve the efforts of printers, typesetters, binders, illustrators, and authors. All of these parties undoubtedly leave a physical trace of their work as the book moves from one stage of creation to the next, and these residual elements remind readers that the object before their eyes is composed of many parts and was originally nothing more than rags, metal, and ink. Borges and Bioy Casares's works, beyond a simple layering of erasure and rewriting, present readers with snippets of other works and in the process become a metaphorical palimpsest through which we can occasionally catch glimpses of their reading preferences and their consciousness of being inscribed within a complex cultural circumstance.

Conclusion
Books after Borges

[U]n libro es más que una estructura verbal, o que una serie de estructuras verbales; es el diálogo que entabla con su lector y la entonación que impone a su voz y las cambiantes y durables imágenes que deja en su memoria.

[A book is more than a verbal structure or series of verbal structures; it is the dialogue that it establishes with its reader and the intonation that it imposes upon his voice and the changing and durable images that it leaves in his memory.]

—Jorge Luis Borges, *Otras inquisiciones*

The book is a fundamental object for Borges. It serves as a source of inspiration for his carefully crafted narratives, and it is also the motivating force behind the diverse forms of his employment throughout his career. During the most productive period of his early years, we see Borges constantly engaged with this medium, from its initial stages of creation and editing to its various printed forms. Furthermore, his deep-seated engagement with the publishing industry throughout the 1930s and 1940s points to his desire to promote new voices for Latin American readers and also make these works more readily available. As a way of concluding, I put Borges in his proper place as a key precursor of the fields of book history and material studies. More specifically, I reflect on the ways in which Borges's publishing activities and knowledge of the book as object impact contemporary theories of the materiality of the book. In addition, I show how many of Borges's canonical short stories and essays, which were intricately tied to and informed by his behind-the-scenes positions from critic and editor to publisher and publicist, provide the foundation for a marked focus on studies in print culture and book history throughout the latter half of the twentieth century.

Broadly speaking, Borges's influential contributions to scholarly discourse are not unknown. Perhaps the most recognized engagement with his writings outside of the field of literary studies is within the pages of *The New Media Reader* in which his "El jardín de senderos que se bifurcan" [The Garden of Forking Paths] serves as the work's introductory text. As Nick Montfort writes, "Borges was no hacker; nor did he specify the hypertext novel in perfect detail. But computers do not function as they do today *only* because of the playful labor of hackers or because of planned-out projects to program, develop, and reconfigure systems. Our use of computers is also based on the visions of those who, like Borges—pronouncing this story from the growing dark of his blindness—saw those courses that future artists, scientists, and hackers might take."[1] Over the past few decades this interest in linking Borges's ideas with hypertexts and the emergence of our modern-day internet has resulted in an ever-growing corpus of critical works that reflects many of Montfort's claims.[2]

Borges's writings have also been employed in the fields of cognitive science and philosophy of mind. For instance, his well-known essay "Borges y yo" [Borges and I] is the first included in Douglas R. Hofstadter and Daniel C. Dennett's *The Mind's I: Fantasies and Reflections on Self and Soul*. Even though Borges is not a trained philosopher, his succinct encapsulation of a split self—one public, one private—serves as the perfect introduction to the book's opening section, "A Sense of Self." In a similar vein, the collection's fourth section, "Created Selves and Free Will," includes his haunting short story "Las ruinas circulares" [The Circular Ruins], which further emphasizes his influence on fundamental questions of the self and existence. While Borges might normally be associated with other literary authors from around the globe, he fits well with his interlocutors in this volume, such as Alan Turing, Richard Dawkins, Robert Nozick, and Thomas Nagel, since many of his works function in the same way as the thought experiments of these individuals. Alongside Borges's inclusion in these two volumes, we also find his short story "La lotería en Babilonia" [The Lottery in Babylon] in the edited volume *Justice,* which forms a part of the Hackett Readings in Philosophy series. Borges's interest in politics and his political affiliations have been analyzed by scholars in the fields of literary studies and political science.[3] That said, his appearance in *Justice* alongside some of the greatest political thinkers from Plato and Aristotle to Karl Marx and J. S. Mill is quite unusual and telling. These examples demonstrate that Borges's texts inspire disparate lines of thought and inquiry across disparate disciplines from new media and technology to cognitive science, philosophy, and politics.[4]

Similar to Borges's role in shaping these other fields, I suggest that many of Borges's metabibliographical short stories and philosophical essays serve as the point of departure for current scholarship in book history.[5] While a number of bibliographers and book historians reference his works in passing, no two scholars rely on his writings more than Gérard Genette and Roger Chartier.[6] Throughout his two most-cited works, *Paratexts* and *Palimpsests,* Genette turns to Borges's fictions and nonfictions time and time again as a point of departure for his own theoretical conceptions of how we are to understand and approach books and print culture more generally. In fact, the idea of Genette's paratext, which I discussed throughout Chapter 5, is almost entirely derived from Borges's writings. More specifically, at the start of *Paratexts,* Genette defines his neologism as "a *threshold,* or—a word Borges used apropos of a preface—a 'vestibule' that offers the world at large the possibility of either stepping inside or turning back."[7] True to his allusion, this definition of the paratext appears to be drawn straight out of one of Borges's many essays about the prologue or the preface. More specifically, readers will recall Borges's "Palabras finales" [Final Words] for the *Antología de la moderna poesía uruguaya* from Chapter 5 that describes the prologue as a continuation of "las persuasiones de la vidriera, de la carátula, de la faja" [the persuasions of the shop window, of the dust jacket, of the promotional band], which are precisely some of the key material features that Genette turns to in his analysis throughout *Paratexts*.

Similarly, Genette's *Palimpsests* draws heavily on many of the ideas that Borges develops surrounding the palimpsest, which he first defines in "Pierre Menard, autor del Quijote" [Pierre Menard, author of the Quijote]: "He reflexionado que es lícito ver en el Quijote 'final' una especie de palimpsesto, en el que deben traslucirse los rastros—tenues pero no indescifrables—de la 'previa' escritura de nuestro amigo" [I reflected that it is licit to see in the "final" *Quijote* a sort of palimpsest, through which the traces—tenuous but not indecipherable—of [our friends'] "previous" writing should be translucently visible].[8] In a more material sense, Borges's tendency to use and reuse any old scrap of paper for his compositional practices signals how we can also think of the presence of (physical) palimpsests in this writer's life more literally as a reflection on the scarcity of resources that so often affects production processes in the publishing industry and, more generally, arises as a fundamental concern in current book history scholarship.[9] Along with his clear debt to this Borges short story, Genette also uses elements from "El acercamiento a Almotásim" [The Approach to Al-Mu'tasim] as well as his *Historia universal de la infamia* and *Discusión* to think about what he deems the "*pseudosummary*, or fictive summary."[10] In addition, his arguments surrounding pastiche refer to Borges and Bioy Casares's collaborative fictions.[11] As I have shown throughout this book, all of these works showcase Borges's alertness to the book as a physical object and rely on the material aspects of print culture for their creation.

Although Chartier's groundbreaking research in the field of book history focuses mainly on European trends and phenomena up through the eighteenth century, his allusions to and engagements with Borges's writings crop up throughout many of his works. For instance, his chapter on the library in Europe in *The Order of Books* begins with a lengthy epigraph taken from Borges's "La biblioteca de Babel" [The Library of Babel].[12] He references this same short story again in his *Forms and Meanings* when discussing the concept of a universal library, specifically within the context of the digital library: "the extravagant happiness of which Borges spoke is promised us by the libraries without walls, even without specific location, that are undoubtedly in our future."[13] Even though Borges's writings occupy a much different temporal space than those of the literary subjects of most of Chartier's critical works, many of his concise philosophical musings on print artifacts and the cultural record serve as ideal parallels to and referents for Chartier's arguments.

Throughout *Inscription and Erasure,* Chartier engages with Borges's nonfictions—from essays and lectures to interviews—as a way to illuminate the complexities inherent in assessing the material aspects of the written word. In his introduction to the work he cites Borges's 1979 lecture on the book, which I discussed in Chapter 1, yet he takes Borges's words at face value and concludes: "For Borges, books are objects of no interest, whose particularities are of little moment. What counts is the way in which the book, taken to be the universal form of the written work regardless of its specific modality, was regarded—or, more often than not, disregarded, in comparison with the 'wingèd and sacred' spoken word. Borges, in other words, took a 'platonic' view."[14] As I have shown throughout this book, we have good reason to believe that this view of Borges is false, given that Borges's actions reveal a cultivated interest in the book as a physical object. In fact, Chartier continues his analysis of Borges's understanding of the book by describing the writer's engagement with and appreciation of *his* Garnier edition of *Don Quijote,* concluding that "the platonic principle is of little weight compared with the pragmatic return of memory."[15] In short, Borges's reliance on books and their bibliographical details foreshadows material studies and the field of book history as they are understood and practiced today.

Paul Needham writes, "Books and writings are, in general, the foundation of historical knowledge, their other nearest comparanda being such artefacts as coins, household objects, architectural remains, and so forth."[16] As historical records, books tell us about the economic and political constraints placed on their production while simultaneously revealing social trends and interests at a given moment in time. Looking to the physical features of books further helps us to understand the intricate relationship between cultural production and reading practices. Regardless of the path that future bibliographical and material investigations take in Latin American literature, their value cannot be emphasized enough. Even though my work here relies on the production of just one individual, Jorge Luis Borges, it is my hope that this type of case study can provide future researchers with a model for investigations into other writers, or even entire schools of writers or publishing houses. Moreover, I hope to have shown the ways in which Borges forever changed the Latin American book world and paved the way for its entrance into the global marketplace.

Appendix
Books Produced by Editorial Sur (1933-1951)

YEAR AUTHOR, WORK
1933 Aldous Huxley, *Contrapunto* [*Point Counter Point*]
      D. H. Lawrence, *Canguro* [*Kangaroo*]
      Federico García Lorca, *Romancero gitano* [*Gypsy Ballads*]
1934 D. H. Lawrence, *La virgen y el gitano* [*The Virgin and the Gypsy*]
1935 Eduardo Mallea, *Conocimiento y expresión de la Argentina* [*Knowledge and Expression of Argentina*]
      Eduardo Mallea, *Nocturno europeo* [*European Nocturne*]
      Francisco Luis Bernárdez, *El buque* [*The Ship*]
      Igor Stravinsky, *Crónicas de mi vida* [*Chronicles of My Life*]
      Louis-Ferdinand Céline, *Mea culpa seguido de la vida y la obra de Semmelweis* [*Mea Culpa and The Life and Works of Semmelweis*]
      Victoria Ocampo, *Supremacía del alma y de la sangre* [*Supremacy of the Soul and Blood*]
      Victoria Ocampo, *Testimonios. Primera serie (1920-1934)* [*Testimonies. First Series (1920-1934)*]
1936 Aldous Huxley, *¿Cómo lo resuelve Ud.? El problema de la paz constructiva* [*How Do You Resolve It? The Problem of Constructive Peace*]
      André Gide y nuestro tiempo [*André Gide and Our Time*]
      André Gide, *Perséphone*
      André Gide, *Regreso de la U.R.S.S.* [*Return from the USSR*]
      André Malraux, *La condición humana* [*The Human Condition*]
      C. G. Jung, *Tipos psicológicos* [*Psychological Types*]
      Carlos Alberto Erro, *Tiempo lacerado* [*Broken Time*]
      Eduardo Mallea, *La ciudad junto al río inmóvil* [*The City beside the Immobile River*]

YEAR	AUTHOR, WORK
	Igor Stravinsky, *Nuevas crónicas de mi vida* [*New Chronicles of My Life*]
	Jacques Maritain, *Carta sobre la independencia* [*A Letter on Independence*]
	Leopoldo Marechal, *Laberinto de amor* [*Labyrinth of Love*]
	Ramón Gómez de la Serna, *El cólera azul* [*Blue Cholera*]
	Victoria Ocampo, *Domingos en Hyde Park* [*Sundays in Hyde Park*]
	Victoria Ocampo, *La mujer y su expresión* [*Woman and Her Expression*]
	Virginia Woolf, *Un cuarto propio* [*A Room of One's Own*]
1937	Aldous Huxley, *Con los esclavos en la noria* [*Eyeless in Gaza*]
	Alfonso Reyes, *Las vísperas de España* [*The Eves of Spain*]
	André Gide, *Retoques a mi regreso de la U.R.S.S.* [*Retouches to My Return from the USSR*]
	Carlos Alberto Erro, *Diálogo existencial* [*Existential Dialogue*]
	Conrado Nalé Roxlo, *Claro desvelo* [*Clear Insomnia*]
	Eduardo González Lanuza, *La degollación de los inocentes* [*The Massacre of the Innocent*]
	Eduardo Mallea, *Historia de una pasión argentina* [*History of an Argentine Passion*]
	Emile Gouiran, *Prolegómenos de una filosofía de la existencia* [*Introduction to Existentialist Philosophy*]
	Francisco Luis Bernárdez, *Cielo de tierra* [*Heaven of Earth*]
	Gregorio Marañón, *Vida e historia* [*Life and History*]
	Jacques Maritain, *Sobre la guerra santa* [*On the Holy War*]
	James Joyce, *Desterrados* [*Exiles*]
	Julio Irazusta, *Actores y espectadores* [*Actors and Spectators*]
	Silvina Ocampo, *Viaje olvidado* [*Forgotten Trip*]
	Virginia Woolf, *Orlando*
1938	Alain Fournier, *El gran meaulnes* [*Meaulnes the Great*]
	Sir Arthur Stanley Eddington, *La naturaleza del mundo físico* [*The Nature of the Physical World*]
	Emily Brontë, *Cumbres borrascosas* [*Wuthering Heights*]
	Francisco Luis Bernárdez, *La ciudad sin Laura* [*The City without Laura*]
	Gabriela Mistral, *Tala*
	Jacques Maritain, *Los judíos entre las naciones* [*The Jews among Nations*]
	María Luisa Bombal, *La amortajada* [*The Shrouded Woman*]
	Pierre-Henri Simon, *Los católicos, la política y el dinero* [*Catholics, Politics, and Money*]
	Ramón Fernández, *¿Es humano el hombre?* [*Is Man Human?*]
	Robert Aron, *Napoleón venció en Waterloo* [*Napoleon Won in Waterloo*]
	Thomas Mann, *Advertencia a Europa* [*Warning to Europe*]
	Victoria Ocampo, *Emily Brontë (Terra incognita)*
	Victoria Ocampo, *Virginia Woolf, Orlando y Cía*
	Virginia Woolf, *Al faro* [*To the Lighthouse*]

YEAR	AUTHOR, WORK
1939	Hermann de Keyserling, *Del sufrimiento a la plenitud* [*From Suffering to Fulfillment*]
	Leon Chestov, *Las revelaciones de la muerte* [*Revelations of Death*]
	Luis Emilio Soto, *Crítica y estimación* [*Critique and Respect*]
	Oliverio Girondo, *Interlunio* [*Lunarlude*]
	Roger Caillois, *El hombre y el mito* [*Man and Myth*]
	Xavier Villaurrutia, *Nostalgia de la muerte* [*Nostalgia for Death*]
1940	Samuel Eichelbaum, *Pájaro de barro* [*Mud Bird*]
	Charles de Gaulle, *El ejército del porvenir* [*The Army of the Future*]
	Denis de Rougemont, *Diario de Alemania* [*Diary of Germany*]
	Fritz Thyssen, *Thyssen-Hitler. Documentos inéditos relativos a este proceso* [*Thyssen-Hitler. Unedited Documents Related to This Trial*]
1941	Alfredo de la Guardia, *García Lorca: Persona y creación* [*García Lorca: Person and Creation*]
	Denis de Rougemont, *¿Cambiar la vida o cambiar al hombre?* [*To Change Life or to Change Man?*]
	H. G. Wells, *El destino del homo sapiens* [*The Fate of Man*]
	Henri Michaux, *Un bárbaro en Asia* [*A Barbarian in Asia*]
	Jorge Luis Borges, *El jardín de senderos que se bifurcan* [*The Garden of Forking Paths*]
	Roger Caillois, *Le Roman policier* [*The Detective Story*]
	Victoria Ocampo, *338171.TE* [*Lawrence of Arabia*]
	Victoria Ocampo, *Testimonios. Segunda serie* [*Testimonies. Second Series*]
	Virginia Woolf, *Tres guineas* [*Three Guineas*]
1942	André Breton, *Fata Morgana*
	Roger Caillois, *Sociología de la novela* [*Sociology of the Novel*]
	Silvina Ocampo, *Enumeración de la patria y otros poemas* [*Enumeration of My Country and Other Poems*]
	Vicente Barbieri, *La columna y el viento* [*The Column and the Wind*]
	William Faulkner, *Luz de agosto* [*Light in August*]
1943	Eduardo González Lanuza, *Transitable cristal* [*Passable Glass*]
	H. Bustos Domecq, *Seis problemas para don Isidro Parodi* [*Six Problems for Don Isidro Parodi*]
	José Bianco, *Las ratas* [*The Rats*]
1944	Charles Baudelaire, *Journaux intimes* [*Intimate Journals*]
	Fr. Guizot, *Des conspirationes et de la justice politique* [*On Conspiracies and Political Justice*]
	Gérard de Nerval, *Sylvie suivi de les chimères* [*Sylvie and the Chimera*]
	Grévières, *El desdichado* [*The Wretched*]
	Jorge Luis Borges, *Ficciones*
	Jules Supervielle, *La belle au bois* [*Beauty in the Woods*]
	Manuel Peyrou, *La espada dormida* [*The Sleeping Sword*]

YEAR	AUTHOR, WORK
	Paul Valéry, *Un poète inconnu* [*An Unknown Poet*]
	Roger Caillois, *Les impostures de la poésie* [*The Deceptions of Poetry*]
	T. E. Lawrence, *Cartas* [*Letters*]
	T. E. Lawrence, *Los siete pilares de la sabiduría* [*Seven Pillars of Wisdom*]
1945	Victoria Ocampo, *Le vert paradis* [*Green Paradise*]
	Saint-John Perse, *Quatre poèmes (1941-1944)* [*Four Poems (1941-1944)*]
	Silvina Ocampo, *Espacios métricos* [*Metric Spaces*]
1946	Alberto Girri, *Línea de la vida* [*Life Line*]
1947	Jean-Paul Sartre, *El existencialismo es un humanismo* [*Existentialism Is Humanism*]
	Victoria Ocampo, *Henry V y Laurence Olivier*
	Victoria Kent, *Cuatro años en París (1940-1944)* [*Four Years in Paris (1940-1944)*]
1948	Albert Camus, *La Peste* [*The Plague*]
	Christopher Isherwood, *Adiós a Berlín* [*Goodbye to Berlin*]
	George Orwell, *Ensayos críticos* [*Critical Essays*]
	Ernesto Sábato, *El túnel* [*The Tunnel*]
	Jean-Paul Sartre, *Reflexiones sobre la cuestión judía* [*Reflections on the Jewish Question*]
1949	Adolfo Bioy Casares, *La invención de Morel* [*The Invention of Morel*]
	Adolfo Bioy Casares, *La trama celeste* [*The Celestial Plot*]
	Cyril Connolly, *La tumba sin sosiego* [*The Unquiet Grave*]
	Graham Greene, *El revés de la trama* [*The Heart of the Matter*]
	Silvina Ocampo, *Autobiografía de Irene* [*Autobiography of Irene*]
1950	Victoria Ocampo, *Hamlet*
	Victoria Ocampo, *San Isidro (con fotografías de S. Thorlingen)* [*San Isidro (with Photographs by S. Thorlingen)*]
	Victoria Ocampo, *Testimonios. Cuarta serie* [*Testimonies. Fourth Series*]

Notes

Introduction

1. "Undergrounds" commonly refers to the University of Virginia's Special Collections library since the space is physically located underground and the entire UVA campus is known as "grounds."

2. See Balderston, *How Borges Wrote* and *Variaciones Borges* 38 (2014) for questions of manuscript variants and genetic criticism in Borges's work.

3. For an idea of the Americana collecting strength of the University of Virginia, see the Tracy W. McGregor Library of American History, the Clifton Waller Barrett Library of American Literature, and the Thomas Jefferson Papers.

4. Transcribed notes from a telephone conversation between Jared Loewenstein and Borges on April 8, 1980, between 9:15 and 9:40 a.m. The transcription and summary of the conversation is part of the University of Virginia Borges Collection records.

5. Lawrence explores this north-south divide at length with a focus on "the complicated forms of attraction and disavowal that writers across the Americas have displayed toward firsthand experience as the ultimate authority for literary work" (*Anxieties of Experience*, 9). On the question of north-south translation issues, also see Rogers, *Incomparable Empires*.

6. See Abraham, *La editorial Tor*; Cucuzza, Spregelburd, and Artieda, *Historia de la lectura en Argentina*; de Diego, *Editores y políticas editoriales* and *La otra cara de Jano*; Epplin, *Late Book Culture in Argentina*; and Batticuore, *Lectores del siglo XIX*.

7. The term *porteño* commonly refers to the city of Buenos Aires and/or its inhabitants. For more on the Argentine professionalization in the book industry during this time, see Buonocore, *El mundo de los libros* and *Libreros, editores e impresores*; Rivera, "La forja del escritor profesional" and "El auge de la industria cultural"; de Sagastizábal, *La edición de libros*; and de Diego, *Editores y políticas editoriales*.

8. de Diego, *Editores y políticas editoriales*.

9. See Tedesco, *Educación y sociedad en la Argentina*; Gvirtz, *Nuevas y viejas tendencias en la docencia*; and Gvirtz and Beech, eds., *Going to School in Latin America*.

10. Three of the largest publishing firms founded in Buenos Aires by Spanish exiles were Emecé Editores, Editorial Sudamericana, and Editorial Losada.

11. Winship, "Publishing in America," 66.

12. Ibid., 81.

13. Burgin and Borges, *Conversations*, 70.

14. Appiah (*Cosmopolitanism*) and Nussbaum (*For Love of Country*) emphasize these aspects in their important work on cosmopolitanism. Nussbaum's most recent work on cosmopolitanism (*The Cosmopolitan Tradition*) came out while the current book was being finalized. Siskind (*Cosmopolitan Desires*) builds on their work and considers the unique (marginal) aspects of Latin American cosmopolitanisms while still focusing on the moral and political connotations of the term.

15. Diogenes of Sinope famously retorted that he was a "citizen of the world" when asked where he came from. Appiah stresses that this "formulation was meant to be paradoxical, and reflected the general Cynic skepticism toward custom and tradition" (*Cosmopolitanism*, xiv).

16. Critchley, "Cynicism We Can Believe In."

17. Baker, "Cynical Cosmopolitanism," 616.

18. For Diogenes and the Cynics, "counseling the simple and uncomplicated satisfaction of one's natural instincts and desires . . . urges detachment from those things held out by convention to be good" (Parry, "Ancient Ethical Theory"). Balderston echoes these ideas in his analysis of Borges's skepticism toward the category of world literature ("Borges en el mundo").

19. The print version of "El escritor argentino y la tradición" first appeared in the journal *Cursos y conferencias* in 1953 and then in the literary journal *Sur* in 1955; it finally was included in the second edition of Borges's *Discusión* [*Discussion*] in 1957. All of these print versions stemmed from shorthand notes taken during the original class in 1951. Similarly, "Kafka y sus precursores" also originated from class notes at the Colegio Libre de Estudios Superiores.

20. Borges, *Selected Non-Fictions*, 426–27.

21. Ibid., 365. Borges acknowledges his clear allusion to T. S. Eliot in this essay with a footnote to "Tradition and the Individual Talent."

ONE Borges and the Book

1. Borges, *Borges, oral*, 13–14. Unless indicated, all translations are mine.

2. Rosato and Álvarez, *Borges, libros y lecturas*, 25.

3. It is important to distinguish this personal library, which was housed at his last residence in Argentina, Maipú 444, from the collection housed at the National Library in Buenos Aires. Even though the volumes that now comprise the collection at the National Library were once part of his personal library, he donated them to this public institution in 1973 and they were thus not located within the author's home.

4. Sometime during 1929 Borges won a literary prize for *Cuaderno San Martín* (1929), and with the money received he purchased a "second-hand set of the Eleventh Edition of the Encyclopaedia Britannica" (Borges, "Autobiographical Notes," 74).

5. Borges dedicates a short article to his father's library in which he states that this place "ha sido el acontecimiento capital de mi vida. Ahí, por obra de la voz de mi padre, me fue revelada esa cosa misteriosa, la poesía; ahí me fueron revelados los mapas, las ilustraciones, más preciosas entonces para mí que las letras de molde ... Ante todo, enciclopedias, que desde Plinio a Brockhaus, pasando por Isidoro de Sevilla, por Diderot y por la undécima edición de la Británica, cuyos lomos dorados imagino en la inmóvil penumbra de la ceguera, son, para un hombre ocioso y curioso, el más deleitable de los géneros literarios. Las bibliotecas son la memoria de la humanidad" [has been the key event of my life. There, thanks to my father's voice, this strange thing, poetry, was revealed to me; there I was shown maps, the illustrations, more precious at that time to me than print words ... Above all, the encyclopedias, from Pliny to Brockhaus, to Isidoro de Sevilla, to Diderot and to the eleventh edition of the Britannica, whose gold spines I picture in the immobile shadow of blindness, are, for a pleasurable and curious man, the most delightful of the literary genres. Libraries are the memory of humanity] (Borges, "La biblioteca de mi padre," 4).

6. Borges, "Autobiographical Notes," 42. While many critics have shown that there are reasons to doubt the veracity of Borges's testimonies throughout his "Autobiographical Notes," the examples and details that he pulls on here are nonetheless revealing (see Rodríguez Monegal, *Jorge Luis Borges*, 1978, and Balderston, *Out of Context*, 1993).

7. Borges, "Autobiographical Notes," 42.

8. Ibid., 42–43.

9. Buonocore, *Libreros, editores e impresores*, 113.

10. Goñi, "A Novel Oasis."

11. Many of the bookstores included in Rosato and Álvarez's study foreground Borges's lack of interest in Latin American literature and instead his pull toward foreign works: "La ausencia prácticamente total de literatura argentina e hispanoamericana en esta colección es una condición que se repite, hasta donde sabemos, en los demás repositorios donde se conservan partes representativas de su biblioteca" [The almost total absence of Argentine and Hispano-American literature in this collection is something that repeats, as far as we know, in other repositories where parts of [Borges's] library are conserved] (*Borges, libros y lecturas*, 25).

12. "One afternoon, Jorge Luis Borges came to the bookstore accompanied by his eighty-eight-year-old mother ... as he was about to leave, he asked me if I was busy in the evenings because he needed (he said this very apologetically) someone to read to him, since his mother now tired very easily. I said I would.

"Over the next two years I read to Borges, as did many other fortunate and casual acquaintances, either in the evenings or, if school allowed it, in the mornings ... I never had the sense of merely fulfilling a duty in my readings to Borges; instead, the experience felt like a sort of happy captivity. I was enthralled not so much by the texts he was making me discover (many of which eventually became my favorites) as by his comments, which were vastly but unobtrusively erudite, very funny, sometimes cruel, almost always indispensable. I felt I was the unique owner of a carefully annotated edition, compiled for my exclusive sake" (Manguel, *A History of Reading*, 16–19).

13. As we shall see in Chapter 2, Viau y Cía later branched out to start publishing books, some of which were Borges's first titles, under the imprint Viau y Zona.

14. Rosato and Álvarez, *Borges, libros y lecturas*, 29.

15. Canto, *Borges a contraluz*, 31.

16. Borges, *Evaristo Carriego*, 51–52.

17. The index to this specific chapter even describes this initial section as "La idea física de cualquier primer libro" [The physical idea of any first book], which further stresses the material aspect of the book and its importance for Borges.

18. Borges, *Discusión*, 106; Tanselle, *A Rationale of Textual Criticism*, 18.

19. Borges, *Discusión*, 106.

20. The fact that *editar* means "to publish" creates a bit of confusion for discussions of many of these early publications that may or may not have been produced with the help of a publishing firm. Surely Borges would have embraced this level of linguistic ambiguity, especially when the ambiguity involved both of his mother tongues.

21. Borges, *Discusión*, 93.

22. Tanselle, "The Pleasures of Being a Scholar-Collector," 8.

23. The first edition of *Historia de la eternidad*, published by Viau y Zona and printed by Francisco A. Colombo in 1936, contains four essays and two notes; the later edition produced by Emecé (1953), adds two additional essays: "El tiempo circular" [Circular Time] and "La metáfora" [The Metaphor].

24. Borges, *Historia de la eternidad*, 19.

25. Pollard, "Bibliography and Bibliology," 909.

26. This particular question relates the issue at hand to that of the ship of Theseus (i.e., if all the parts of the book, much like Theseus's ship, are replaced with new parts, is it the same object?).

27. Borges, *El jardín de senderos que se bifurcan*, 12.

28. Balderston (*The Literary Universe of Jorge Luis Borges* and *Out of Context*) has proved that most of the books that Borges references are real books.

29. Carrizo and Borges, *Borges, el memorioso*, 222.

30. Pollard, "Bibliography and Bibliology," 909.

31. Borges, *Ficciones*, 15.

32. Bowers, *Principles of Bibliographical Description*, 374n5. Undoubtedly there are geographic and profession-specific preferences for the use of the terms "(re)printing" and "(re)impression." According to Fredson Bowers, "Printing is the term ordinarily used by the book trade ... the word impression is preferable for bibliographical writing" (374n5). For more information regarding the differences between an edition, an impression, an issue, and a state, see Tanselle, "The Bibliographical Concepts of 'Issue' and 'State.'"

33. Bowers, *Principles of Bibliographical Description*, 380.

34. Gaskell, *A New Introduction to Bibliography*, 315.

NOTES TO PAGES 25–30   287

35. De Ricci, *English Collectors of Books and Manuscripts*, 159.

36. de Toro, "Borges and the Construction of 'Reality,'" 282n13.

37. Borges, *Ficciones*, 17. Nicolás Helft has linked these black and gold spines with the eleventh edition of the *Encyclopedia Britannica*, but they could just as easily match up with the tenth (or an even earlier) edition, especially when we consider the drastic physical changes that this work underwent with the eleventh edition. More specifically, the most novel feature of the eleventh edition was its use of India paper, which made the volumes thinner, lighter, and easier to handle and read. In addition, these new volumes were available in four different binding styles, with the India paper and three with ordinary book paper.

38. Borges, *Ficciones*, 18–19. The book described is addressed to Herbert Ashe, not the narrator.

39. Ibid., 35.

40. Ibid., 48.

41. "He dicho que la obra *visible* de Menard es fácilmente enumerable. Examinado con esmero su archivo particular" [I have said that Menard's *visible* work is easily enumerated. Examining his particular archive with care] (*Ficciones* 48). The phrase "obra *visible*" [*visible* work] appears on three separate occasions throughout the work when the writings of Menard are being discussed, which seems to show a similar link to bibliography since, in its broadest sense, it is the study of books as observable physical objects (*Ficciones* 47, 48, 51).

42. Borges, *Ficciones*, 52.

43. Ibid.

44. See Grafton, *Forgers and Critics*.

45. Borges, *Ficciones*, 55.

46. Ibid., 52–53.

47. Here again we see the pull between manuscripts and printed forms in the creation process.

48. Borges, *Ficciones*, 38.

49. Ibid.

50. One such reference appears in a short story in *Ficciones*, "El milagro secreto" [The Secret Miracle], in which a playwright, Hladík, is arrested for his translation of the *Sepher Yezirah* "para la editorial Hermann Barsdorf; el efusivo catálogo de esa casa había exagerado comercialmente el renombre del traductor" [for Editorial Hermann Barsdorf; the effusive catalogue for this firm had commercially exaggerated the fame of the translator] (*Ficciones* 166). Similar to the British publishing firm that appears in "El acercamiento a Almotásim," Hermann Barsdorf is also a real publishing house (in this case in Germany). More interesting, perhaps, is the fact that, during the Second World War, many Nazi soldiers used catalogues from this German publishing house to identify Jewish authors and subsequently to persecute them.

51. Borges, *Ficciones*, 38.

52. Here again we see the conflation of real and imaginary worlds with the juxtaposition of the invented Herbert Quain and the "real" author of detective fiction, Ellery

Queen (which was, however, a pseudonym for Frederic Dannay [Daniel Nathan] and Manfred Bennington Lee [Emanuel Lepofsky]).

53. The passage in question from "Examen de la obra de Herbert Quain" is the following: "*todos creyeron que el encuentro de los dos jugadores de ajedrez había sido* casual. Esa frase deja entender que la solución es errónea. El lector, inquieto, revisa los capítulos pertinentes y descubre otra solución, que es la verdadera. El lector de ese libro singular es más perspicaz que el *detective*" [*everyone believed that the meeting between the two chess players was* chance. That phrase leads one to believe that the solution is wrong. The reader, restless, looks over the relevant chapters and finds another solution, that is the true one. The reader of this unique book is keener than the *detective*] (*Ficciones*, 61); Borges's review in *El Hogar* states the following: "'y todos creyeron que el encuentro de ese hombre y de esa mujer había sido casual'—que indicara o dejara suponer que la solución era falsa. El lector, inquieto, revisaría los capítulos pertinentes y daría con otra solución, con la verdadera. El lector de ese libro imaginario sería más perspicaz que el 'detective'" ['and everyone believed that the meeting between that man and that woman was chance'—which indicated or led one to believe that the solution was false. The reader, restless, would look over the relevant chapters and would come up with another solution, with the true one. The reader of his imaginary book would be keener than the 'detective'] ("Excellent Intentions," 26).

54. Marcano, "La reseña bibliográfica," 466.
55. Borges, *Ficciones*, 91.
56. Ibid., 93–94.
57. Ibid., 94.
58. Ibid., 96.
59. Ibid.
60. Pollard, *Books in the House*, 8.
61. Borges, *Ficciones*, 97.
62. Ibid., 100.
63. Pollard, "Bibliography and Bibliology," 911.
64. Editorial Sur first published *Ficciones* in 1944, and it consisted of two parts: *El jardín de senderos que se bifurcan* and "Artificios" [Artifices]. When Emecé Editores published the second edition of *Ficciones* in 1956, three new stories were added to "Artificios": "El fin" [The End], "La secta del fénix" [The Sect of the Phoenix], and "El sur" [The South].
65. Borges, *Ficciones*, 119.
66. Ibid., 128.
67. The named books in Yarmolinsky's collection are the following: "una *Vindicación de la cábala*; un *Examen de la filosofía de Robert Fludd*; una traducción literal de *Sepher Yezirah*; una *Biografía del Baal Shem*; una *Historia de la secta de los Hasidim*; una monografía (en alemán) sobre el Tetragrámaton; otra, sobre la nomenclatura divina del Pentateuco" [a *Vindication of the Cabala*; an *Examination of the Philosophy of Robert Fludd*; a literal translation of the *Sepher Yezirah*; a *Biography of the Baal Shem*; a *History of the Sect of Hasidim*; a monograph (in German) about the Tetragrammaton; another, on

the divine nomenclature of the Pentateuch] (*Ficciones*, 149). The translation of the *Sepher Yezirah* is also mentioned in another story in *Ficciones*, "El milagro secreto" [The Secret Miracle].

68. Borges and Bioy Casares, *Seis problemas*, 71.

69. Editorial Losada first published *El Aleph* in 1949. When this same firm published the second edition in 1952, four new stories were added: "Abenjacán el Bojarí, muerto en su laberinto" [Abenjacán el Bojarí, Dead in His Labyrinth], "Los dos reyes y los dos laberintos" [The Two Kings and the Two Labyrinths], "La espera" [The Wait], and "El hombre en el umbral" [The Man on the Threshold].

70. Borges, *El Aleph*, 7. The fact that the manuscript in question was found in a physical book raises the question of whether or not these additional pages were tipped-in (or bound with the other pages) or simply inserted loosely after the text block was bound. If this phrase is understood as meaning that the manuscript pages were physically bound into the book, then we must also take into consideration the possibility that the reader might have bound these pages in separately after purchase.

71. Instead of being released all at once, each of the six volumes came out annually, which "allowed the publisher, Bernard Lintot (1675–1736), to pay for the production of only one volume, the sales of which would eventually provide the capital for the second volume, and so on to the sixth and last. Indeed, the success of this system depended on the abilities of authors and publishers to gather a fair number of subscribers in order to finance the projected volumes" (Álvarez, "Collection Highlight"). In addition to the financial advantages that Pope's *Iliad* introduced to England, the selection of a quarto format (offered in both ordinary and thick paper) introduced a change in aesthetics since, before its publication, most major works tended to appear in folio format. In addition to the quarto options for Pope's *Iliad,* small- and large-paper folios also were available.

72. Borges, *El Aleph*, 165.

73. Ibid., 167. This is a joke drawing on the mythological figure of Procrustes to indicate that Daneri's work is either warped or distorted to fit an arbitrary standard in order to be published. This allusion might also be an erudite reference to the guillotining of the edges of book paper after binding.

74. Molloy, *Signs of Borges*, 106.

75. Ibid., 110–11.

76. For similar work on the blurring of boundaries between the real and the fictitious, see White, *The Content of the Form*; González Echevarría, *Myth and Archive*; Jasper and Smith, eds., *Between Truth and Fiction*; and Doran, ed., *Philosophy of History After Hayden White*.

77. See Tcherepashenets, *Place and Displacement in the Narrative Worlds of Jorge Luis Borges and Julio Cortázar*; Block de Behar, *Borges*; Wolf, *Building Imaginary Worlds*; and Sassón-Henry, *Borges 2.0*.

78. See Fishburn, "A Footnote to Borges Studies," and Waisman, *Borges and Translation*.

79. This line of thought is complementary to Balderston's work in *Out of Context*.

80. The most comprehensive study of such apocryphal books is Allen Ruch's "The

Crimson Hexagon: Books Borges Never Wrote" (1996), which seeks to catalogue all of the imaginary books that Borges mentions throughout his writings.

81. Waisman, *Borges and Translation*, 231n10.

82. See Bell-Villada, *Borges and His Fiction*; de Costa, *Humor in Borges*; Martín, "Humor y parodia en Borges"; Blanco, "Parodia y política"; and González, *Borges and the Politics of Form*.

83. Rodríguez Monegal, *Jorge Luis Borges*, 90.

84. He even went on to say "I am sick of Borges" during this same conversation with Loewenstein.

85. Carrizo and Borges, *Borges, el memorioso*, 218.

86. Ibid. The sum Borges received for his position as codirector of the *Revista Multicolor* is quite a bit more than his salary while employed at the Municipal Miguel Cané Library a few years later. This difference in earnings might be the result of the types of positions he held at each of these establishments as well as the overall revenue of these places, which would determine how much they could pay their employees.

87. Petit de Murat, *Borges*, 140–41.

88. Balderston, "'His Insect-Like Handwriting.'"

89. Although it is quite difficult to determine the format of the first edition copies of this work from the UVA collection (both of which have been rebound), they each have sixty-four pages, plus an additional insert of a drawing of Borges by Silvina Ocampo, which would indicate that a fourth "pliegue," or gathering, was added to Borges's initial calculations. Even more puzzling is the fact that of the list of possible poems in this manuscript, only ten appear in the printed first edition of *Cuaderno San Martín*, which seems to suggest a *reduction* in the necessary number of pages, as opposed to an increase.

90. Editorial Proa, or the Sociedad Editorial Proa, was an Argentine publishing firm founded by Oliverio Girondo, Ricardo Güiraldes, and Evar Méndez in 1924.

91. It is also important to highlight that *Cuaderno San Martín* was Borges's first book of poems to include notes.

TWO Borges as Author

1. There have been several great, in-depth studies of individual venues in which Borges published during the early 1930s, but no comparative study looks at all of these firms collectively.

2. Louis, *Jorge Luis Borges*, 25.

3. Ibid., 28.

4. Although the printed volumes of this edition do not contain information regarding the specific number of copies in the print run, similar works produced at the time would range between 250 and 300, which is a safe estimate for this book.

5. Cháneton, "El libro de lujo en Argentina," 47.

6. I consider the question of luxury editions and printed material for the elite classes in Chapter 5.

7. The Amigos del Arte began their own "actividades editoriales" [editorial activities] in 1930 (Cháneton, "El libro de lujo en Argentina," 51).

8. Even after Colombo's death in 1953, the printing firm continued production, as a family operation, under his name: "Vivos están en ellas el supremo cuidado en la impresión que prodiga Emilio Colombo, el rigor en la diagramación tipográfica de Alejandro A. Zampieri, y la generosa comprensión de Osvaldo Colombo, digno heredero de quien iniciara ésta labor maravillosa" [In them are alive a supreme quality of printing bestowed by Emilio Colombo, an exactitude in typographical diagramming by Alejandro A. Zampieri, and the generous understanding of Osvaldo Colombo, the worthy heir from whom this marvelous work started] (Larrauri, *El arte del libro*, 5).

9. The only other printer that produced luxury editions in Argentina during this time was Ghino Fogli, "el artesano de vocación y profesión, el técnico de rica experiencia y ciencia, el discípulo fiel a las severas enseñanzas de ese magnífico instituto de artes gráficos que se llama Escuela del Libro de Milán" [the artisan of vocation and profession, the expert of rich experience and science, the faithful disciple of the strict teachings of that magnificent institute of graphic arts that is called the School of the Book of Milan] (Buonocore, *Libreros, editores e impresores*, 189).

10. Thompson, "La sociedad de bibliófilos," 396. The first work printed for the Sociedad de Bibliófilos Argentinos was Domingo F. Sarmiento's *Facundo* in 1933 (1935 according to its colophon), which Colombo printed on Japanese paper in a run of 105 copies with etchings by Alfredo Guido; from that moment forward each print run would be limited to 100 copies, which indicates their primary function as collectors' items.

11. One important aspect of the commercial relationship between Colombo and Güiraldes is the influence of Parisian stylistic tendencies. Previously mentioned as an important factor in the emergence of luxury editions in Argentina during the 1920s, the use of French design techniques in Colombo's editions can be traced directly to Güiraldes since he wrote his novel *Don Segundo Sombra*, which would later be published with Colombo, in Paris. His preference for special paper and numbered copies can be linked to his exposure to French luxury editions.

12. *Francisco A. Colombo en sus cincuenta años de labor gráfica*, 10.

13. Larrauri, *El arte del libro*, 4. According to one of Colombo's catálogues, Güiraldes's *Rosaura* was "el primer libro en edición de lujo compuesta a mano e impresa por Francisco A. Colombo en San Antonio de Areco" [the first book in a luxury edition set by hand and printed by Francisco A. Colombo in San Antonio de Areco]. Alberto Güiraldes designed the cover, and it was printed in a run of two hundred numbered copies that were not for sale.

14. Ros, "La sociedad de bibliófilos argentinos," 71.

15. Marqués, "La plaqueta artística en La Argentina," 21. Before Colombo, the main printers of fame were Guillermo Kraft, Jacobo Peuser, Lorenzo J. Rosso, and F. G. Profumo. While certain aspects of Kraft's work were elegantly printed, they were nowhere near the quality of Colombo's books, and none of these earlier printers was ever described as a luxury printer.

16. Cháneton, "El libro de lujo en Argentina," 55.

17. Colombo also printed his earlier *Cuaderno San Martín* (1929).

18. *Francisco A. Colombo en sus cincuenta años de labor gráfica*, 41–42.

19. King, *Sur*, 46.

20. Buonocore, *Libreros, editores e impresores*, 189.

21. In fact, the only collection of published poetry during the time frame this book explores (1930–1951) is a reissuing (with slight changes) of his previous three collections (*Fervor de Buenos Aires* [1923], *Luna de enfrente* [1925], and *Cuaderno San Martín* [1929]) in one volume: *Poemas (1922–1943)* (Editorial Losada, 1943).

22. di Giovanni, *The Lesson of the Master*, 94.

23. Di Giovanni also suggests an earlier precedent in Borges's *Luna de enfrente* (1925) where Carriego serves as a key link to understanding a few of the poems in the collection.

24. In addition to di Giovanni's study, see Balderston, "'Las variantes raleaban,'" and Canala, "Lecturas y relecturas de un comienzo."

25. Borges, "Autobiographical Notes," 74. Besides the production and printing of *Fervor de Buenos Aires* (1923), which was completely financed by his father, this is the only other (personal) reference to the monetary backing of one of his books.

26. Ibid.

27. Sara del Carril, who worked closely with Borges at Emecé Editores, notes that virtually all of his earlier books that this firm republished in the 1950s and 1960s "salieron con tapa gris tipográfica (a Borges no le gustaban las tapas ilustradas)" [came out with gray, typographically designed covers (Borges did not like illustrated covers)] ("Borges en Emecé," 125). When I met with del Carril during the summer of 2015, she confirmed this statement and shared several anecdotes about Borges's dislike of such visual ornamentation on the covers of any of his books.

28. The typeface used on the cover of *Evaristo Carriego* is most likely a variant of either Garamond or Bodoni, both of which were fairly widespread among fine printers at this time.

29. According to each of their respective colophons, *Inquisiciones* was printed by the Talleres Gráficos "El Inca," *El tamaño de mi esperanza* was printed by the Talleres Gráficos de E. A. Petenello, and, as we have already established, *Evaristo Carriego* was printed by Francisco A. Colombo.

30. Manuel Gleizer, the publisher for both *Discusión* and *Evaristo Carriego*, will be discussed in the next section on accidental publishers.

31. "Discusión sobre Borges."

32. Ibid., 19. Although there is no lack of articles or critical investigations dedicated to the essays and contents of this collection, virtually no studies are dedicated to the collection as a whole, aside from this very early critical response and Irby, "Textual Series in *Discusión*."

33. "Discusión sobre Borges," 13. See Bastos, *Borges ante la crítica argentin*, for a more detailed study of the importance of this special issue.

34. Borges, *Discusión*, 9. Similar to much of Borges's published works from these earlier years, the reedited, republished editions from the 1950s and 1960s show several marked differences. In addition to emendations to the already included essays in *Discusión*, many of the later editions include new pieces such as "La poesía gauchesca" [Gau-

chesque Poetry], "Nota sobre Walt Whitman" [Note on Walt Whitman], "Avatares de la tortuga" [Avatars of the Tortoise], "Vindicación de 'Bouvard et Pécuchet'" [Vindication of "Bouvard and Pécuchet"], "Flaubert y su destino ejemplar" [Flaubert and His Exemplary Destiny], and "El escritor argentino y la tradición" [The Argentine Writer and Tradition] (Emecé Editores, 1957). Given my time frame, I consider the contents of only the first edition of *Discusión* (1932).

35. Borges, *Obras completas* (2007–2011), 1:790. "Noticia de los kenningar [Note about Kennings]," *Sur* 6 (1932): 202–8. This essay later appeared in Borges's *Historia de la eternidad* (1936). The typographical error of the definite article (*los* instead of *las*) might explain Borges's desire to reprint the essay as a stand-alone piece.

36. The only piece of criticism that I have been able to locate on this specific essay (Lynn and Shumway, "Borges y *Las Kenningar*") refers solely to the version of the work included in *Historia de la eternidad* (1936); the authors of this piece assign the collection an incorrect publishing date of 1933, which possibly alludes to their knowledge of the earlier publication of this essay, but there is no mention of Colombo or any of the physical details of the text. Instead, as with any passing references to *Las Kenningar* in critical studies, Lynn and Shumway focus on the influence of Icelandic sagas and Old Norse on Borges's writings and how this essay can be seen as an early antecedent for his later writings on these cultures.

37. Emecé's later edition of this work (1953) adds two additional essays: "El tiempo circular" [Circular Time] and "La metáfora" [The Metaphor].

38. Buonocore confirms these characteristics: "Textos en gran papel, con amplios márgenes, caracteres exclusivamente diseñados, tintas de calidad en dos o más colores e ilustraciones originales a cargo de artistas de notoria reputación" [Texts on large paper, with wide margins, exclusively designed type, quality ink in two or more colors, and original illustrations undertaken by artists with notorious reputations] (*Libreros, editores e impresores*, 187).

39. Velarde, *El editor Domingo Viau*, 52.

40. Buonocore, *Libreros, editores e impresores*, 196.

41. Sixty-eight titles were published under the name Viau y Zona (1927–1937), twenty-two published under Domingo Viau y Cía (1934–1942), nineteen under El Bibliófilo (1937–1945), thirty-five under Domingo Viau-editor (1936–1947), and eight with the description of "editados por la casa" [edited by the publishing house] (*Catálogo*).

42. Velarde, *El editor Domingo Viau*, 47–48.

43. King, *Sur*, 89.

44. Sotheby's London, *Medieval and Renaissance Manuscripts*, 83.

45. As one source notes, Gleizer "va a transformarse en librero por azar" [would transform himself into a bookseller by chance] and later "en 1922 pasó de librero a editor" [in 1922 transitioned from bookseller to editor] (de Diego, *Editores y políticas editoriales*, 82–83).

46. García Costa, "El último romántico de los editores," 5.

47. Bär, "Manuel Gleizer."

48. One of the interviewees in Raquel Goldenberg's study of Gleizer empha-

sizes the impact of this publisher on Argentine culture: "No puede dejar de recordarse la valiosa obra de difusión cultural de aquel pionero de las impresiones de libros en nuestra ciudad que se llamó Manuel Gleizer" [One cannot forget the valuable work of cultural dissemination of Manuel Gleizer, who was a pioneer in book publishing in our city] ("Manuel Gleizer," 322).

49. "Mapa celeste de editoriales."
50. Goldenberg, "Manuel Gleizer," 329.
51. Ibid., 330.
52. Bär, "Manuel Gleizer."
53. Ibid.
54. Goldenberg, "Manuel Gleizer," 328. Goldenberg also notes that Colombo's son, Osvaldo, said: "guardo aún en la casa de Areco, documentos comerciales 'pagarés,' firmados y nunca 'protestados'—los he guardado por conservar la firma de Gleizer—. Este tenía un olfato muy especial para descubrir el talento de los jóvenes poetas argentinos" [In our Areco house I still hang onto these commercial "promissory note" documents, signed and never "refused"—I've saved them to conserve the signature of Gleizer. He had a real sense for discovering the talent of young Argentine poets] (ibid.).

55. The short-lived commercial relationship between Gleizer and Colombo, started in 1930 and ended in 1933, raises the question of whether Borges was a key link in their connection, especially when we consider the fact that all three of Borges's works from 1930 to 1933 were printed by Colombo, and all but one (*Las Kenningar*) were published by Gleizer.

56. Akin to other publishers that were named after their founders, Editorial TOR was originally called Editorial Torrendell, "pero ante los frecuentes errores por parte de los clientes y proveedores... se optó por la versión simplificada" [but after frequent errors by both clients and providers... he opted for the simplified version] (Abraham, *La editorial Tor*, 34).

57. "El uso de rotativas permitió que la empresa publicase libros y revistas en cantidades masivas y a muy bajo precio. Por ejemplo, si en la etapa anterior el precio promedio de los libros oscilaba entre 1 y 3 pesos, en esta oscila entre 20 y 30 centavos... Y, en vez de publicar solo cuando aparecía un texto interesante o provechoso, se debió hacer funcionar las máquinas de modo constante y regular a fin de aprovechar la capacidad instalada, lo que obligó a buscar constantemente nuevos textos para las diversas colecciones" [The use of rotary presses allowed the firm to publish books and magazines in massive quantities and at a very low cost. For example, if in their previous phase the average cost of the books oscillated between one and three pesos, in this phase it oscillated between twenty and thirty cents... And, in terms of publishing only when an interesting or profitable title appeared, the machines were now operated nonstop so that they could make the best of their investment, which required them to search constantly for new texts for their diverse collections] (Abraham, *La editorial Tor*, 67).

58. de Diego, *Editores y políticas editoriales*, 73.
59. Abraham, *La editorial Tor*, 45.
60. It is even more curious when we consider the fact that Borges himself cites

this collection of fiction as the start of his literary career: "The real beginning of my career as a story writer starts with the series of sketches entitled 'Historia universal de la infamia' ('A Universal History of Infamy')" ("Autobiographical Notes," 78).

61. Abraham, *La editorial Tor,* 91. In addition to Borges's *Historia universal de la infamia,* the Colección Megáfono also included Ignacio Anzoátegui's *Vidas de muertos* [*Lives of the Dead*] (1934), Julio Irazusta's *Ensayo sobre Rosas* [*Essay about Rosas*] (1935), and Sigfrido Radaelli's *Irreverencia histórica* [*Historical Irreverence*] (1934).

62. "Discusión sobre Borges," 18.

63. Rodríguez Monegal, *Jorge Luis Borges,* 255.

64. Waisman, *Borges and Translation,* 91.

65. Borges, *Obras completas* (2007–2011), 1:597.

66. Alazraki, "Génesis de un estilo"; Balderston, *El precursor velado* and *Out of Context*; Molloy, *Signs of Borges*; and Waisman, *Borges and Translation.*

67. Petit de Murat, *Borges,* 140.

68. Part of the sensational and larger-than-life aspects of the *Revista Multicolor* can be traced to Botana's desire to compete with *La Nación*'s various supplements, which had appeared in print starting in 1902. As a result, Botana ensures his loyal readers that the supplement for *Crítica* will appear on Sundays, just like *La Nación.*

69. Sarlo, *The Technical Imagination,* 59.

70. Ibid., 60. Borges goes so far as to describe the literary supplement as "heavily and even gaudily illustrated" ("Autobiographical Notes," 80).

71. Saítta, "Recorrido"; Atena Green, *Borges y Revista multicolor de los sábados*; and Louis, *Jorge Luis Borges.*

72. In addition to Helft's digital edition and Balderston's *El precursor velado,* Zangara's edited edition of *Borges en la Revista Multicolor* contains "obras, reseñas y traducciones inéditas de Jorge Luis Borges" [unedited works, reviews and translations by Jorge Luis Borges] that appeared in the literary supplement (with a few misattributions), yet no discussion of the physical qualities or aspects of it. Atena Green's *Borges y Revista multicolor de los sábados* focuses almost entirely on the writings that become part of *Historia universal de la infamia* yet does not discuss the material changes from one medium to the next, nor does she discuss any variants or alterations in the texts themselves. De los Ángeles Mascioto's recent work on the *Revista Multicolor* dedicates space to the visual elements of the periodical, yet her focus is on genre formation and textual mutations across mediums ("Suplemento *de* literatura" and "La *Revista Multicolor de los Sábados*").

73. Louis, *Jorge Luis Borges,* 164.

74. Helft, ed., *Crítica,* [3].

75. Rivera, "Los juegos de un tímido," 21.

76. The images in question can be accessed online through the Archivo Histórico de Revistas Argentinas: https://www.ahira.com.ar/revistas/revista-multicolor-de-los-sabados/.

77. Borges, "El impostor inverosímil Tom Castro," 1.

78. Borges, "El rostro del profeta," 6. Virtually all of the illustrations show a similar focus on the central figures and themes of the stories they accompany: the sinister

depiction of Monk Eastman reflects his status as a New York gangster; the portrayal of Kotsuké no Suké reflects the importance of honor; the cartoonlike images in "El brujo postergado" [The Deferred Sorcerer] correspond with don Illán de Toledo, the bishop, and the role of magic.

79. Cited in Ciabattari, "Is Borges the 20th Century's Most Important Writer?" Sarlo's *Jorge Luis Borges: A Writer on the Edge* is the most developed study of the writer's interest in both elite and popular cultures: "I have wanted to highlight this tension which, in my opinion, runs through Borges's work and defines it: a game on the edge of various cultures, which touch on the borders, in a space that Borges would call *las orillas*" (2). That said, her study focuses almost entirely on the 1920s. For more studies on similar topics of high and low cultures, see Rodríguez Monegal, *Jorge Luis Borges*; de Costa, *Humor in Borges*; and Díaz, *Borges*.

THREE Borges as Critic and Collaborator

1. Borges, "¿Por qué los escritores argentinos no viven de su pluma?," 167.

2. Ann Keen was the previous director of this section of *El Hogar*. In an interview with Enrique Sacerio-Garí, Borges noted that he thought that this name was most likely a pseudonym since he had never heard of such a person.

3. In this chapter I focus exclusively on the book reviews that Borges wrote for *Sur*. See Chapter 5 for an in-depth analysis of his relationship with Ocampo's journal and publishing house of the same name.

4. Pablo De Santis notes that Editorial TOR published various French authors, such as Gastón Leroux, Maurice Leblanc, and George Simenon, whose works were in opposition to those that Borges and Bioy Casares sought for the Séptimo Círculo (Seventh Circle) series. Readers also will recall from Chapter 2 that Editorial TOR was known for its cheap paperback editions of profitable literature. Thus, it is quite clear that "la colección de Tor—tapas chillonas, traducciones a menudo deficientes—no era la estrategia más adecuada para la revalorización que pretendían Borges y Bioy" [TOR's collection—garish covers, often deficient translations—wasn't the most adequate strategy for the reevaluation that Borges and Bioy Casares hoped for] (De Santis, "Los mejores asesinatos de la literatura").

5. The most comprehensive study of Borges and Bioy Casares's collaborative fictions is Parodi, *Borges-Bioy en contexto*.

6. Vaccaro, *Borges*, 335.

7. "La dinastía de los Huxley" [The Dynasty of the Huxleys], 8; "Presencia de Miguel de Unamuno" [The Presence of Miguel de Unamuno], 8; "Kipling y su autobiografía" [Kipling and His Autobiography], 9; "Vindicación de la *María* de Jorge Isaacs" [The Vindication of Jorge Isaacs's *María*], 9; "La máquina de pensar de Raimundo Lulio" [Raymond Llull's Thinking Machine], 14; "Una alarmante historia de la literatura" [An Alarming History of Literature], 14.

8. Milanesio, *Workers Go Shopping in Argentina*, 79.

9. Although Borges published a few pieces in *El Hogar* after the July 7, 1939, issue, the above dates mark his employment with the magazine as a full-time staff member.

10. Rodríguez Monegal, *Jorge Luis Borges*, 288.
11. Ibid.
12. Ibid., 342.
13. The countries of several writers mentioned throughout the pages of *El Hogar* are not represented in the figure in the text in an effort to make the findings clearer. All of the following countries, not included in the figure, are represented by a writer one time during Borges's position as director of the "Libros y autores extranjeros" page: Poland, Japan, Colombia, Sweden, Wales, Egypt, China, Brazil, New Zealand, Hungary, Tibet, The Netherlands, and Denmark. Other critics note this tendency toward European authors, particularly English writers, but to date, none has statistically analyzed these striking preferences, nor have they shown the exact degree to which English authors dominated Borges's column. See Yates, *Jorge Luis Borges*; Aizenberg, *Borges and His Successors*; and Malamet, *The World Remade*.
14. In the previously mentioned article from February 1937, Borges even describes England as "el más literario de los países" [the most literary of all the countries] ("Los escritores y Buenos Aires," 5).
15. There was a separate review column dedicated to "Libros y autores de idioma español" [Books and Authors in the Spanish Language] in the weeks that Borges's column was not published in *El Hogar*, but this column did not have one dedicated editor, nor did it maintain a consistent format. In any case, the question of who counts as a foreign author still stands.
16. This same issue also contains one of Borges's literary review pages.
17. Palacio, "¿Por qué no se leen libros argentinos?," 32. Palacio's discussion of the profitability of publishing is as follows: "El libro argentino *no es negocio*. Salvo contadas excepciones, que no coinciden exactamente con la excelencia literaria, la colocación de nuestros libros en el mercado no da resultados que compensen el esfuerzo de los autores ni es riesgo de los editores. Su publicación significa, pues, casi siempre, un sacrificio realizado en aras de la gloria. Sacrificio que, como es natural, recae sobre el autor mismo, convertido en editor de su obra, ya que ningún negociante acomete la empresa lírica de invertir un capital, así sea ínfimo, en ediciones argentinas" [The Argentine book *is not a business*. With few exceptions that do not coincide exactly with literary excellence, the placement of our books in the market does not give results that reflect the efforts of the authors nor the risks of the publishers. Their publication signifies, thus, almost always, a sacrifice on the altar of glory. A sacrifice that, as is natural, falls to the author himself, converted into editor/publisher of his own work, considering that no businessman undertakes the lyrical venture of investing capital, which is negligible, in Argentine editions] (ibid.).
18. Ibid. As we shall see in the next chapter, this is precisely the work that Borges undertakes throughout the 1940s in an effort to elevate the abandoned literature of his native Argentina.
19. Since Chapter 5 discusses this periodical and Ocampo's publishing house of the same name, I do not detail the entire history and formation of these venues at this point.

20. Several of the more prominent writers in the detective fiction genre that Borges includes in his page in *El Hogar* and that do not appear in the Séptimo Círculo series can be accounted for by royalty issues. Bioy Casares writes at length about this in his *Memorias* [*Memories*]: "el trabajo en la editorial nos asomó a los problemas de los derechos de autor, que hasta entonces habíamos ignorado ... Nos enteramos así de que algunas novelas que deseábamos incluir en El Séptimo Círculo no estaban libres" [the work in the publishing house opened our eyes to the problems of authors' rights, that we had ignored until then ... We discovered that some novels that we wanted to include in the Seventh Circle series were not free] (101). He names a few key authors and books that they hoped, but ultimately were unable, to include: Agatha Christie, *Asesinato de Roger Ackroyd* [*The Murder of Roger Ackroyd*]; Milward Kennedy, *El Socorro de la muerte* [*Death to the Rescue*]; Eden Phillpotts, *Monkshood*; and works by Dorothy Sayers.

21. The Séptimo Círculo series, and Borges and Bioy Casares's roles as its directors, extended well beyond 1951, but I have chosen this date as a cutoff in light of the scope of the current book. Some critics have looked at certain overlaps between the latter three publications, but *El Hogar* is not included in any of these studies (Fernández Vega, "Una campaña estética"; Parodi, "Borges y la subversión del modelo policial"; and Miranda, "More Than the Sum of Its Parts").

22. I return to this idea, as well as all of the anthologies mentioned, in the next chapter, which is dedicated entirely to the collections that Borges edited between 1937 and 1951.

23. It was quite common to publish works as part of a larger series or collection in not only Argentine markets, but also Spanish-speaking markets more broadly. This is most certainly the case for both Editorial Sudamericana and Editorial Losada as well as other publishing houses, including Emecé Editores, and still others not analyzed here, such as Espasa-Calpe (de Sagastizábal, *La edición de libros*, 108).

24. "Agosto 18 de 1938."

25. In terms of the transatlantic link made between Editorial Losada and Spain, "los editores de la Argentina que habían llegado a estas tierras desde España, volvían allí a través de los libros que aquí editaban" [the publishers in Argentina that arrived in these lands from Spain, returned there through the books that they published here] (de Sagastizábal, *La edición de libros*, 119).

26. The most recent, and most panoramic, study of the publishing industry in Argentina (de Diego, *Editores y políticas editoriales*), cites only the Pajarita de Papel series as one of many that Losada created during its early years and the fact that Borges's translation of Kafka's *La metamorfosis* serves as the initial volume.

27. Leonor Acevedo de Borges translated the following works for the Pajarita de Papel series: Katherine Mansfield, *En la bahía* [*At the Bay*] (1938); D. H. Lawrence, *La mujer que se fué a caballo* [*The Woman Who Rode Away*] (1939); and Aldous Huxley, *El joven Arquímedes* [*Young Archimedes*] (1943). In addition to these works, Borges's mother also translated Herbert Read's *El significado del arte* [*The Meaning of Art*] for Editorial Losada (1954), William Saroyan's *La comedia humana* [*The Human Comedy*] for Inter-

americana (1943), and Eden Phillpotts's *El señor Digweed y el señor Lumb* [*Mr. Digweed and Mr. Lumb*] for Emecé's Séptimo Círculo series (1946).

28. *Catálogo general* (1950), 5.

29. Baines, *Penguin by Design,* 20. The Penguin Books series used specific colors to stand for genres and subject matter ("orange for fiction, green for crime, dark blue for biography, cerise for travel & adventure, red for plays" [ibid.]). I soon dismissed my initial desire to find a similar organization theory for the works produced for Colección Horizonte because of the sheer number of works included in the series. Moreover, since virtually every volume was published in various editions, and each new edition presented readers with a new combination of colors on its cover, I decided that this project was much too large (and somewhat distracting) to undertake.

30. In light of the fact that there are virtually no extant publishers' records for all of the major Argentine publishing houses operating during this time, these prices are a vital piece of data that reveals a great deal about the sales and cost of production, especially when we compare the prices from various editions of the same work. For instance, the second edition of William Faulkner's *Las palmeras salvajes* [*The Wild Palms*] was priced at $3.50 Argentine pesos (with a total of 368 pages), while the third edition of this same work jumped in price to $9 Argentine pesos (and contained only 324 pages).

31. In order to clarify any confusion for readers that are familiar with Emecé's catalogue, this publishing house also produced another series titled Colección la Quimera (Chimera Collection), but unlike the Cuadernos de la Quimera, it focused on novels and larger narratives, not the novella.

32. Borges not only mentions Chaucer and Ayala in his *Sur* contributions, but also explicitly reviews their works that Emecé publishes in its Cuadernos de la Quimera series.

33. According to Juan José Saer, the nouvelle is normally between "veinte a ciento veinte páginas más o menos" [20 and 120 pages more or less], which gives it "la ventaja de ser suficientemente amplias como para dejarle a la imaginación muchas opciones constructivas" [the advantage of being sufficiently long to leave room for the imagination to create constructive options] ("Onetti y la novela breve," xv). Saer also notes that this form fell out of favor after the 1960s in Latin America because of "el mercado anglosajón, plegándose en el contenido y en el formato a sus normas comerciales" [the Anglo-Saxon market, to which it folded in terms of the commercial norms for content and form] (ibid.).

34. The only exception is the last work by Henry James, which I include since Borges wrote its prologue.

35. Similar to *El Hogar, La Nación,* founded by Bartolomé Mitre, was known for its connections to the conservative (and religious) public of Argentina.

36. Borges also published a large portion of his creative fictions with *Sur,* but I am solely interested here in his book reviews that appeared in this periodical. Furthermore, none of the essays, poems, or short stories that he published in *La Nación* during the 1940s appears in *Sur.*

37. Vázquez, *Borges, sus días y su tiempo,* 133–34.

38. Silvina Ocampo had been a friend of Norah Borges for some time (mainly because both were painters of a similar style) before spending time with her brother, Jorge Luis, and his newly discovered friend, Adolfo, who would later become Silvina's husband.

39. King, "Adolfo Bioy Casares," 48.

40. The fact that Colombo printed this pamphlet is a detail that tends to be overlooked. Parodi's "Borges, Bioy y el arte de hacer literatura con leche cuajada" is the only critical piece to date on this pamphlet, and although she does not directly mention this Argentine printer, she includes a subtle reference to it in her bibliography: "*La leche cuajada de La Martona. Estudio dietético sobre las leches ácidas. Folleto con recetas.* s/a Buenos Aires: Talleres Gráficos Colón, s/f." As we saw in the last chapter, Colombo's printing workshop was also known as "Colón," thus establishing the link.

41. Aside from passing references to *Destiempo*, the only detailed study of this periodical is Fabiana Sabsay-Herrera's "Para la prehistoria de H. Bustos Domecq." Sabsay-Herrera notes the extreme scarcity of copies of *Destiempo* as a reason for the lack of studies. Luckily, copies of all three numbers are now available in a digitized format through the Archivo Histórico de Revistas Argentinas.

42. Borges published several poems and short pieces in various issues of *ULTRA* and also within the initial numbers of *Martín Fierro*, which highlights his knowledge of and familiarity with both periodicals.

43. The first few issues of *Martín Fierro* (1924–1925) had a serif typeface for the title, but the publisher changed to a more modern, sans serif typeface with equal stress throughout each of the letters. Another interesting aspect of the publication of *Destiempo* is that Francisco A. Colombo printed all three issues, which speaks to the quality of this periodical. Considering that Colombo's work would have been costly, it is quite probable that Bioy Casares financed the printing of *Destiempo*. This idea is further supported by the fact that the only advertisements found throughout any of its pages are those for Bioy Casares's family business La Martona.

44. Along with his appearance in the *Antología de la literatura fantástica*, Manuel Peyrou also worked with Borges at *Los Anales de Buenos Aires* [Annals of Buenos Aires], and his work was published as part of the Séptimo Círculo series (*El estruendo de las rosas* [Thunder of the Roses] [1948]).

45. The authors published in *Destiempo* that also appear in the above-mentioned series are Erskine Caldwell, Angel J. Battistessa (translator), and Jules Supervielle. Another key aspect of the literary magazine *Destiempo* is the fact that it is also the starting point for the publishing house Editorial Destiempo, created by both Borges and Bioy Casares, which advertises six forthcoming books in the last issue of their periodical. This publishing firm will be discussed in greater detail in Chapter 6, along with Borges and Bioy Casares's other publishing house.

46. Schwartz, "Reading and Writing 'A Destiempo,'" 301.

47. Borges first used a similar name, "F. Bustos," to sign "Hombre de las orillas" in the *Revista Multicolor de los Sábados*.

48. The playful name "Biorges" is sometimes used to refer to both writers. It was first used in Rodríguez Monegal, "Nota sobre Biorges."

49. Romera, "H. Bustos Domecq"; Hernández Martín, "Dialogism and Parody in the Detective Story"; Sabsay-Herrera, "Para la prehistoria de H. Bustos Domecq"; Pellicer, "Borges, Bioy y Bustos Domecq"; Domínguez, "Seis problemas para don Isidro Parodi"; and Lafon, "Bioy and Borges."

50. Hernández Martín, "Textual Polyphony," 13. For more on this branch of criticism, see Yates, "The Argentine Detective Story"; Margery Peña, "Seis problemas para don Isidro Parodi"; Lafforgue and Rivera, eds., Asesinos de papel; Close, Contemporary Hispanic Crime Fiction; Lafon, "Bioy and Borges"; Setton, Los orígenes de la narrativa policial; and Miranda, "More Than the Sum of Its Parts." Critics have heavily explored the relationship between the genre of detective fiction and Borges's writings, and as a result the books and articles discussed here can be seen as a point of departure for interested readers. In addition to these works, the most detailed study of the figure of Honorio Bustos Domecq and all (invented) figures associated with him is Parodi, Borges-Bioy en contexto. Borges later uses the form of the detective story as an instrument of philosophical exploration.

51. An exception to this statement would be the Portuguese poet and writer Fernando Pessoa (1888–1935). Throughout his career he created for himself as many as seventy-five unique pseudonyms, or "heteronyms" as he called them, which speaks to the fact that these were not just names, but entire personas with specific styles and biographies. I use the word "synthetic" as a possible way of thinking about the dual meaning behind Borges's "biografías sintéticas" for El Hogar.

52. In later editions of Seis problemas para don Isidro Parodi, Adelia Puglione's name is swapped out for Adelma Badoglio, who is supposedly an Argentine educator but in reality is another invention of the two writers. In addition to this change in name, there is one other notable difference in the text of the first edition and later printed editions. One phrase in the first edition reads "Durante el gobierno de Iriondo" [During the government of Iriondo], while the same sentence in the next printed edition by Editorial Sur reads "Durante la intervención de Labruna" [During the intervention of Labruna]. Both names refer to soccer players famous during the first part of the twentieth century, Iriondo in Spain and Labruna in Argentina. This subtle alteration might be just another way that Borges and Bioy Casares try to reach their contemporary Argentine readers.

53. Entre libros y papeles, "The American Magazines of Buenos Aires," was published in 1932, two years before the date cited in Bustos Domecq's bibliography; it was dedicated to literary studies.

54. "Citizen Kane (cuyo nombre en la República Argentina es El Ciudadano) tiene por lo menos dos argumentos. El primero, de una imbecilidad casi banal, quiere sobornar el aplauso de los muy distraídos … El segundo es muy superior. Une al recuerdo de Koheleth el de otro nihilista: Franz Kafka … Me atrevo a sospechar, sin embargo, que Citizen Kane perdurará como 'perduran' ciertos films de Griffith o de Pudovkin, cuyo valor histórico nadie niega, pero que nadie se resigna a rever. Adolece de gigantismo, de pedantería, de tedio. No es inteligente, es genial: en el sentido más nocturno y más alemán de esta mala palabra" [Citizen Kane (whose name is The Citizen in Argentina) has at least two arguments. The first, of an almost banal stupidity, wants to bribe the applause

of the distracted ... The second is very much superior. It unites the memory of Koheleth to another nihilist: Franz Kafka ... I dare suspect, however, that *Citizen Kane* will live on as certain films of Griffith or Pudovkin "live on," whose historic value is denied by none, but no one can bear to see them a second time. It suffers from gigantism, from pedantry, from tedium. It is not intelligent, it is brilliant: in the nocturnal and German sense of this bad word] ("Un film abrumador" [An Overwhelming Film], 64–65).

55. This line of thinking would also directly relate to my arguments regarding the marketing strategies of Borges during this time.

56. Borges and Bioy Casares, *Seis problemas*, 8.

57. In addition to the above-mentioned apocryphal titles penned by Bustos Domecq are the following: *Fata Morgana* (1919), *El aporte santafecino a los Ejércitos de la Independencia* [*The Santa Fe's Contribution to the Armies of the Independence*] (n.d.), and *Astros nuevos: Azorín, Gabriel Miró, Bontempelli* [*New Stars: Azorín, Gabriel Miró, Bontempelli*] (n.d.).

58. Borges and Bioy Casares, *Seis problemas*, 10.

59. Ibid., 10–11.

60. See Chapter 1 for references to Whatman paper and the Devil's Bible format in this short story.

61. The emphasis on certain metafictional elements throughout the work, particularly in the preliminary materials and occasions in which Parodi steps outside of himself and makes an aside on his work at hand, not only are a foreshadowing of Borges's most canonical work, *Ficciones* (1944), but also seem to hark back to earlier trends in twentieth-century literature, most notably Miguel de Unamuno's *Niebla* [*Mist*]. The striking similarities between these two works is especially clear when we compare the figures of Gervasio Montenegro and Victor Goti.

62. Borges and Bioy Casares, *Seis problemas*, 67.

63. Ibid., 69.

64. In addition to the above described book references, there are several instances in which people are compared to a book. For example, "Le habló como un libro abierto" [He spoke to him like an open book] or "vecinos que dormían como una rectilínea biblioteca de libros clásicos" [neighbors who slept like a rectilinear library of classic books] (Borges and Bioy Casares, *Seis problemas*, 90, 120).

65. As we shall see in Chapter 5, Borges was a member of the original editorial board for the literary journal *Sur* and also very much involved in the publishing firm of the same name. As a result, he published many articles (both fiction and nonfiction) in this periodical starting in 1931 and also published a number of his books with the firm of the same name. The first book bearing his name and that of Editorial Sur is a translation he did of Virginia Woolf's *Un cuarto propio* [*A Room of One's Own*] (1936). Borges's canonical *El jardín de senderos que se bifurcan* [*The Garden of Forking Paths*] (1941), which later becomes part of his *Ficciones* (1944), appeared in the same year as *Seis problemas para don Isidro Parodi*, but since this chapter deals exclusively with works in collaboration, I leave the discussion of these books for Chapter 5.

FOUR Borges as Editor and Anthologist

1. Borges, *"The Albatross Book of Living Prose,"* 26.
2. Ibid.
3. De Maeseneer and Logie, "Antologías del cuento dominicano de la última década (2000–2010) y canon," 17.
4. Balderston reiterates many of these claims in his introduction to Balderston, ed., *The Latin American Short Story,* ix.
5. Diehl, "'Antología clásica,'" 128.
6. Reyes, "Teoría de la antología," 138. Reyes first wrote this piece in 1930, but it was not published until 1938 in *La Prensa*.
7. Palacio, "¿Por qué no se leen libros argentinos?," 32.
8. Ibid.
9. I bring up Borges's ultraist phase intentionally since, when discussing the value of Baldomero Fernández Moreno's poetry in "La lírica argentina contemporánea," he arrives at many of his critical opinions with this point of view in mind: "Como ultraísta que soy..." [Like the ultraist that I am...] (138). Borges traditionally rejects much of his work from this stage in his life, which makes such an overlap all the more meaningful.
10. Palacio, "¿Por qué no se leen libros argentinos?," 32.
11. Borges and Henríquez Ureña, eds., *Antología clásica,* 7.
12. This idea is echoed further by Diehl's review of this anthology: "Pedro Enríquez [sic] Ureña, Jorge Luis Borges. No necesita leerse la obra para juzgarla. Podemos estar seguros, de que no serán sorprendidos en un solo descuido, en una sola falla y olvido" [Pedro Enríquez [sic] Ureña, Jorge Luis Borges. You don't have to read the work to judge it. We can be sure that we won't be surprised with a single mistake, with a single error or oversight] ("'Antología clásica,'" 128).
13. Borges and Henríquez Ureña, eds., *Antología clásica,* 8.
14. Ibid.
15. Ibid.
16. Ibid.
17. Ibid., 440.
18. Tanselle, *A Rationale of Textual Criticism.*
19. Shillingsburg, "Text as Matter, Concept, and Action."
20. Borges and Henríquez Ureña, eds., *Antología clásica,* 236.
21. A review of the recent critical edition of *Martín Fierro* shows the problematic textual history of this poem: "La edición del *Martín Fierro* realizada por ARCHIVOS ilustra una circunstancia ciertamente paradojal: uno de los textos más notorios de la literatura argentina, e inclusive hispanoamericana, fue asediado desde sus orígenes (1872 y 1879 respectivamente) por reediciones plagas de erratas y omisiones que prácticamente las inutilizaban para una lectura confiable, y no digamos erudita" [The ARCHIVOS edition of *Martín Fierro* illustrates a truly paradoxical situation: one of the most well-known texts in Argentine literature, and even in Hispano-American literature, besieged from its start (1872 and 1879, respectively) by reeditions full of errors and omissions that made it

practically impossible to produce a trustworthy reading, let alone an erudite one] (Rivera, "José Hernández," 1).

22. Borges and Henríquez Ureña, eds., *Antología clásica*, 440.

23. Ibid., 236.

24. For instance, at one moment in the text, the footnote that accompanies a verse does not state just the change in a later edition (1878) but also includes the following descriptor: "Hernández mejoró después este verso" [Hernández improved this verse] (243n11). The rest of the notes that bring readers' attention to differences among editions simply read, "En la edición de 1878" [In the 1878 edition].

25. Melgarejo, "Sello tradicional."

26. The *Boletín bibliográfico argentino* started in 1937 to remedy the "falta de una biografía nacional, fuente obligada para la compilación de bibliografías especializadas" [lack of a national bibliography, which is a necessary resource for compiling specialized bibliographies] (Camou, Tortti, and Viguera, eds., *La Argentina democática*, 418). It was published until 1956 under various titles, and there was a general sense of irregularity among the issues. The title of *Boletín bibliográfico argentino* was used for the first twenty-six issues (1937–1951, covering from 1937 to 1949); it changed to the *Boletín bibliográfico nacional* [National Bibliographical Bulletin] for issues twenty-seven through thirty-three (1952–1963, covering from 1950 to 1956) (Bell, *An Annotated Guide*, 8–9). In addition to giving readers a sense of the types of work being produced and published at this time in Argentina, the *Boletín bibliográfico argentino* is an extremely useful source since it tends to include the prices of each of the volumes described.

27. *Boletín bibliográfico argentino*, 21–23.

28. The most curious aspects of Beltrán's *Antología de poetas y prosistas americanos* are the overlaps with Borges and Henríquez Ureña's *Antología clásica*. More specifically, the entire second volume of Beltrán's anthology is dedicated to "la poesía gauchesca en el río de la plata" [Gauchesque poetry of the River Plate region]. The purpose of these volumes, as stated by Beltrán in his prólogo, also aligns with that of the *Antología clásica*: that of education.

29. The act of bringing texts from authors who were previously in the public domain into the private domain of copyright also speaks to an interest in the marketing and commercialization of works for profit.

30. Borges and Henríquez Ureña, eds., *Antología clásica*, 11.

31. Ibid., 21.

32. *Catálogo número 4*, 168. Even though Antonio López Llausás managed Editorial Sudamericana shortly after it was founded in 1939, it should be noted that the above sentiment, with regards to making the most important works of world literature known to the most readers, is reflected in the original group of intellectuals responsible for the creation of this publishing house: "Victoria Ocampo, Carlos Mayer, Oliverio Girondo, Antonio Santamarina y un grupo de intelectuales con el propósito de divulgar autores contemporáneos" [Victoria Ocampo, Carlos Mayer, Oliverio Girondo, Antonio Santamarina, and a group of intellectuals with the purpose of divulging contemporary authors] (Vaccaro, *Borges*, 341).

33. *Catálogo número 4,* 168.

34. Borges, Bioy Casares, and Ocampo, eds., *Antología poética argentina,* 7.

35. Inside flap of Borges, Bioy Casares, and Ocampo, eds., *Antología de la literatura fantástica.*

36. Another aspect of this poetry anthology that elevates it from other works and suggests a learned, elite reader is the fact that all of Gloria Alcorta's poems are printed in French with no translations.

37. Borges, Bioy Casares, and Ocampo, eds., *Antología poética argentina,* 7. Many of the ideas expressed in this introduction bring to mind the debates surrounding Octavio Paz's edited poetry anthology, *Laurel,* which was published in the same year as the *Antología poética argentina* and included work by Borges: "A mí se me ocurrió la idea de hacer la antología. Con ella quería mostrar la continuidad y la unidad de la poesía de nuestra lengua. Era un acto de fe. Creía (y creo) que una tradición poética no se define por el concepto político de nacionalidad sino por la lengua y por las relaciones que se tejen entre los estilos y los creadores" [The idea of creating an anthology came to me. With it I wanted to show the continuity and the unity of the poetry in our language. It was an act of faith. I believed (and I still believe) that a poetic tradition is not defined by the political concept of nationality but rather by the language and relations that are woven between styles and creators] (Paz, *Xavier Villaurrutia en persona y en obra,* 16–17).

38. Borges, Bioy Casares, and Ocampo, eds., *Antología poética argentina,* 8.

39. Ibid., 10–11.

40. Ibid., 11.

41. This same work comments on the important role of others in editing its contents, especially the poets themselves, which is a very different approach from what we saw in Borges and Henríquez Ureña's *Antología clásica.*

42. Beltrán, *Antología de poetas y prosistas americanos,* 8.

43. For instance, González Carbalho, ed., *Índice de la poesía argentina contemporánea,* cites Borges's birth year as 1900 and prints his poetry collection, *Luna de enfrente,* as *Luna de enrente.*

44. Borges, Bioy Casares, and Ocampo, eds., *Antología poética argentina,* 66, 188.

45. Bioy Casares, *Memorias,* 89.

46. There is a typographical error in the title of the first work as it appears in the *Antología poética argentina*; it is actually *La Salamanca* (Editorial Losada, 1943). The second work is published in 1941.

47. This is the case for the following poets' works printed as "en preparación": Juan Carlos Dávalos, Ezequiel Martínez Estrada, Pedro Miguel Obligado, Miguel Andrés Camino, María Alicia Domínguez, Horacio Schiavo, Córdova Iturburu, Emilia Bertolé, Eduardo Keller, Ulyses Petit de Murat, Wally Zenner, Ignacio B. Anzoátegui, and Elvira de Alvear.

48. Rodríguez Monegal, *Jorge Luis Borges,* 357.

49. Gerhardt, "Temas y autores argentinos," 5.

50. One of the only references to this collection of texts by Borges and Bull-

rich Palenque is in Alazraki, "Borges"; Bioy Casares mentions Bullrich in passing in his *Memorias* as the person who introduced Borges to Emecé.

51. Seoane and Cuadrado worked exclusively with this collection until 1942, when they left Emecé to start their own publishing house: Editorial Nova. This firm creates a similar series, Colección Mar Dulce, that appears to imitate the Colección Buen Aire in terms of themes and physical presentation of the volumes. See Chapter 5 for a detailed discussion of Editorial Nova.

52. Gerhardt, "Temas y autores argentinos," 6.

53. Ibid. The majority of the volumes are organized into the following categories: "Viajes y crónicas" [Travels and Chronicles], "Poesía y cancioneros" [Poetry and Collections of Verse], "Paisajes y ciudades" [Landscapes and Cities], "Memorias y recuerdos" [Memories and Souvenirs], "Leyenda y folklore" [Tales and Folklore], "Temas y documentos de historia" [Historical Topics and Documents], "Biografías" [Biographies], "Impresiones sobre América" [Impressions of America], and "Teatro americano" [American Theater].

54. Ibid.

55. Several important figures associated with Argentine publishing history surface for their role in helping produce various works in this collection, such as José Bonomi (cover illustrator), Imprenta López (printer), and J. Hay Bells (printer).

56. Borges and Bullrich Palenque, *El compadrito*, 7. Although it is likely that Bullrich Palenque had some role in crafting the prologue to *El compadrito*, only Borges's initials are included at its close, and for that reason I attribute this introductory text to him.

57. Ibid.

58. Ibid., 8.

59. Ibid.

60. Ibid., 7.

61. Lafforgue and Rivera, eds., *Asesinos de papel,* 134. Lafforgue and Rivera's foundational study of the evolution of the genre of detective fiction in Argentina is the first place to start for any further investigations into this topic. Also see Yates, "The Argentine Detective Story"; Molloy, *Signs of Borges*; Bennett, "The Detective Fiction of Poe and Borges"; Hart, *The Spanish Sleuth*; Cortínez, "De Poe a Borges"; Arenas Cruz, "Borges y la literatura policial"; Sarabia, "'La muerte y la brújula'"; Fernánez Vega, "Una campaña estética"; Parodi, "Borges y la subversión del modelo policial"; and Close, *Contemporary Hispanic Crime Fiction*. In addition to these works, a large number of published interviews with Borges touch on the topic of detective fiction in his writings, including Burgin and Borges, *Conversations with Jorge Luis Borges*; Alifano, *Borges*; and Borges and Ferrari, *Libro de diálogos*.

62. The most detailed studies of the evolution of Borges's detective fiction stories and his general interest in this genre are Yates, "The Argentine Detective Story"; Rodríguez-Luis, "La intención política en la obra de Borges"; Arenas Cruz, "Borges y la literatura policial"; Lafforgue and Rivera, eds., *Asesinos de papel*; and Fernández Vega, "Una campaña estética."

63. Hernández Martín, *Readers and Labyrinths*, 49.

64. Borges, Bioy Casares, and Ocampo, eds., *Antología de la literatura fantástica*, 14–15.

65. Ibid., 8–10.

66. Ibid., 8.

67. Ibid., 10. The term "Yellow Peril" refers to a form of xenophobia against East Asia. In his introduction, Bioy Casares alludes to the Yellow Peril in the context of H. G. Wells's work: "Wells hubiera caído en el peligro amarillo si hubiera hecho, en vez de un hombre invisible, ejércitos de hombres invisibles que invadieran y dominaran el mundo (plan tentador para novelistas alemanes)" [Wells would have fallen into the Yellow Peril if he had made, instead of an invisible man, an army of invisible men that invaded and dominated the world (a tempting plan for German novelists)] (Ibid).

68. Ibid., 10–14.

69. Rodríguez Monegal, *Jorge Luis Borges,* 350.

70. The figure of George Loring Frost appears to be an apocryphal author as his works are nowhere to be found except in the pages of the *Antología de la literatura fantástica,* yet Balderston contends that he is real (*Out of Context,* 140).

71. Also see Balderston, "La *Antología de la literatura fantástica* y sus alrededores."

72. Chesterton, Borges, Peyrou, and Poe all appear in *Los mejores cuentos policiales,* and Peyrou also appears as part of the Séptimo Círculo series.

73. Suarez, "The Production and Consumption of the Eighteenth-Century Poetic Miscellany," 218–19.

74. Another important aspect of these three writers is the fact that they all appear in Borges's literary review page for *El Hogar*. In fact, Hsue-Kin's work (*El sueño del aposento rojo*) is precisely the work reviewed by Borges in *El Hogar* on November 19, 1937. He curiously ends his review with the following description of Hsue-Kin's work: "Abunda lo fantástico: la literatura china no sabe de 'novelas fantásticas,' porque todas, en algún momento, lo son" [The fantastic is plentiful: Chinese literature doesn't know about "fantastic novels," because all of them, at some point, are just that] ("*El sueño del aposento rojo,*" 24).

75. Each of the two excerpted texts from the other three authors in this group are from different works: Bloy, *Le Mendiant Ingrat* [*The Ungrateful Beggar*] and *Le Vieux de la Montage* [*The Old Man from the Mountain*]; Gómez de la Serna, "Peor que el infierno" [Worse Than Hell] and "La sangre en el jardín" [Blood in the Garden]; Kafka, *Josefina la cantora o El pueblo de los ratones* [*Josephine the Singer, or the Mouse Folk*] and "Ante la ley" [Before the Law].

76. Batt, "Miscellanies," 799.

77. Several authors come from countries not included in the figure in an effort to make the findings clearer. All of the following countries (not included in the figure) are represented by a writer one time in the anthology: Austria, Chile, Italy, Scotland, and Sweden. In addition, there is one piece by an anonymous author and another from the Roman Empire.

78. The only writers included in this anthology who do not have a short biography are W. W. Skeat, Herbert Allen Giles, and Richard Wilhelm. The latter two omissions

can be explained when we consider their correlation with Chuang Tzu's entry: "Hay versiones inglesas de Giles y de Lege; alemena, de Wilhelm" [There are English versions by Giles and by Lege; German, by Wilhelm] (Borges, Bioy Casares, and Ocampo, eds., *Antología de la literatura fantástica*, 240).

79. María Luisa Bombal's and Pilar de Lusarreta's biographies include no birthplace or birth year; the entries for Olaf Stapleton and W. W. Jacobs have only birth years (no places); and the entry for May Sinclair includes only a birthplace (no year).

80. Vaccaro, *Borges*, 343.

81. Bioy Casares, *Memorias*, 89. Rodríguez Monegal also claims that "the anthology was the least successful venture attempted by Borges and the Bioys" (*Jorge Luis Borges*, 357). In light of the fact that there are no extant publishers' archives for Editorial Sudamericana, it would be quite difficult to determine whether this work sold well or not in the early 1940s in Argentina.

82. Borges and Bioy Casares, eds., *Los mejores cuentos policiales*, inside flap.

83. The first edition was published in 1943 and shortly after a second (1944) and a third edition (1947) followed. The second series of *Los mejores cuentos policiales* was published in 1951 and introduced ten new short stories by several authors who were not present in the first series.

84. Bioy Casares, *Memorias*, 100.

85. This colorful design is not printed on a dust jacket for the third edition of the first series of *Los mejores cuentos policiales* but rather on the actual cover. This change appears to be the first step (of many) toward cutting costs and producing more economical paperback editions. The quality of the paper used for this third edition is noticeably cheaper than that of the first two editions as well.

86. The biographies of Chesterton, Poe, and Peyrou appear to be lifted directly from the *Antología de la literatura fantástica*.

87. Stevenson's short story in *Los mejores cuentos policiales* is excerpted from *The Master of Ballantrae*. While the examples given pertain to only the first series of *Los mejores cuentos policiales*, similar examples are found throughout the second series. For instance, Peyrou's biography mentions his *El estruendo de las rosas*, which forms part of the Séptimo Círculo series, Chesterton's biography highlights the presence of two of his works in the Colección "Grandes Ensayistas"; and Phillpotts's biography has been updated to include three new additions to the Séptimo Círculo series.

88. The first edition of the second series was priced at $16 Argentine pesos, and the second edition of this same work (1952) lists its price as $18 Argentine pesos. The third edition, which had a new cover design on much thicker cardstock, was a whopping $46 Argentine pesos.

89. Lafforgue and Rivera, eds., *Asesinos de papel*, 121.

90. Ibid., 123.

91. Nobilia and Valerga, eds., *José Bonomi y El Séptimo Círculo*, 9.

92. Bioy Casares also notes that "con nuestras novelas policiales los editores conocieron el encanto de las buenas ventas y perdieron las ganas de volver a las aventuras prestigiosas" [the editors recognized the charm of good sales with our detective fic-

tions and they lost their motivation to return to prestigious ventures] (*Memorias,* 100). Another factor that might have aided in the large success of this series was the eventual use of a pocketsize format for its books.

93. Bonomi quoted in Lafforgue and Rivera, eds., *Asesinos de papel,* 128n2.

94. Bioy Casares, *Memorias,* 100.

95. Editorial TOR's Serie amarilla was published during the 1940s and 1950s, which shows an important overlap with Emecé's Séptimo Círculo. The jarring yellow covers, which reflect the title of the series, and cheap quality of the paper and production pale in comparison to the types of books produced by Borges and Bioy Casares, Bonomi, and Emecé.

96. Miranda, "More Than the Sum of Its Parts," 32.

97. Lafforgue and Rivera, eds., *Asesinos de papel,* 131n6.

98. Miranda calculates that "90 per cent of the 63 writers included [in this series] were imports" ("More Than the Sum of Its Parts," 32). She also focuses on the importance of translation(s) for much of Argentine culture during the 1940s, which she aptly ties to the boom of the Argentine publishing industry.

99. Bioy Casares, *Memorias,* 107.

100. Miranda, "More Than the Sum of Its Parts," 34–35.

101. Borges, *Selected Non-Fictions,* 426–27.

102. King, *Sur,* 90.

103. Ibid., 43. King's foundational study of *Sur* is still the most detailed to date. See also Gramuglio, "Bioy, Borges y *Sur,*" "'Sur,'" and "SUR en la década del treinta"; Parodi, "El proyecto cultural de la revista 'Sur'"; Chiappini, *Borges y la revista Sur*; Zuleta, "Sur entre cultura y política"; Pasternac, *Sur*; Gómez López-Quiñones, *Borges y el nazismo*; Majstorovic, "An American Place"; and Willson, *La constelación del Sur.*

104. King, *Sur,* 55–56.

105. Ibid., 56.

106. King stresses the fact that "there were very few Latin American [authors] published [in *Sur*], save for certain writers who were mainly included through personal friendship (Mistral and Bombal)" (ibid., 84).

107. Both issues physically reflect their area of study with distinct red, white, and blue covers.

108. The University of Pittsburgh's Borges Center refers to these special issues as the "Anthology of North American Poetry" and the "Anthology of French Literature," respectively.

109. A poem by Marianne Moore ("En desconfianza de méritos" [In Distrust of Merits]) is also included in this anthology, but its translation is attributed to Ricardo Baeza, not Borges and Bioy Casares.

110. Ocampo, "Introducción" (1944), 10.

111. Zabel, "La literatura en los Estados Unidos," 18.

112. Zabel emphasizes this general interest in books and the publishing industry: "los libros se imprimen, se compran y se leen en cantidades enormes" [books are printed, purchased, and read in enormous quantities] (ibid., 19).

113. Ibid., 25.

114. Ibid., 27.

115. Borges and Bioy Casares, "Antología de poesía norteamericana," 68–71. All included translations from this anthology are Borges and Bioy Casares's.

116. Ibid., 118–19.

117. A few other passing comments made by Zabel in his panorama emphasize the importance of the above selection of poets for this section in the journal: "La poesía de Wallace Stevens... trató de imponer un orden de sensibilidad e inteligencia sobre el caos de la experiencia y el escepticismo modernos" [The poetry of Wallace Stevens... tries to impose a sensible order and intelligence over the chaos of experience and modern skepticism]; "Apareció la obra temprana de los poetas del sur—John Crown Ransom, Allen Tate, Robert Penn Warren—y pronosticó la parte significativa que esos hombres y sus colegas desempeñarían más recientemente en el estudio del problema total de la tradición americana a través del lente de una historia y una experiencia regional particular" [The early works of the southern poets appeared—John Crowe Ransom, Allen Tate, Robert Penn Warren—and these poems predicted the significant part that those men and their colleagues would carry out most recently in their study of the entire problem of American literature through the lens of history and regional experience]; "El individualismo poético alcanzó el ingenio más sutil y la originalidad satírica en la poesía de E. E. Cummings" [The poetic individual achieves the most subtle ingenuity and satiric originality in the poetry of e. e. cummings] ("La literatura de los Estados Unidos," 39–46).

118. There is also an extensive note about the acquisition of materials for this issue: "SUR expresa su vivo reconocimiento al Dr. Henry Allan Moe, de la Guggenheim Foundation, que prestó su generosa ayuda a Victoria Ocampo, directora de la revista, para obtener los materiales reunidos en este número; a Mr. Bowden Broadwater, cuya buena voluntad y discernimiento le fueron indispensables en la elección de los mismos; a Mr. Monroe Wheeler, del 'Museum of Modern Art,' y a Mr. Glenway Wescott, que tan gentilmente facilitaron su tarea" [SUR expresses its deep recognition of Dr. Henry Allan Moe, of the Guggenheim Foundation, who offered his generous help to Victoria Ocampo, director of the magazine, to obtain the materials collected in this issue; to Mr. Bowden Broadwater, whose goodwill and discernment were indispensable in the selection of these texts; to Mr. Monroe Wheeler, from the Museum of Modern Art, and to Mr. Glenway Wescott, who so graciously made this work possible] (*Sur* 113-14 (1944): 283). A very stringent statement regarding the republication of the translations in this volume also appears in these closing pages: "Todos los materiales han sido exclusivamente traducidos para SUR. Queda prohibido reproducir íntegra o fragmentariamente cualquiera de ellos sin autorización especial o sin mencionar su procedencia" [All of the materials have been exclusively translated for SUR. It is prohibited to reproduce any of them in part or whole without special authorization or without mentioning their origin] (ibid., [285]).

119. Ocampo, "Introducción" (1947), 7.

120. Ibid.

121. Rodríguez Monegal, *Jorge Luis Borges*, 398.

122. Ibid., 399.

123. *Los Anales de Buenos Aires,* 1, [3].

124. There were a total of thirty-nine book reviews in the entire run of the periodical. The titles listed in Table 15 make up 18 percent of all of the books.

125. Rodríguez Monegal, *Jorge Luis Borges,* 400.

126. *Catálogo general perpetuo.* Reprinted in Borges and Bioy Casares, *Museo,* 115.

127. Ibid.

128. Ricardo Baeza (Cuba, 1890–Madrid, 1956) was a key figure in the publishing world in both Latin America and Spain throughout the twentieth century. From journalist and poet to editor and translator, he held a number of positions behind the scenes at various periodicals (*Revista de Occidente, Atenea, El Sol,* and *Sur,* among others) and publishing houses (Emecé, Editorial Sudamericana, Editorial Sur, Editorial Losada, and W. M. Jackson, among others).

129. Ballester Peña also illustrated several volumes in the Séptimo Círculo series, and Orlando Pierri contributed to various issues of *Los Anales de Buenos Aires.*

130. This description of the Breviarios collection comes from the back cover of Borges and Ingenieros, eds., *Antiguas literaturas germánicas.*

131. The second director of Fondo de Cultura Económica, Arnaldo Orfila Reynal (1897–1997), who also created the Breviarios collection, was a native Argentine and directed Fondo de Cultura Económica's Argentine branch before heading the entire publishing house in 1948. This connection might have fueled Borges's work for this firm.

132. The description of the collection on each dust jacket is as follows: "Redactados por especialistas de crédito universal, cada uno de estos *Breviarios* constituirá un tratado sumario y completo sobre la materia que anuncie su título; en su conjunto, cuidadosamente planeado, formarán esa biblioteca de consulta y orientación que la cultura de nuestro tiempo hace indispensable" [Edited by specialists of universal credit, each one of these *Breviarios* consists of a brief and complete treaty on the subject announced by its title; as a whole, carefully planned, they will form part of a library of consultation and orientation that is indispensable for the culture of our time].

133. The other topics covered are the following: art (magenta), philosophy (purple), social sciences (blue), science and technology (yellow), and economics (dark green).

134. Borges and Ingenieros, eds., *Antiguas literaturas germánicas,* dust jacket flap.

135. Even the bibliography is presented in a quasi-narrative form, making it much more approachable for readers: "Sobre Ulfilas, puede consultarse el trabajo de C. A. Scott: Ulfilas, *Apostle of the Goths* (1885)" [For more about Ulfilas, consult the work of C. A. Scott: Ulfilas, *Apostle of the Goths* (1885)]; "De la Edda Mayor cabe indicar dos versiones alemanas" [There are two German versions of the *Elder Edda*]; "es un agudo estudio general de la literatura nórdica" [is a sharp general study of Nordic literature] (Borges and Ingenieros, eds., *Antiguas literaturas germánicas,* 173), etc.

136. Ibid., 14. The fact that this work provides a lengthy explanation and description of the form of the kenning, along with ample examples, reminds readers of Borges's *Las Kenningar.* There is a good amount of overlap between that earlier work and the statements that he makes in *Antiguas literaturas germánicas.* He also includes a curi-

ous example that seems to draw connections to one of the previous anthologies studied (*El compadrito*): "Los compadritos de Buenos Aires llaman Quinta del Ñato (Quinta del Chato, Quinta de la Calavera) al cementerio, y sobretodo de madera al ataúd" [The *compadres* from Buenos Aires call the cemetery The Neighborhood of the Short-Nosed (The Neighborhood of the Short-Sighted, The Neighborhood of the Skulls), and refer to the coffin as a wooden overcoat] (ibid., 94).

137. Ibid., dust jacket flap.

138. The most prominent examples are his translations of Virginia Woolf's *Un cuarto propio* [*A Room of One's Own*] (Editorial Sur, 1936) and *Orlando* (Editorial Sur, 1937) as well as William Faulkner's *Las palmeras salvajes* [*The Wild Palms*] (Editorial Sudamericana, 1940). I discuss these works in greater detail in Chapter 5.

139. The detailed colophon from this first edition states: "Este libro se acabó de imprimir el día 14 de septiembre de 1951, en los talleres de Gráficas Panamericana, S. de R. L., Pánuco 63, México, D.F. De él se tiraron 8.000 ejemplares. En su composición se utilizaron tipos Janson de 11:12, 10:11 y 9:10. Se encuadernó en la Encuadernación Cabrera, Comonfort 29-A. La edición estuvo al cuidado de Alí Chumacero" [This book was printed on September 14, 1951, in the Graphic Workshops Panamericana, LCC, Pánuco 63, Mexico, D.F. It was part of a print run of eight thousand copies. They used the typeface Janson in a variety of body sizes, 11:12, 10:11, and 9:10. It was bound in the Cabrera Bindery, Comonfort 29-A. The edition was overseen by Alí Chumacero] (Borges and Ingenieros, eds., *Antiguas literaturas germánicas*, 181).

FIVE Borges as Publicist and Promoter

1. Pereda Valdés, ed., *Antología de la moderna poesía uruguaya*, 221.

2. Although the literary journal of the same name (*Sur*) was founded by Victoria Ocampo in 1931, I have chosen to focus entirely on the publishing house and the production of books, especially since much work has already been dedicated to the literary journal, and not as much attention has been paid to Editorial Sur.

3. Genette, *Paratexts*, 1–2.

4. Although Genette does not specifically state so in his work, I would argue that blurbs on the inside flaps and back covers of books are part of a book, not accessory to it.

5. Genette, *Paratexts*, 197. Emphasis in original.

6. Kristal, *Invisible Work*, 1.

7. Consider, for instance, Borges's preface to Valéry's *El cementerio marino* [*The Graveyard by the Sea*] (1931): "Presuponer que toda recombinación de elementos es obligatoriamente inferior a su original, es presuponer que el borrador 9 es obligatoriamente inferior al borrador H—ya que no puede haber sido borradores. El concepto de texto *definitivo*, no corresponde sino a la religión o al cansancio" [To presuppose that every recombination of elements is always inferior to the original is to presuppose that draft 9 is always interior to draft H—considering that they could not have been drafts. The concept of a *definitive* text does not correspond to anything but religion or exhaustion] (5). This same passage appears in his later essay "Las versiones homéricas" (*Discusión*, 1932).

8. Kristal, *Invisible Work*, 2.

9. Ibid.

10. The Spanish word *prólogo* can be translated as either "prologue" or "preface." I see these two terms as slightly different. While they both are placed before the text of the book, a prologue tends to focus on an approach to the words that follow, whereas a preface might include an additional account of how the idea for the book came about. Thus, I use "prologue" to describe these short introductory works unless they are characterized as a *prefacio* in the book.

11. Cited in Genette, *Paratexts*, 196.

12. Ibid. Emphasis in the original. Genette also includes a sixth option that relates to apocryphal texts and fictional persons: *"fictional prefaces"* (196). Since I am dealing only with prologues written by Borges, I do not delve into this final category. That said, a clear example would be Gervasio Montenegro's preface to Borges and Bioy Casares's *Seis problemas para don Isidro Parodi*.

13. The frame novel (and the epistolary novel) had a major vogue in the eighteenth century, which raises the question of how this early form might have helped to establish the allographic preface.

14. Genette, *Paratexts*, 264–65. Genette uses Borges's assorted collections as prime examples of this idea of unity in the prologue, which is a fundamental characteristic of the original authorial preface (ibid., 204–5).

15. Ibid., 265.

16. Ibid., 270.

17. These are not the only publishing houses for which Borges crafts translations and prologues during this period, but I focus solely on their publications for reasons of space. A complete inventory of all of Borges's translations and prologues from this time period, along with his own creative fictions, can be found in Benedict, "Mapping Borges," the digital appendix to this book. In addition to the titles and authors of these works, readers will find a full description of the unique physical features of these books.

18. Readers will recall from Chapter 3 that Leonor's own translations appeared alongside those of her son in Editorial Losada's Pajarita de Papel series.

19. Borges, "Las dos maneras de traducir," 4.

20. In addition to Levine, "Borges sobre la traducción," see Gargatagli Brusa, "Jorge Luis Borges y la traducción," which provides a thorough bibliography of works related to Borges and translation.

21. Meyer, *Victoria Ocampo*, 100. During her travels to Europe she was also introduced to the works of Virginia Woolf, which would become paramount pieces of literature for her.

22. Cited in ibid., 106.

23. Ibid., 107.

24. In a 1930 letter to José Ortega y Gasset, whose literary efforts, especially his *Revista de Occidente*, had a large impact on the conceptualization of *Sur*, Ocampo writes: "He aquí mi proyecto: publicar una revista que se ocupe principalmente de problemas americanos, bajo varios aspectos, y donde colaboren los americanos que tengan algo que

decir y los europeos que se interesen en América. El *leitmotiv* de la revista será ése pero, naturalmente, tratará también otros temas" [This is what I propose to do: publish a journal devoted principally to American problems, in various aspects, to which Americans who have something to say can contribute as well as Europeans who are interested in America. That will be the *leitmotiv* of the journal, but naturally it will address other topics as well] ("Vida de la revista *Sur*," 6–7).

25. Along with Borges, the initial editorial board consisted of Eduardo González Lanuza, Eduardo Bullrich, Oliverio Girondo, Alfredo González Garaño, and María Rosa Oliver. The board of foreign consultants consisted of Ernest Ansermet, Pierre Drieu la Rochelle, Leo Ferrero, Waldo Frank, Pedro Henríquez Ureña, Alfonso Reyes, Jules Supervielle, and José Ortega y Gasset. Nicolás Helft graciously provided me with a copy of the original document that lists each of these individuals.

26. King, *Sur*, 90.

27. See King, *Sur*; Gramuglio, "Bioy, Borges y *Sur*," "'Sur,'" and "SUR en la década del treinta"; Parodi, "El proyecto cultural de la revista 'Sur'"; Chiappini, *Borges y la revista Sur*; Zuleta, "*Sur* entre cultura y política"; Pasternac, *Sur*; López-Quiñones, *Borges y el nazismo*; Majstorovic, "An American Place"; and Willson, *La constelación del Sur*.

28. King, *Sur*, 50; Majstorovic, "An American Place," 175.

29. García Lorca, *Romancero gitano*, [4]. All of the authors in this preliminary list first publish works with Editorial Sur between 1935 and 1936. The only exception is Molinari, who does not publish anything with Editorial Sur until 1964 (*Un día, el tiempo, las nubes* [*A Day, Time, the Clouds*]).

30. *Sur* 8, 157.

31. A curious trait of Editorial Sur's books that speaks to Ocampo's goal of creating unity between the Americas can be found on the interior flaps, which normally highlight the firm's recently published works. While one of the flaps tends to list the "últimas ediciones de 'SUR'" [latest publications from "SUR"], the other flap frequently changes the headings that adorn the works listed there. Thus, Virginia Woolf's *Orlando* (1937) prints "Últimos éxitos editoriales de 'SUR'" [Latest Publishing Successes for "SUR"], while Conrado Nalé Roxlo's *Claro desvelo* [*Clear Insomnia*] (1937) opts for "Otros libros de autores hispanoamericanos" [Other Books by Spanish-American Authors] and Gabriela Mistral's *Tala* (1938) similarly chooses "Libros americanos" [American Books].

32. García Lorca, *Romancero gitano*, [2].

33. The close examination of other works published by Editorial Sur reveals a similar tendency toward multiple, differing editions. For instance, José Bianco's *Las ratas* [*The Rats*] (1943) informs readers that two distinct editions were printed.

34. See Larrea Rubio, *Federico García Lorca en Buenos Aires*, and García Lorca, *Primer romancero gitano*.

35. Villa Ocampo in Argentina has conserved the few surviving records related to Editorial Sur. In addition to this rare pamphlet, it also possesses a number of cashbooks (mainly dating from the 1960s until the 1980s) as well as a fair number of original contracts between published authors and Editorial Sur (mainly dating from the 1960s to the 1980s).

36. "Para la constitución de una sociedad editorial," [2–3].
37. Ibid., [3].
38. Ibid.
39. If we look to Ortega y Gasset's *Revista de Occidente,* the source of inspiration for Ocampo's literary magazine, we also can identify parallels in the creation of a sister publishing house, especially in terms of the prevalence of translations in both. That said, Ortega y Gasset's publishing firm produced works much more sporadically and does not seem to have created multiple types of editions. See López Campillo, *La 'Revista de Occidente' y la formación de minorías.*
40. de Sagastizábal, *La edición de libros,* 108.
41. *Catálogo 1944,* 160.
42. A number of advertisements in the literary journal *Sur* alert readers when certain works produced by Editorial Sur are sold out and therefore the firm will be issuing a second (or third) edition in light of the popularity of the works.
43. I say "also translated by Borges" here, but we can infer that Editorial Sudamericana is using the same translation that Borges provided for Editorial Sur. A quick perusal of Editorial Sudamericana's catalogues from the late 1940s reveals that they were producing "new" editions of not only *Orlando* for the Colección Horizonte, but also several other translated works that originated with Editorial Sur. These works would then be reproduced in other collections with Editorial Sudamericana, including its Piragua collection. As a result, it is clear that these translations were a way to bring in new readers and encourage them to buy other works in the same collection. See Chapter 3 for more details on Editorial Sudamericana's Colección Horizonte.
44. Borges's translation of Gide's *Perséphone* appeared in the literary journal *Sur* (no. 19, April 1936) one month before the production of the free edition, which suggests a type of reverse marketing to attract potential subscribers by giving them access to a (successful) sample of the type of material that the firm publishes.
45. Imprenta López also occupied the following addresses throughout its early years: Perú 538 and Tacuarí 761.
46. *Homenaje a Don José López García,* 10.
47. Ibid.
48. Ibid., 13.
49. Ibid., [33].
50. *Quién es quién,* 945.
51. *Cómo se imprime un libro,* 2.
52. Woolf, *Un cuarto propio,* [134]. A large number of the works translated for Editorial Sur contain similar messages in their colophons, which might explain why these specific translations circulate to other publishing houses. That said, the lack of a publisher's archive for Editorial Sur (or for any other of the firms in question, such as Editorial Sudamericana and Editorial Losada) makes it impossible to know for certain the costs, use, and implications of the subsequent printings of these first translations by other publishing houses.
53. As we see later in this chapter, Editorial Losada is not the only publishing

house that Editorial Sur names as an authorized distributor; Emecé, Editorial Nova, and Editorial Sudamericana are also named as distributors of other works published by Ocampo's firm.

54. I have yet to examine every work produced by Editorial Sur from 1933 to 1950, but I can say for certain that at the very least, all of Borges's translations lack a prologue.

55. See Willson, "Página impar."

56. Aside from an occasional introductory note by the author of the work itself, virtually no other prologues exist, save a few short introductions by Ocampo that appear in a sparse number of books. In light of the fact that she was the editor of this firm, many of these notes reflect her decision to publish (or translate) certain works and at times provide a type of warning for readers (see, for instance, her prologue to Lawrence's widely censored *El Troquel* [*The Mint*]).

57. Borges also translated William Faulkner's *Las palmeras salvajes* [*The Wild Palms*] for Editorial Sudamericana's Colección Horizonte (1940). See Chapter 3 for more details on this collection and Benedict, "Mapping Borges," for more details on these specific books.

58. Borges, *Prólogos*, 8. In this same work Borges outlines a few types of prologues: "El prólogo, en la triste mayoría de los casos, linda con la oratoria de sobremesa o con los panegíricos fúnebres y abunda en hipérboles irresponsables, que la lectura incrédula acepta como convenciones del género. Otros ejemplos hay . . . que enuncian y razonan una estética . . . El de muchas obras que el tiempo no ha querido olvidar es parte inseparable del texto" [The prologue, in the sad majority of cases, borders on a long after-dinner speech or a funeral panegyric and is full of irresponsible hyperboles, which the skeptical reading accepts as conventions of the genre. There are other examples . . . that sketch out and explain a certain kind of aesthetic. Those of many works that time has not forgotten are an inseparable part of the text] (8–9).

59. de Alvear, *Reposo*, 13–14.

60. Borges, *Prólogos*, 8.

61. See Jauretche, *El Paso de los Libres*; Alcorta, *Prison de l'enfant*; Kafka, *La metamorfosis*; Sarmiento, *Recuerdos de provincia*; James, *La humillación de los Northmore*; and Zenner, *Antigua lumbre*.

62. See Valéry, *El cementerio marino,* and Borges, Bioy Casares, and Ocampo, eds., *Antología de la literatura fantástica*.

63. Borges, *Prólogos*, 75.

64. del Carril, "Borges en Emecé," 125.

65. Bioy Casares, *Memorias*, 100.

66. In addition to the Séptimo Círculo series, Borges contributed to Emecé's Colección Buen Aire (*El compadrito* [1945]) and directed the firm's Puerta de Marfil with Bioy Casares (see Chapter 4).

67. *Catálogo general perpetuo.* Each volume in this catalogue details specific collections or series that Emecé produces (I. Biblioteca Emecé; II. Colección Buen Aire; III. Clásicos Emecé, Grandes Ensayistas, Cuadernos de Grandes Ensayistas, Sophia, Biblioteca del Peregrino, Historiadores de Indias, and El Crucero; IV. La Quimera, Cuadernos

de la Quimera, Colección Hórreo, El Navío, Los Libros Evocadores, Los Románticos, Colección Dorna, and Teatro del Mundo; V. Maestros de la Ciencia, Ciencia Divulgada, Ciencia e Investigación, and Fondo de Obras Técnico-Científicas; VI. Anaquel de Ediciones Varias and Libros en Distribución; VII. El Séptimo Círculo and La Puerta de Marfil).

68. The textual presentation of works also consists of "traducciones fieles a la letra y al espíritu ... [e] índices onomásticos o analíticos cuando la índole del libro así lo requiere" [faithful translations in letter and in spirit ... and onomastic and analytic indexes when the nature of the book requires it] (*Catálogo general perpetuo*).

69. *Catálogo. XXV aniversario*, 6.

70. Ibid.

71. *Papel, Libro, Revista* 1, 12.

72. *Papel, Libro, Revista* 14-15, 510-19.

73. de Sagastizábal, *La edición de libros*, 85-86.

74. "El domingo se recordará a Eduardo Mallea."

75. Cane, *The Fourth Enemy*, 41.

76. Melville, *Bartleby*, 12.

77. Sarmiento, *Recuerdos de provincia*, 9.

78. This is one of the few collections that presented its books in a hardcover format with dust jackets that corresponded in color to the specific subject of the work.

79. *Catálogo general perpetuo*.

80. Ibid.

81. Borges provided a prologue for a different work by Carlyle, *De los héroes*, for the publishing house W. M. Jackson in 1949 (Ralph Waldo Emerson's *Hombres representativos* [*Representative Men*] appears alongside Carlyle's work in this edition, with a preface by Borges as well). He also wrote an "estudio preliminar" [preliminary study] for W. M. Jackson's edition of Dante's *Divina comedia* (1949). Even though these works fall within the general scope of the current book, I have chosen not to include materials published by W. M. Jackson for reasons of space. That said, Borges's preface to Dante's work is extremely important and, reminiscient of the *Antología clásica de la literatura argentina*, has a much more scholarly angle.

82. Carlyle, *Sartor Resartus*, 12.

83. Werfel, *Juárez y Maximiliano*, 7.

84. *Catálogo general perpetuo*.

85. Borges and Bioy Casares picked the selections and wrote all of the notes included in the work as well.

86. "Agosto 18 de 1938."

87. The other initial members were Francisco Romero, Lorenzo Luzuriaga, Teodoro Becú, and Felipe Jiménez de Asúa. Losada also established a good relationship with Imprenta López.

88. The works of Rafael Alberti, Federico García Lorca, and Vicente Aleixandre all appeared in Buenos Aires with Editorial Losada.

89. de Sagastizábal, *La edición de libros*, 111.

90. The overlap in quality among certain editions produced by Editorial Losada, Editorial Sur, and Emecé can be explained by the fact that Rossi was the artistic director not only for Editorial Losada, but also for Imprenta López, which printed the majority of the works of all three firms (*Papel, Libro, Revista* 2, 52).

91. *Papel, Libro, Revista* 1, 13.

92. Cited in de Sagastizábal, *La edición de libros*, 114.

93. This work was republished a few years later as part of a different collection for Editorial Losada, its Biblioteca Clásica y Contemporánea (Classic and Contemporary Library), which speaks to the financial success of this work. Its republication also illustrates possible promotional strategies since the Pajarita de Papel series would have been slightly more expensive, given its hardback covers, illustrated endpapers, and decorative typographic ornaments throughout.

94. Kafka, *La metamorfosis*, 8.

95. Borges also contributed a critical essay, "Nota sobre 'La tierra purpúrea'" [Note about 'The Purple Land'], to Editorial Losada's "*Antología* de Guillermo E. Hudson" (1941), but since this work is not a prologue, I do not discuss it here.

96. I return to the unique editorial fruits of this particular friendship in Chapter 6 with a discussion of their own publishing houses.

97. *Papel, Libro, Revista* 3, 727.

98. Borges, "Jorge Luis Borges to Attilio Rossi."

99. *Papel, Libro, Revista* 3, 727.

100. Bioy Casares, *La invención de Morel*, 7.

101. Ibid.

102. Ibid., 8.

103. Rossi, *Buenos Aires en tinta china*, 7.

104. Borges, "Jorge Luis Borges to Attilio Rossi."

105. Ibid.

106. See, for example, Michaux, *Un bárbaro en Asia,* and De la Guardia, *García Lorca.* From the advertisements for these works, we can date the role of Editorial Losada as the "concesionario exclusivo para la venta" [exclusive authorized dealer for sale] for Editorial Sur from as early as 1941 to as late as 1946.

107. The few surviving cashbooks for Editorial Sur indicate that specific funds were allocated for distribution (around $2,000 Argentine pesos for September and October 1952). What is more, on October 6, 1952, there is an entry for funds "recibido de Editorial Nova por liquidación de distribución de libro" [received from Editorial Nova for the liquidation of its book distribution] in the amount of $24,058.25 Argentine pesos.

108. Pérez Rodríguez, "Luis Seoane, editor."

109. Gerhardt, "Exiliados gallegos en el mercado del libro argentino," 5.

110. Ibid., 7.

111. The price of each volume, in both collections, also appears printed on each back cover.

112. del Campo, *Fausto*, 8.

113. Risso Platero, *Arquitecturas del insomnio*, 9.

114. Ibid., 10.

115. Borges's prologue is introduced as a "Foreword" on the title page of *Ferment*, yet the table of contents for this same work refers to it as a "Prólogo." This curious shift in language reflects the work as a whole since the entire book is in English—even the more ornamental phrases indicating the "page"—with the exception of Borges's opening words, which are in Spanish.

116. Shand, *Ferment*, 9.

117. Ibid.

118. A striking 75 percent of *El jardín de senderos que se bifurcan* is previously published material. The only new short stories in this collection are "La biblioteca de Babel" [The Library of Babel] and "El jardín de senderos que se bifurcan."

119. Although I have been unable to track down images or physical copies of the advertising bands for most of the works published by Editorial Sur, I found a curious overlap between the wording on the bands that I have seen and the advertisements for these works in *Sur*. My working theory is that the texts for these bands were duplicated below the titles of each advertised work in the journal, and as a result, even if we do not have the original bands, we can look to extant copies of *Sur* for a better idea of its promotional framing.

120. We see a similar trend with the promotional band that adorns Borges's *Historia universal de la infamia*, published by Editorial TOR in 1935: "Toda la escoria del mundo" [All of the dregs of the world]. That said, there are virtually no extant bands from other works published by this firm, which makes it nearly impossible to draw any conclusions about its use of such bands.

121. Much like the previously cited band texts, the following examples from Editorial Sur's edition of *Ficciones* (1944) are taken from advertisements in the literary journal *Sur*.

122. Aside from the entirety of *El jardín de senderos que se bifurcan*, which is the first part of *Ficciones*, all of the stories in the second part of the work—*Artificios* [Artifices]—appear in *Sur*.

123. The Sociedad Argentina de Escritores (SADE) still awards this prize to writers.

124. The first edition of Camus's work appeared in December 1948, and the second edition appeared in November 1949. A series of advertisements in *Sur* reveal that this work was first priced at $9 Argentine pesos (*Sur* 167), promptly sold out (*Sur* 178), and then appeared in a new edition with a higher price of $12 Argentine pesos (*Sur* 182). The extant Editorial Sur cashbooks reveal that Ocampo advertised heavily in other venues as well, including Emecé, Editorial Sudamericana, Editorial Losada, Fondo de Cultura Económica, and even Harrod's. Her publicity in these outlets from July to December 1951 amounted to $2,950 Argentine pesos, while that from September and October 1952 amounted to a whopping $4,920 Argentine pesos.

125. The following five additional poems appear in this collection under the heading "otros poemas": "Prose Poems to I. J.," "Insomnio" [Insomnia], "Noche cíclica" [Cyclical Night], "Del infierno y del cielo" [Of Hell and Heaven], and "Poema conjetural" [Con-

jectural Poem]. Similar to the republication of his earlier volumes in this new collection for Editorial Losada, four of these five poems are previously published in other journals or newspapers.

126. See Cajero, *Palimpsestos del joven Borges,* and Hernaiz, "Borges y sus editores."

127. The second edition of *El Aleph* adds four new short stories to the collection: "Abenjacán el Bojarí, muerto en su laberinto" [Ibn Hakkan al-Bokhari, Dead in His Labyrinth], "Los dos reyes y los dos laberintos" [The Two Kings and Their Two Labyrinths], "El hombre en el umbral" [The Man on the Threshold], and "La espera" [The Wait].

128. The second edition of *El Aleph* (1952) contains a more elaborate version of the design of the first (not by Rossi), but this latter edition is outside the scope of the current book.

129. "Agosto 18 de 1938."

130. The first edition of *Ficciones* cost $4 Argentine pesos, the first edition of *El Aleph* cost $7 Argentine pesos, and the first edition of *La muerte y la brújula* costa $14 Argentine pesos.

131. In each of these three collections, the newly added material amounts to no more than 25 percent of the whole work.

SIX Borges as Publisher

1. Winship, "Publishing in America," 67.

2. For an extensive overview and analysis of *Destiempo,* see Sabsay-Herrera, "Para la prehistoria de H. Bustos Domecq." Digital copies of all three issues of this journal can be found on the Archivo Histórico de Revistas Argentinas website (https://www.ahira.com.ar/revistas/destiempo/).

3. One of the early references to Editorial Destiempo appears in Sabsay-Herrera, "Para la prehistoria de H. Bustos Domecq," 118. Also see de los Ángeles Mascioto, "Borges editor."

4. Sabsay-Herrera, "Para la prehistoria de H. Bustos Domecq," 107–8.

5. Aside from being featured in the three issues of *Destiempo,* three of these writers appear in Borges and Bioy Casares's *Antología poética argentina* (Ulyses Petit de Murat, Carlos Mastronardi, Ezequiel Martínez Estrada), which is discussed in Chapter 4. Readers will also recall from Chapter 2 that Borges and Petit de Murat worked as codirectors of the *Revista Multicolor de los Sábados* from 1933 to 1934. Borges was known to have a close relationship with Alfonso Reyes, who frequently contributed to the literary journal *Proa* and was even placed in charge of the projected third installment of this journal, which never saw the light of day. Furthermore, Reyes oversaw Editorial Proa's Cuadernos de la Plata (Notebooks from the [River] Plate), which published Borges's *Cuaderno San Martin* (1929) as its second work in the series.

6. Cited in Bosco, *Borges y los otros,* 80.

7. In my research of Bioy Casares's *Luis Greve, muerto,* I discovered two variations on the first edition of this work, also published with Editorial Destiempo: one with a yel-

low cover and a few typographical errors, and one with a blue cover: https://borgestodoe lanio.blogspot.com/2019/01/jorge-luis-borges-luis-greve-muerto-de.html; https://www .abebooks.com/servlet/BookDetailsPL?bi=30256144830&searchurl=sortby%3D17%26tn %3Dluis%2Bgreve%2Bmuerto&cm_sp=snippet-_-srp1-_-image2#&gid=1&pid=1.

8. Borges, "*Luis Greve, muerto.*"

9. King, *Sur,* 91.

10. "Adolfo Bioy Casares, *Luis Greve, muerto.*"

11. Petit de Murat, *Marea de lágrimas,* 6.

12. Bioy Casares, *Luis Greve, muerto,* 155. The variations in cover color and typography must reflect these differing print runs.

13. All of these prices appear on the inside flap of *Mallarmé entre nosotros.* Olivari's *Diez poemas sin poesía* is also listed, but without a price.

14. Barbieri, *Cabeza yacente,* 6.

15. Both *Continuación de la nada* and *Teseo fatal* are described as "en preparación" [in preparation] on the inside flap for Reyes's *Mallarmé entre nosotros* (1938).

16. Charles, "Apocryphal Literature," 176.

17. Bioy Casares, *Borges,* 1328. Alberto Casares, an Argentine antiquarian bookseller, describes Editorial Oportet & Haereses in a similar way: "Este nombre elegido por Borges y Bioy Casares para identificar su propia editorial, proviene seguramente de un poema de Paul Verlaine que forma parte de la obra *Liturgies intimes* (1892), titulado precisamente Oportet Haereses Esse. Que podría traducirse 'Conviene que haya herejías.' Asimismo esta frase proviene de San Pablo, I, Corintios, XI, 18" [This selected name by Borges and Bioy Casares to identify their own publishing house surely comes from a poem by Paul Verlaine that forms part of *Liturgies Intimes* (1892), titled precisely Oportet Haereses Esse. That could be translated "It's in our interest to have heretics." This phrase also comes from Saint Paul, I, Corinthians, XI, 18].

18. 1 Cor. 9:19: "For though I am free from all, I have made myself a servant to all, that I might win more of them" (ESV); 1 Cor. 11:19: "For there must be factions among you in order that those who are genuine among you may be recognized" (ESV).

19. This more accurate translation and use of terminology reflects the New King James Version of the Bible as well as the English Standard Version and the Reina Valera Spanish translation, the latter of which Borges used throughout his life (see Adur Nobile, "Las biblias de Borges").

20. Cited on the back cover of Borges and Bioy Casares, *Dos fantasías memorables. Un modelo para la muerte.*

21. Ibid.

22. Borges and Bioy Casares, *Obras completas en colaboración,* 136.

23. Ibid., 137.

24. Bioy Casares, *Borges,* 599, and also cited in Parodi, *Borges-Bioy en contexto,* 153.

25. Hermida, "Coleccionar para educar," 18.

26. Ibid., 22.

27. Alcorta, *Instrucción secundaria,* 9.

28. Ibid., 100–101. Eduardo Wilde played a key role in developing and enacting the foundational Law 1420, which established free, secular education in Argentina (1884).

29. This type of indirect critique is a common strategy that Borges and Bioy Casares employ in their collaborative writings. In other words, they frequently refer to earlier problems in Argentine history that echo many contemporary issues (especially those involving Perón).

30. Plotkin, *Mañana es San Perón,* 20. By 1952, the "Peronization" of the educational system had gone so far as passing a law (14.126) that required the use of Eva Perón's biography, *La razón de mi vida* [*The Reason for My Life*], as a primary textbook for all school levels (ibid., 108).

31. Some sources refer to Jacobsen's firm as the Librería Europa, while others call it the Librería Europea. I use this latter name because most sources, including Buonocore's *Libreros, editores e impresores,* use it.

32. Sabor Riera, "Contribución al estudio histórico del desarrollo de los servicios bibliotecarios," 26.

33. de Diego, "Editores alemanes en Argentina," 229.

34. Buonocore, *Libreros, editores e impresores,* 42. Jacobsen first opened his shop on Florida 242, moved after a few years between Florida and Lavalle, and a few years later made one final move to Charcas (today know as Marcelo T. de Alvear).

35. "Danesa."

36. Borges and Bioy Casares, *Obras completas en colaboración,* 138.

37. Ibid., 139.

38. For a more detailed study of these works, see Parodi, *Borges-Bioy en contexto,* 158–60.

39. Ibid., 159–60.

40. Borges and Bioy Casares, *Obras completas en colaboración,* 140. Curiously, Don Wenceslao serves time at the Penitencia Nacional in cell number 272, which just happens to be the cell adjacent to that of Don Isidro Parodi in *Seis problemas para don Isidro Parodi.*

41. Gen. 9:13, NRSV.

42. Borges and Bioy Casares, *Obras completas en colaboración,* 140.

43. Ibid., 140–41.

44. Ibid., 142. This grotesque use of food imagery also brings to mind the epic battle between Doña Cuaresma and Don Carnal in *El libro de buen amor* [*The Book of Good Love*].

45. Since both stories open with an acknowledgment of this figure of Lumbeira, they can be seen as two parts of one conversation between this figure and Mascarenhas.

46. Borges and Bioy Casares, *Obras completas en colaboración,* 131.

47. Ibid., 132.

48. The demolition of this home, in tandem with its mysterious basement, echoes what transpires in "El Aleph."

49. Isa. 6:5, NRSV. I should note that "El testigo" is the first story in *Dos fantasías memorables.*

50. Borges and Bioy Casares, *Obras completas en colaboración*, 149.

51. Ibid., 129.

52. This connection further emphasizes the earlier mentioned link of the adjacent prison cells for Don Wenceslao and Don Isidro Parodi.

53. Borges and Bioy Casares, *Obras completas en colaboración*, 145.

54. Ibid., 147. The phrase "presidente de *povo irmão*" is an example of the hybrid, transitional language *cocoliche*—except here it is a Portuñol/Portunhol overlap instead of the traditional Spanish-Italian—that Borges and Bioy Casares use throughout the work. The use of Portuguese might allude to the somewhat parallel political situation in Brazil under Getúlio Vargas as a sort of foreshadowing of Perón's rule. Also see Parodi, *Borges-Bioy en contexto*.

55. Ibid., 147. The fact that Bustos Domecq is too busy writing "bocetos biográficos" [biographical sketches] also recalls Borges's "biografías sintéticas" in *El Hogar*. While the entirety of Borges's column in *El Hogar* is dedicated to literary reviews, we see this form arising from certain "Bibliografía" [Bibliography] sections in the *Revista Multicolor de los Sábados* in which he and Petit de Murat review current works. In particular, the January 6, 1934, issue of the *Revista Multicolor* contains a "Bibliografía" section that is virtually identical to what we later find in Borges's columns in *El Hogar*. A few articles that Borges pens throughout the *Revista Multicolor* are also signed "F. Bustos" or "Francisco Bustos," which further strengthens this link.

56. MacAdam, "*Un modelo para la muerte*," 548–49.

57. Although the *Revista Multicolor* was not dedicated exclusively to detective fiction, several works that appear in its pages fall into this category. Some examples include G. K. Chesterton, "El muerto de la casa del pavo real" [The Death of the Peacock House] (December 30, 1933; p. 1); Víctor Juan Guillot, "El detective magnífico" [The Magnificent Detective] (October 28, 1933; p. 8); Pedro Devaux, "Sabios detectives" [Wise Detectives] (February 24, 1934; p. 8); and a review of Ramón Doll's "Policía intelectual" [Intellectual Police] (December 9, 1933; p. 5).

58. Chesterton, "La profecía del perro," 2.

59. MacAdam, "*Un modelo para la muerte*," 547.

60. Borges and Bioy Casares, *Obras completas en colaboración*, 153.

61. MacAdam, "*Un modelo para la muerte*," 549.

62. Borges, "Libros nuevos," 30; Borges, "*The Wild Palms*," 62.

63. These images accompany the following texts: "El asno de tres patas" [The Three-Legged Ass], "El Behemoth," "El dragón chino" [The Chinese Dragon], "El Golem," "El T'ao-T'ieh" [The Taotie], and "El Uroboros." While they are not attributed to any artist, the style of these illustrations is reminiscent of much of Xul Solar's work.

64. Borges, *Nueva refutación del tiempo*, 16.

65. See Bartoloni, "The Problem of Time in the Critical Writings of Jorge Luis Borges" and "Spatialised Time and Circular Time"; Donnelly, "Mirror of Time"; Johnson, "Time for Borges"; Moure, "Borges y la refutación (poética) del tiempo"; Sieber, "Time, Simultaneity, and the Fantastic in the Narrative of Jorge Luis Borges"; and Šišmišová, "Los juegos de Borges con el tiempo."

66. Each of the first edition printings of *Dos fantasías memorables* and *Un modelo para la muerte* were limited to a numbered run of three hundred copies.

67. A handful of early twentieth-century Argentine books show similar marbled paper boards (with quarter-bound leather spines and no paper spine labels), but the majority of these works have been rebound in this style and were not originally produced in such a way.

68. Peterson, *The Kelmscott Press*, 121.

69. Inherent in such discussions are artists' books, the *livre d'artiste*, bibliophilic tendencies, and book collecting. For more on the difficulty of reading these works, which have never been translated into English, see Parodi, *Borges-Bioy en contexto*.

70. The last work published by Editorial Destiempo, Bioy Casares's *Homenaje a Francisco Almeyra*, echoes this classic style of printing as well.

71. del Carril, "Borges en Emecé."

72. Rodríguez Monegal, *Jorge Luis Borges*, 64. Another link between these two can be found in the inscribed editions of *El Aleph* ("Dear Mandie / Happy Xmas with best greetings from / Jorge Luis Borges / 1951, Buenos Aires / What if this friend happened to be God?") and *La muerte y la brújula* ("To Mandie from your lazy friend / Jorge Luis Borges—1951") that Borges gifted to Molina Vedia: http://www.securenet.net/tbcl/TBCL_AHOME_Borges1.htm.

73. Borges, *Obras completas*, 328.

74. Borges, *Ficciones*, 58–59.

Conclusion

1. Montfort and Wardrip-Fruin, eds., *The New Media Reader*, 29–30.

2. Davison, "Literary and Electronic Hypertext"; Lapidot, "Borges between the Printing Press and the Hypertext"; and Sassón-Henry, "Borges and His Legacy in Hyperfiction" and *Borges 2.0*.

3. Salinas, *Liberty, Individuality, and Democracy*; González, *Borges and the Politics of Form*; Rosa, *Comienzos para una estética anarquista*; and Benedict, "Censorship and Political Allegory."

4. Borges's ideas and writings also influence jazz composition. More specifically, his short story "Pierre Menard, autor del Quijote" [Pierre Menard, Author of the Quijote], was printed as the liner notes for Mostly Other People Do the Killing's album *Blue* (2014), a note-for-note reproduction of Miles Davis's *Kind of Blue*.

5. In an earlier essay I define metabibliography in relation to Borges's writings as "a reflective study of how bibliographical analysis is understood, conducted, and written about. The purpose of establishing metabibliography as a theoretical framework is to understand what bibliography might mean in a given context—here, in the work of Borges. Rather than conducting bibliographical analysis, I argue that Borges writes about these types of research methods and uses the evidence that they provide to enrich his creative fictions" (Benedict, "Books about Books," 3).

6. McGann, *The Textual Condition*; McCarl, "Discourse of Data?"; Darnton, *The Case for Books*; and Cullen, *Editors, Scholars, and the Social Text*.

7. Genette, *Paratexts*, 1–2.

8. Borges, *Ficciones*, 58–59.

9. See Balderston, *How Borges Wrote*, for specific examples of the various types of paper scraps and objects that he would use for drafts of his short stories, essays, and poems. Genette also returned to "Pierre Menard" in his discussions of imitation, copy, parody, and "hyperesthetic passages" in the final section of *Palimpsests* (393–94).

10. Genette, *Palimpsests*, 252.

11. Ibid., 131.

12. Chartier, *The Order of Books*, 61–62.

13. Chartier, *Forms and Meanings*, 21.

14. Chartier, *Inscription and Erasure*, ix–x.

15. Ibid., x. Chartier also mentions Borges's "Magias parciales del Quijote" [Partial Magic in the Quijote] in his chapter "The Press and Fonts: Don Quixote in the Print Shop," which shows Borges's and Cervantes's ability to fuse "the world of the book with that of the reader" (ibid., 40).

16. Needham, "Fragments in Books," 87.

Bibliography

Abraham, Carlos Enrique. *La editorial Tor: Medio siglo de libros populares.* Argentina: Tren en movimiento, 2012.

Achugar, Hugo. "El poder de la antología/La antología del poder." *Cuadernos de Marcha* 46 (1989): 55–63.

"Adolfo Bioy Casares, *Luis Greve, muerto.*" Agencia Literaria Carmen Balcells. Accessed January 30, 2020. http://www.agenciabalcells.com/pt/autores/obra/adolfo-bioy-casares/luis-greve-muerto/.

Adur Nobile, Lucas Martín. "Las biblias de Borges." *Variaciones Borges* 41 (2016): 3–25.

"Agosto 18 de 1938. Nace Editorial Losada." *Primera Plana* 296 (August 20, 1968): 88.

Aguilar, Gonzalo Moisés. "Una historia local de la infamia. (Sobre *Seis problemas para don Isidro Parodi* de H. Bustos Domecq)." *Tramas para leer la literatura argentina* 5 (1996): 69–80.

Aizenberg, Edna. "Borges, Postcolonial Precursor." *World Literature Today* 66, no. 1 (1992): 21–26.

———. *Borges and His Successors: The Borgesian Impact on Literature and the Arts.* Columbia: University of Missouri Press, 1990.

Alazraki, Jaime. "Borges: Entre la modernidad y la postmodernidad." *Revista Hispánica Moderna* 41 (1988): 175–79.

———, ed. *Critical Essays on Borges.* Boston: G. K. Hall, 1987.

———. "Génesis de un estilo: *Historia universal de la infamia.*" *Revista Iberoamericana* 123–24 (1983): 247–61.

———. "Lectura estructuralista de 'El Sur' de Borges." *Escritura* 2, no. 3 (1977): 109–19.

———. "El texto como palimpsesto: Lectura intertextual de Borges." *Hispanic Review* 52 (1984): 281–302.

Alcorta, Amancio. *Instrucción secundaria.* Buenos Aires: La Cultura Argentina, 1916.

Alcorta, Gloria. *Prison de l'enfant*. Buenos Aires: self-published, 1935.
Alifano, Roberto. *Borges: Biografía verbal*. Barcelona: Plaza & Janés, 1988.
Alonso, Ricardo N. "Libros, libreros de viejo y bibliófilos." *El Tribuno*, April 24, 2011. http://www.eltribuno.info/libros-libreros-viejo-y-bibliofilos-n17380.
Alonso Estenoz, Alfredo. *Los límites del texto: Autoría y autoridad en Borges*. Madrid: Verbum, 2013.
Álvarez, Pablo. "Collection Highlight: Pope. The Iliad of Homer." University of Rochester, River Campus Libraries. http://rbscp.lib.rochester.edu/3948.
Los Anales de Buenos Aires 1–23 (1946–1948).
Antología de poetas argentinos. Buenos Aires: Imprenta Mercatali, 1926.
Appiah, Kwame Anthony. *Cosmopolitanism: Ethics in a World of Strangers*. New York: W. W. Norton, 2007.
Araujo, Carlos. "Librerías de viejo." *El Buenos Aires que se fue* (blog), November 14, 2012. http://blogs.monografias.com/el-buenos-aires-que-se-fue/2012/11/14/librerias-de-viejo/.
Arenas Cruz, Elena. "Borges y la literatura policial." *Castilla: Boletín del Departamento de Literatura Española* 17 (1992): 7–20.
Arrieta, Rafael Alberto. *La ciudad y los libros: Excursión bibliográfica al pasado porteño*. Buenos Aires: Librería del Colegio, 1955.
Ascher, James P. "Bibliographical Awareness in Art: Joel Swanson's Spacebar." *Media Archaeology Lab* (blog), December 3, 2013. https://mediaarchaeologylab.com/blog/bibliographical-awareness-art-joel-swansons-spacebar/.
Atback, Philip G., and Edith S. Hoshino, eds. *International Book Publishing: An Encyclopedia*. New York: Garland, 1995.
Atena Green, Raquel. *Borges y Revista multicolor de los sábados: Confabulados en una escritura de la infamia*. New York: Peter Lang, 2010.
Baines, Phil. *Penguin by Design: A Cover Story, 1935–2005*. London: Penguin, 2005.
Baker, Gideon. "Cynical Cosmopolitanism." *Theory & Event* 21, no. 3 (2018): 607–26.
Balderston, Daniel. "La *Antología de la literatura fantástica* y sus alrededores." In *El oficio se afirma. Historia crítica de la literatura argentina* 9, edited by Sylvia Saítta, 217–27. Buenos Aires: Emecé Editores, 2004.
———. "Biografías infames: Reflexiones sobre cuatro manuscritos de los cuentos de *Historia universal de la infamia*." *Variaciones Borges* 42 (2016): 213–31.
———. *Borges: Realidades y simulacros*. Buenos Aires: Editorial Biblos, 2000.
———. "Borges and *The Gangs of New York*." *Variaciones Borges* 16 (2003): 27–33.
———. "Borges en el mundo, el mundo en Borges." *Revista chilena de literatura* 96 (2017): 55–66.
———. "'Demasiado evanescente y extático': Reflexión sobre unas anotaciones de Borges en un ejemplar de las *Noches áticas* de Aulio Gellio." *Variaciones Borges* 37 (2014): 69–79.
———. "Detalles circunstanciales: Sobre dos borradores de 'El escritor argentino y la tradición.'" *Cuadernos LIRICO* 9 (2013): 1–13.

———. "'His Insect-Like Handwriting': Marginalia and Commentaries on Borges and Menard." *Variaciones Borges* 31 (2011): 125–36.
———. "Historical Situations in Borges." *MLN* 105 (1990): 331–50.
———. *How Borges Wrote*. Charlottesville: University of Virginia Press, 2018.
———. *Innumerables relaciones: Cómo leer con Borges*. Buenos Aires: Universidad Nacional del Litoral, 2010.
———, ed. *The Latin American Short Story: An Annotated Guide to Anthologies and Criticism*. Westport, CT: Greenwood, 1992.
———. *The Literary Universe of Jorge Luis Borges: An Index to References and Allusions to Persons, Titles, and Places in His Writings*. Westport, CT: Greenwood, 1986.
———. "Los manuscritos de Borges: 'Imaginar una realidad más compleja.'" *Variaciones Borges* 28 (2009): 15–26.
———. *Out of Context: Historical Reference and the Representation of Reality in Borges*. Durham, NC: Duke University Press, 1993.
———. "Palabras rechazadas: Borges y la tachadura." *Revista Iberoamericana* 246 (2014): 81–93.
———. *El precursor velado: R. L. Stevenson en la obra de Borges*. Buenos Aires: Editorial Sudamericana, 1985.
———. "'Las variantes raleaban': Two Drafts of *Evaristo Carriego*." *Variaciones Borges* 38 (2014): 81–97.
Bär, Ana Ojeda. "Manuel Gleizer: El último de los editores románticos." *La Nación*, April 2, 2006. http://www.lanacion.com.ar/793369-manuel-gleizer-el-ultimo-de-los-editores-romanticos.
Barbieri, Vicente. *Cabeza yacente*. Buenos Aires: Editorial Destiempo, 1945.
Barnatán, Marcos Ricardo. *Borges: Biografía total*. Madrid: Temas de Hoy, 1995.
Barnstone, William. *Borges at Eighty: Conversations*. Bloomington: Indiana University Press, 1982.
Bartoloni, Paolo. "The Problem of Time in the Critical Writings of Jorge Luis Borges." *Modern Greek Studies: Australia and New Zealand* 11–12 (2003–2004): 317–33.
———. "Spatialised Time and Circular Time: A Note on Time in the Work of Gerald Murnane and Jorge Luis Borges." *Australian Literary Studies* 18, no. 2 (1997): 185–91.
Bastos, María Luisa. *Borges ante la crítica argentina, 1923–1960*. Buenos Aires: Ediciones Hispamérica, 1974.
Batt, Jennifer. "Miscellanies." In *The Encyclopedia of British Literature, 1660–1789*, 799–805. Chichester: Wiley Blackwell, 2015
Batticuore, Graciela. *Lectoras del siglo XIX: Imaginarios y prácticas en la Argentina* Buenos Aires: Editorial Ampersand, 2017.
Baudelaire, Charles. *La Fanfarlo*. Translated by Aurora Bernárdez. Buenos Aires: Emecé Editores, 1944.
Baum, Vicki. *Marión*. Translated by Miguel de Hernani. Buenos Aires: Editorial Sudamericana, 1943.

Beaudry, Mary Carolyn, and Dan Hicks, eds. *The Oxford Handbook of Material Cultural Studies*. Oxford: Oxford University Press, 2010.
Becco, Horacio Jorge. *Jorge Luis Borges: Bibliografía total, 1923–1973*. Buenos Aires: Casa Pardo, 1973.
Bell, Barbara L. *An Annotated Guide to Current National Bibliographies*. Alexandria, VA: Chadwyck-Healey, 1986.
Bell-Villada, Gene H. *Borges and His Fiction: A Guide to His Mind and Art*. Chapel Hill: North Carolina University Press, 1981.
Beltrán, Oscar R., ed. *Antología de poetas y prosistas americanos*. Buenos Aires: Ediciones Anaconda, 1937.
Benedict, Nora C. "Books about Books and Books as Material Artifacts: Metabibliography in Jorge Luis Borges's *El jardín de senderos que se bifurcan*." *Revista Canadiense de Estudios Hispánicos* 42, no. 3 (2018): 451–72.
———. "Censorship and Political Allegory in Jorge Luis Borges's 'Viejo hábito argentino.'" *Bulletin of Hispanic Studies* 96, no. 1 (2019): 87–105.
———. "Mapping Borges in the Argentine Publishing Industry." http://norabenedict.github.io/borges.
———. "La novela negra en Borges: Una aproximación nueva a 'El muerto.'" *Variaciones Borges* 39 (2015): 143–58.
Bennett, Maurice J. "The Detective Fiction of Poe and Borges." *Comparative Literature* 35, no. 3 (1983): 266–75.
Bianco, José. *Las ratas*. Buenos Aires: Editorial Sur, 1943.
———. *Sombras suele vestir*. Buenos Aires: Emecé Editores, 1944.
Bioy Casares, Adolfo. *Borges*. Barcelona: Ediciones Destino, 2006.
———. *Homenaje a Francisco Almeyra*. Buenos Aires: Editorial Destiempo, 1954.
———. *La invención de Morel*. Buenos Aires: Editorial Losada, 1940.
———. *Luis Greve, muerto*. Buenos Aires: Editorial Destiempo, 1937.
———. *Memorias: Infancia, adolescencia, y cómo se hace un escritor*. Barcelona: Tusquets, 1994.
———. *El perjurio de la nieve*. Buenos Aires: Emecé Editores, 1944.
Blanco, Mariela. "Parodia y política en la escritura en colaboración de Borges." *Variaciones Borges* 23 (2007): 85–103.
Block de Behar, Lisa. *Borges: The Passion of an Endless Quotation*. Albany: New York State University Press, 2003.
Bloom, Harold. *Jorge Luis Borges*. Broomhall, PA: Chelsea House, 1986.
Boletín bibliográfico argentino. Buenos Aires: Comisión Nacional de Cooperación Intelectual, 1937–1949.
Boletín bibliográfico nacional. Buenos Aires: Ministerio de Educación de la Nación, 1950–1963.
"Book Publishing in Argentina." *United States Department of Commerce Publications, Catalog, and Index Supplement*. US Department of Commerce, July 1949: 1–4.
Bonet, Juan. "El *Índice de la nueva poesía americana*, 'Who is Who' de la vanguardia con-

tinental." In *Vanguardias sin límites: ampliando los contextos de los movimientos hispánicos*, 5–24. Budapest: Universidad Eötvös Loránd, 2012.

Borges, Jorge Luis. "Una alarmante Historia de la literatura." *El Hogar*, April 8, 1938, 14.

———. "The Albatross Book of Living Prose." *El Hogar*, April 1, 1938, 26.

———. *El Aleph*. Buenos Aires: Editorial Losada, 1949.

———, trans. "Antología de la literatura francesa." *Sur* 147–49 (1947): 222–23.

———. "Antología expresionista." *Cervantes* (Madrid) (October 1920): 100–112.

———. "Autobiographical Notes." *New Yorker*, September 19, 1970, 40–99.

———. "La biblioteca de mi padre." *El Correo* (1985): 4.

———. *Borges, oral*. Buenos Aires: Emecé Editores, 1979.

———. *Borges en El Hogar, 1935–1958*. Buenos Aires: Emecé Editores, 2000.

———. *Borges en Revista Multicolor: Obras, reseñas y traducciones inéditas de Jorge Luis Borges*. Edited by Irma Zangara. Buenos Aires: Editorial Atlántida, 1995.

———. *El círculo secreto: prólogos y notas*. Edited by Sara Luisa del Carril and Mercedes Rubio de Socchi. Buenos Aires: Emecé Editores, 2003.

———. "La dinastía de los Huxley." *El Hogar*, January 15, 1937, 8.

———. *Discusión*. Buenos Aires: Manuel Gleizer, 1932.

———. "Las dos maneras de traducir." *La Prensa*, August 1, 1926.

———. "Los escritores y Buenos Aires." *El Hogar*, February 12, 1937, 5.

———. *Evaristo Carriego*. Buenos Aires: Manuel Gleizer, 1930.

———. "Excellent Intentions." *El Hogar*, April 15, 1938, 26.

———. *Ficcionario: Una antología de sus textos*. Edited by Emir Rodríguez Monegal. Mexico City: Fondo de Cultura Económica, 1985.

———. *Ficciones*. Buenos Aires: Editorial Sur, 1944.

———. "Un film abrumador." *Sur* 83 (1941): 64–65.

———. *Historia de la eternidad*. Buenos Aires: Viau y Zona, 1936.

———. *Historia universal de la infamia*. Buenos Aires: Editorial TOR, 1935.

———. "Homenaje a Carriego." *Martín Fierro* 39 (1927): 8.

———. "El impostor inverosímil Tom Castro." *Crítica: Revista Multicolor de los Sábados*, September 30, 1933, 1.

———. *Inquisiciones*. Buenos Aires: Editorial Proa, 1925.

———. *El jardín de senderos que se bifurcan*. Buenos Aires: Editorial Sur, 1941.

———. *Jorge Luis Borges en Sur, 1931–1980*. Buenos Aires: Emecé Editores, 1999.

———. "Jorge Luis Borges to Attilio Rossi." 1951. Manuscript in the Borges Collection of the Albert and Shirley Small Special Collections Library, University of Virginia.

———. *Las Kenningar*. Buenos Aires: Colombo, 1933.

———. "Kipling y su autobiografía." *El Hogar*, March 26, 1937, 9.

———. "Libros nuevos." *El Hogar*, June 24, 1938, 30.

———. "La lírica argentina contemporánea." *Cosmópolis* 36 (1921): 641–51.

———. "Luis Greve, muerto." *Sur* 39 (1927): 85–86.

———. "La máquina de pensar de Raimundo Lulio." *El Hogar*, October 15, 1937, 14.

———. *El "Martín Fierro."* Buenos Aires: Columba, 1953.

———. *La muerte y la brújula*. Buenos Aires: Emecé Editores, 1951.
———. "Noticia de los kenningar." *Sur* 6 (1932): 202–8.
———. *Nueva refutación del tiempo*. Buenos Aires: Editorial Oportet & Haereses, 1947.
———. *Obras completas*. Buenos Aires: Emecé Editores, 2001.
———. *Obras completas*. Vols. 1–3. Edición crítica. Edited by Rolando Costa Picazo and Irma Zangara. Buenos Aires: Emecé Editores, 2007–2011.
———. *Otras inquisiciones, 1937–1952*. Buenos Aires: Editorial Sur, 1952.
———. "La perpetua carrera de Aquiles y la tortuga." *La Prensa*, January 1, 1929.
———. *Poemas [1922–1943]*. Buenos Aires: Editorial Losada, 1943.
———. *Poesía completa*. New York: Vintage, 2012.
———. "¿Por qué los escritores argentinos no viven de su pluma?" *El Hogar*, July 12, 1946, 167–69.
———. "Presencia de Miguel de Unamuno." *El Hogar*, January 29, 1937, 8.
———. *Prólogos con un prólogo de prólogos*. Buenos Aires: Torres Agüero, 1975.
———. "El rostro del profeta." *Crítica: Revista Multicolor de los Sábados,* January 20, 1934, 6.
———. *Selected Non-Fictions*. Edited by Eliot Weinberger. New York: Penguin, 2000.
———. "El sueño del aposento rojo." *El Hogar*, November 19, 1937, 24.
———. *El tamaño de mi esperanza*. Buenos Aires: Editorial Proa, 1926.
———. *Textos cautivos: Ensayos y reseñas en "El Hogar."* Edited by Enrique Sacerio-Garí and Emir Rodríguez Monegal. Barcelona: Tusquets, 1986.
———. *Textos recobrados: 1931–1955*. Edited by Sara Luisa del Carril and Mercedes Rubio de Socchi. Buenos Aires: Emecé Editores, 2001.
———. "Two Covers of a Cuaderno Chacabuco with Manuscript Notes and Original Drawings by the Author." N.d. Manuscript in the Borges Collection of the Albert and Shirley Small Special Collections Library, University of Virginia.
———. "Vindicación de *María* de Jorge Isaacs." *El Hogar*, May 7, 1937, 9.
———. "The Wild Palms." *El Hogar*, May 5, 1939, 62.
Borges, Jorge Luis, and Adolfo Bioy Casares, trans. "Antología de poesía norteamericana." *Sur* 113–14 (1944): 62–135.
———. *Dos fantasías memorables*. Buenos Aires: Editorial Oportet & Haereses, 1947.
———. *Dos fantasías memorables. Un modelo para la muerte*. Buenos Aires: Emecé Editores, 1998.
———, eds. *Los mejores cuentos policiales*. Buenos Aires: Emecé Editores, 1943.
———, eds. *Los mejores cuentos policiales. Segunda Serie*. Buenos Aires: Emecé Editores, 1951.
———. *Un modelo para la muerte*. Buenos Aires: Editorial Oportet & Haereses, 1946.
———. *Museo: Textos inéditos*. Edited by Sara Luisa del Carril and Mercedes Rubio de Socchi. Buenos Aires: Emecé Editores, 2002.
———. *Obras completas en colaboración*. Buenos Aires: Emecé Editores, 2001.
———. *Seis problemas para don Isidro Parodi*. Buenos Aires: Editorial Sur, 1942.
Borges, Jorge Luis, Adolfo Bioy Casares, and Silvina Ocampo, eds. *Antología de la literatura fantástica*. Buenos Aires: Editorial Sudamericana, 1940.

———. *Antología poética argentina*. Buenos Aires: Editorial Sudamericana, 1941.
Borges, Jorge Luis, and Sylvina Bullrich Palenque. *El compadrito*. Buenos Aires: Emecé Editores, 1945.
Borges, Jorge Luis, and Ronald Christ. "The Art of Fiction: Jorge Luis Borges." *Paris Review* 40 (1967): 116–64.
Borges, Jorge Luis, and Osvaldo Ferrari. *Libro de diálogos*. Buenos Aires: Editorial Sudamericana, 1986.
Borges, Jorge Luis, and Margarita Guerrero. *Manual de zoología fantástica*. Mexico City: Fondo de Cultura Económica, 1957.
Borges, Jorge Luis, and Delia Ingenieros, eds. *Antiguas literaturas germánicas*. Mexico City: Fondo de Cultura Económica, 1951.
Borges, Jorge Luis, and Pedro Henríquez Ureña, eds. *Antología clásica de la literatura argentina*. Buenos Aires: Editorial Kapelusz y Cía, 1937.
Bornstein, George. *Material Modernism: The Politics of the Page*. Cambridge: Cambridge University Press, 2001.
Bosco, María Angélica. *Borges y los otros*. Buenos Aires: Editorial Fabril, 1967.
———. "Manual de conjuradores: Jorge Luis Borges o la colectividad imposible." In *Jorge Luis Borges: Políticas de la literatura*, edited by Juan Pablo Dabove, 251–70. Pittsburgh: Instituto Internacional de Literatura Iberoamericana, 2008.
Bottaro, Raúl H. *La edición de libros en Argentina*. Buenos Aires: Ediciones Troquel, 1964.
Bourdieu, Pierre. *The Field of Cultural Production*. New York: Columbia University Press, 1993.
Bowers, Fredson. *Principles of Bibliographical Description*. New Castle, DE: Oak Knoll, 2012.
———. *Textual and Literary Criticism*. Cambridge: Cambridge University Press, 1966.
Braun, David Maxwell. "Devil's Bible Darkest Secrets Explained." *National Geographic* (blog), December 17, 2008. https://blog.nationalgeographic.org/2008/12/17/devils-bible-darkest-secrets-explained/.
Brown, Bill. *A Sense of Things: The Object Matter of American Literature*. Chicago: Chicago University Press, 2003.
Buonocore, Domingo. *Bibliografía literaria y otros temas sobre el editor y el libro*. Buenos Aires: Universidad Nacional del Litoral, 1956.
———. *Diccionario de bibliotecología: Términos relativos a la bibliología, bibliografía, bibliofilia, biblioteconomía, archivología, documentología, tipografía y materias afines*. Buenos Aires: Ediciones Marymar, 1984.
———. *Libreros, editores e impresores de Buenos Aires*. Buenos Aires: El Ateneo, 1944.
———. *Libreros, editores e impresores de Buenos Aires: Esbozo para una historia del libro argentino*. Buenos Aires: Bowker Editores, 1974.
———. *El mundo de los libros: Páginas sobre el libro, el escritor, la imprenta, la lectura, la biblioteca, el bibliotecario, el bibliófilo y el librero*. Santa Fe, Argentina: Castellví, 1955.
———. *Vocabularios bibliográficos: Términos relativos al libro, al documento, a la biblioteca y a la imprenta, para uso de escritores, bibliógrafos, bibliófilos, bibliotecarios,*

archivistas, libreros, editores, encuadernadores y tipógrafos. Santa Fe, Argentina: Castellví, 1952.
Burgin, Richard, and Jorge Luis Borges. *Conversations with Jorge Luis Borges.* New York: Holt, Rinehart and Winston, 1969.
Butler, Rex. "Everything and Nothing: On Jorge Luis Borges's 'Kafka and His Precursors.'" *Romance Quarterly* 57 (2010): 129–41.
Cajero Vázquez, Antonio. *Palimpsestos del joven Borges: Escritura y reescrituras de Fervor de Buenos Aires (1923).* San Luis Potosí, Mexico: El Colegio de San Luis, 2013.
Calvo, Hortensia. "Latin America." In *A Companion to the History of the Book,* edited by Simon Eliot and Jonathan Rose, 138–52. Malden, MA: Blackwell, 2007.
Camaña, Raquel. *El dilettantismo sentimental.* Buenos Aires: La Cultura Argentina, 1916.
———. *Pedagogía social.* Buenos Aires: La Cultura Argentina, 1916.
Camou, Antonio, Cristina Tortti, and Aníbal Viguera, eds. *La Argentina democrática: Los años y los libros.* Buenos Aires: Prometeo Libros, 2007.
Canala, Juan Pablo. "Lecturas y relecturas de un comienzo: sobre las ediciones de *Evaristo Carriego.*" *Variaciones Borges* 38 (2014): 99–120.
Cane, James. *The Fourth Enemy: Journalism and Power in the Making of Peronist Argentina, 1930–1955.* University Park: Pennsylvania State University Press, 2012.
Canto, Estela. *Borges a contraluz.* Madrid: Espasa Calpe, 1989.
Carlyle, Thomas. *De los héroes.* Translated by Jorge Luis Borges. Buenos Aires: W. M. Jackson, 1949.
———. *Sartor Resartus: Vida y opiniones de Herr Teufelsdröckh.* Translated by Joaquín Ojeda. Buenos Aires: Emecé Editores, 1945.
Carrizo, Antonio, and Jorge Luis Borges. *Borges, el memorioso: Conversaciones de Jorge Luis Borges con Antonio Carrizo.* Mexico City: Fondo de Cultura Económica, 1983.
Carter, John, and Nicholas Barker. *ABC for Book Collectors.* New Castle, DE: Oak Knoll, 2004.
Catálogo. Buenos Aires: Viau y Zona, 1935.
Catálogo. XXV aniversario, 1939–1964. Buenos Aires: Emecé Editores, 1964.
Catálogo general. Buenos Aires: Editorial Sudamericana, 1950.
Catálogo general perpetuo. Buenos Aires: Emecé Editores, n.d.
Catálogo 1944. Buenos Aires: Editorial Sudamericana, 1944.
Catálogo número 4. Buenos Aires: Editorial Sudamericana, [1949].
Catelli, Nora. "Dos hombres solos hablan: *Borges* de Bioy Casares." *Variaciones Borges* 34 (2012): 27–37.
Centro Cultural Borges. *Borges, a través de sus libros: Homenaje décimo aniversario.* Buenos Aires: Centro Cultural Borges, 1996.
Cervantes, Miguel de. *Novelas ejemplares.* Buenos Aires: Emecé Editores, 1946.
Cesco, Andréa. "Bibliografía sobre Jorge Luis Borges." *Fragmentos (Florianópolis)* 28/29 (2005): 433–521.
Cháneton, Abel. "El libro de lujo en la Argentina: Itinerario para bibliófilos." *El libro en la Argentina* 89–90 (1943): 47–60.

Charles, Robert Henry. "Apocryphal Literature." In *Encyclopedia Britannica,* 175–83. Cambridge: Cambridge University Press, 1910–1911.

Chartier, Roger. *Forms and Meanings: Text, Performances, and Audiences from Codex to Computer.* Philadelphia, PA: University of Pennsylvania Press, 1995.

———. *Inscription and Erasure: Literature and Written Culture from the Eleventh to the Eighteenth Century.* Translated by Arthur Goldhammer. Philadelphia: University of Pennsylvania Press, 2008.

———. *The Order of Books: Readers, Authors, and Libraries in Europe between the Fourteenth and Eighteenth Centuries.* Translated by Lydia G. Cochrane. Cambridge: Polity, 1994.

Chesterton, G. K. "La profecía del perro." *Crítica: Revista Multicolor de los Sábados,* May 12, 1934, 2.

Chiappini, Julio O. *Borges y la revista Sur.* Rosario, Argentina: Editorial Zeus, 1994.

———. *Los prólogos de Borges.* Rosario, Argentina: Editorial Zeus, 1991.

Ciabattari, Jane. "Is Borges the 20th Century's Most Important Writer?" BBC, September 2, 2014. http://www.bbc.com/culture/story/20140902-the-20th-centurys-best-writer.

50 años Emecé Editores: 1939–1989. Buenos Aires: Emecé Editores, 1989.

Close, Glen S. *Contemporary Hispanic Crime Fiction: A Transatlantic Discourse on Urban Violence.* New York: Palgrave Macmillan, 2008.

Cómo se imprime un libro. Buenos Aires: López y Cía, 1942.

Congreve, William. *The Way of the World.* Cambridge: Proquest, 2011.

Corral, Rose. "Acerca del 'primer Borges.'" *Nueva Revista de Filología Hispánica* 42, no. 1 (1994): 151–59.

Cortínez, Verónica. "De Poe a Borges: La creación del lector policial." *Revista Hispánica Moderna* 48, no. 1 (1995): 127–36.

Critchley, Simon. "Cynicism We Can Believe In." *New York Times,* March 31, 2009.

Cucuzza, Héctor Rubén, Roberta Paula Spregelburd, and Teresa L. Artieda. *Historia de la lectura en Argentina: Del catecismo colonial a las netbooks estatales.* Buenos Aires: Editoras del Calderón, 2012.

Cuento, Sergio, and Alberto Giordano. *Borges y Bioy Casares, ensayistas.* Rosario, Argentina: Ediciones Paradoxa, 1988.

Cullen, Darcy, ed. *Editors, Scholars, and the Social Text.* Toronto: University of Toronto Press, 2012.

Damon-Moore, Helen. *Magazines for the Millions: Gender and Commerce in the Ladies' Home Journal and the Saturday Evening Post, 1880–1910.* Albany: State University of New York Press, 1994.

"Danesa. Una historia de los inmigrantes daneses en la Argentina (1848–1939), tal cual lo explica María M. Bjerg en su libro Entre Sofie y Tovelille." https://web.archive.org/web/20140518120835/http://www.buenosaires.gob.ar/derechoshumanos/observatorio/colectividad-danesa.

Darnton, Robert. *The Case for Books: Past, Present, and Future.* New York: PublicAffairs, 2010.

Davison, Ned J. "Literary and Electronic Hypertext: Borges, Criticism, Literary Research, and the Computer." *Hispania* 74, no. 4 (1991): 1159–61.
de Alvear, Elvira. *Reposo*. Buenos Aires: Manuel Gleizer, 1934.
de Castro, Juan E. "Christopher Isherwood Meets Jorge Luis Borges: On the Value of South American Cultures." *MLN* 119 (2004): 329–43.
———. "De Eliot a Borges: Tradición y periferia." *Iberoamericana* 7, no. 26 (2007): 7–18.
de Costa, René. *Humor in Borges*. Detroit: Wayne State University Press, 2000.
de Diego, José Luis. "Actualidad del mercado del libro: El caso argentino." *Revista Hispánica Moderna* 71, no. 2 (2018): 131–50.
———. "Editores alemanes en Argentina." In *Ideas viajeras y sus objetos: El intercambio científico entre Alemania y América austral,* edited by Gloria Chicote and Barbara Göbel, 223–30. Madrid: Vervuert/Iberoamericana, 2011.
———, ed. *Editores y políticas editoriales en Argentina (1880–2010)*. Mexico City: Fondo de Cultura Económica, 2014.
———. *La otra cara de Jano. Una mirada crítica sobre el libro y la edición*. Buenos Aires: Editorial Ampersand, 2015.
de la Guardia, Alfredo. *García Lorca: Persona y creación*. Buenos Aires: Editorial Sur, 1941.
de los Ángeles Mascioto, María. "Borges editor." *Anclajes* 22, no. 2 (2018): 57–68.
———. "Del *Magazine* a la *Revista Multicolor,* un camino hacia la especificidad literaria." *Jornadas sobre la Historia de las Políticas Editoriales en la Argentina* (2015): n.p.
———. "Literatura fantástica entre el diario *Crítica* y la Editorial Sudamericana: Políticas editoriales, materialidad de los textos y modos de escritura." *Revista chilena de literatura* 93 (2016): 127–53.
———. "La *Revista Multicolor de los Sábados* como contexto formativo de un tipo de literatura policial de enigma." In *Tiempos de papel. Publicaciones periódicas argentinas (siglos XIX–XX),* edited by Verónica Delgado and Geraldine Rogers, 127–40. La Plata, Argentina: Universidad Nacional de la Plata, 2016.
———. "Suplemento *de* literatura: Cultura impresa y ficción en la *Revista Multicolor de los Sábados*." In *Tramas impresas. Publicaciones periódicas argentina (XIX–XX),* compiled by Verónica Delgado, Alejandra Mailhe, and Geraldine Rogers, 207–20. La Plata, Argentina: Universidad Nacional de la Plata, 2014.
De Maeseneer, Rita, and Ilse Logie. "Antologías del cuento dominicano de la última década (2000–2010) y canon." *Confluencia* 31, no. 1 (2015): 17–27.
de Maturana, José. *Naranjo en flor*. Buenos Aires: La Cultura Argentina, 1918.
De Ricci, Seymour. *English Collectors of Books and Manuscripts (1530–1930) and Their Mark of Ownership*. Bloomington: Indiana University Press, 1960.
de Sagastizábal, Leandro. *La edición de libros en la Argentina. Una empresa de cultura*. Buenos Aires: Editorial Universidad de Buenos Aires, 1995.
De Santis, Pablo. "Los mejores asesinatos de la literatura." *La Nación,* April 13, 2003. http://www.lanacion.com.ar/487962-los-mejores-asesinatos-de-la-literatura.
de Toro, Alfonso. "El productor 'rizomórfico' y el lector como 'detective literario': La aventura de los signos o la postmodernidad del discurso borgesiano (intertextualidad-

palimpsesto deconstrucción-rizoma)." In *Jorge Luis Borges. Variaciones interpretativas sobre sus procedimientos literarios y bases epistemológicas,* edited by Karl Alfred Blüher and Alfonso de Toro, 145–83. Madrid: Vervuert/Iberoamericana, 1992.

de Toro, Fernando. "Borges and the Construction of 'Reality.'" *Semiotica* 195 (2013): 277–304.

de Torre Borges, Miguel. *Borges: Fotografías y manuscritos.* Buenos Aires: Ediciones Renglón, 1987.

del Campo, Estanislao. *Fausto.* Buenos Aires: Editorial Nova, 1946.

del Carril, Sara Luisa. "Borges en Emecé." *Proa* 42 (1999): 125–27.

Dennett, Daniel C., and Douglas R. Hofstadter, eds. *The Mind's I: Fantasies and Reflections on Self and Soul.* New York: Basic Books, 2010.

di Giovanni, Norman Thomas. *The Lesson of the Master: On Borges and His Work.* London: Continuum, 2003.

Díaz, Hernán. *Borges, between History and Eternity.* London: Continuum, 2012.

Dickens, Charles. *El velo negro.* Buenos Aires: Emecé Editores, 1945.

Diehl, Adán L. "'Antología clásica de la literatura argentina.' Selección de Pedro Henríquez Ureña y Jorge Luis Borges. Editorial Kapelusz y Cía., Buenos Aires." *Caras y Caretas* 2 (1937): 128–29.

"Discusión sobre Borges." *Megáfono* 11 (1933): 13–33.

"El domingo se recordará a Eduardo Mallea." *La Nación,* August 8, 2003. http://www.lanacion.com.ar/517653-el-domingo-se-recordara-a-eduardo-mallea.

Domínguez, Marta Susana. *Las parodias satíricas de Jorge Luis Borges y Adolfo Bioy Casares.* Bahía Blanca, Argentina: Editorial de la Universidad Nacional del Sur, 2010.

———. "*Seis problemas para don Isidro Parodi*: Del relato policial a la sátira." In *Actas de Primeras Jornadas literatura, crítica, medios: Perspectivas,* edited by Amelia Arancet Ruda, Mariano García Valera Melchiorre, and Lucía Puppo, 215–20. Buenos Aires: Universidad Católica Argentina, 2004.

Donnelly, Jennifer. "Mirror of Time." *Contemporaneity: Historical Presence in Visual Culture* 2 (2012): 75–86.

Doran, Robert, ed. *Philosophy of History after Hayden White.* London: Bloomsbury Academic, 2013.

Dos Passos, John. *Hombre joven a la ventura.* Translated by Clara Diament. Buenos Aires: Editorial Sudamericana, 1951.

———. *El número uno.* Translated by María Rosa Oliver. Buenos Aires: Editorial Sudamericana, 1943.

Elbanowski, Adam. "Del margen al texto: Las notas en la obra de Jorge Luis Borges." *Thesaurus* 51, no. 1 (1996): 487–516.

Eliot, T. S. "Tradition and the Individual Talent." In *The Sacred Wood and Major Early Essays,* 27–33. Mineola, NY: Dover, 1998.

Emerson, Ralph Waldo. *Hombres representativos.* Translated by Jorge Luis Borges. Buenos Aires: W. M. Jackson, 1949.

Epplin, Craig. *Late Book Culture in Argentina*. London: Bloomsbury Academic, 2014.
Esteban, Ángel. "Borges y las bibliotecas. El escritor en su laberinto." *Mi Biblioteca* 1 (2005): 14–17.
Faulkner, William. *Las palmeras salvajes*. Translated by Jorge Luis Borges. Buenos Aires: Editorial Sudamericana, 1943.
Fernández Vega, José. "Una campaña estética. Borges y la narrativa policial." *Variaciones Borges* 1 (1996): 27–66.
Ferrero, Corinne. "Adolfo Bioy Casares y Jorge Luis Borges: Una colaboración inédita y anecdótica." *Recto/Verso* 3 (2008): 1–10.
Fishburn, Evelyn. "A Footnote to Borges Studies: A Study of the Footnotes." *Institute of Latin American Studies Occasional Papers* 26 (2002): 1–23.
Fishburn, Evelyn, and Psiche Hughes. *A Dictionary of Borges*. London: Duckworth, 1990.
Foster, David William. *A Bibliography of the Works of Jorge Luis Borges*. Tempe: Center for Latin American Studies, Arizona State University, 1971.
———. *Jorge Luis Borges: An Annotated Primary and Secondary Bibliography*. New York: Garland, 1984.
———, ed. *El legado de Borges*. Mexico City: El Colegio de México, 2015.
Francisco A. Colombo en sus cincuenta años de labor gráfica: Palabras pronunciadas en su homenaje. Buenos Aires: Colombo, 1942.
Galasso, Norberto. *Jorge Luis Borges: Un intelectual en el laberinto semicolonial*. Buenos Aires: Editorial Colihue, 2012.
Gambini, Hugo. *Historia del peronismo: El poder total (1943–1951)*. Buenos Aires: Planeta, 1999.
García Costa, Víctor O. "El último romántico de los editores." In *Manuel Gleizer. Librero y editor*, 3–11. Buenos Aires: Peña del Libro "Trenti Rocamora," 2008.
García Lorca, Federico. *Primer romancero gitano, 1924–1927*. Edited by Mario Hernández. Madrid: Alianza Editorial, 1983.
———. *Romancero gitano*. Buenos Aires: Editorial Sur, 1933.
Gargatagli Brusa, Ana. "Jorge Luis Borges y la traducción." PhD diss., Universidad Autónoma de Barcelona, 1993.
Gaskell, Philip. *A New Introduction to Bibliography*. New Castle, DE: Oak Knoll, 2012.
Genette, Gérard. *Palimpsests: Literature in the Second Degree*. Translated by Channa Newman and Claude Doubinsky. Lincoln: University of Nebraska Press, 1997.
———. *Paratexts: Thresholds of Interpretations*. Translated by Jane E. Lewin. Cambridge: Cambridge University Press, 1997.
Gerhardt, Federico. "Exiliados gallegos en el mercado del libro argentino: Sellos y colecciones editoriales de la década del 40." *Jornadas sobre la Historia de las Políticas Editoriales en la Argentina* (2015): 1–15.
———. "Temas y autores argentinos y latinoamericanos en proyectos editoriales de los exiliados gallegos en la Argentina durante la década del cuarenta." *Kamchatka. Revista de análisis cultural* 7 (2016): 73–96.
Giardinelli, Mempo. *El género negro*. Mexico City: Universidad Autónoma Metropolitana, 1984.

Gide, André. *Perséphone*. Translated by Jorge Luis Borges. Buenos Aires: Editorial Sur, 1936.
———. *Regreso de la U.R.S.S.* Translated by Rubén Darío Sánchez. Buenos Aires: Editorial Sur, 1936.
Gilardoni, José. *Borgesiana: Catálogo bibliográfico de Jorge Luis Borges, 1923–1989*. Buenos Aires: Catedral al Sur Editores, 1989.
Glass, Loren. *Authors Inc.: Literary Celebrity in the Modern United States, 1880–1980*. New York: New York University Press, 2004.
Goldenberg, Raquel. "Manuel Gleizer: Un editor 'legendario' y 'el ultimo de los románticos.'" In *Ensayos sobre judaísmo latinoamericano*, 319–38. Buenos Aires: Milá, 1990.
Gómez López-Quiñones, Antonio. *Borges y el nazismo: SUR (1937–1946)*. Granada: Universidad de Granada, 2004.
Goñi, Uki. "A Novel Oasis: Why Argentina Is the Bookshop Capital of the World." *The Guardian,* June 19, 2015. https://www.theguardian.com/world/2015/jun/19/argentina-books-bookstores-reading.
González, José Eduardo. *Borges and the Politics of Form*. New York: Garland, 1998.
González Carbalho, José, ed. *Índice de la poesía argentina contemporánea*. Santiago: Ediciones Ercilla, 1937.
González Echevarría, Roberto. *Myth and Archive: A Theory of Latin American Narrative*. Cambridge: Cambridge University Press, 1990.
González Stephan, Beatriz. *Contribución al estudio de la historiografía literaria hispanoamericana*. Caracas: Academia Nacional de la Historia, 1985.
Goyena, Pedro. *Crítica literaria*. Buenos Aires: La Cultura Argentina, 1917.
Grafton, Anthony. *Forgers and Critics: Creativity and Duplicity in Western Scholarship*. Princeton, NJ: Princeton University Press, 1990.
Gramuglio, María Teresa. "Bioy, Borges y *Sur,* diálogos y duelos." *Punto de Vista* 34 (1989): 11–16.
———. "'Sur': Constitución del grupo y proyecto cultural." *Punto de Vista* 17 (1983): 7–10.
———. "SUR en la década del treinta: Una revista política." *Punto de Vista* 28 (1986): 32–39.
Greco, Martín. "Presentación de la revista [*Martín Fierro*]." *Archivo Histórico de Revistas Argentinas*. Accessed January 30, 2020. https://www.ahira.com.ar/revistas/martin-fierro/.
Green, Julien. *Adriana Mesurat*. Translated by Lysandro Z. D. Galtier. Buenos Aires: Editorial Sudamericana, 1939.
Greenblatt, Stephen. *Renaissance Self-Fashioning: From More to Shakespeare*. Chicago: University of Chicago Press, 1980.
Gutiérrez Viñuales, Rodrigo. "Seoane en el centro. Algunos itinerarios por el arte en Buenos Aires (1936–1963)." In *Buenos Aires, escenarios de Luis Seoane,* edited by Rodrigo Guitérrez Viñuales and Miguel Anxo Seixas Seoane, 1–39. Buenos Aires: Fundación Luis Seoane, 2007.

Gvirtz, Silvina. *Nuevas y viejas tendencias en la docencia (1945-1955)*. Buenos Aires: Centro Editor de América Latina, 1991.
Gvirtz, Silvina, and Jason Beech, eds. *Going to School in Latin America*. Westport, CT: Greenwood, 2008.
Hansen, Anne Mette. *The Book as Artefact, Text and Border*. Amsterdam: Rodopi, 2005.
Hart, Patricia. *The Spanish Sleuth: The Detective in Spanish Fiction*. Rutherford, NJ: Fairleigh Dickinson University Press, 1987.
Harte, Francis Bret. *Bocetos californianos*. Translated by D. E. de Vaudray and D. F. de Arteaga. Buenos Aires: Emecé Editores, 1946.
Helft, Nicolás. *Borges: Postales de una biografía*. Buenos Aires: Emecé Editores, 2013.
———, ed. *Crítica: Revista Multicolor de los Sábados, 1933-1934. Edición completa en CD-ROM*. Buenos Aires: Fondo Nacional de las Artes, 1999.
———. "History of the Land Called Uqbar." *Variaciones Borges* 15 (2003): 151-80.
———. *Jorge Luis Borges: Bibliografía e índice*. Buenos Aires: Ediciones Biblioteca Nacional, 2013.
Hermida, Carola. "Coleccionar para educar. Acerca de 'La Cultura Argentina' (1915-1928)." *Estudios de Teoría Literaria* 1, no. 2 (2012): 17-30.
Hernaiz, Sebastián. "Borges y sus editores: itinerarios de *Fervor de Buenos Aires* (1923-1977)." *Orbis Tertius* 20, no. 22 (2015): 1-8.
Hernández, José. *Martín Fierro*. Edited by Élida Lois and Ángel Núñez. Paris: Allca XX, 2001.
Hernández Martín, Jorge. "Dialogism and Parody in the Detective Story: Honorio Bustos Domecq's *Seis problemas para don Isidro Parodi*." *Revista Canadiense de Estudios Hispánicos* 21, no. 2 (1997): 295-311.
———. *Readers and Labyrinths: Detective Fiction in Borges, Bustos Domecq, and Eco*. New York: Garland, 1995.
———. "Textual Polyphony and Skaz in *Seis problemas para don Isidrio Parodi* by Bustos Domecq." *Variaciones Borges* 6 (1998): 13-32.
Herzovich, Guido. "Towards a Modern Synergy: Cultural Massification and the Compartmentalization of Books and Publics in Argentina and Brazil (1920-1960)." *Revista Hispánica Moderna* 71, no. 2 (2018): 163-77.
Hidalgo, Alberto, Vicente Huidobro, and Jorge Luis Borges, eds. *Índice de la nueva poesía americana*. Buenos Aires: Sociedad de Publicaciones El Inca, 1926.
Homenaje a Don José López García. XXX° aniversario de la fundación de la Imprenta López. Buenos Aires: López y Cía, 1938.
Hudson, Guillermo E., ed. *Antología*. Buenos Aires: Editorial Losada, 1941.
Huxley, Aldous. *Con los esclavos en la noria*. Translated by Julio Irazusta. Buenos Aires: Editorial Sudamericana, 1945.
———. *Contrapunto*. Translated by Lino Novás Calvo. Buenos Aires: Editorial Sur, 1933.
———. *El joven Arquímedes*. Translated by Leonor Acevedo de Borges. Buenos Aires: Editorial Losada, 1943.
———. *El tiempo debe detenerse*. Translated by Miguel de Hernani. Buenos Aires: Editorial Sudamericana, 1945.

Ibarra, Nestor. "Jorge Luis Borges, poeta." *Sintesis. Artes, Ciencias y Letras* 34 (1930): 11–32.
Irby, James E. "Borges, Carriego y el arrabal." *Nueva Revista de Filología Hispánica* 19 (1971): 119–23.
———. "Textual Series in *Discusión*." *Variaciones Borges* 31 (2011): 1–12.
James, Henry. *La humillación de los Northmore*. Translated by Haydée Lange. Buenos Aires: Emecé Editores, 1945.
James, William. *Pragmatismo*. Translated by Vicente P. Quintero. Emecé Editores, 1945.
Jasper, David, and Allen Permar Smith, eds. *Between Truth and Fiction: A Narrative Reader in Literature and Theology*. Waco, TX: Baylor University Press, 2010.
Jauretche, Arturo. *El Paso de los Libres*. Buenos Aires: La Boina Blanca, 1934.
Jefferson, Thomas. *The Jefferson Cyclopedia*. Edited by John P. Foley. New York: Russell & Russell, 1967.
Jennings, A. L. "'El libro' en la obra de Jorge Luis Borges." *Nueva Narrativa Hispano-americana* 3 (1973): 275–80.
Johnson, David E. "Time for Borges." *CR: The New Centennial Review* 9, no. 1 (2009): 209–26.
Kafka, Franz. *Informe para una academia*. Translated by María Rosa Oliver. Buenos Aires: Emecé Editores, 1945.
———. *La metamorfosis*. Translated by Jorge Luis Borges. Buenos Aires: Editorial Losada, 1938.
King, John. "Adolfo Bioy Casares: A biographical sketch." In *Adolfo Bioy Casares: Borges, Fiction and Art,* edited by Karl Posso, 38–57. Cardiff: University of Wales Press, 2012.
———. *Sur: A Study of the Argentine Literary Journal and Its Role in the Development of a Culture, 1931–1970*. Cambridge: Cambridge University Press, 1986.
Kingery, W. D. *Learning from Things: Method and Theory of Material Cultural Studies*. Washington, DC: Smithsonian Institution Press, 1996.
Kleingeld, Pauline, and Eric Brown. "Cosmopolitanism." *The Stanford Encyclopedia of Philosophy,* Fall 2014 Edition, edited by Edward N. Zalta. Substantive revision July 1, 2013. https://plato.stanford.edu/archives/fall2014/entries/cosmopolitanism/.
Kristal, Efraín. *Invisible Work: Borges and Translation*. Nashville: Vanderbilt University Press, 2002.
Lafforgue, Jorge, and Jorge B. Rivera, eds. *Asesinos de papel. Ensayos sobre narrativa policial*. Buenos Aires: Ediciones Colihue, 1995.
Lafon, Michel. "Bioy and Borges: From the Third Man to the World of Bustos Domecq." In *Adolfo Bioy Casares: Borges, Fictions and Art,* edited by Karl Posso, 73–88. Cardiff: University of Wales Press, 2012.
Lagarde, Pierre. *La Politique de l'édition du livre en Argentine*. Toulouse: Service des Publications de l'Université de Toulouse-Le Mirall, 1981.
Lapidot, Ema. "Borges between the Printing Press and the Hypertext." In *Jorge Luis Borges: Thought and Knowledge in the XXth Century,* edited by Alfonso de Toro and Fernando de Toro, 327–52. Madrid: Vervuert/Iberoamericana, 1999.
Larrauri, Agustín O. *El arte del libro*. Buenos Aires: Colombo, 1954.

Larrea Rubio, Pedro. *Federico García Lorca en Buenos Aires.* Sevilla: Renacimiento, 2015.
Lawrence, D. H. *Canguro.* Translated by Lino Novás Calvo. Buenos Aires: Editorial Sur, 1933.
———. *La mujer que se fué a caballo.* Translated by Leonor Acevedo de Borges. Buenos Aires: Editorial Losada, 1939.
———. *El Troquel.* Translated by Victoria Ocampo. Buenos Aires: Editorial Sur, 1955.
———. *La virgin y el gitano.* Translated by Eduardo Uribe. Buenos Aires: Editorial Sur, 1934.
Lawrence, Jeffrey. *Anxieties of Experience: The Literatures of the Americas from Whitman to Bolaño.* Oxford: Oxford University Press, 2018.
Levine, Suzanne Jill. "Borges sobre la traducción." *Teoría de la Educación. Educación y Cultura en la Sociedad de la Información* 13, no. 1 (2012): 9–39.
Libertella, Mauro. "Los Cuadernos de la Quimera." *Página 12,* August 7, 2005.
Loewenstein, C. Jared. Conversation Recorded between Jorge Luis Borges and C. Jared Loewenstein. April 8, 1980. Memorandum in the Borges Collection of the Albert and Shirley Small Special Collections Library, University of Virginia.
———. *A Descriptive Catalogue of the Jorge Luis Borges Collection at the University of Virginia.* Charlottesville: University Press of Virginia, 1993.
Loewenstein, C. Jared, and Donald L. Shaw. "Five Manuscript Poems by Borges in the Virginia Collection." In *Convergencias hispánicas,* edited by Elizabeth A. Scarlett and Howard B. Wescott, 141–58. Newark: Juan de la Cuesta, 2001.
López Campillo, Evelyne. *La "Revista de Occidente" y la formación de minorías (1923–1936).* Madrid: Taurus, 1972.
López Llovet, Gloria. *Sudamericana. Antonio López Llausás, un editor con los pies en la tierra.* Madrid: Random House/Mondadori, 2004.
Louis, Annick. *Borges ante el fascismo.* New York: Peter Lang, 2007.
———. "Definiendo un género. La *Antología de la literatura fantástica* de Silvina Ocampo, Adolfo Bioy Casares y Jorge Luis Borges." *Nueva Revista de Filología Hispánica* 2 (2001): 409–37.
———. *Jorge Luis Borges. Obras y maniobras.* Santa Fe, Argentina: Ediciones UNL, 2013.
———. "Las revistas literarias como objeto de estudio." In *Almacenes de un tiempo en fuga. Revista culturales en la modernidad hispánica,* edited by Hanno Ehrlicher and Nanette Ribler-Pipka, 31–57. Aachen: Shaker, 2014.
Lynn, Karen, and Nicolas Shumway. "Borges y *Las Kenningar.*" *Texto Crítico* 28 (1984): 122–30.
MacAdam, Alfred. "El espejo y la mentira, dos cuentos de Borges y Bioy Casares." *Revista Iberoamericana* 37 (1971): 357–74.
———. "*Un modelo para la muerte*: La apoteosis de Parodi." *Revista Iberoamericana* 46 (1980): 545–52.
Maier, Linda S. *Borges and the European Avant-garde.* New York: Peter Lang, 1996.
Majstorovic, Gorica. "An American Place: Victoria Ocampo's Editorial Politics, the Foundation of *Sur,* and Hemispheric Alliances." *Arizona Journal of Hispanic Cultural Studies* 9 (2005): 171–80.

Malamet, Elliott. *The World Remade: Graham Greene and the Art of Detection.* New York: Peter Lang, 1998.
Manguel, Alberto. *A History of Reading.* London: HarperCollins, 1996.
———. *A Reader on Reading.* New Haven, CT: Yale University Press, 2010.
Mann, Thomas. *Las cabezas trocadas.* Translated by Francisco Ayala. Buenos Aires: Editorial Sudamericana, 1942.
Mansfield, Katherine. *En la bahía.* Translated by Leonor Acevedo de Borges. Buenos Aires: Editorial Losada, 1938.
"Mapa celeste de editoriales." Museo del libro y de la lengua. https://web.archive.org/web/20160322091710/http://museo.bn.gov.ar/museo/mapa-celeste-de-editoriales.
Marcano, Nashieli. "La reseña bibliográfica y la inestabilidad textual en 'Examen de la obra de Herbert Quain' (1941), de Jorge Luis Borges." *Revista de Estudios Hispánicos* 50, no. 2 (2016): 463–83.
Margery Peña, Enrique. "*Seis problemas para don Isidrio Parodi.* Notas para su interpretación con alcances sobre el género policial." *Filología y Lingüística* 13, no. 2 (1987): 61–91.
Marqués, Rodolfo Santiago. "La plaqueta artística en La Argentina." PhD diss., Instituto Universitario Nacional del Arte, 2012.
Martín, Marina. "Humor y parodia en Borges: Versiones de lo inverosímil." *Variaciones Borges* 18 (2004): 43–61.
Martínez Estrada, Ezequiel. *La inundación.* Buenos Aires: Emecé Editores, 1943.
Mateos, Zulma. *Borges y los argentinos.* Buenos Aires: Biblos, 2010.
Mattalia, Sonia. *La ley y el crimen: Usos del relato policial en la narrativa argentina (1880–2000).* Madrid: Vervuert/Iberoamericana, 2009.
Matthews, Nicole, and Nickianne Moody, eds. *Judging a Book by Its Cover: Fans, Publishers, Designers, and the Marketing of Fiction.* Aldershot: Ashgate, 2007.
Maugham, William Somerset. *La otra comedia.* Translated by Juan Axpe. Buenos Aires: Editorial Sudamericana, 1941.
McCarl, Clayton. "Discourse of Data? Theorizing the Electronic Edition of Antonio de León Pinelo's 1629 Bibliography of the Indies." In *Latin American Textualities: History, Materiality, and Digital Media*, edited by Heather J. Allen and Andrew R. Reynolds, 177–96. Tucson: University of Arizona Press, 2018.
McGann, Jerome J. *The Textual Condition.* Princeton, NJ: Princeton University Press, 1991.
McKenzie, D. F. *Bibliography and the Sociology of Texts.* Cambridge: Cambridge University Press, 1999.
McKerrow, Ronald B. *An Introduction to Bibliography for Literary Students.* Oxford: Clarendon, 1927.
———. "Notes on Bibliographical Evidence for Literary Students and Editors of English Works of the Sixteenth and Seventeenth Centuries." *Transactions of the Bibliographical Society* 12 (1911–1913): 211–318.
Melgarejo, Graciela. "Sello tradicional. Kapelusz celebra sus 100 años de vida fomentando

la lectura." *La Nación,* October 6, 2005. http://www.lanacion.com.ar/744995-kape lusz-celebra-sus-100-anos-de-vida-fomentando-la-lectura.

Melville, Herman. *Bartleby.* Translated by Jorge Luis Borges. Buenos Aires: Emecé Editores, 1944.

Meyer, Doris. *Victoria Ocampo: Against the Wind and the Tide.* New York: G. Braziller, 1979.

Miceli, Sergio. *Ensayos porteños: Borges, el nacionalismo y las vanguardias.* Translated by Ada Solari. Bernal: Universidad Nacional de Quilmes, 2012.

Michaux, Henri. *Un bárbaro en Asia.* Translated by Jorge Luis Borges. Buenos Aires: Editorial Sur, 1941.

Milanesio, Natalia. *Workers Go Shopping in Argentina: The Rise of Popular Consumer Culture.* Albuquerque: University of New Mexico Press, 2015.

Miller, Daniel. *Materiality.* Durham, NC: Duke University Press, 2005.

Miranda, Carolina. "More Than the Sum of Its Parts: Borges, Bioy Casares and the Phenomenon of the *Séptimo Círculo* Collection." In *Serial Crime Fiction: Dying for More,* edited by Jean Anderson, Carolina Miranda, and Barbara Pezzotti, 31–40. New York: Palgrave, 2015.

Mistral, Gabriela. *Tala.* Buenos Aires: Editorial Sur, 1938.

Molloy, Sylvia. *Signs of Borges.* Translated by Oscar Montero. Durham, NC: Duke University Press, 1994.

Montfort, Nick, and Noah Wardrip-Fruin, eds. *The New Media Reader.* Cambridge, MA: Massachusetts Institute of Technology Press, 2003.

Mora, Rosa. "La histórica editorial argentina Losada se instala en España." *El País,* April 13, 2002.

Morelli, Gabriele. *Historia y recepción de la* Antología *poética de Gerardo Diego.* Valencia: Pre-Textos, 1997.

Moure, Clelia. "Borges y la refutación (poética) del tiempo." *Variaciones Borges* 35 (2013): 245–64.

Mueller, Joanne M. "Jorges [sic] Luis Borges: The Writer as Political Conscience." Paper presented at the International Congress of the Latin American Studies Association (LASA), University of Wisconsin, spring 1973.

Nalé Roxlo, Conrado. *Claro desvelo.* Buenos Aires: Editorial Sur, 1937.

Needham, Paul. "Fragments in Books: Dutch Prototypography in the Van Ess Collection." In *"So precious a foundation": The Library of Leander van Ess at the Burke Library of Union Theological Seminary in the City of New York,* edited by Milton Gatch, 85–110. New York: Grolier Club, 1996.

Nobilia, Patricia, and Ricardo Valerga, eds. *José Bonomi y El Séptimo Círculo.* Buenos Aires: Museo de Arte Español "Enrique Larreta," 2014.

Noé, Julio, ed. *Antología de la poesía argentina moderna (1896–1930).* Buenos Aires: El Ateneo, 1931.

———, ed. *Antología de la poesía argentina moderna (1900–1925).* Buenos Aires: Nosotros, 1926.

Nussbaum, Martha C. *The Cosmopolitan Tradition. A Noble but Flawed Ideal.* Cambridge, MA: Harvard University Press, 2019.
———. *For Love of Country: Debating the Limits of Patriotism.* Edited by Joshua Cohen. Boston: Beacon, 1996.
Ocampo, Victoria. "Introducción." *Sur* 113–14 (1944): 7–10.
———. "Introducción." *Sur* 147–49 (1947): 7–8.
———. "Vida de la revista *Sur.* 35 años de una labor." *Sur* 303–5 (1966–1967): 1–22.
O'Flaherty, Liam. *El alucinado.* Translated by Román A. Jiménez. Buenos Aires: Editorial Sudamericana, 1939.
Olea Franco, Rafael, ed. *Borges: Desesperaciones aparentes y consuelos secretos.* Mexico City: El Colegio de México, 1999.
Olivari, Nicolás. *Diez poemas sin poesía.* Buenos Aires: Editorial Destiempo, 1938.
Omil, Alba. "A medio siglo de 'Hombre de la esquina rosada.'" *Sur* 348 (1981): 63–67.
Orgambide, Pedro G. *Borges y su pensamiento político.* Mexico City: Comité de Solidaridad con el Pueblo Argentino, Casa Argentina, 1978.
Ortiz, Rodolfo. "Las deslecturas de Borges: Eliot, el traductor argentino y la tradición." *Variaciones Borges* 37 (2014): 37–50.
O'Ryan, Mariana Casale. *The Making of Jorge Luis Borges as an Argentine Cultural Icon.* London: Modern Humanities Research Association, 2014.
Osuna, Rafael. *Las revistas literarias: Un estudio introductorio.* Cádiz: Universidad de Cádiz, 2004.
Othoniel Rosa, Luis. *Comienzos para una estética anarquista: Borges con Macedonio.* Santiago: Editorial Cuarto Propio, 2016.
Palacio, Ernesto. "¿Por qué no se leen libros argentinos?" *El Hogar,* March 19, 1937, 32.
Palma, Dante Augusto. *Borges.com: La ficción de la filosofía, la política y los medios.* Buenos Aires: Biblos, 2010.
Papel, Libro, Revista 1–23 (1942–1945).
"Para la constitución de una sociedad editorial." Buenos Aires: Editorial Sur, 1937.
Parodi, Cristina. "Borges, Bioy y el arte de hacer literatura con leche cuajada." In *Reescrituras,* edited by Luis Rodríguez Carranza and Marilene Nagle, 259–72. Amsterdam: Rodopi, 2004.
———. *Borges-Bioy en contexto: Una lectura guidada de H. Bustos Domecq y B. Suárez Lynch.* Pittsburgh: Borges Center, 2018.
———. "Borges y la subversión del modelo policial." In *Borges: Desesperaciones aparentes y consuelos secretos,* edited by Rafael Olea Franco, 79–97. Mexico City: El Colegio de México, 1999.
———. "Una fantasía memorable: 'El signo.' Fragmentos de una enciclopedia de Bustos Domecq y Suárez Lynch." *Variaciones Borges* 37 (2014): 177–205.
———. "El proyecto cultural de la revista 'Sur' (1931–1970) en la obra literaria de Victoria Ocampo." PhD diss., University of Berlin, 1987.
Parry, Richard. "Ancient Ethical Theory." In *The Stanford Encyclopedia of Philosophy,* Fall 2014 Edition, edited by Edward N. Zalta. https://plato.stanford.edu/archives/fall2014/entries/ethics-ancient/.

Pasternac, Nora. *Sur, una revista en la tormenta: Los años de formación, 1941–1944*. Buenos Aires: Paradiso, 2002.
Paz, Octavio. *Xavier Villaurrutia en persona y en obra*. Mexico City: Fondo de Cultura Económica, 1978.
Pellicer, Rosa. "Borges, Bioy y Bustos Domecq: Influencias, confluencias." *Variaciones Borges* 10 (2000): 5–28.
Pereda Valdés, Ildefonso, ed. *Antología de la moderna poesía uruguaya*. Buenos Aires: El Ateneo, 1927.
Pérez Rodríguez, María Antonia. "Luis Seoane, editor: Nova. Bos Aires 1942–1947." Fundación Luis Seoane, November 13, 2013/February 23, 2014. http://www.fundacionluisseoane.gal/fundacionls/es/agenda/luis-seoane-editor-nova-bos-aires-1942-1947.
Peterson, William S. *The Kelmscott Press: A History of William Morris's Typographical Adventure*. Oxford: Clarendon, 1991.
Petit de Murat, Ulyses. *Borges, Buenos Aires*. Buenos Aires: Municipalidad de la Ciudad de Buenos Aires, Secretaría de Cultura, 1980.
———. *Marea de lágrimas*. Buenos Aires: Editorial Destiempo, 1937.
Phillpotts, Eden. *El señor Digweed y el señor Lumb*. Translated by Leonor Acevedo de Borges. Buenos Aires: Emecé Editores, 1945.
Pickenhayn, Jorge Oscar. *Borges total: En prosa y verso*. Buenos Aires: Corregidor, 1991.
Plotkin, Mariano Ben. *Mañana es San Perón: A Cultural History of Perón's Argentina*. Wilmington, DE: SR Books, 2003.
Pollard, A. W. "Bibliography and Bibliology." In *Encyclopedia Britannica*. 11th ed., 909–12. Cambridge: Cambridge University Press, 1911.
———. *Books in the House: An Essay on Private Libraries and Collections for Young and Old*. London: Arthur L. Humphreys, 1907.
Quaritch, Bernard. *A General Catalogue of Books, Offered to the Public at the Affixed Prices*. London: G. Norman & Son, 1880.
Quevedo, Francisco de. *Prosa y verso*. Buenos Aires: Emecé Editores, 1948.
Quién es quién en la Argentina. Buenos Aires: Editorial Kraft, 1968.
Read, Herbert. *El significado del arte*. Translated by Leonor Acevedo de Borges. Buenos Aires: Editorial Losada, 1954.
Reyes, Alfonso. *Mallarmé entre nosotros*. Buenos Aires: Editorial Destiempo, 1938.
———. "Teoría de la antología." In *Obras completas de Alfonso Reyes*, Vol. 14, 137–41. Mexico City: Fondo de Cultura Económica, 1983.
Risso Platero, Ema. *Arquitecturas del insomnio*. Buenos Aires: Ediciones Botella al Mar, 1948.
Rivera, Jorge B. "El auge de la industria cultural (1930–1955)." In *El escritor y la industria cultural*, 94–127. Buenos Aires: Centro Editor de América Latina, 1981.
———. *La forja del escritor profesional (1900–1930). Los escritores y los nuevos medios masivos*. Capítulos 56 y 57: La historia de la literatura argentina. Buenos Aires: Centro Editor de América Latina, 1967.

———. "José Hernández, Martín Fierro Francia, ALLCA XX, Université Paris X, 2001, Edición crítica Élida Lois y Ángel Núñez (coordinadores), Colección Archivos 51, 429 páginas." *Orbis Tertius* 8, no. 9 (2002-2003): 1-2.

———. "Los juegos de un tímido. Borges en el suplemento de *Crítica*." *Crisis* (1976): 20-27.

Rodríguez-Luis, Julio. "La intención política en la obra de Borges: Hacia una visión de conjunto." *Cuadernos Hispanoamericanos* 361-362 (1980): 170-98.

Rodríguez Monegal, Emir. *Jorge Luis Borges: A Literary Biography*. New York: E. P. Dutton, 1978.

———. "Nota sobre Biorges." *Mundo Nuevo* 22 (1968): 89-93.

Rogers, Gayle. *Incomparable Empires: Modernism and the Translation of Spanish and American Literature*. New York: Columbia University Press, 2018.

———. *Modernism and the New Spain: Britain, Cosmopolitan Europe, and Literary History*. Oxford: Oxford University Press, 2014.

Romera, Ricardo. "H. Bustos Domecq: Un modelo opuesto a J. L. Borges y A. Bioy Casares." *Vericuetos* 9 (1993): 168-93.

Romero, Luis Alberto. "Buenos Aires en la entreguerra: Libros baratos y cultura de los sectores populares." In *Mundo urbano y cultura popular: Estudios de historia social argentina,* compiled by Diego Armus, 40-67. Buenos Aires: Editorial Sudamericana, 1990.

Ros, Vicente. "La sociedad de bibliófilos argentinos." *Infodiversidad* 15 (2010): 65-80.

Rosarivo, Raúl M. *Historia general del libro impreso desde el origen del alfabeto hasta nuestros días*. Buenos Aires: Ediciones Áureas, 1964.

Rosato, Laura, and Germán Álvarez. *Borges, libros y lecturas*. 2nd ed. Buenos Aires: Biblioteca Nacional, 2017.

Rossi, Attilio. *Buenos Aires en tinta china*. Buenos Aires: Editorial Losada, 1951.

Royano, Lourdes. "Jorge Luis Borges, la lectura como reescritura." *Norte* 454-55 (2006): 10-14.

Ruch, Allen. "The Crimson Hexagon: Books Borges Never Wrote." *Variaciones Borges* 1 (1996): 121-31.

Sabor Riera, María Ángeles. "Contribución al estudio histórico del desarrollo de los servicios bibliotecarios de la Argentina en el siglo XIX." Chaco: Universidad Nacional del Nordeste, 1974.

Sabsay-Herrera, Fabiana. "Para la prehistoria de H. Bustos Domecq. *Destiempo,* una colaboración olvidada de Jorge Luis Borges y Adolfo Bioy Casares." *Variaciones Borges* 5 (1998): 106-22.

Sacerio-Garí, Enrique. "La crítica de Borges en 'El Hogar.'" *Revista Interamericana de Bibliografía* 33 (1983): 171-90.

Saer, Juan José. "Onetti y la novela breve." In *Novelas cortas,* critical edition, edited by Daniel Balderston, xv-xx. Córdoba: Alción Editora, 2009.

Saítta, Sylvia. "Recorrido." In *Crítica: Revista Multicolor de los Sábados, 1933-1934. Edición completa en CD-ROM,* edited by Nicolás Helft, 10-37. Buenos Aires: Fondo Nacional de las Artes, 1999.

Salas, Horacio. *Borges: Una biografía*. Buenos Aires: Planeta, 1994.
———. "Borges y su paso por *Crítica*." In *Crítica: Revista Multicolor de los Sábados, 1933-1944. Edición completa en CD-ROM,* edited by Nicolás Helft, 7–8. Buenos Aires: Fondo Nacional de las Artes, 1999.
Salinas, Alejandra. *Liberty, Individuality, and Democracy in Jorge Luis Borges*. Lanham, MD: Lexington Books, 2016.
Sarabia, Rosa. "'La muerte y la brújula' y la parodia borgeana del género policial." *Journal of Hispanic Philology* 17 (1992): 12–13.
Sarlo, Beatriz. *Jorge Luis Borges: A Writer on the Edge*. London: Verso, 1993.
———. *The Technical Imagination: Argentine Culture's Modern Dreams*. Stanford, CA: Stanford University Press, 2008.
Sarmiento, Domingo Faustino. *Recuerdos de provincia*. Buenos Aires: Emecé Editores, 1944.
Saroyan, William. *La comedia humana*. Translated by Leonor Acevedo de Borges. Buenos Aires: Editora Inter-americana, 1943.
Sassón-Henry, Perla. "Borges and His Legacy in Hyperfiction: A Study through the Lenses of Deleuze and Guattari's Rhizome Theory." *Latin American Essays* 18 (2005): 148–56.
———. *Borges 2.0: From Text to Virtual Worlds*. New York: Peter Lang, 2007.
Schrjver, Frans. *Regionalism after Regionalisation: Spain, France and the United Kingdom*. Amsterdam: Amsterdam University Press, 2006.
Schwartz, John Pedro. "Reading and Writing 'A Destiempo': The Figure of the Museum in Borges." *Bulletin of Hispanic Studies* 92, no. 3 (2015): 299–318.
Setton, Román. *Los orígenes de la narrativa policial en la Argentina. Recepción y transformación de modelos genéricos alemanes, franceses e ingleses*. Madrid: Vervuert/Iberoamericana, 2012.
Shand, William. *Ferment*. Buenos Aires: Ediciones Botella al Mar, 1950.
Shillingsburg, Peter. "Text as Matter, Concept, and Action." *Studies in Bibliography* 44 (1991): 31–82.
Sieber, Sharon Lynn. "Time, Simultaneity, and the Fantastic in the Narrative of Jorge Luis Borges." *Romance Quarterly* 51, no. 3 (2004): 200–211.
Siskind, Mariano. *Cosmopolitan Desires: Global Modernity and World Literature in Latin America*. Evanston, IL: Northwestern University Press, 2014.
Šišmišová, Paulína. "Los juegos de Borges con el tiempo." *Verba Hispanica* 20, no. 2 (2012): 325–35.
Sorrentino, Fernando. "El kafkiano caso de la *Verwandlung* que Borges jamás tradujo." *Espéculo: Revista de estudios literarios* 10 (1998): n.p.
———. *Seven Conversations with Jorge Luis Borges*. Philadelphia: Whitston, 1982.
Sotheby's London. *Medieval and Renaissance Manuscripts and Continental and Russian Books*. Auction catalogue. London: Sotheby's, 2018.
Steiner, Bill. *Audubon Art Prints: A Collector's Guide to Every Edition*. Columbia: South Carolina University Press, 2003.

Stravinsky, Igor. *Crónicas de mi vida.* Translated by Guillermo de Torre. Buenos Aires: Editorial Sur, 1935.

———. *Nuevas crónicas de mi vida.* Translated by Leopoldo Hurtado. Buenos Aires: Editorial Sur, 1936.

Suarez, Michael. "The Production and Consumption of the Eighteenth-Century Poetic Miscellany." In *Books and Their Readers in Eighteenth-Century England: New Essays,* edited by Isabel Rivers, 217–251. London: Leicester University Press, 2001.

Sur 1–364/371 (1931–1992).

Tanselle, G. Thomas. *Bibliographical Analysis: A Historical Introduction.* Cambridge: Cambridge University Press, 2009.

———. "The Bibliographical Concepts of 'Issue' and 'State.'" *Papers of the Bibliographical Society of America* 69, no. 1 (1975): 17–66.

———. *Book-Jackets: Their History, Forms, and Use.* Charlottesville: Bibliographical Society of the University of Virginia, 2011.

———. "The Concept of Format." *Studies in Bibliography* 53 (2000): 67–115.

———. "A Description of Descriptive Bibliography." Washington, DC: Library of Congress, 1992.

———. "The Pleasures of Being a Scholar-Collector." *Nikirk Lectures* 5 (2005): 1–29.

———. *A Rationale of Textual Criticism.* Philadelphia: University of Pennsylvania Press, 1989.

Tcherepashenets, Nataly. *Place and Displacement in the Narrative Worlds of Jorge Luis Borges and Julio Cortázar.* New York: Peter Lang, 2008.

Tedesco, Juan Carlos. *Educación y sociedad en la Argentina (1880–1945).* Buenos Aires: Siglo Veintiuno, 2009.

Thompson, Lawrence S. "La sociedad de bibliófilos." In *Encyclopedia of Library and Information Science,* Vol. 39, supplement 4, edited by Allen Kent, 396–97. New York: Dekker, 1985.

"The Tragedy of Argentina: A Century of Decline." *Economist,* February 17, 2014.

Vaccaro, Alejandro. *Borges: Vida y literatura.* Buenos Aires: Edhasa, 2006.

Valéry, Paul. *El cementerio marino.* Buenos Aires: Ediciones Schillinger, 1931.

Vallely, Charles, John Wronoski, and Saúl E. Roll-Vélez. *Jorge Luis Borges: A Catalogue of Unique Books and Manuscripts.* Brookline, MA: Lame Duck Books, 2003.

Van Nostrand, Albert. *Major Book Markets in South America. Reports to the U.S. Information Agency.* Providence: Brown University, 1962.

Vázquez, María Esther. *Borges: Esplendor y derrota.* Barcelona: Tusquets, 1996.

———. *Borges, sus días y su tiempo.* Buenos Aires: Javier Vergara, 1984.

Velarde, Max. *El editor Domingo Viau y otros escritos.* Buenos Aires: Alberto Casares, 1998.

Waisman, Sergio Gabriel. *Borges and Translation: The Irreverence of the Periphery.* Lewisburg, PA: Bucknell University Press, 2005.

Waugh, Evelyn. *Decadencia y caída.* Translated by Floreal Mazía. Buenos Aires: Editorial Sudamericana, 1955.

———. ¡ . . . Más banderas! Translated by Horacio Laurora. Buenos Aires: Editorial Sudamericana, 1947.
———. Retorno a Brideshead. Translated by Clara Diament. Buenos Aires: Editorial Sudamericana, 1948.
———. Los seres queridos. Translated by Pedro Lecuona. Buenos Aires: Editorial Sudamericana, 1953.
Werfel, Franz. Estafa de cielo. Translated by D. J. Vogelmann. Buenos Aires: Editorial Sudamericana, 1947.
———. Juárez y Maximiliano. Translated by Elvira Martín and Annie Reney. Buenos Aires: Emecé Editores, 1946.
Westphal, Jonathan, ed. Justice. Indianapolis: Hackett, 1996.
White, Hayden. The Content of the Form: Narrative Discourse and Historical Representation. Baltimore: Johns Hopkins University Press, 1987.
Williamson, Edwin. Borges: A Life. New York: Penguin, 2005.
———, ed. The Cambridge Companion to Jorge Luis Borges. Cambridge: Cambridge University Press, 2013.
Willson, Patricia. La constelación del Sur: Traductores y traducciones en la literatura argentina del siglo XX. Buenos Aires: Siglo Veintiuno, 2004.
———. "Página impar: El lugar del traductor en el auge de la industria editorial." In Historia crítica de la literatura argentina 9, edited by Sylvia Saítta, 123–42. Buenos Aires: Emecé Editores, 2014.
Winship, Michael. "Publishing in America: Needs and Opportunities for Research." In Needs and Opportunities in the History of the Book: America, 1639–1876, edited by David D. Hall and John B. Hench, 61–102. Worcester, MA: American Antiquarian Society, 1987.
Wolf, Mark J. P. Building Imaginary Worlds: The Theory and History of Subcreation. New York: Routledge, 2013.
Woodall, James. Borges: A Life. New York: Basic Books, 1997.
———. The Man in the Mirror of the Book: A Life of Jorge Luis Borges. London: Hodder & Stoughton, 1996.
Woolf, Virginia. Un cuarto propio. Translated by Jorge Luis Borges. Buenos Aires: Editorial Sur, 1936.
———. Orlando. Translated by Jorge Luis Borges. Buenos Aires: Editorial Sur, 1937.
Yates, Donald A. "The Argentine Detective Story." PhD diss., University of Michigan, 1960.
———. "La colaboración de Jorge Luis Borges y Adolfo Bioy Casares." AIH. Actas IV (1971): 855–63.
———. Jorge Luis Borges: Life, Work, and Criticism. Fredericton: York Press, 1985.
———. "The Spanish American Detective Story." Modern Language Journal 40, no. 5 (1956): 228–32.
Zabel, Morton Dauwen. "La literatura en los Estados Unidos: Panorama de 1943." Translated by Frida Weber. Sur 113–14 (1944): 17–61.

Zenner, Wally. *Antigua lumbre.* Buenos Aires: Francisco A. Colombo, 1949.
Zuleta, Emilia de. "*Sur* entre cultura y política: 1931–1960." In *Cuando opinar es actuar. Revistas argentinas del siglo XX,* edited by Noemí Girbal-Blacha and Iriana Quatrocchi-Woisson, 193–221. Buenos Aires: Academia Nacional de la Historia, 1999.

Index

Page numbers in *italics* refer to illustrations.

Abad, Vicente Diego, 176
"El acercamiento a Almotásim," 29–30, 38, 275
Acevedo de Borges, Leonor, 101, 190
Acosta Van Praet, Marta, 177
Advertisements, 7, *76*, 201, 209–10, 224, 228, 239–40, 245–47
Aisenson, Aída, 177
"Alba desdibujada," 233
The Albatross Book of Living Verse, 121
Alcorta, Amancio, 249–53
"El Aleph," 37, 236, 259n48
El Aleph, 4, 41, 55, 109, 171; bibliographical details in, 36–37; book design of, 233, *235*–37
"Algunos pareceres de Nietzsche," 110
Almafuerte, 56
Alonso, Amado, 218, 233
Álvarez, Germán, 14, 16n11, 17
Amigos del Arte, 51
Amorim, Enrique, 92–94
Los Anales de Buenos Aires, 170–75, 179, 182, 233
Antiguas literaturas germánicas, 181–84

Antología clásica de la literatura argentina, 114, 127–32, 134, 140, 144, 146, 150; biographies in, 152; book design of, 138; reference style in, 169; review of, 123
Antología de cuentos irreales, 243–44
Antología de la literatura fantástica, 132–33, 148–53, 244; biographies in, 168–69; other collection overlaps with, 96, 98–99, 114, 155, 173
"Antología de la literatura francesa," 165, 169–70
Antología de la moderna poesía uruguaya, 185, 237, 274–77
Antología de la poesía argentina moderna (1896–1930), 136–37
Antología de la poesía argentina moderna (1900–1925), 136–37
"Antología de la poesía norteamericana," 165–70
Antología de poetas argentinos, 136–37
Antología de poetas y prosistas americanos, 130, 136–37
Antología de poetas y prosistas españoles, 130

"Antología expresionista," 125–26
Antología poética argentina, 126, 132–39, 140, 146, 151–52, 169, 240n5, 244
Anzoátegui, Ignacio B., 62, 146
Apocryphal, 40, 45, 77, 116, 188n12, 247–48
Apollinaire, Guillaume, 156
Argentine educational system, 251–54; Borges's critique of, 8, 11, 116–17, 239, 246; changes to, 5; books used in, 130
Argentine literature, 11, 122, 126–46, 151, 181, 193–94, 211, 254; Editorial Sur editions of, 193–94; figure of the gaucho in, 118; lack of literary criticism for, 94–95, 124
Aristotle, 216, 274
Aron, Robert, 280
Arrieta, Rafael Alberto, 126
"El arte narrativo y la magia," 63
Artsybashev, Mikhail, 176
Ascasubi, Hilario, 56
"El asesino desinteresado Bill Harrigan," 83
"Autobiographical Notes," 15–16, 56
Avant-garde, 73, 89, 113–14, 165–66, 24
Ayala, Francisco, 108
Azul, 63

Baeza, Ricardo, 176, 178
Baker, Gideon, 8
Balchin, Nigel, 174, 177
Ballester Peña, J. A., 179
Banchs, Enrique, 126
Barbieri, Vicente, 243–46, 281
Baudelaire, Charles, 108, 281
Bauer, Elvira, 95–97
Baum, Vicki, 104
Bautista, Juan, 200
Beerbohm, Max, 149, 151
Beltrán, Oscar R., 130, 136–37
Berdiaeff, Nikolai, 191
Berkeley, Anthony, 86, 99, 157
Berkeley, George, 267

Bernárdez, Francisco Luis, 193, 279–80
Besouchet, Lidia, 212
Best sellers, 72, 75, 159–60, 164
Beutelspacher (bookstore), 17
Bianco, José, 108, 195n33, 211, 281
Bible, 248, 256–59
El Bibliófilo (Viau y Zona), 67–68
Bibliography, 3, 5, 14–15, 19–20, 23–24, 30–39, 276; descriptive, 24, 26–27, 29, 32 (*see also* Book format); enumerative, 27–30, 32; textual, 28–31, 127–30
Bibliophile, 14–15, 19, 51–52
Biblioteca contemporánea (Losada), 101
"La biblioteca de Babel," 31–34, 37, 41, 275
Biblioteca Emecé, 158, 207, 214–17, 220
Biblioteca Gallega (Emecé), 141
Biblioteca Miguel Cané, 141
Biblioteca Nacional Mariano Moreno, 14, 17, 253
Bioy Casares, Adolfo, 53, 98–99, 108, 157, 173, 211, 263–68; as co-director of Puerta de Marfil series, 175–79; as co-director of Séptimo Círculo series, 96, 159–61, 164; as co-editor, 96, 113–14, 133, 138, 153, 164, 207, 212; collaborations between Borges and, 10, 87–88, 115–18, 120, 147, 150, 153–55, 271; friendship between Borges and, 54, 109, 112–13; *La invención de Morel*, 221–23, 282; as publisher, 238–50, 253, 255, 257, 259–60; prologues by, 148–49; *Seis problemas para don Isidro Parodi*, 35–36; *La trama celeste*, 282; translations by, 165–67, 169
Bishop, Elizabeth, 170
Bishop, John Peale, 165, 167–68
Blake, Nicholas (Cecil Day-Lewis), 98–99, 116
Blomberg, Héctor Pedro, 126
Bloom, Harold, 8
Bloy, Léon, 9, 150–51
Bogan, Louise, 167
Boissonnas, Edith, 169–70

INDEX

Boletín bibliográfico argentino, 130
Bombal, María Luisa, 99, 280
Bonomi, José, 160–64, 179
Book design, 140, 182, 208; of bindings, 17, 51, 200–201, 208, 217, 268, 269; of covers, 57–69, 77–78, 105–7, 120, 138–40, 160–63, 198–99, 244–46; of dust jackets, 154, 182, 215n78, 223–24; of endpapers, 101–2, 217; of hardcovers, 101–2, 131–32, 142–43, 179–80, 213, 217, 226, 268–69; illustrations in, 62, 100–102, 179, 223–29, 242–46, 264, 265–66, 267 (*see also* cover illustrations); logos and, 101, 107, 120, 161, 212, 217, 221, 242–43; of luxury editions, 17, 51–55, 67–69, 192–95, 202–3, 214, 245, 268–70; page layout and, 44–45, 68, 133, 142, 149, 151–53, 202–3, 225–27; paper and, 57, 67–69, 78, 131–33, 202–3, 214, 245–46, 268; paperbacks and, 51, 72, 75, 158, 179, 218; poor quality of, 2, 48, 50–51, 75, 78, 80, 131, 158; print runs and, 68–69, 72, 159–60, 184, 214, 194–95, 245–46, 248; promotional bands and, 231–32
Book format, 22, 26, 35–37, 68, 75
Book history, 3, 5, 12, 273–76
Book pricing, 7, 105, 133, 158, 192, 200, 232–33, 245
Book reviews, 40, 67, 120, 147, 217, 220, 242; in "El acercamiento a Almotásim," 30; of The Albatross Book of Living Prose, 121; in "Examen de la obra de Herbert Quain," 30–31; of Excellent Intentions, 30; in *El Hogar,* 4, 10, 30, 67, 87–109, 127, 172, 217; of *Luis Greve, muerto,* 242–44; of *The Moonstone,* 264; in *Sur,* 95–109, 172, 217; of *The Wild Palms,* 264
Borges, Jorge Luis, as anthologist, 11, 87–88, 96, 109, 114, 120–58, 165–70; as book collector, 20–21; bookstores and, 16–18, 72; citation styles of, 38–40, 128–29; as collaborator, 10–11, 87–88, 109, 112–20, 127–64, 165–69, 175–84, 238–71; as editor, 44, 78–79, 87–88, 127–64, 170–84; income of, 42, 69, 87, 141; libraries of, 14–16, 21; manuscripts of, 42, 43, 44–45; politics and, 8, 88, 274; as publisher, 238–71; as translator, 100, 104, 108, 126, 165–70, 186–87, 190–204, 237; work in print shop by, 41–42, 78–79, 89. *See also titles of individual works*
Borges de Torre, Norah, 54, 100–101, 113n38, 223, 270
"Borges y yo," 273
Botana, Helvio I., 72–73
Botana, Natalio, 72–73, 78–79
Bradley, Francis, 216
Braun Menéndez, Carlos, 140–41
Breton, André, 204, 281
Breviarios collection, 181–84
Brontë, Emily, 280
Brown, George Douglas, 177
Browning, Robert, 9
"El brujo postergado," 82
Buitrago, Guillermo, 179
Bullrich Palenque, Sylvina, 141–46
Buonocore, Domingo, 16, 54–55
Bustos Domecq, Honorio, 88, 115–20, 260–62, 281

Caillois, Roger, 169, 204, 281–82
Cain, James M., 174–77
Camaña, Raquel, 251, 253–54
"La cámara de las estatuas," 82
Camus, Albert, 169, 204, 233, 282
"Caña de ámbar," 233
Cancela, Arturo, 72
Cané, Miguel, 253
Canto, Estela, 17–18, 176
Caprile, A., 176
Carlyle, Thomas, 151, 215–16
Carr, John Dickson, 98–99, 119, 157
Carriego, Evaristo, 50, 53, 55–57, 61, 137–38, 144–46
"Carriego y el sentido del arrabal," 56

Carrizo, Antonio, 41–42
Carybé, 243, 245
Cascella, Armando, 62
Caspary, Vera, *163,* 175–76
Céline, Louis-Ferdinand, 279
Censorship, 218–19, 238–39, 248–52; pornography and, 254–56
"Cercanías," 233
Cervantes (Madrid), 125, 131
Cervantes, Miguel de, 28–29, 215–16
Chambers' *Encyclopaedia,* 16
Chartier, Roger, 12, 274–76
Chaucer, 108
Chesterton, G. K., 86, 99, 150–51, 156, 262–64
Chestov, Lev, 191, 281
Christie, Agatha, 156
Ciancaglini, Jorge, 176
Citizen Kane, 116
"Ciudad," 233
Clásicos Emecé, 207, 217–18
Claudel, Paul, 100, 217
Cleaver, Hylton, 156
Cocteau, Jean, 99, 151, 211, 217
Codex Gigas, 35–36
Cognitive science, 273–74
Colección Austral (Espasa-Calpe), 218, 221
Colección Buen Aire (Emecé), 141–43, 144–46, 179, 226–27
Colección de nuevos escritores argentinos (Gleizer), 61–62
Colección Dorna (Emecé), 226
Colección "Grandes Ensayistas" (Emecé), 158
Colección Horizonte (Sudamericana), 11, 103–6, 114, 198, 204n57
Colección Hórreo (Emecé), 226
Colección Laberinto (Sudamericana), 132–39, 140, 148–53, 155
Colección "La Quimera" (Emecé), 155, 158
Colección Mar Dulce (Nova), 226–27

Colección Megáfono (TOR), 62, 75, 77, 8
Colegio Libre de Estudios Superiores, 8
Coleridge, Samuel Taylor, 44–45
Collins, Wilkie, 99, 156, 174, 263–64
Colombo, Francisco A., 7, 44, 48–69, 77, 120, 201–2, 270; *Destiempo* and, 244–46; Editorial Destiempo and, 244–46; Gleizer's work with, 73–74; La Martona (pamphlet) and, 113
Colombo, Osvaldo, 74
Compadre, 142, 144, 146, 227
El compadrito, 141–43, 144–46, 183n136, 226
Conan Doyle, Arthur, 156
Connolly, Cyril, 282
Conrad, Joseph, 174–78
Coppola, Horacio, 61
Copyright, 5, 102–3, 178, 203
"El coronel Ascasubi," 63
Cosmópolis (magazine), 126, 131
Cosmopolitanism, 7–9
Cover illustrations, of *Antología poética argentina, 139;* of *Buenos Aires en tinta china,* 223–24; of Colección Mar Dulce, 226; of *El Aleph,* 233, 235–36; of *El compadrito,* 142–43; of *Ferment,* 229–30; of *La invención de Morel,* 223–24; of *La muerte y la brújula,* 270; of *Los mejores cuentos policiales,* 154; of *Poemas (1922–1943),* 233–34, 236; of Puerta de Marfil serie, 179–80; of Séptimo Círculo series, 160–61, *163*
Crane, Hart, 165
Critchley, Simon, 8
Crítica, 48, 72, 78–85, 88–89
Cuaderno Chacabuco, 43–45
Cuaderno San Martín, 43–45, 47, 233
Cuadernos de la Quimera (Emecé), 105, 107–8, 114, 204, 207, 211–12, 214
Cuadernos del Plata (Editorial Proa), 44
Cuadrado, Arturo, 141–42, 225–31
La Cultura Argentina, 251, 253–54
cummings, e. e., 165, 167

Dabove, Santiago, 152
Darío, Rubén, 253
David-Néel, Alexandra, 149–50
Dawkins, Richard, 274
de Alvear, Elvira, 204–5
de Diego, Juan Mateos, 176
De Ferkin, Susana W., 177
de Gaulle, Charles, 281
de la Guardia, Alfredo, 281
de las Casas, Álvaro, 140–41
de l'Isle-Adam, Villiers, 119, 132, 152
De Luaces, J. G., 177
de Nerval, Gérard, 281
De Rougemont, Denis, 281
de Sagastizábal, Leandro, 209–10
de Toro, Fernando, 25
de Torre, Guillermo, 100–101, 218, 220–21, 233
del Campo, Estanislao, 226–27
del Carril, Sara Luisa, 206
Dennett, Daniel C., 273
Destiempo, 11, 113–15, 172, 239–41, 244, 246–47
Detective fiction, 16, 173; Borges's rebranding of, 87–88, 98–99, 120, 146–64, 184; hard-boiled tradition of, 88, 117–18, 161, 164; in Borges's anthologies, 4, 11, 122, 146–64, 206–7; *Un modelo para la muerte* and, 260–64, 267; *novela enigma* style of, 147–48, 161, 164; pseudonyms in, 88, 115–16, 247, 260–61; *Seis problemas para don Isidro Parodi* and, 115–19
di Giovanni, Norman Thomas, 55, 69
Díaz de Guzmán, Ruy, 131
Dickens, Charles, 98, 108, 223
"Dictamen," 233
Diehl, Adán C., 123, 127n12
Diogenes of Sinope, 8
Discusión, 47, 49, 55, 63, 67–68, 74, 216, 275; bibliographical details in, 20–21; design features of, 62, 64–65; reception of, 61–62

"Un doble de Mahoma," 83
Don Quijote, 16, 20, 27–29, 276
Dos fantasías memorables, 247, 249–60, 263, 267–68
"Dos libros de este tiempo," 110
"Las dos maneras de traducir," 190
Dos Passos, John, 104
Drieu la Rochelle, Pierre, 191, 211
Dunsany, Lord (Edward Plunkett), 9, 99
"La duración del infierno," 63

"Eastman, el proveedor de iniquidades," 82
Echeverría, Esteban, 52–53
Eco, Umberto, 8
Eddington, Sir Arthur Stanley, 280
Ediciones Botella al Mar, 227–31
Editorial Destiempo, 11, 238–46, 270–71
Editorial Kapelusz y Cía, 130
Editorial Losada, 138, 189, 204, 218–25, 270; Borges's publications with, 36n69, 233, 234–35, 236–37; Editorial Sur book distribution with, 196, 203, 228; Pajarita de Papel series of, 11, 100–103, 114
Editorial Montaner y Simón, 178
Editorial Nova, 196, 225–29, 250
Editorial Oportet & Haereses, 11, 238, 246–71
Editorial Proa, 44, 59–60
Editorial Sudamericana, Colección Horizonte of, 11, 102–6, 109, 114, 198; Colección *Laberinto* of, 132–39, 140, 148, 153, 155; other firms working with, 196, 228; sales catalogues of, 196–98
Editorial Sur, 164–65, 172, 186, 239, 245; books published by, 169, 279–82; Borges's work with, 104, 189, 191–204, 206, 210, 231–33, 237; book distribution for, 224–25, 228–29; *La invención de Morel* and, 222–23; *Seis problemas para don Isidro Parodi* and, 88, 120
Editorial theory, 27–30, 127–30. *See also* Bibliography: textual

Editorial TOR, 74–75, *76*, 88n4, 130, 195; Borges's work with, 7, 48–50, 62, 77–78, 80, 232n120; Colección Megáfono of, 62, 75, 80; Serie amarilla of, 161–62
Eichelbaum, Samuel, 281
Eliot, T. S., 39, 167, 217, 229
Emecé Editores, 140–41, 207–10, 222–23, 233; Biblioteca Emecé of, 158, 207, 214–17, 220; Borges's work with, 7, 109, 172–73, 189; Clásicos Emecé of, 207, 217–18; Colección Buen Aire of, 141–43, 144–46, 179, 226–27; Colección Dorna of, 226; Colección "Grandes Ensayistas" of, 158; Colección Hórreo of, 226; Colección "La Quimera" of, 155, 207; *El compadrito* and, 141–43, 144–46; Cuadernos de la Quimera of, 105, 107–8, 114, 204, 207, 210–12, 214; Editorial Nova and, 225–26; *Los mejores cuentos policiales* and, 96, 98–99, 153–58, 161, 164, 206; *La muerte y la brújula* and, 236–37; El Navío of, 207, 212–13, 214; Piragua series of, 158; Puerta de Marfil of, 174–*80*; Selección Emecé de Obras Contemporáneas of, 158; Séptimo Círculo series of, 96, 98–99, 153–55, 159, *163*–64, 174, 206–7; Teatro del Mundo of, 174, 207, 217
Emerson, Ralph Waldo, 2
Encyclopedia Britannica, 15, 21–22, 25, 33, 56, 184, 212, 247
Entre libros y papeles, 116
Erro, Carlos Alberto, 193, 279–80
"El escritor argentino y la tradición," 8–9
"Los escritores argentinos y Buenos Aires," 89
"El espantoso redentor Lázarus Morell" ("El atroz redentor Lázarus Morell"), 77, 81–82
Espasa-Calpe, 218, 221
"El espejo de tinta," 82
Evaristo Carriego, 18–20, 41, 49–50, 55–*58*, 61–62, 64, 74

"Examen de la obra de Herbert Quain," 29–31, 35

Fantastic literature, 132, 148–52, 184, 227–29, 242, 244, 257–59
Fargue, Léon-Paul, 191
Faulkner, William, 4, 86, 99, 104, 157, 204n57, 264, 281
Fernández, Macedonio, 73, 114, 126, 151, 246–47
Fernández, Ramón, 280
Fernández Moreno, Baldomero, 126
Fervor de Buenos Aires, 47, 233, 270
Ficciones, 4, 41, 55, 109–11, 236, 281; bibliographical details in, 34–37, 45; marketing of, 231–33
Fijman, Jacobo, 73
"Films," 63
Fingerit, Julio, 62
"La flor de Coleridge," 111
Fondane, Benjamin, 191
Fondo de Cultura Económica, 181–84
"La forma de la espada," 35, 110
Foucault, Michel, 8
Fournier, Alain, 280
Frank, Waldo, 191–92
Frazer, James George, 99
Frías, Carlos V., 159–60, 164
Fundación Internacional Jorge Luis Borges, 14
"Funes el memorioso," 34–35, 110

Galindo, Marco Aurelio, 176–77
García Lorca, Federico, 193–95, 219, 279
Gaucho, 118, 142, 144, 241
Genette, Gérard, 12, 186–89, 205, 274–75
Gerhardt, Federico, 142
Gide, André, 169, 195, 198–99, 200, 211, 279–80
Girondo, Oliverio, 52–53, 196, 281
Girri, Alberto, 282
Gleizer, Manuel, 7, 48–50, 61–62, 64, 71–74, 130

Glusberg, Samuel, 72
Godel, Roberto, 206
Goethe (bookstore), 17
Golding, Louis, 174, 176, 178
Gollancz, Victor, 30, 38
Gómez de la Serna, Ramón, 113–14, 150–51, 211, 280
González Carbalho, José, 136–37
González Garaño, Alfredo, 196
González Lanuza, Eduardo, 280–81
Gouiran, Emile, 280
Goyena, Pedro, 251, 254
Green, Julien, 104, 108
Greene, Graham, 98–99, 156, 282
Grévières, 281
Groussac, Paul, 20–21, 248, 253
Guardiola, Antonio, 177
Guasp, Gonzalo, 176
Guerrero, Margarita, 267
Guilmain, Andrés, 177
Güiraldes, Ricardo, 52–54, 146
Guizot, François, 281

"Hallazgo," 233
Harper's Bazaar, 90
Harte, Francis Bret, 215–17
Hawthorne, Nathaniel, 4, 156
Helft, Nicolás, 80
Henríquez Ureña, Pedro, 114, 123, 127–32, 150, 218
Henschke, Alfred, 90
Hernández, José, 129–30
Hernández, Rafael, 227
Hidalgo, Alberto, 136–37
High modernism, 87, 98, 183, 204
"Historia de la eternidad," 21–22, 37
Historia de la eternidad, 49, 55, 67, 110–11, 216; bibliographical details in, 21–22; design features of, 68–69, 70, 246, 270
Historia universal de la infamia, 40–41, 47–50, 62, 75–84, 236, 275
Hofstadter, Douglas R., 273
El Hogar, 79, 121, 151, 211, 261; Borges's work for, 10, 30–31, 67, 86–109, 114–15, 147, 151, 261 (see also "Libros y autores extranjeros"); design features of, 90–91; other publications linked to, 172–73, 179, 186, 216–17; "¿Por qué no se leen libros argentinos?" in, 124–25, 127, 140; promotion of detective fiction in, 147, 164, 183, 264; promotion of high modernism in, 183, 204
"Hombres de las orillas," 82
"Homenaje al Carriego," 56
Hopenhaym, Benjamín, 177
Hsue-Kin, Tsao, 150
Huidobro, Vicente, 136–37
Hull, Richard, 30, 98–99
Hume, David, 267
Huxley, Aldous, 90, 100, 104, 193, 197–98, 204, 211, 279–80

"El idioma analítico de John Wilkins," 110
El idioma de los argentinos, 56, 73
"El impostor inverosímil Tom Castro," 81–82
Imprenta López, 7, 200–203, 226, 228–29, 250
"El incivil maestro de ceremonias Kotsuké no Suké," 83
Índice de la nueva poesía americana, 136–37
Índice de la poesía argentina contemporánea, 136–37
Ingenieros, Delia, 181–84
Ingenieros, José, 251, 253
Inicial (magazine), 90
"El inmortal," 36–37
Innes, Michael (J. I. M. Stewart), 98–99, 116, 157
Inquisiciones, 47, 57, 59
Irazusta, Julio, 280
Irish, William, 156
Isaacs, Jorge, 90, 92–94
Isherwood, Christopher, 282

Jacobsen, Luis, 252–53
James, Henry, 108, 175, 177, *180*, 212, 228
James, William, 215–16
Jammes, Francis, 177, 179
"El jardín de senderos que se bifurcan," 41, 273
El jardín de senderos que se bifurcan, 22–34, 36, 38, 47, 231–32, 236–37, 281
Joyce, James, 99, 150–51, 183, 204, 280
Jung, Carl G., 204, 279

Kafka, Franz, 4, 99–100, 108, 114, 149–51, 204, 220
"Kafka y sus precursores," 8–9
Kant, Immanuel, 7
Kapelusz, Adolfo, 130
Kelmscott Press, 268
Kemelman, Harry, 157
Kennedy, Milward, 98–99, 155, 157
"Las Kenningar," 67
Las Kenningar, 48–49, 55, 64, 66–69, 183n36, 246, 270
Kennings, 4, 64, 183
Kent, Victoria, 282
Kessel, Joseph, 176, 178
Keyserling, Hermann von, 197–98, 204, 281
Kierkegaard, Søren, 9
King, John, 192
Kipling, Rudyard, 86, 90, 99, 151
Knox, Ronald, 157
Kodama, María, 14
Koetz, Edgar, 179
Koremblit, Bernardo Ezequiel, 72
Kristal, Efraín, 187–88

Ladies' Home Journal, 90
Lafforgue, Jorge, 161, 164
Lange, Haydée, 108
Lawrence, D. H., 193–94, 279
Lawrence, T. E., 282
Leprêtre, Julien, 214

Leroux, Gaston, 148
Levine, Suzanne Jill, 190–91
Librería Europa (Librería Europea), 252–53
Librería La Cultura, 72
"El libro," 13–14
El libro de arena, 47
"Libros y autores extranjeros" (*El Hogar*), 67, 87, 89, 93–94, 109
Lins do Rego, José, 212
"La lírica argentina contemporánea," 125–26, 136
"Llamarada," 233
Llull, Ramón, 90, 92–93
Loewenstein, C. Jared, 41
London, Jack, 156
López García, José, 200–201
López Llausás, Antonio, 153, 196
López Soto, José, 250
Loring Frost, George, 149
Losada, Gonzalo Pedro, 101, 218–21
"La lotería en Babilonia," 274
Louis, Annick, 48–50, 80
Lugones, Leopoldo, 53–54, 56, 134, 146, 151, 214, 227
Luna de enfrente, 47, 233

MacAdam, Alfred, 261–64
Machen, Arthur, 174, 177, 179
Mackern's (bookstore), 16–18, 211
Mallea, Eduardo, 62, 107, 192–93, 211–13, 214, 279–80
Mallea, Enrique, 62
Malraux, André, 169, 279
Manguel, Alberto, 17
Mann, Thomas, 100, 104, 204, 280
Manual de zoología fantástica, 267
Marañón, Gregorio, 211, 280
Marcano, Nashieli, 30–31
Marechal, Leopoldo, 193, 280
Maritain, Jacques, 280
Marquina, Rafael, 176

"El *Martín Fierro*," 63
Martín Fierro, 129–30, 144
Martín Fierro (magazine), 56, 89–90, 113–14
Martínez Estrada, Ezequiel, 108, 146, 240n5, 246–47
Marx, Karl, 274
Mastronardi, Carlos, 114, 240n5, 246–47
Maturana, José de, 251, 254
Maugham, William Somerset, 104
Maupassant, Guy de, 151
Mazo, Marcelo del, 126, 146
Medina del Río, Mariano, 140–41
Megáfono (magazine), 61–62, 77
Los mejores cuentos policiales, 153–54, 164, 169, 212; design features of, 154–55; other publications linked to, 96, 98–99, 150, 155, 161; promotion of detective fiction in, 88, 150; sales of, 158, 175, 206–7
Melián Lafinur, Álvaro, 126
Melville, Herman, 108, 204, 211–12
Michaux, Henri, 198, 203, 231, 281
Mill, John Stuart, 274
Millar, Margaret, 174, 177
Milongas, 144–45
Miró, Gabriel, 191
Miscellanies, 149–50
Mistral, Gabriela, 280
Mitchell's (bookstore), 16–18
Un modelo para la muerte, 247, 259–64, 265–66, 267–69
Molina Vedia, Amanda, 270
Molinari, Ricardo E., 52–54, 193
Molloy, Sylvia, 38
Montfort, Nick, 273
Montherlant, Henry de, 217
Moore, Marianne, 167
Morris, William, 6, 268
Moyano, Osvaldo, 177
"La muerte y la brújula," 34–35, 157, 270
La muerte y la brújula, 236
Mujica Láinez, Roberto, 176

Muñoz, Gori, 246
Muñoz, Melgarejo, 52–53
"Música patria," 233

La Nación, 8, 79, 87, 107–11, 211, 217, 236
Nagel, Thomas, 274
Nalé Roxlo, Conrado, 280
El Navío (Emecé), 207, 212–13, 214
Needham, Paul, 276
Nelson, Beatriz Florencia, 177
The New Media Reader, 273
Nietzsche, Friedrich, 67
"La noche cíclica," 110
Noé, Julio, 136–37
Nosotros, 63, 88–89
"Nota sobre (hacia) Bernard Shaw," 270–71
"Nota sobre 'The Purple Land,'" 110
Novalis, 247
Novella, 107, 211
Nozick, Robert, 274
"Nuestras imposibilidades," 63
Nueva refutación del tiempo, 247, 267–68, 270
"Las 'nuevas generaciones' literarias," 89–90

Ocampo, Silvina, 98–99, 113–14, 133, 150, 211, 244, 280–82
Ocampo, Victoria, 54, 112–13, 172, 231, 237, 279–82; Editorial Sur and, 191–98, 224–25, 231, 237, 279–82; *Sur* and, 54, 87, 95, 164–70, 172, 191–92, 237
O'Flaherty, Liam, 104
Olivari, Nicolás, 114, 243–44
O'Neill, Eugene, 151
Ortega y Gasset, José, 125, 196n39, 211
Orwell, George, 282
Otras inquisiciones, 47, 110–11, 171, 216
El otro, el mismo, 110–11
"El otro Whitman," 63
Oyuela, María Antonia, 177

El País, 190
Pajarita de Papel (Losada), 11, 100–103, 105, 114, 220–21
Palacio, Ernesto, 94–95, 124–25, 127, 131, 140, 146, 170
Papel, Libro, Revista, 76, 208–10, 219–21
Papini, Giovanni, 151
"Para la constitución de una sociedad editorial," 195–96
Parmenides, 216
Parodi, Cristina, 250, 255
Parpagnoli, Guido, 81
"Paul Groussac," 20–21, 63
Paz, General José María, 212
Penguin Books, 105, 182, 215, 221
"La penúltima versión de la realidad," 63
Perés, Ramón D., 176–77
Perón, Juan, 88, 175, 238–39, 244, 248, 250–53, 256, 263
"La perpetua carrera de Aquiles y la tortuga," 63, 220
Perry, George Sessions, 176
Perse, Saint-John, 282
Petit de Murat, Ulyses, 42, 61–62, 114, 239–40, 243–46
Peuser, Jacobo, 18–19
Peyrou, Manuel, 98–99, 114, 157, 281
Phillpotts, Eden, 98–99, 155–56
philosophy of mind, 273–74
"Pierre Menard, autor del Quijote," 27–29, 35, 191, 274n4, 275
Pierri, Orlando, 179
Piragua series (Emecé), 158
Pissavini, Ernesto, 239–40
Plato, 67, 216, 274
Pliny, *Naturalis Historia,* 21, 35, 37
Plotinus, 67, 216
Poe, Edgar Allan, 2, 155, 228; Borges's reviews of, 86, 99; detective fiction and, 4, 99, 119, 132, 151–52, 156
"Poema conjetural," 111
Poemas (1922–1942), 233–34, 236–37

Poetas de España y América (Losada), 233, *234*
Political science, 274
Pollard, Alfred W., 15, 22, 24, 32–34
Ponge, Francis, 169–70
Pope, Alexander, 36–37
Porter, Katherine Anne, 167
Portnof, G., 176
"La postulación de la realidad," 63
La Prensa, 63, 79, 88–89, 190
"Las previsiones de Sangiácomo," 35–36, 119
Prisma (magazine), 89–90
Proa (magazine), 89–90
Prólogos con un prólogo de prólogos, 110–11, 204–5
"El propósito de Zarathustra," 111
Publishers' catalogues, 7, 86; of Bernard Quaritch, 25–26; of Editorial Sudamericana, 103–4, 132, 196; of Editorial TOR, 75; of Emecé Editores, 175, 178–79, 207–8, 210–12, 215–16, 218
Publishing industry, 4–7, 20, 51, 69, 71; Borges's jobs in, 1–2, 41–42, 78–79, 87, 89, 206–7, 237; distribution methods of, 7, 69, 196–98, 203, 224–25, 228, 237; problems faced by, 208–9, 219–20; trends in Argentina in, 225
Puerta de Marfil (Emecé), 174–*80*
Pygmalion (bookstore), 17

Quaritch, Bernard, 25–26
Queen, Ellery (Frederic Dannay and Manfred Bennington Lee), 4, 30, 86, 98–99, 116, 156–57
Quevedo, Francisco de, 217–18

Rabelais, François, 151
Radaelli, Sigfrido A., 62
Ravel, Maurice, 191
Repertorio Americano (San José, Costa Rica), 63

Revista Argentina, 254
Revista Multicolor de los Sábados, Borges as co-director of, 41–42, 49, 62, 78–79, 89, 261–62; Borges's contributions to, 67, 87; design features of, 79–81, 84; *Historia universal de la infamia* and, 75, 82–83
Reyes, Alfonso, 44, 123, 240, 243–45, 280
Reyles, Teresa, 177
Risso Platero, Ema, 227–29
Rivas Cherif, Cipriano de, 176
Rivera, Jorge B., 161, 164
Rivero Olazábal, Raúl, 62, 77
Rodríguez Monegal, Emir, 40, 90, 140, 149, 153n81, 173, 270
Rojas, Ricardo, 138
Rosato, Laura, 14, 16n11, 17
Rossi, Attilio, 101, 218–19, 221–24, 233, 234–35, 236, 270
"El rostro del profeta" ("El tintorero enmascarado Hákim de Merv"), 81, 83–84
"Las ruinas circulares," 273

Sábato, Ernesto, 282
Sabsay-Herrera, Fabiana, 239–40
Saint-Exupéry, Antoine de, 169
Samet, Jacobo, 72
Santayana, George, 100
Sarmiento, Domingo F., 212–13, 214
Sartre, Jean-Paul, 204, 282
Schonbach, Friedrich (Fritz), 236
Schopenhauer, Arthur, 67
Seis problemas para don Isidro Parodi, 35, 88, 115–20, 256n40, 260, 263, 281
Selección Emecé de Obras Contemporáneas, 158
Seoane, Luis, 141–42, 225–29
Séptimo Círculo series (Emecé), 153, 159, 169, 174–75, 178, 206–7; design features of, 160–61, *163,* 179; other publications linked to, 96, 98–99, 150, 155, 161; promotion of detective fiction in, 150, 164
Serie amarilla (TOR), 161–62
Shakespeare, 3, 18–19
Shand, William, 227, 229–*30*
Shapiro, Karl J., 165, 168
Shaw, George Bernard, 104
"El signo," 249–57, 259–60
Simenon, Georges, 99, 157
Simon, Pierre-Henri, 280
Síntesis (magazine), 63, 88–89
"Sobre el Vathek de William Beckford," 111
"Sobre una alegoría china," 111
Sociedad Argentina de Escritores (SADE), 140, 232
Sociedad de Bibliófilos Argentinos, 51–52
El Sol (Madrid), 63
Solar, Xul, 40, 77, 114, 267n63
Soto, Luis Emilio, 281
Spanish Civil War, 5, 93–94, 173, 218, 225
Spilimbergo, Lino Enea, 52–53
Spotorno, Juan Antonio, 208
Stapledon, Olaf, 99
Stevens, Wallace, 165, 167
Stevenson, Robert Louis, 156, 158
Stoics, 7–8
Storni, Alfonsina, 126
Stravinsky, Igor, 198, 200, 279–80
Strong, L. A. George, 177
Suárez Lynch, Benito, 88, 115, 260–61, 269
"La supersticiosa ética del lector," 63
Supervielle, Jules, 100, 114, 211, 281
Sur (magazine), 63, 112–13, 120, 172, 197, 217, 221, 237; advertisements in, 224, 228; "Antología de la literatura francesa" in, 165, 169–70; "Antología de la poesía norteamericana" in, 165–70; Borges's book reviews in, 87, 95–109, 217, 242; Borges's publications in, 233, 267; design features of, 54, 192, 201; editorial board of, 196

El tamaño de mi esperanza, 56–57, *60*
tango, 135, 144
Tanselle, G. Thomas, 20–21
Tate, Allen, 167
Teatro del Mundo (Emecé), 174, 207, 217
Tejeda, Luis de, 131
"Tema del traidor y del héroe," 35
"El teólogo," 83
"Teoría de Almafuerte," 110
Terry, George S., 95
"El testigo," 257–60
Thompson, Dustan, 165
Thoreau, Henry David, 212
Thyssen, Fritz, 281
Times Literary Supplement, 89
"Tlön, Uqbar, Orbis Tertius," 23–27, 34, 37, 39
Torrendell, Juan Carlos, 74–75
Torroba, José, 176
"Los traductores de las 1001 noches," 191
"Tres formas del eterno regreso," 110
"Tres versiones de Judas," 35
Turing, Alan, 274
Twain, Mark, 77, 212
Typography, 9; errors in, 137; in *Antología clásica de la literatura argentina,* 131–32; in Colección Buen Aire, *143,* 226; in Colección Horizonte, 105–6; in Colección Laberinto, 132–33, *139,* 151; in Colección Mar Dulce, 226; in Cuadernos de la Quimera, 107; in *Un cuarto propio,* 202–3; of Editorial Destiempo, 242, 244–46; of Editorial Oportet & Haereses, 268; of Editorial TOR, 77–78; of Francisco A. Colombo, 53, 57–*58,* 62, 64, *65*–66, 67–69, 120, 270; of Imprenta López, 201–3; in *Los mejores cuentos policiales,* 154–55; in *Orlando,* 202–3; in *Perséphone,* 198–99; in *Recuerdos de provincia,* 212–13, 214; in *Seis problemas para don Isidro Parodi,* 120; of Viau y Zona, 67–69

"La última invención de Hugh Walpole," 111
ULTRA (magazine), 113–14
Ultraism, 126
Unamuno, Miguel de, 90, 92–93, 119n61
University of Virginia Borges Collection, 2–3, 41–*43,* 69

Valéry, Paul, 100, 169, 191, 282
Valoraciones, 90
Vázquez Zamora, R., 176
Vega, Carlos, 138
Velázquez, Marta, 177
Verlaine, Paul, 248
Veroni, Raúl, 52–53, 179
"Las versiones homéricas," 20, 63, 187n7, 190–91
Very Short Introduction series (Oxford), 184
Viau, Domingo, 67
Viau y Cía (bookstore), 17
Viau y Zona, 7, 48–49, 67–*70*
La Vida Literaria (magazine), 63
Villaurrutia, Xavier, 281
"Una vindicación de la cábala," 63
"Una vindicación del falso Basílides," 63
"La viuda Ching," 82

Waisman, Sergio, 40, 187
Walpole, Hugh, 98–99
Warren, Robert Penn, 165, 167–68
Waugh, Evelyn, 104, 108
Wells, H. G., 95, 132, 151–52, 174–75, 177, 204, 231–32, 281
Werfel, Franz, 100, 104, 174, 179, 217
Whitman, Walt, 100, 212
Wilde, Eduardo, 251–53
Wilde, Oscar, 108, 190
Winship, Michael, 238
Wolfe, Thomas, 212
Woolf, Virginia, 6, 86, 197–98; *Al faro,* 280; as publisher, 6; *Un cuarto propio,*

198, 200, 202–3, 280; high modernism and, 183, 204; *Orlando,* 104, *106,* 198, 202–3, 280; *Tres guineas,* 231, 281

World literature, 11, 86–87, 120, 122, 132, 151–52, 164–84, 216; Austrian literature, 164, 173; English literature, 2–3, 16–18, 89, 91–92, 164, 173, 178; foreign literature, 93–95, 100, 164–79, 184, 193, 204, 221, 237; French literature, 89–91, 151, 165–70, 178; German literature, 16–17, 89–90, 183; Icelandic sagas, 41, 183; Irish literature, 92, 151; Italian literature, 151, 159, 190; North American literature, 2–3, 17, 88, 165–68, 178; Russian literature, 164, 173, 178; Scottish literature, 92, 151, 178

Yeats, William Butler, 229
Yu, Han, 9

Zabel, Morton Dauwen, 166–67, 168n117
Zamora, Antonio, 72
Zeno, 9, 220
Zia, Lisardo, 62
Zona, Alejandro, 67